NEW LEFT, NEW RIGHT AND BEYOND

New Left, New Right and Beyond

Taking the Sixties Seriously

Edited by

Geoff Andrews
Senior Lecturer in Politics
University of Hertfordshire

Richard Cockett
Lecturer in History
Royal Holloway College
University of London

Alan Hooper
Senior Lecturer in Politics
University of Hertfordshire

and

Michael Williams
Lecturer in Politics and Public Policy
University of Hertfordshire

First published in Great Britain 1999 by
MACMILLAN PRESS LTD
Houndmills, Basingstoke, Hampshire RG21 6XS and London
Companies and representatives throughout the world

A catalogue record for this book is available from the British Library.

ISBN 0–333–74147–1

First published in the United States of America 1999 by
ST. MARTIN'S PRESS, INC.,
Scholarly and Reference Division,
175 Fifth Avenue, New York, N.Y. 10010

ISBN 0–312–22035–9

Library of Congress Cataloging-in-Publication Data
New left, new right and beyond : taking the sixties seriously / edited
by Geoff Andrews . . . [et al.].
p.   cm.
Includes bibliographical references and index.
ISBN 0–312–22035–9
1. United States—Politics and government—1961–1963.   2. United
States—Politics and government—1963–1969.   3. Right and left
(Political science)—History—20th century.   I. Andrews, Geoff,
1961–   .
E841.N44   1999
320.51'3'097309046—dc21   98–32036
                                                          CIP

This book is printed on paper suitable for recycling and made from fully managed and
sustained forest sources.

10   9   8   7   6   5   4   3   2   1
08   07   06   05   04   03   02   01   00   99

Printed and bound in Great Britain by Antony Rowe Ltd, Chippenham, Wiltshire

Contents

v

Acknowledgements

The idea for this book emerged from a course at the University of Hertfordshire, entitled Contemporary Political Movements and Ideas, which takes as its starting-point the legacies of the 1960s. Two public lecture series – 'Twenty-Five Minutes from King's Cross' (1997) and 'The Sixties and their Political Legacies' (1998) – helped to provide the impetus for the book and included earlier versions of contributions to this volume from Peter Saunders, Anne Showstack Sassoon, Richard Cockett and Paul Hirst.

We would like to thank Sandy McLean for secretarial support, Wayne Diamond for technical advice and support, and colleagues in the Social Sciences Department who participated in the staff seminar where many of these ideas were discussed. We are grateful to Rosemary Bechler, editor of *New Times*, for publishing an initial statement of our views and for allowing us to adapt an earlier version of Paul Hirst's piece which first appeared in *New Times*. *The New Statesman* has sponsored many of our events and we are grateful for their continuing support for our work. We would also like to thank our students for their interest, enthusiasm and tolerance of occasional reminiscence. Our colleague Vassilis Fouskas has been an enthusiastic supporter of our project and we are grateful to him for organising a seminar at the London School of Economics on our behalf.

Notes on the Contributors

Geoff Andrews is Senior Lecturer in Politics at the University of Hertfordshire and an Associate Lecturer at the Open University. He has written for a range of journals and newspapers, including *The New Statesman*, *The Times Higher Education Supplement*, *Renewal* and *Marxism Today*. He is the editor of *Citizenship* (1991) and co-editor (with Nina Fishman and Kevin Morgan) of *Opening the Books: Essays on the Social and Cultural History of the British Communist Party* (1995).

Richard Cockett completed his PhD at the University of London and is a Lecturer in History at Royal Holloway College, University of London. He has published several books, including *David Astor and the Observer* and *Thinking the Unthinkable*, on aspects of modern British history. He has also contributed to academic journals and is a regular contributor to the national press, especially *The New Statesman*, *The Economist*, the *Independent on Sunday* and *The Times Educational Supplement*. He lives in London and is too young to have any direct memories of the 1960s.

Marvin Gettleman is Emeritus Professor of History at Brooklyn Polytech, a member of the editorial board of the Marxist scholarly quarterly *Science & Society*, and a Staff Associate of the Veterans of the Abraham Lincoln Brigade. He was active in the Civil Rights and anti-Vietnam War movements, as well as the now-defunct New American Movement, precursor of the present Democratic Socialists of America. Author and editor of a dozen books, he is now at work on a historical study of the US Communist Party's educational work before 1957.

Paul Hirst is Professor of Social and Political Theory at Birkbeck College, University of London. His recent publications include *Associative Democracy* (1994), *Globalization in Question* (1996, with Grahame Thompson) and *From Statism to Pluralism* (1997). He is also Chair of the Council of Charter 88.

Alan Hooper is Senior Lecturer in Politics, University of Hertfordshire, and author of essays on modern British history and contemporary Brazilian politics.

Tariq Modood is Professor of Sociology, Politics and Public Policy at the University of Bristol. His many publications include (as co-author) *Ethnic Minorities in Britain: Diversity and Disadvantage* (1997), (as editor) *Church, State and Religious Minorities* (1997), (as joint editor) *Debating Cultural Hybridity* (1997) and *The Politics of Multiculturalism in the New Europe* (1997).

Peter Saunders is Professor of Sociology at the University of Sussex, and has held visiting academic positions in Australia, New Zealand, Germany and the United States. He is author of nine books and over fifty articles, most of them in the areas of urban sociology, political sociology and social stratification. His current research is on social mobility and meritocracy in Britain. He was an active member of the British Labour Party until the early 1980s, since when he has belonged to no party organisation, although he describes himself as sympathetic to the classical liberal position. He is currently on the editorial board of the Institute of Economic Affairs Health and Welfare Unit, and his most recent book is *Unequal but Fair?* (1996).

Anne Showstack Sassoon is Professor of Politics and Co-Director of the European Research Centre at Kingston University. She was educated in the United States, Italy and the United Kingdom. She has written widely on Gramsci, women's new socio-economic roles and, more recently, New Labour politics. A collection of her essays *Beyond Pessimism of the Intellect* is shortly to be published.

Tom Steele is a Senior Lecturer in Adult Education at the University of Glasgow. He was Organising Tutor for the WEA at the Swarthmore Centre in Leeds from 1973 to 1987 and Lecturer in Adult Education in the Department of Adult Continuing Education at the University of Leeds from 1990 to 1996. His previous publications include *Alfred Orage and the Leeds Art Club* (1990), *Learning Independence: a Political Outline of Indian Adult Education* (with Richard Taylor, 1995) and *The Emergence of Cultural Studies: Adult Education, Cultural Politics and the 'English' Question* (1997). He is currently working on a study of European popular education movements and popular knowledge.

Hilary Wainwright is editor of the journal *Red Pepper*, Senior Research Fellow at the Institute of Labour Studies, University of Manchester and Fellow of the Transnational Institute, Amsterdam. Publications include *Beyond the Fragments* (with Sheila Rowbotham and Lynne Segal) (1979), *Labour: a Tale of Two Parties* (1987) and *Arguments for New Left* (1992).

Wendy Wheeler is Reader in English at the University of North London, where she teaches English literature and critical theory. She has published many essays on literature, culture and politics, and is currently finishing her first book, *A New Modernity?* – on politics, identity, culture and science at the end of the twentieth century – for publication in 1999.

Michael Williams lectures in politics and public policy at the University of Hertfordshire and elsewhere. Before then he spent twenty years as a civil servant in what is now the Department of the Environment, Transport and the Regions. He has published papers on privatisation and the role of management consultants in shaping public policy.

Introduction
Alan Hooper and Michael Williams

Should we take the sixties seriously? People on the right often emphasise the frivolity and irresponsibility of the period – but they also insist on its baneful impact on society and culture. People on the left criticise the period for inflated rhetoric and negligible achievement. It can be seen as the climax of a short golden age of peace and prosperity, sandwiched between the extremes of earlier and later periods, and thus more occasion for nostalgia than for celebration or inspiration. Altogether the sixties can easily be dismissed as an era of bourgeois solidity tarnished only by occasional youthful or bohemian excess – mere froth upon the daydream.

But such an assessment would be to ignore other aspects of the period – those savage wars of peace in Algeria and Vietnam which still reverberate today; the wind of change that released most of Africa from European rule, the solid construction of the foundations of the European Union which can now be seen as Europe's greatest adventure since 1945. Might it not be that, as Marx observed of the 'so-called revolutions' of 1848, such 'poor incidents, small fractures and fissures' as, for example, the Berkeley Free Speech Movement or the London School of Economics gates incident when students tore down barriers separating two parts of the college (and countless similar manifestations), released 'oceans of liquid matter' which would subsequently 'rend into fragments' the 'hard rock' of complacency and placidity and precipitate the landslide of political dissolution and intellectual disarray of the century's last decades? (Fernbach: 279).

The essays in this volume seek to investigate this possibility through an exploration of the dialectic – dialectic of liberation, indeed – between those twin progeny of the period, the New Left and New Right, during subsequent decades. As such, they are concerned with the diffuse legacy of the sixties – social, political and cultural – and the way in which these contrasting but related political formations sought to channel the energies of the decade. The focus, therefore, is more upon the political appropriation of the period in ideological and organisational terms than upon its diverse expressions in subsequent 'new' social movements – though many of the essays are certainly informed by the link between the personal and the political which those movements sought to evoke. Equally, the editors have not sought to impose a single definition of either of the protean and diverse movements which constitute the New Left and the New Right.

Despite obvious differences, these two movements contributed to the erosion and ultimate dissolution of that mid-century stability which has been described – perhaps too easily – as the post-war consensus. That consensus was founded on a belief that the state had both the capacity and the need to plan social and economic development. It was that conviction that the New Left, riding the crest of wider social and economic changes, called into question in the name of participatory democracy. It was those questions to which the New Right – in the ensuing dialectic of liberation – delivered their own distinctive replies in the name of the supposed superior democracy of the free market.

Today the outcome of this dialectic is not so obvious as it might have seemed in 1990 at the climax of a decade of 'bourgeois triumphalism' (in Peregrine Worsthorne's memorable phrase). The 'emotional revolutionism' of the first phase of New Right militancy represented by Thatcher and Reagan faded and the faith became 'part of the conventional phraseology of political philistines' like Bush and Major (Weber, 1919: 125). John Redwood's and Newt Gingrich's attempt to revive the original insurgent impulse confirmed Hegel's remarks about tragedy and farce. Instead a suitably repackaged and chastened left has reoccupied the seats of what passes for political power in the global market-place that the Anglo-American right has bequeathed to the world.

This new left (deliberately uncapitalised) represents neither the old left nor the New Left but rather seeks to transcend both categories, and to leap beyond the old dichotomies accepted by New Right and New Left alike in a true *Aufhebung* – that untranslatable German word conveying both abolition and incorporation of contending opposites in a process of resolution in a higher plane – which Hegel saw as the third moment in the dialectic. This process has been described more prosaically (albeit with unconscious echoes of the triune dialectic) as 'triangulation' and a 'third way'. The project is as ambitious as it may be nebulous, with Blair seeking to join Clinton and other, more improbable, acolytes in an attempt to manage – from a 'centre-left perspective' – 'social change in the global economy'. As Blair put it: 'The old left resisted that change. The new right did not want to manage it. We have got to manage that change to produce social solidarity and prosperity' (Kettle, 1998).

The rhetoric echoes the concern of much American and certainly some British social theory in the 1990s with the danger of social disintegration. There is much controversy over the source of this development. The right, especially in the US, laid responsibility at the door of the sixties and an alleged over-emphasis on rights. Some on the left are disposed to see the development as the all-too-predictable outcome of the 'creative destruction' of unrestricted global capitalism celebrated by the right. Whatever the explanation the problem evokes a common response – on left and right alike – in terms of a concern with 'community'. However, this concern with community fails to answer the question of exactly what kind of community is being identified or proposed. Are we to conceive of community as some form of government-sponsored national cohesiveness with all its authoritarian implications and potential for intensifying division by stigmatising minorities, or some more pluralistic conception – of communities rather than community? Whatever the answer, the present concern about cohesion invokes the very concept of community which, however defined, was central to the New Left in the 1950s and 1960s – even though its critics today might be reluctant to agree.

Can we identify in these contemporary developments an emerging new consensus in which old divisions are healed and new understandings forged? Kondratiev's theories of long waves of capitalist development may point to the beginning of a new economic upswing arriving, on the dot, 50 years after the onset of the post-war boom. The current 'boom' of the Anglo-American economies has certainly encouraged some to hold out a prospect of sustained non-inflationary growth. Can we see a new institutional order in the making which will provide the necessary framework for the sort of sustained growth which, if it cannot restore the golden age from 1948 to 1973, will at least overcome the disruptions of the subsequent landslide and avoid the need for renewed shock therapy? Such is the formula widely propagated in the form of the 'Washington consensus' of free markets, civil societies and good governance – Yankee Hegelianism, perhaps. Thus far it has been mainly imposed on societies in Latin America and Africa – and more recently – east Asia that are unable to resist. How far the advanced capitalist countries – notably Japan and Germany – will be able – or indeed wish – to achieve a similar 'structural adjustment' remains to be seen.

For the moment the focus seems to be as much upon attitudinal as upon institutional change. Recent soul-searching by the likes of Michael Portillo or Peregrine Worsthorne, in which old racial or sexual chauvinism is renounced and new sympathies declared, does seem to point to a new 'era of good feelings' in inter-personal and inter-cultural relations. Here surely is evidence of the beneficial legacy of the sixties. Yet a common concern on the part of New Labour and New Democrat alike to reform the behaviour of the poor and dependent (while currying favour with the rich and glamorous) arouses echoes of an earlier age – and of the intervening Thatcher/Reagan era. Superficial associations with the sixties may disguise a harsher spirit, more in tune with the requirements of the 'Washington consensus', than with the more expansive and generous spirit of that time.

The chapters in this work explore the dialectic of New Right and New Left since the 1960s in a variety of ways. For Alan Hooper, writing about what he calls the long sixties – 1956 to 1976 – the popular insurgency of the time can be seen as a 'modernism in the streets' aroused by a modernising impulse from above which eventually evoked a repressive response. In a sense the crisis of the left of the 1970s represents an internecine (and intergenerational) conflict from which the right benefited and in which the New Left's search for community receded before market imperatives in a 'globalising' mode.

Tom Steele demonstrates in his chapter about the British reception of Gramsci that the Italian Marxist aroused such a strong response precisely because his broader conception of the role of the party complemented the concern with culture as community so characteristic of what has been called the first New Left around Edward Thompson and Raymond Williams. A fascinating example of an earlier dialectic between right and left can be seen in Williams' intellectual debt to T.S. Eliot who drew inspiration from Karl Mannheim – who in turn sat at the feet of the eminent Hungarian Marxist Georg Lukács who was 'rediscovered' by the New Left, first as a literary critic and then as a political theorist. For Lukács the Communist Party represented precisely such a recovery of lost community.

Wendy Wheeler picks up this theme in her discussion of the British counter-culture of the sixties. For her too the animating spirit of the movement lay in its search for a community of authenticity and principle in opposition to the atomisation of the market. Tony Blair as a child of this era can awaken a widespread response when he stresses the need for a new community of rights and obligations.

In his account of what he calls the three New Lefts in Britain, Geoff Andrews points to their common engagement with notions of culture and community. He argues that the third New Left (around *Marxism Today*) was attempting to engage with the consequences of the failure of their predecessors to recapture a lost commonality in the face of the wave of consumerism and individualism unleashed by the sixties and ridden so skilfully by their opponents.

Marvin Gettleman's chapter on the American New Left finds its animating impulse in a search for 'beloved community' which found more diffuse expression in the counter-culture – which has contributed its own distinctive strand to Silicon Valley-style capitalism and a proportion of the more soft-centred management theory of the 1980s and 1990s. Recent research has shown that increasing numbers of Americans feel more 'at home' at work than at home (Griffith, 1997).

Richard Cockett explores the central theme of a dialectic between New Right and New Left. He argues that the New Right may have won the economic battle but the New Left won the cultural battle. Tony Blair's New Labour can be taken to represent a synthesis of the economic liberation celebrated by the New Right and the personal liberation celebrated by the New Left.

Peter Saunders offers a rather different perspective on New Labour which points to a social liberalism which goes beyond a discredited social conservatism against which both New Left and New Right revolted and the liberal conservatism of the New Right itself which has been emphatically rejected by the electorate of both Britain and the US. Invoking Emile Durkheim, he sees the main thrust of New Labour as an attempt to overcome social fragmentation through a new social solidarity in which exclusion is overcome by 'welfare to work' and inequality justified by merit.

Michael Williams attempts to set Alan Hooper's long sixties in the context of the century as a whole by an examination of the work of two leading historians – Eric Hobsbawm on the left and Robert Skidelsky on the right – who have also played a prominent role in political debates since the 1960s. Despite very different points of departure both historians have made a significant contribution to New Labour – the one by stressing the need for a broad coalition against the right through themes of inclusion, and the other through policies designed to reconstruct the welfare state. The need to rebuild community has been a major theme of publications from the Social Market Foundation headed by Skidelsky.

Paul Hirst picks up the theme of community in his chapter on associative democracy. Against the authoritarian impulse lurking within the social liberalism discerned by Saunders, Hirst offers a more pluralistic conception which arouses echoes of the more generous, utopian impulses of the sixties. Hilary Wainwright explores another legacy of the sixties, investigating the extent to which the various movements that are associated with the Bennite left point beyond the twin antinomies of social democracy and stalinism – and thus, like Hirst, towards a new relationship between the institutions of state and market and popular social initiatives.

Tariq Modood advances another kind of pluralism in his discussion of changes in the conceptualisation of black identity in Britain since the 1960s. He argues for the existence of a range of identities and against a simple polarity of black and white. Like Hirst, Modood points to the problems of an imposed community – and of a single, over-arching community, however defined. Anne Showstack Sassoon shows the extent to which the first and second New Lefts in the 1960s were inspired by what one might call the 'heroic community' of the 1930s and 1940s. She also points to the need to transcend past heroics and embrace the search for a new settlement which New Labour claims to represent.

The chapters in this volume illustrate the diversity and eclecticism of the sixties themselves and the complex lineages of descent to today's uncertainties. Community is just one of the themes of the decade refracted through different lenses in the chapters that follow. They illustrate the contested nature of the concept while pointing towards some possible solutions. But they also touch upon a host of unresolved issues, broadly registered around the concern with 'modernisation' and cognate preoccupations with modernity and postmodernism, that may be traced back to that turbulent decade. The questions were first posed in their current form in the sixties themselves and until they have been resolved we shall need to take the decade as seriously as we can.

REFERENCES

Fernbach, D. (ed.) (1973), *Karl Marx. Surveys from Exile. Political Writings*, vol. II, Penguin.

Griffith, V. (1997), 'Satanic Mills', *Financial Times*, 7 May.

Kettle, M. (1998), 'The Next Step: a Blueprint for New Labour's World role', *The Guardian*, 7 February.

Weber, M. (1919), 'Politics as a Vocation', H.H. Gerth and C. Wright Mills (eds), *From Max Weber: Essays in Sociology*, Routledge & Kegan Paul, 1948.

1 A Politics Adequate to the Age: the New Left and the Long Sixties

Alan Hooper

The sixties continue to trouble friend and foe alike but while opponents are frequently intemperate in their criticism sympathisers often prove no more than lukewarm in their appreciation. Thus E.J. Hobsbawm considers the climacteric of the decade – 1968 – 'was neither an end nor a beginning but only a signal'. When we look for what it heralded, however, we are disappointed, Hobsbawm suggesting only that it cautioned past hubris – 'it served as a warning, a sort of *memento mori* to a generation that half-believed it had solved the problems of Western society for good' – rather than promised future hope (Hobsbawm, 1995: 286). If the message is largely a negative one it does highlight an important feature of the period, namely that those who invested their hopes in the sixties included not only the masses but also the ruling elites. Might Marx's comment on an earlier revolution, that it 'paralyses its own representatives and endows only its opponents with passion and forcefulness', apply to the later one as rulers seek to distance themselves from their own failures as much as to denounce the follies of their subordinates? (Marx, 1973: 171). What is crucial to understanding the sixties is a sense of the magnitude of what was at stake; the subsequent disdain heaped upon the decade by its opponents should be seen as evidence of the scale of its challenge rather than as confirmation of its futility.

It is just such recognition that informs Samuel Beer's analysis of the twin forces which expressed a 'culture of modernity' common to all western countries and resulted in 'a general transformation of political culture in Western countries' from the 1960s – a rationalistically inspired technocratic initiative from above and a rebellious and romantic populism from below. Beer describes the latter as a form of 'populistic democracy' but it is his characterisation of its goals as the 'quality of life, participation and decentralization' which is especially relevant for it is not unreasonable to describe them as a restatement of the historic formula of liberty, equality and fraternity (Beer, 1982: 111, 147). The sixties brought together many of the key challenges of the modern era – especially the possibilities of democracy in a libertarian mode, culture in an egalitarian compass and community in a fraternal embrace – and tested their implications in a style that was as exhilarating in manner as it was problematic in outcome. This essay explores the way in which this engagement of the forces of the left with the modern condition unfolded in the 'long 1960s' in Britain and America. It begins with modernity's greatest challenge, the revolutions which were like a 'flash of truthfulness lighting up the world's political landscape', as Hans Konig observes in comparing 1968 with 1848 (Konig, 1988: 15).

The comparison of 1968 with 1848 is a telling one for, rather as 'all the doctrines developed after 1830 met their challenge in 1848', so too the aspirations of the sixties were put to the test in 1968; there was an *avant Mai* to match the earlier *vorMarz* and their illumination highlighted both past and future (Lichtheim, 1968: 61). Just as an 'unmistakable tang of modernity' emerged in 1848 so 1968 gave strong intimations of postmodernity (Elton, 1931: 138; Young, 1977: 93). As such, both compelled consideration of the significance of the 'modern': while the political aspect involved an engagement with the legacy of 1789 the social dimensions were no less significant. For 1968 came at the end of the greatest economic boom in the history of capitalism and a period of profound social change. As one observer noted in 1968, 'work has new meaning, personal space is compressed, leisure looms large, consumption has a different function' (Kopkind, 1995: 153). The changes involved the working-out of many of the issues first raised around 1848, in particular questions of 'culture', as an emerging 'post-industrial' society focused attention upon the consequences of information and education for the 'social individual'. The sixties represented an engagement with these changes not only by the left but also the hegemonic capitalist societies, Britain and the United States, whose rulers sought a liberal, as opposed to a revolutionary, solution to the democratic implications of social and political change. Their political strategies – the left drawing upon the revolutionary tradition of rights asserted by the masses in 1848, and the elites upon a liberal conception codified by T.H. Marshall a century later – unfolded in the shadow of the destructive rivalries of the Cold War as well as the liberating possibilities of an economic boom and gave to the period that peculiar mix of elation and desperation which came to a climax in 1968 (Cronin, 1996: 170–2; Nuttall, 1970: 20).

The challenge of 1848 and 1968 was felt most intensely on the left whose need to define both the means to its goals and the identity of the popular sectors led to something like a 'revolution in the revolution'. There were, however, key differences in the answers, for while '48 simplified options by finding a focus for change in the state and an agency in the labour movement, '68 confirmed an increasing disenchantment with both by enlarging political perspectives to a point of indefinition as it sought to energise social forces in association with or even against the state and labour movement. As such '68 not only identified a 'forward march of labour halted' some ten years before the claim but also called into question the achievements of that march during its century of advance from 1848 to 1948. It did so in a spirit that owed as much to the 'communalism' of '48 and values – feminism, environmentalism and romanticism – which had blossomed with the growth of the early socialist movement, as the more influential communism which pushed such values to the margins in the social changes and movements of the following century (Lichtheim, 1968: 70–1, 75, 234, 243). If 1848 proved to be a culmination which presaged retreat, 1968 testified to the sixties rediscovery of what had been deferred and of what became an imperative, the search for fraternity.

For the rulers, and especially their intellectuals, it was the question of equality which emerged most powerfully from the two years. While 1848 held out the promise of the equalisation of cultural access, 1968 and the sixties seemed to signal its imminent realisation. In doing so they posed afresh the dilemma, analysed by de Tocqueville in *Democracy in America* and Matthew Arnold in *Culture and Anarchy*, as to whether democracy in its American/egalitarian mode would entail cultural levelling and debasement. It was a challenge which issued from the popular insurgencies of the 1830s and 1840s – Jacksonian and Chartist – and which lent urgency to the answers of both; by the second half of the nineteenth century, however, the question seemed to have been settled in a manner which accommodated popular aspirations while preserving elite privileges. Chartist goals were largely assimilated within Gladstonian liberalism, while Jacksonian ambitions were channelled into a capacious Republican party. While the energies of the 1830s and 1840s found powerful cultural expression in Whitman and Ruskin, cultural practice remained more restrained. Arnold's concern with the anarchy that would follow the 'Englishman's right to do what he likes' proved largely unfounded in his own century and his own country (Arnold, 1869: 231). When British workers did seek to do what they wished it was largely in private, in institutions of their own creation – co-operatives, friendly societies, pubs – and in a manner which left other classes largely undisturbed; the one exception being their trade unions but here too, though with significant periods of disruption, it proved possible to achieve long periods of national accommodation. The energies of an

American(ising) working class could be contained by that country's geographic and economic expansiveness during the second half of the century.

Arnold's 'grave question' concerning the 'tone' of a democratic society re-emerged in the twentieth century in the form of a modernist aesthetic which promised a revolutionary combination of political and artistic radicalism (Arnold, 1861: 113). Its first manifestation occurred in the opening decade of the century when, in John Berger's 'Moment of Cubism', it seemed that a 'transformed world (had) become theoretically possible and (that) the necessary forces of change could already be recognised as existing'. The conjunction of those 'necessary forces' was rarely achieved, however. In part this was a consequence of the political attitudes of the modernists themselves for, as Berger notes, '(t)he Cubists imagined the world transformed, but not the process of transformation'. But more important in the failure of the classic modernism of the early twentieth century were the wider political circumstances which conspired against the modernists' ambitions, the fortunes of the Bauhaus being emblematic of modernism's fate during the first half of the century. However, the material abundance of the 'affluent' societies like the US in the 1950s promised not only 'a peaceful, "evolutionary" transition to the new Utopia' but also a renewal of the radical energies and inclusive aspirations of early modernism (Berger, 1970: 145, 161; Fuller, 1980: 145). In short, an egalitarian culture to complement the democratic politics which, following fascism's defeat, had become a norm for the world's states.

Fulfilling democratic promise raised not only the issue of equality but also the question of the libertarian possibilities of a political community. Once again it did so in a manner which evoked 1848 and again it was the Anglo-American societies which faced the most urgent challenges. In seeking to reinforce their liberal credentials in the face of an expansive communism and to define their world role in a period when one had lost an empire and the other acquired one, the ruling class of both countries sought to renew their socio-political arrangements. In doing so they not only opened the door to the libertarian energies of the 1960s but called into question the very institutional arrangements created to close the phase of libertarian activity of the period around 1848. In both societies the second half of the nineteenth century witnessed a recomposition and rehabilitation of the ruling-elites following the mid-century turmoil (the 'hungry forties' in Britain; the civil war in the US) resulting in a set of institutions and practices which proved highly successful formulas of political rule until the middle of the twentieth century. In Britain there emerged that aristocratically-based 'Establishment' whose identity was recognised in the mid-1950s; in the US the corresponding elite were those patrician progressives whose presidential representatives, from Theodore Roosevelt to Franklin D. Roosevelt, guided the country from regional power to global hegemony (Harris, 1984: 38, 194; Lasch, 1974: 84, 87, 95; Hewison, 1997: 75–8; Blum, 1980: 17–19).

Neither regime was without its exclusions, however. Such exclusions had been shaped by a mid-nineteenth century public/private divide which placed a predominantly male elite in the public sphere and 'minorities' – women, gays and blacks – in the private. In the mid-twentieth century 'personal troubles' arising from such exclusions became 'public' – even international – issues as a result of the Cold War. It was in seeking to redress these in the 1950s – by adding J.S. Mill's tolerance to Arnold's guidance – that both formulas and the elites who managed them were tested to something close to self-destruction in the 1960s. In the case of America this involved the most flagrant exclusion, the slavery which had tarnished the country's democratic credentials since its inception; in Britain's case the exclusions were more subtle and in so far as they bore a name it was the 'Victorianism' which censored or punished behaviour transgressing moral codes derived from that era. In both cases legal decisions signalled the search for a new settlement, the Supreme Court judgment of 1954 outlawing segregated schooling in one and the non-prosecution for obscenity of the publishers of *Lady Chatterley's Lover* in 1960 in the other (Marable, 1984: 17; Marwick, 1982: 151). The 1960s saw the Anglo-American democracies committed to fulfilling the libertarian potential of their democratic precepts as a way of overcoming exclusions which, in the context of the Cold War struggle for allegiance, had become an embarrassment or worse. With the egalitarian promise of expanding economies and the fraternal aspirations which emerged during the decade the 1960s promised a revolutionary agenda – whether it prompted a revolutionary response is the issue to which I shall now turn.

Defining the sixties is not simply a question of placing them in an historical perspective but also of establishing their duration. For just as 1956 was not simply a year but also, in Stuart Hall's words, a 'conjuncture' so too the 1960s cannot be understood if they are confined to their chronological limits; rather they can be seen as a period which was generational in scope, beginning in 1956 and ending with a set of events around the mid-1970s which we may fix in 1976 (Hall, 1989: 13). Such a periodisation helps to capture the content of the sixties by framing it in a span which was as distinctive as it was paradoxical. It highlights not only the manner in which the sixties brought together the challenges from the modern era but also how they were contested and contained. As such the period saw a complex interplay of the political and the cultural, of modernist aspiration and post-modernist critique, issues which can be approached through the most systematic attempt to define the nature and scope of the period, Frederic Jameson's essay 'Periodizing the 60's'.

'Modernism in the streets'. Such was the reported comment of Lionel Trilling concerning the youth movements of the 1960s and the 'adversary culture' of which they were an expression (Lasch, 1985: 200). It is an apt description in so far as it captures the insurgent nature of the popular forces of the decade but it misleads if it deflects attention from the modernism which was also to be found in the councils of the power-holders. For as Beer stressed, the sixties began as much with an elite-inspired 'assertion of the values of scientific rationalism' and of 'technocracy' as they did with popular insurgency; in a spirit of modernising renewal from above as well as modernist aspiration from below. Beginning in 1956 and continuing through to the mid-1960s power-centres with global pretensions sought to modernise their beliefs and practices to meet the challenge of the unfolding and apparently unending 'long boom'. For the cold war rivals – following Khrushchev's Twentieth Party Congress speech and Kennedy's New Frontier programme – this was especially urgent but left reassessment (in Crosland's *The Future of Socialism* and German Social Democracy's renunciation of Marxism) and right regimes (in the persons of Macmillan and de Gaulle) showed the extent of the imperative. Each sought to respond to the human and material possibilities of an expansive economy and, in the name of 'modernisation', to embrace a liberating science and technology which were to be directed to popular advantage by elites newly empowered by a faith in planning.

Stressing that the sixties were launched on a wave of elite renewal is not to underplay the popular energies that were decisive in the formation of the period. In identifying 1956 as the starting-point of the sixties I am not simply taking up a suggestion of a number of writers that the middle years of the fifties marked a watershed, but also pointing to a range of popular actions which caused that shift (Lukacs, 1990: 188; Barraclough, 1967: 36–8; Jameson, 1984: 180). Many are familiar and need no emphasis; they have been compellingly documented in Christopher Booker's *The Neophiliacs*. Two do need to be recalled, however, for they are central to my argument: first, and well-known, the emergence of the New Left from the twin international crises of Suez and Hungary; second, and less familiar, the first major exhibition of the group of artists called the Independent Group who together created Pop Art in Britain. The appearance of these two movements in 1956 points to the breadth and vitality of popular concerns in that year and also to an issue which was central to the prospects of the popular movements in the sixties, the renewal and possible combination of Marxism and modernism as expressions of political and aesthetic modernity.

This emphasis upon the western origins of the sixties and on the interplay between the political and the cultural as a central preoccupation contrasts with that of Frederic Jameson. He suggests that the decisive sources of the energies of the sixties derived from the anti-colonial struggles of the emergent Third World – with the civil rights movement in the US part of that de-colonising wave – and took the form of a cultural rather than political challenge in the west (Jameson, 1984: 180, 182–3). Neither claim is without plausibility but both capture only part of the story. Thus while it would be foolish not to recognise the crucial importance of events in the Third World – the emergence of the post-colonial world was the greatest revolution in the second half of the century – my claim would be that the sixties were a global phenomenon, not simply in the sense implied by Jameson that events in one part of the globe impacted upon the rest, but that societies, and especially the Anglo-American ones, were responding to a shared global challenge represented by the long boom and the competitive struggles between systems and ideologies which it entailed. Similarly, while recognising the centrality of the cultural in any definition of the sixties I would also stress the political character of the period, not only in identifying its origins in the elites' adoption of modernising strategies but also the manner of the period's closure and the reasons for its abrupt termination.

For while Jameson highlights a series of major political events during the years 1972–74 as marking the end of sixties – including the US withdrawal from Vietnam, the coup in Chile and the formation of the Trilateral Commission in 1973 – he places decisive emphasis, following Ernest Mandel, upon the 'world-wide economic crisis'. Thus he sees the sixties as a period characterised by linkages from economy to culture – the 'mechanization of the superstructure' involving, in a famous image, an 'immense and inflationary issuing of superstructural credit' in the form of popular energies – and from Third World to First as movements in the former inspired the mass culture of the latter. It is an analysis premised upon a view of the period as one in which the 'active political categories no longer seemed to be those of social class' (Jameson, 1984: 205–9). My claim is that the sixties not only began around 1956 with a class initiative – the elites' reformation – but that they ended around 1976 with a class defeat – of the masses' rebellion – and that both possessed fundamental political significance.

The manner in which the rebellion from below was checked and defeated will be examined later; given the importance of cultural issues to the sixties, however, it is vital to consider the cultural resources of the subordinate classes, in particular the modernism available for their purposes as the elites had defined a modernism for their needs. What was this popular modernism? For Beer it was a 'romantic revolt' imbued with radical-democratic ideas and a populist spirit in which the affinities between popular culture, especially pop music, and the political radicalism of the 1960s displayed the 'liberating spirit of modernity' (Beer, 1982: 139–40). Another expression of this was the Pop Art movement which began almost simultaneously in Britain and the US in the mid-1950s. It was the former that witnessed the first major public appearance of the movement at the 'This is Tomorrow' exhibition in 1956. A key exhibit on this occasion was Richard Hamilton's collage 'Just what is it that makes today's homes so different, so appealing?' which, with its images of modern man and woman surrounded by the objects and symbols of affluence in its industrial-capitalist mode, captured many of the concerns of the movement that was to flourish in the 1960s (Appleyard, 1989: 127; Hewison, 1981: 191). What did such a movement offer in the renewal of modernism and in relation to the aspirations of the masses?

The most positive aspect of Pop Art was its desire to embrace contemporary experience – 'simply to wake up to the very life we're living' as a related figure, John Cage, put it – thereby adding aesthetic dignity to what was socially popular. In so doing it connected with the concern of twentieth-century cultural and social modernism – from Freud to Trotsky – with the conditions of everyday life and with the nature of human experience in the context of industrialising, 'mass' societies. In seeking to express what Eduardo Paolozzi, one of its leading exponents, called the 'sublime of everyday life' it renewed the aspiration of early modernism to encompass the world of the masses and the 'real' and to end that divorce between the aesthetic and quotidian worlds which had afflicted modernism following its defeats at the hands of fascism and Stalinism. At its best Pop Art aspired to be inclusive and democratic and represented an heroic attempt to embrace the world and to put art at its service; together with ' "serious" pop music and the "alternative" society' it expressed a 'conviction that old cultural distinctions were worthless and had to be replaced by a new acceptance of the totality of modern experience' (Russell, 1969: 21; Appleyard, 1989: 126, 131).

Such was the promise but it was not without its problems. One was a political innocence which it shared with classic modernism: though it was a movement which connected with popular energies – with the mass and above all the young – and could be seen as a 'resistance movement: a classless commando … directed against the Establishment', it no more forged 'necessary' conjunctions with political radicalism than its early twentieth-century forerunner. The involvement of the Situationists or the Provos with what a key text of the former movement called *The Revolution of Everyday Life* (1963–65) and the explosive events of May 1968 did enable imagination briefly to seize power. Moreover the concerns of New Left figures like Raymond Williams and E.P. Thompson with culture, and especially the category of 'experience', pointed to the possibility of an 'integral lived politics' which would bring together the 'dissociated halves' of political and aesthetic radicalism which had frozen into 'Leninist' and 'avant garde' caricatures (Pinkney, 1989: 26). But a fusion of a renewed Marxism and a restored modernism proved problematic. For Pop Art's embrace of consumer society, its very non-judgemental quality, led to a mood of fatality rather than freedom before the universal reign of commodities. Williams had for some years expressed his reservations concerning modernism on the grounds not only of its tendency to self-regarding elitism but also because, in contrast to his preferred naturalism, it tended to be distant from 'experience … within its real environment'. If he became more sympathetic to modernism's radical political potential it was not without recognition of how its potential for an 'innovatory inclusion of a diversity of voices' contrasted with the 'self-absorbed miming of others' or the difference between the 'everyday vernacular' and the 'Vox Pop'. It was precisely the inability of sixties aesthetic modernism to maintain this distinction between an open, democratic modernism and a closed, technocratic one that led Peter Fuller to break with his erstwhile modernist allegiance, based upon his sympathy for the writings of John Berger, and to move towards what would later be seen as recognisably post-modern preferences for the 'natural' and the 'spiritual' (Williams, 1989: 61–2, 79–80, 113; Fuller, 1988, 1990).

This move would become a fashion but it did highlight a growing doubt as to whether a renewed modernism could encompass an increasingly diverse social experience. Such doubts had been expressed at the beginning of the sixties when in 1959 three American observers, Peter Drucker, C. Wright Mills and Irving Howe, spanning the US political spectrum from conservative through radical to socialist, identified changes which pointed to a condition which tentatively they were calling 'post-modern' (Drucker, 1959: ix; Wright Mills, 1970: 184; Bertens, 1995: 22). By the late 1960s a sense of the dissolution of the modern – and with it the modernist project of social self-determination – was finding echoes elsewhere as the optimism of the early part of the decade gave way to the travails at its end. The writings of John Lukacs were especially striking in this respect. His *The Passing of the Modern Age* (1970) gave sophisticated expression to the vulgar conservative cry 'more will mean worse'. Identifying a process of generalised inflation or what he was later to call 'insidious devolution', Lukacs noted that whether 'it is money or books or degrees or sex, where there is more and more of something it is worth less and less' and that a 'decline of taste and judgement, of truthfulness and reason was inseparable from this devolution' in areas like politics and education (Lukacs, 1990: 265; 1993: 286). These views do more than prefigure the conservative cultural critique which has dominated recent American debate; they also connect with the post-modern sentiment that modernity, as a consequence of its own evolution and elaboration, has achieved a baroque complexity or 'involution' before which 'modern' solutions are doomed to be unavailing. As such it posed a clear challenge to the artistic and political radicalism of the sixties and to the attempt of thinkers like Wright Mills and Raymond Williams to define a politics adequate to the age. It is to that politics that I now turn.

The New Left shared with Pop Art not only its origins in the year 1956 but also its concern to deepen and make relevant ambitions which had atrophied over the course of the century; in its case, though initially at least more so in Britain than America, Marxism. The twin crises of 1956 in Suez and Hungary suggested the moral bankruptcy of a capitalism reformed in a social democratic guise and of a communism incapable of discarding its Stalinist habits. More fundamentally, however, and of continuing relevance to the critique of both systems as they entered their 'modernising' phases in the 1960s, was the sense that state-led and 'planned' industrial societies were not only incapable of addressing old grievances – especially those of race, sex and class – but that the solutions they could offer simply entailed patterns of social relations which were dispiriting and dehumanising. In this sense the New Left questioned modernity in its elite-led modernising mode, counterposing to its massification of society and its pluralist politics a more radical sense of the modern, involving the search for new forms of political community and popular participation. It was a search that proved to be as disruptive for the left as it was dramatic for society. By the end of the 1960s, the extremities of the period, the inadequacies of the left and a sense of the intractibilities of the modern condition, drove the movement into a phase of self-criticism whose destructive impact was only obscured by the buoyancy which derived from a period of wide-ranging working-class mobilisation. When this crumbled in the mid-1970s before the elites' counter-offensive, and opened the way to what proved a generation of New Right domination, the left was in full retreat.

At the outset the New Left was informed by a mood of intelligent pessimism offset by a conviction that creative optimism could achieve change. It was a mood which drew equally on critical detachment and pragmatic engagement, the balance of either reflecting the contrasting political legacies of the left in Britain and the US. Thus while the British New Left – at least in its ex-communist form around E.P. Thompson – sought the renewal of Marxism, Wright Mills in the US was disposed to question a central proposition of Marxism, what he famously called the 'labor metaphysic'. Nevertheless both movements shared a commitment to a sense of community and new forms of political action, seeking what Wright Mills called a 'community of publics' and Williams a 'knowable community', or what the Port Huron Statement, the 1962 testament of the US Students for a Democratic Society, described as '... a democracy of individual participation, governed by two central aims: that the individual share in those social decisions determining the quality and direction of his life; that society be organised to encourage independence in men and provide the media for their common participation' (Jacobs and Landau, 1967: 117; Wright Mills, 1959: 300; Williams, 1974: 13–14; Teodori, 1970: 167). Freed of its conventional gender – a freeing that was to be part of the left's subsequent, often anguished, self-discovery – it expressed a fraternity to inform both the left's more usual strategic concerns with equality and liberty and to guide its tactical choices.

That it was more than a pious aspiration was evident in the two great movements which gave the New Left political anchorage in the late 1950s and early 1960s – CND and the Civil Rights movement. Drawing on traditions of political mobilisation – pacifist and anti-slavery – whose roots were deep in the first half of the previous century, they also absorbed not a little of the religiosity that had inspired these movements, the personal witness of CND and its offshoots being matched by the search for 'the beloved community' amongst civil rights activists. The momentum of both carried them through to the mid-1960s with some sense of real achievement: the Test-ban treaty of 1963 and the Civil Rights Act of 1964 were testimony to their impact. Both, perhaps inevitably, fell short of their goals: the bomb was not banned and racism not eradicated and from the mid-1960s, in what are widely regarded as the decade's climacteric of 1965–68, disillusionment with Wilson's Labour Government and Johnson's Democratic Presidency, dramatised in both cases by the agony of Vietnam, drove the New Left in search of new responses (Burner, 1996: 155–7; Young, 1977: 157–9).

It was a search that proved as dramatic as it was destructive. Both were fully evident in the 'summer of love' of 1967, of hippiedom and psychedelia. Today the best remembered, and easiest mocked, phase of the sixties it was the most assimilable to the imperatives of capital accumulation. Nevertheless, it arose from the same impulse as movements, of which black power was the first, which were concerned to explore the relationship between self and society and which produced one of the most famous slogans of the period, the 'personal is political'; its legacy was not simply the cultivation of lifestyle but also the emergence of the feminist and gay movements. A second and related response in these years was the establishment of communes for living or collectives for service-provision. Such (anti) institution building drew upon traditions which had been nurtured in Europe in the years before 1848 and often found a lasting home only in the United States during the nineteenth century; it was there that they received the greatest support and perhaps their lasting achievements. Often representing an attempt to rethink the nature of professional practice – as in moves to establish centres of artistic, psychiatric and academic provision in Britain by Wesker, Laing and Cooper – their more exploitable energies could be commodified by capitalist entrepreneurs as in Silicon Valley. Equally, the same region, perhaps the leading centre for such communal experiment, could also nurture a gay community which, if it could not create an alternative society, did sustain a sense of alternative values (Hewison, 1986: 17–18, 138–9, 155–6; Berman, 1996: 166–8; Roszak, 1988: 161–4).

The most dramatic attempt on the part of the left to meet the challenge of the explosive mid-1960s period, however, came in movements which sought to look outwards rather than inwards and to give an encompassing meaning to the notion of community rather than one based upon individual or group identity. As a sense of crisis intensified, above all in the US but also in a wave of military coups in the Third World and the unravelling of Stalinism in Czechoslovakia and Gaullism in France, so the left looked to total explanations and solutions. A desire for 'sweeping summations' has been noted as a feature of the period and by the latter part of the decade, and especially around 1968, this reached a peak. It was as evident in the writings of newly discovered gurus like Marshall McLuhan and Buckminster Fuller as it was in the practice of artists like Stockhausen and Cage; politically it found its clearest expression in the revival of interest in the Marxism of Lukacs and the humanistic analysis of the French and British New Left (Appleyard, 1989: 203, 213). It represented an attempt to engage with the 'totality' of socio-political circumstances facing societies transformed by the long boom and apparently experiencing an equally comprehensive crisis, revolutionary in its ramifications and in the response it seemed to require.

'1968' was that response. It took place at a time when the 'organised' forces of the New Left, the SDS and the May Day Manifesto initiative in Britain, were entering a deep and terminal crisis (Young, 1977: 87, 160). Nevertheless, spontaneous organisation, as in France in May, seemed both adequate to the task and more in keeping with the spirit of events whose spread was as rapid as it was unpredictable. Moreover, the events seemed to reveal that fusion of culture and totality whose dimensions the New Left had sought to define. The spirit was captured in much of the art produced during the turmoil but we also possess, in the accounts of Tom Nairn and Henri Lefebvre, compelling witness to what was at stake. Thus Nairn noted the actuality of totality: '(1) ate capitalist society is infinitely more united than the conventional categories allow for, and this unity (because the system remains divisive at the same time) is itself an omnipresent contradiction', while Lefebvre identified the cultural dimensions of the crisis – 'a certain conception of learning ... a certain rationality ... is disintegrating' – and saw as the solution 'self-management' not just of 'learning' but 'of the totality of social life' (Nairn, 1968: 162–3; Lefebvre, 1969: 140–1). Such eloquence testifies not only to the revolutionary spirit of the May 'events', but also suggests their character as an attempt to realise that fraternal embrace, egalitarian culture and libertarian democracy which was the historic significance of the sixties. That they failed will come as no surprise to those for whom goals of this magnitude are bound to seem as delusive as the forces seeking their realisation were nugatory. In turning in the final section of this chapter to the defeat of the left I want to suggest that the manner of the defeat is itself testimony to the enormity of the challenge posed by the movements of the long 1960s and that it is in defeat that we learn as much about the character of the period's aspirations as in success.

The defeat of the left, and with it the close of the sixties, seems so easily accounted for that it might be described, in a word that reverberated throughout the left in the 1970s, as 'over-determined'. Such an interpretation runs the risk of failing to give adequate attention to left opportunities because of an only-too-easy temptation to accept right inevitabilities. To do so would be to ignore the very real sense of crisis which afflicted western political economies in the mid-1970s, one expression of which was the 'crisis of democracy' literature of the period (Crozier *et al.*, 1975). Because that crisis has now been resolved, for the moment at least, the left's insurgency at the time looks both implausible and insignificant. In seeking to document the left's failure it is necessary to avoid a narration which makes defeat appear pre-ordained. Only by giving back to the period a sense of the possible can we restore to the sixties and to the left a sense of their continuing significance.

By the late 1960s there was clear evidence that the energies of the decade were in danger of self-destructing. I have noted the crisis of the New Left organisations which, paradoxically, co-incided with the climax of mass mobilisation in 1968; equally, however, there was a sense of waning cultural confidence. The promise of an aesthetic modernism was called into question not simply from the right but also from the left, from Peter Fuller as well as John Betjeman. The urban environment, key to any modernist artistic and political project, was the focus. Already in the early sixties, in a text that can now been seen as a precursor of the post-modernist turn, Jane Jacobs had warned of the destructive effects of comprehensive urban planning; the fate of the high-rise blocks at Ronan Point, East London and Pruitt-Igoe, St Louis in 1968 and 1972 respectively, quickly becoming symbols for the failings of an overweening modernism. It was an unfair charge, for it conveniently ignored the political and economic constraints on both architect and planner, but it was one which stuck. Modernism had failed to connect with popular sensibilities: an international style attuned to national sensibility, of the sort proposed by the 'arch-modernist' Nikolaus Pevsner, was not achieved (Appleyard, 1989: 122–5; Curtis, 1996: 499).

A similar dissociation of the modern and the popular, the cosmopolitan and the local, afflicted Marxism. The political equivalent of the New Brutalism in architecture was the Althusserianism that swept the Anglo-American left in the 1970s. Not only did it marginalise what was now increasingly called the 'old' New Left – Thompson and Williams being rejected for their 'romantic populism' – but it also had adverse political consequences for the left as a whole. A key legacy of 1968 was, as we have seen, the discovery of new social identities which blossomed into the new social movements that came to dominate much left politics in the 1970s. This could be seen, at the very least, as a necessary development for the left, remedying its own exclusions – of blacks, women and gays – of the past century and reconnecting with the diverse concerns and romantic energies of the era of 1848. However, in its Althusserian inflection it countenanced, if it did not actively encourage, the fragmentation of the left and, as Jameson has noted, a 'semi-autonomous cultural politics'.

This development, understandable in so far as it reflected the surge of energies of movements engaged in what were increasingly perceived as struggles against millenial-long oppressions, took a heavy toll on the left's confidence. For not only did the 'centrifugal force of the critique of totality' lead it to 'self-destruct', in Jameson's words, but the avowed anti-humanism of Althusser and his epigones identified the left, fairly or not, with the anti-democratic, technocratic and inhuman features of modernity against which the New Left impulse had first emerged. With the counter-culture increasingly identifying such forms of 'modernity' with the Enlightenment the way was open for a veritable surge of post-modernist 'spirituality': Thompson's bitter polemic and Berger's embarrassed retractions could not stem a tide which made Prince Charles the defender of the values of community and drove Peter Fuller in search of the 'lost illusions' of Nature and God (Jameson, 1984: 191–2; Thompson, 1978; Jencks, 1988; Dyer, 1986: 139).

This disarray among the left assumed epidemic proportions in the 1980s for by then the countervailing force of an insurgent working-class was in decline. For the early 1970s had seen a wave of labour militancy of a sort that many on the New Left had thought a thing of the past; a product of the crisis of the western political-economies which unfolded between 1968 and 1973, and perhaps of the student 'signal' of 1968, its political repercussions were felt in the crisis of governability in Britain and the United States – the miners' strikes and the Watergate crisis respectively – and throughout Western Europe in the form of Eurocommunist advance and the crisis of the dictatorships – Italy and Portugal being the key instances. A full narration of these events is beyond the scope of this essay but two fundamental political consequences may be noted. First, the development of the New Right. As a political formation its emergence may be dated from the election of Margaret Thatcher in May 1975, its American annunciation following with Ronald Reagan's unsuccessful campaign for the Republican Presidential nomination in 1976. Both were to achieve preeminence in the 1980s when their versions of free market liberalism, reinforced where necessary by reactionary moralism and aggressive militarism, established the supremacy of an Anglo-American version of capitalism whose global extension proved to be one of the most remarkable features of the latter part of the century. Second, and related to the emergence of the New Right, was the role of the 'old left' in the mid-1970s crisis. For if the New Right were the ultimate beneficiaries of the end of the post-war era it was the old left that oversaw its initial death-throes. It was Wilson and Carter who guided Britain and the US through the 'present danger', seeing off the challenge of those imperfect embodiments of New Left energies, Benn and

McGovern, while the course of the 'transition' crises in Europe were decisively influenced by left politicians – communist and socialist – in Italy, Spain and Portugal (Pimlott, 1993: 659–63; 1995: 243–4). While the old left claimed to be defining a new popular settlement, the outcome was not only a disabling of left organisations and energies but an opportunity for an emboldened New Right to seek an 'irreversible shift in the balance of wealth and power' to the possessing classes.

Writing five years after 1968, of a different but not unrelated conjuncture – 1945 – E.P. Thompson noted that the reforms of that year and those which followed 'if sustained and enlarged by an aggressive socialist strategy, might well have affected such a cancellation of the logic of capitalism that the system would have been brought to a point of crisis'. So far so familiar perhaps but then he added: 'a crisis not of despair and disintegration but a crisis in which the necessity for a peaceful revolutionary transition to an alternative socialist logic became daily more evident and more possible' (Thompson, 1978: 144). Was it not 'despair and disintegration' which set in from the mid-1970s and which has gathered apace for the socialist left thereafter? And was there not an absence of 'aggressive socialist strategy' which could have carried forward the energies of the sixties and at least have challenged if not cancelled the 'logic of capitalism'? Instead that logic has assumed new and perhaps unprecedented momentum in what is now called 'globalisation'. It represents a stark contrast to the ambitions of the sixties left for, as George Katsiaficas has put it, '(p)eriods of revolutionary crisis bear little resemblance to crises produced by economic breakdown' for while the latter have their roots in the irrational organization of the economy and the state ... general strikes and revolutions are essentially attempts to provide rational alternatives', so that while economic breakdown eventuates in a reassertion of the 'blind hand of change' resting solely 'on the internal development of the economy' revolutions seek a process by which Nature becomes History (Katsiaficas, 1987: 10, 96). Was it not just such a reconciliation of that which the New Right sought to sunder – the 'natural' and the 'cultural' – that was sought by the New Left in theory and by the sixties in practice in their quest for 'totality' and 'community' and are we not living with the consequences of their failure in a world from which the values of libertarian or participatory democracy, egalitarian cultural practice and, above all, fraternal social relations are absent? Let the last word – of modernist aspiration to set against post-modern dissolution – come from the founding statement of the American New Left which is even more relevant today than it was then: a 'new left must transform modern complexity into issues that can be understood and felt close-up by every human being. It must give form to … feelings of helplessness and indifference, so that people may see the political, social and economic sources of their private troubles and organize to change society' (Teodori, 1970: 172).

REFERENCES

Appleyard, B. (1989), *The Pleasures of Peace. Art and Imagination in Post-War Britain*, Faber & Faber.
Archer, R., Bubeck, D., Glock, H. *et al.* (eds) (1989), *Out of Apathy. Voices of the New Left Thirty Years On*, Verso.
Arnold, M. (1861), 'The Popular Education of France' in *Matthew Arnold: Selected Prose* (ed. P.J. Keating), Penguin, 1970.
Arnold, M. (1869), 'Culture and Anarchy' in *Matthew Arnold: Selected Prose* (ed. P.J. Keating), Penguin, 1970.
Barraclough, G. (1967), *An Introduction to Contemporary History*, Penguin.
Beer, S. (1982), *Britain Against Itself. The Political Contradictions of Collectivism*, W.W. Norton.
Berger, J. (1970), 'The Moment of Cubism' in *The Look of Things* (ed. N. Stangos), Penguin.
Berman, P. (1996), *A Tale of Two Utopias. The Political Journey of the Generation of 1968*, W.W. Norton.
Bertens, H. (1995), *The Idea of the Postmodern*, Routledge.
Blum J. Morton (1980), *The Progressive Presidents. Theodore Roosevelt, Woodrow Wilson, Franklin D. Roosevelt, Lyndon B. Johnson*, W.W. Norton.
Booker, C. (1970), *The Neophiliacs. A Study of the Revolution in English Life in the Fifties and Sixties*, Fontana.
Burner, D. (1996), *Making Peace with the 60s*, Princeton University Press.
Cronin, J.E. (1996), *The World the Cold War Made. Order, Chaos and The Return of History*, Routledge.
Crozier, M.J., Huntington, S.P. and Watanuki, J. (1975), *The Crisis of Democracy*, New York University Press.
Curtis, W.J.R. (1996), *Modern Architecture since 1900*, 3rd edn, Phaidon.
Drucker, P. (1959), *The Landmarks of Tomorrow*, William Heinemann.
Dyer, G. (1986), *Ways of Telling. The Work of John Berger*, Pluto Press.
Elton Lord (1931), *The Revolutionary Idea in France, 1789–1871*, Edward Arnold.
Fernbach, D. (1973), *Surveys from Exile, Political Writings,* vol. 2, Penguin.
Fuller, P. (1980), *Art and Psychoanalysis*, Writers and Readers Publishing Co-op.
Fuller, P. (1983), *Aesthetics after Modernism*, Writer and Readers Publishing Co-op.
Fuller, P. (1988), *Seeing through Berger*, Claridge Ltd.
Fuller, P. (1990), *Images of God. The Consolations of Lost Illusions*. Hogarth.
Hall, S. (1989), 'The First New Left: Life and Times' in *Out of Apathy. Voices of the New Left Thirty Years On* (ed. R. Archer), Verso.
Harris, J. (1984), *Private Lives, Public Spirit: Britain 1870–1914*, Penguin.

Hewison, R. (1981), *In Anger. Culture in the Cold War 1945–60*, Weidenfeld & Nicolson.

Hewison, R. (1986), *Too Much. Art and Society in the Sixties, 1960–75*, Methuen.

Hewison, R. (1997), *Culture and Consensus. English Art and Politics since 1940*, Methuen.

Hobsbawm, E.J. (1995), *Age of Extremes. The Short Twentieth Century 1914–1991*, Abacus.

Jameson, F. (1984), 'Periodizing the 60s' in *The 60s Without Apology* (ed. S. Sayres), University of Minnesota Press.

Jacobs, P. and Landau, S. (1967), *The New Radicals*, Penguin.

Jencks, C. (1988), *The Prince, the Architects and the New Wave Monarchy*, Academy Editions.

Katsiaficas, G. (1987), *The Imagination of the New Left: a Global Analysis of 1968*, South End Press.

Keating, P. (1970), edited and introduced, *Matthew Arnold: Selected Prose*, Penguin.

Konig, H. (1988), *1968. A Personal Report*, Unwin Hyman.

Kopkind, A. (1995), *The Thirty Years' War. Dispatches and Diversions of a Radical Journalist, 1965–1994*, Verso.

Lasch, C. (1974), *The World of Nations. Reflections on American History, Politics and Culture*, Vintage.

Lasch, C. (1985), *The Minimal Self. Psychic Survival in Troubled Times*, Pan.

Lefebvre, H. (1969), *The Explosion. Marxism and the French Upheaval*, Monthly Review Press.

Lichtheim, G. (1968), *The Origins of Socialism*, Weidenfeld & Nicolson.

Lukacs, J. (1990), *Confessions of an Original Sinner*, Ticknor & Fields.

Lukacs, J. (1993), *The End of the Twentieth Century and the End of the Modern Age*, Ticknor & Fields.

Marable, M. (1984), *Race, Reform and Rebellion: the Second Reconstruction in Black America*, Macmillan.

Marwick, A. (1982), *British Society since 1945*, Penguin.

Marx, K. (1973), '18th Brumaire of Louis Napoleon' in *Surveys from Exile, Political Writings*, vol. 2 (ed. D. Fernbach), Penguin.

Mills, C. Wright (1959), *The Power Elite*, Oxford University Press.

Mills, C. Wright (1970), *The Sociological Imagination*, Penguin.

Nairn, T. (1968), 'Why it Happened' in *The Beginning of the End. France, May 1968* (eds A. Quattrochi and T. Nairn), Panther Books.

Nuttall, J. (1970), *Bomb Culture*, Paladin.

Pimlott, B. (1993), *Harold Wilson*, Harper Collins.

Pimlott, B. (1995), *Frustrate their Knavish Tricks*, Harper Collins.

Pinkney, T. (1989), 'Introduction' in *The Politics of Modernism. Against the New Conformists*, Verso.

Quattrochi, A. and Nairn, T. *The Beginning of the End. France, May 1968*. Panther Books.

Roszak, T. (1988), *The Cult of Information. The Folklore of Computers and the True Art of Thinking*, Paladin.

Russell, J. (1969), 'Introduction' in *Pop Art Redefined* (eds J. Russell and S. Gablik), Thames & Hudson.

Sayres, S. (ed.) (1984), *The 60s Without Apology*, University of Minnesota Press.

Stangos, N. (1970), edited and introduced. *The Look of Things*, Penguin.
Teodori, M. (ed.) (1970), *The New Left: A Documentary History*, Jonathan Cape.
Thompson, E.P. (1978), *The Poverty of Theory and Other Essays*, Merlin.
Williams, R. (1974), *The English Novel. From Dickens to Lawrence*, Paladin.
Williams, R. (1989), *The Politics of Modernism. Against the New Conformists*, Verso.
Young, N. (1977), *An Infantile Disorder? The Crisis and Decline of the New Left.* Routledge & Kegan Paul.

2 Hey Jimmy! The Legacy of Gramsci in British Cultural Politics

Tom Steele

The legacy of Gramsci in the British New Left is both profound and puzzling. It's now almost 50 years since the first translations of Gramsci's work were made but still the 'war of position' and the 'organic intellectual' read as enigmatic metaphors rather than political realities. In the absence of a proletarian revolutionary party, or 'Modern Prince', which was central to Gramsci's project, the cultural struggle initiated by the New Left has only fitfully grounded itself in any social movements. Despite an impressive body of solid cultural analysis, the caricature of academic cultural studies as looping psychotically between mandarin theoretical discourses and an uncritical populism, is not without some truth. Such a grounding in political economy and social movements, which was the aim of the old New Left, has yet to be made. The moment may have passed. Class as an organising myth of solidarity has given way before the claims of gender, ethnicity, sexuality, disability and a variety of issue-based politics, much of which, it has to be said, have been made visible by the new forms of cultural analysis. Academic cultural studies, indeed, ushered in the politics of New Times in which post-Marxists so successfully deconstructed their own foundations, that they left themselves without party or central direction. Failing to materialise, the 'rainbow coalition' faded into the dull blur of New Labour. But, not to be too gloomy, there are what Raymond Williams called 'resources of hope' here. The desubordination of women has profoundly affected everyday life in the post-1960s decades through making the politics of the personal central to 'family' life and increasingly unavoidable at the workplace. Older forms of industrial struggle, as the 1984–85 Miners' Strike graphically displayed, were transformed into struggles for lives and communities by the critical engagement of women – culture as a form of life. What the new politics have also shown moreover is the importance of place and locality rather than the abstractions of state and nation. Beginning with demands for quality of life, cultural struggle is centrally about here and now.

'Hey, Jimmy! Huv ye nae heer't o' Gramsky?' In February and March, 1968, the *Scotsman* published an angry correspondence between two old comrades which announced a new star in the night sky of the British Left. The Scottish poet, Hugh MacDiarmid, responding to a reference his friend, Hamish Henderson, had made to his brief flirtation with fascism in the 1920s, wrote that it was amusing that Henderson should have used 'the great name of Gramsci' to confute him. Henderson's rebuke was that if MacDiarmid had a wanted a true political hero why, instead of Il Duce, did he not contemplate the career of Antonio Gramsci. MacDiarmid replied that of course he already knew about Gramsci, who 'dealt primarily with the 'superstructure' – the whole complex of political, social and cultural institutions and ideals – rather than its 'economic foundations' (quoted in Henderson, 1997: 167). MacDiarmid was remarkably familiar with Gramsci's ideas:

> Gramsci believed that 'cultural' problems were especially important in periods following revolutionary activity, as in Europe after 1815 and again after 1921. At such times, he said, there are not pitched battles between classes: the class struggle becomes a 'war of position' and the 'cultural front' the principal area of conflict. But a 'cultural' battle was not easy: Marxism had retained too many elements of materialism, determinism and economism.' (Henderson, 1997: 168)

He then quoted a rather puzzling paragraph about something called 'the philosophy of praxis' and revealed just how it was that he knew so much about a long-dead Italian communist of whom few, outside of the minuscule British New Left, had heard:

> The quotation is from Gramsci's *Quaderni del Carcere* – as perhaps Mr Henderson knows, since he told me about twenty years ago that he had been entrusted with the translation of Gramsci's works into English – a project of which, so far as Mr Henderson is concerned, nothing quite characteristically has been heard since. (Henderson, 1997: 168)

Twenty years! And thirty years since 1968. Yet looking back, without 'Gramsci' the shape of the British New Left would have been almost unimaginable. He was placed in the vanguard of what was to become a significant stream of European Marxist intellectual influences, invoked by the New Left to restore the intellectual deficit at the heart of British culture, the famous 'absent centre' described by Anderson in 1967, and to repair the theoretical defects of Marxism itself (Anderson, 1991).

In the 'New Left' an entirely new politics had been conjured up to deal with, by the end of the 1960s, an increasingly prosperous and markedly unrevolutionary British working class, easing comfortably into the post-war welfare state; a Communist Party in terminal decline from its war-time high water mark of 60 000 members; a Labour Left abruptly disaffected from Harold Wilson's 1966 government and, stemming from the expansion of the Robbins Report, a rebellious libertarian student population.

But, despite MacDiarmid, it was in large part Henderson's proselytising that brought Gramsci to the attention of the notoriously insular British Left. During the latter part of World War Two he had served in Italy with the partisans and, on his return to Britain, his friend Amleto Micozzi sent him the volumes of Gramsci's writings as they appeared in Italian, which included the 'Letters from Prison' in 1947, 'Historical Materialism and the Philosophy of Benedetto Croce' in 1948 and 'Notes on Machiavelli, Politics and the Modern State' in 1949. Henderson 'began the translation of them straightaway, as a labour of love, and without (at first) a thought of a publisher' (Henderson, 1997: 168). No publisher was immediately forthcoming. The newly founded Instituto Gramsci had also approved Louis Marks to make a translation of selections from the prison notebooks and he discussed the problems of translation with Henderson. Lawrence and Wishart eventually published them as *The Modern Prince* in 1957, effectively the first text of Gramsci's in English to get a thorough airing. Extensive extracts from Henderson's translations were however published in 1959 in successive numbers (9 and 10) of the *New Reasoner* which Edward Thompson and John Saville were then publishing from Yorkshire.

THE OLD NEW LEFT AND SOCIALIST HUMANISM

Thompson and Saville had begun the *New Reasoner* as a critical organ within the Communist Party but after Khrushchev's public exposure of Stalin's crimes and the suppression of the Hungarian uprising in 1956, they left the party. Tentatively, they made contact with the group of former Oxford University students, which included Stuart Hall and Raphael Samuel, who ran the *Universities and Left Review* (Dworkin, 1997: 66). The resulting collaboration produced *New Left Review* which became the primary intellectual organ of the emergent British New Left. The *New Reasoner* was explicitly a journal of 'Socialist Humanism', the guiding rationale of which was a trenchant critique of the Stalinised economistic marxism which characterised the ideology of the Communist Party of Great Britain (CPGB). In effect it opened the cultural front within British Marxism itself. While the issue of culture had never been entirely absent from the CPGB, until the end of the war it had been more or less marginalised to the party's intellectual groupings. Although intellectuals and writers were encouraged to form sections for literature, writing, history and so on, they were not expected to engage with the political decisions taken by the party's central committee.

One of the British Communist Party's more congenial aspects for intellectuals had been precisely its cultural activity (Croft, 1995). The party was indeed a source of patronage and education for young writers during the 1930s, for whom it could offer publication in literary journals and introduction to left publishing houses like Lawrence and Wishart. At the same time its most energetic historians' group, under Dona Torr and Christopher Hill, was attempting to reconstitute a British social history along marxist lines and based on popular sources (here it paralleled the more social democratic social history of R.H. Tawney, G.D.H. Cole and others whose centre was in adult education) (Steele, 1997). It also enabled a cosmopolitan atmosphere into which other European refugees from Nazism could discuss non-Soviet European Marxism, like that of the Lukács group, so long as they were discreet about it. The party acted both as a club and mentor group. Dissident intellectuals and writers were attracted to it in part because it provided alternative arenas for serious cultural debate to those commanded by Bloomsbury and the aesthetic elite but also offered a partisanship with working people. Although, between the World Wars, the party adopted a relatively laissez-faire approach to its cultural groups and allowed them considerable rein, later disputes between the groups and the party leadership grew bitter. With the onset of the Cold War, in 1947, however, the leadership began to realise the growing political significance of culture and established a National Cultural Committee, under the chairmanship of Emile Burns, to 'co-ordinate' the work of the ten specialist cultural groups, including the Writers' Group. The Cold War in Britain was, inevitably, given the overdetermined influence of 'English' writers in the national culture, shaping up on the literary high ground – as exemplified by Crossman's *The God that Failed* – and the party's view increasingly was that culture was too important to be left to intellectuals (Croft, 1995).

As orthodox Marxist models of economic determinism came increasingly under attack from defenders of the 'open society', the party had become more sensitised to the power of ideologies and representations in forming class consciousness. Moreover, inspired by the Chinese Revolution in 1948 and the importance given to the cultural struggle in the writings of Mao Tse Tung, the Twenty-Second Party Congress called for a cultural front alongside the political struggle. 'The British Road to Socialism', the party's new political programme, which stressed the independent national dimension, had to be supported by some more developed understanding of what Britishness, or Englishness, actually was. Under the auspices of *Arena*, the most important of the party's cultural journals, a seminal series of conferences on aspects of culture were held, to which many of the party's intellectuals contributed, including the young Edward Thompson.

These conferences were important for mapping the ground on which the cultural struggle should be fought. In tune with growing anti-colonial movements, they attempted to construct an alternative sense of national identity to that associated with imperialism and oppression, which revalued the radical tradition of Paine, Cobbett and Morris. It was clear that, in these conferences, the idea of a militant 'class' culture was strategically giving ground to that of a national 'common' culture. George Thomson, the classicist and one of the party's most respected intellectuals, argued that it was wrong to think of 'culture' as class-bound only since, in Britain, so-called bourgeois culture was also the heritage of socialism. Tommy Jackson, the proletarian philosopher, argued that it was even a revolutionary culture and English literary realism, as Gorky had said, was 'pioneering' in its ability to lay bare the injustices suffered by working people. However, at this stage, George Thomson's ambitions for the cultural struggle were relatively limited. He wanted the party to encourage 'worker-writers', so that writing was seen not simply as a class-bound activity. He encouraged intellectuals not only to unite with the workers but be tempered by them and he also wanted intellectuals to interpret the British cultural heritage in the light of Marxism–Leninism.

But, by quoting from the heretical communist literary critic of the 1930s, Christopher Caudwell, that the struggle should 'drag the past into the present and force the realisation of the future', Thomson seriously offended the party leadership. They, in turn, drummed up a fierce debate in the pages of the party's journal *The Modern Quarterly* during 1950–51, intended to bring dissident party intellectuals into line. This had the opposite effect on Edward Thompson who was inspired into re-thinking the role played by culture in the class struggle. He was completely persuaded by Caudwell's refusal of the reduction of consciousness to passive reflection and mechanical materialism and of the galvanic power of poetry (Thompson, 1977). This broke with the conventional Marxist base and superstructure analogy and allowed a much more flexible interpretation of cultural determinants to be developed.

In his own contribution to the *Arena* conference on 'The American Threat to British Culture', Edward Thompson made perhaps his first major intervention into the party's cultural debate with a talk called 'William Morris and the Moral Issues of Today'. Here, he argued that party could not wait until a new kind of 'socialist man' appeared after the revolution: 'We must change people now, for that is the essence of all our cultural work' (Thompson, 1951). Morris's 'moral realism' was clearly in his sights at this time and the significance of the talk is that he interpreted the political project of the party as in major part to be achieved through educational and cultural objectives. Thompson's work as a university staff tutor in adult education at the University of Leeds, in the West Riding of Yorkshire from 1948 to 1965, gave him a base for putting this policy into practice. Here he produced two seminal works which were to create new mental maps for the emergent new left, *William Morris. From Romantic to Revolutionary* in 1955 and *The Making of the English Working Class* in 1963 (this last was to attract a truly popular readership only when it was published by Pelican in 1968).

While the CPGB's strategy was to reconstruct a radical vision of Britain primarily through new historical narratives, Thompson had long known that orthodox marxist economism had little to offer. Thus *The Making* pursued the Caudwell heresy in implying a relative autonomy of the cultural sphere. The working class was not just passively shaped by economic forces, it shaped itself. In Thompson's account, it moved, through its own agency, from being a class in itself, in the Hegelian sense, to being a class for itself. 'William Morris' became a key sign, which signalled the power of culture to inspire both anti-stalinist and anti-capitalist energies in the political struggle, through what Thompson called 'moral realism' and 'socialist humanism'.

Thus in part the New Left began to emerge in Britain through the invocation of significant writers on culture and centred in the practice of education, particularly adult education. The seminal texts such as *The Making of the English Working Class*, Richard Hoggart's *The Uses of Literacy*, Raymond Williams's *Culture and Society* and *The Long Revolution*, were all written during the ten to fifteen years that their authors worked in university adult education. It is important to emphasise that these works were not isolated events but were nested in a widespread culture of experiment in adult education which had begun with the debates over arts and literature teaching in the mid- to late-1930s (Steele, 1997). In one of his last essays Raymond Williams noted:

> when I moved into internal university teaching, when at about the same time Richard Hoggart did the same, we started teaching in ways that had been absolutely familiar in Extra Mural and WEA classes, relating history to art and literature, including contemporary culture, and suddenly so strange was this to the Universities they said 'My God, here is a new

subject called Cultural Studies'. But we are beginning I am afraid, to see encyclopaedia articles dating the birth of Cultural Studies from this or that book in the late 'fifties. Don't believe a word of it. That shift of perspective about the teaching of arts and literature and their relation to history and to contemporary society began in Adult Education, it didn't happen anywhere else. (Williams, 1989: 162)

Williams believed that the basis for a New Left politics was the constituency of working-class and lower middle-class students who came to adult education classes and he envisaged a new culturally based left politics. Williams's own short-lived journal, *Politics and Letters*, and a companion volume called the *Critic*, were attempts to engage in that arena which Williams increasingly saw as the 'decisive' world for his political work: 'Virtually every WEA tutor was a Socialist of one colour or another. We were all doing adult education ourselves. So we saw the journals as linked to this very hopeful formation with a national network of connection to the working-class movement. If there was a group to which *Politics and Letters* referred, it was the adult education tutors and their students.' (Williams, 1979: 69) Although he was familiar with members of the Communist Party's Historians Group, especially Eric Hobsbawm, Williams had only briefly been a member before the war and was never a committed Marxist. Indeed, precisely to displace Marxism (to use Stuart Hall's term derived from Gramsci) from the centre of his intellectual work, he had all but constructed his own radical tradition in the Tawney mode, which he called the 'Romantic critique of capitalism', which was the burden of his epochal book *Culture and Society*. Paradoxically, Williams almost certainly gained his understanding of the significance of this kind of cultural political work, not from any left theorist but from F.R. Leavis and from T.S. Eliot's recently published *Notes Towards a Definition of Culture*, which he rather admired. For him, Eliot was a conservative for whom radicals should be grateful. (But, in an interesting intellectual loop, Eliot in his turn was indebted to the work of Karl Mannheim, with whom he had regularly come into contact in Oxford Christian Socialist networks.)

While the contemporary significance of William Morris and the adult education constituency had been where Williams and Thompson and the old New Left met, it was of no interest to the young turks who, in the early 1960s, ousted the founders of *New Left Review* from the editorial board, and this signified a conceptual break in the notion of the cultural struggle. The project for this new New Left then became less one of 'nostalgically' rehistoricising Britain, national identity or a new Englishness, than of

'Europeanising' the Left and constructing marxist intellectual cadres. Perry Anderson and his colleagues on NLR were convinced that the intellectual hardware for conducting the cultural struggle could not be resurrected from domestic sources. They embarked on an ambitious programme of translating European marxist, revisionist and post-marxist theorists, while simultaneously dumping the non-theoretical and popular cultural issues of the journal into the out-tray. Of Anderson, Thompson wrote: 'we found we had appointed a veritable Dr. Beeching of the socialist intelligentsia. ... Old Left steam engines were swept off the tracks: way side halts ("Commitment", "What Next for C.N.D.?", "Women in Love") were boarded up; and the lines were electrified for the speedy traffic from the marxistentialist Left bank. ... Finding ourselves redundant we submitted to dissolution' (Thompson, 1978: 35).

As we have seen, Thompson had already published some of the first translations of Gramsci by Henderson in the *New Reasoner*. But there were other important European precursors. As immigrants to Britain in the 1930s, Jewish intellectuals on the run from nazi persecution had by the mid-1950s, by and large, secured for themselves academic appointments and were publishing significant 'cultural' sociology in English: for example, Karl Polanyi's *The Great Transformation*, Karl Mannheim's *Ideology and Utopia* and Arnold Hauser's *Social History of Art*. Although Norbert Elias's *Involvement and Detachment* was published in 1956, most of his work had to wait until the last twenty years to be read in English despite his position in an English university (Kilminster, 1993). Adolf Löwy was another refugee from the 'other' Frankfurt to gain intellectual influence in Britain (Pels, 1993).

However, what characterised this group of European intellectual was their indebtedness to German philosophical idealism, the Hegelian–Marxist dialectic and Weberian sociology. This group prepared the way for the reception of George Lukács, translated and published during the 1960s by the Merlin Press, one base of the old New Left (see also Watnick, 1962). While many years earlier in the Budapest *Sonntagkreis* his *History and Class Consciousness* had stimulated Mannheim's engagement with the sociology of consciousness, it now resonated strongly with Thompson's re-examination of working-class consciousness. Goode remarks that the translation of Lukács's work was an important precursor for the reading of Thompson's and that 'Thompson's concept of consciousness as historical agent teaches us more about the actual behaviour of literary texts in history than most of the analyses of the behaviour of signifiers' (Goode, 1990: 190).

While the younger New Left took a considered interest in this strand of Euro-marxism, it became fascinated by the more radical Frankfurt School of Benjamin, Horkheimer and Adorno. Many in the student movement took up Herbert Marcuse with relish because they read his dialectics of liberation as implying that students now replaced the working class as the agents of revolution and 'Students of the World Ignite!' became the slogan which sparked off campus occupations across Britain. But its main preoccupation was with what Thompson called the 'marxistentialist Left Bank', ie Parisian theory. Initially this centred on Sartre's later work, particularly *The Problem of Method*, which was sharply critical of Lukács, and the *Temps Modernes* writers such as André Gorz. But, in his turn, Sartre was critiqued and translations of Louis Althusser and Jacques Lacan followed, along with a turn towards structuralist and linguistic methods. Although Deleuze had announced in *Nietzsche et la philosophie* (1962) that the labour of the dialectic must be replaced by the play of difference, the widespread English dissemination of French deconstructionist and post-structuralist writers did not take off until more than a decade later – and then on the rebound from the United States.

FROM LEAVIS TO GRAMSCI: THE BIRMINGHAM CENTRE FOR CONTEMPORARY CULTURAL STUDIES

Without doubt, however, the seminal institutional innovation in the project of advancing the cultural struggle was the foundation by Richard Hoggart in the mid-1960s of the Centre for Contemporary Cultural Studies at the University of Birmingham. A shoestring post-graduate set-up, castigated by some of his elitist colleagues as 'Hoggart's line in cheap hats', the Birmingham Centre produced some of the most acute cultural criticism and analysis of popular culture yet to appear in Britain. Significantly, the centre grew from Hoggart's less politicised pre-occupation with working-class and popular culture, much of it based on reflecting on his own background in, and emigration from, the urban working class. It was determined much more by Hoggart's engagement with literary criticism, particularly Leavisite methods, a reading of Orwell's radical journalism, and marked by an explicit hostility to Marxism, which he regarded as methodologically too crude to deal with cultural questions. Ironically, Hoggart did not see this work as political but, if anything, anthropological, or an extension of literary critical methods into an analysis of popular culture already begun by Orwell. He was sceptical of socialist utopian claims and unhappy with Williams's term 'common culture' (Corner, 1991). He put this down to the difference in their understanding of the value of their class background despite the apparent identity of being 'working-class'. In a conversation with Williams, Hoggart confessed,

> I felt from your book [*Culture and Society*] that you were surer, sooner than I was, of your relationship to your working-class background. With me, I remember, it was a long and troublesome effort. It was difficult to escape a kind of patronage, even when one felt one was understanding the virtues of the working-class life one had been brought up in – one seemed to be insisting one these strengths in spite of all sorts of doubts in one's attitudes, (Hoggart and Williams, 1960: 26).

However, he recruited Stuart Hall from *New Left Review* to increase the sociological edge of the new centre. Hall may have been glad to escape the feuding on the journal's editorial board but clearly had a different agenda from that of Hoggart and, although he followed the emphasis Hoggart placed on working-class culture as resistance, he gradually dislocated it from Hoggart's vision. What Hall did was to bring a sociological perspective and a personal determination to explore non-Soviet and revisionist marxist theory for ways round the utterly disabling base-and-superstructure metaphor.

His rediscovery of Gramsci in the early 1970s, even more than Althusser – 'this profound misreading, this superstructuralist mistranslation, of classical marxism' (Hall, 1996: 266) – was a breakthrough. Gramsci, he said, radically displaced some of the inheritances of marxism in cultural studies; his work was a necessary detour around the blockages to a marxist study of culture. From Gramsci cultural studies in the British context learned 'immense amounts about the study of culture itself, about the discipline of the conjunctural, about the importance of historical specificity, about the enormously productive metaphor of hegemony, about the way in which one can think questions of class relations only by using the displaced notion of ensemble and blocs' (Hall, 1996: 267). So more than two decades after Hamish Henderson's initial attempts to translate and publish Gramsci in Britain, he finally arrived.

Hall's project at the Birmingham Centre fitted somewhere between the Thomson/Williams 'long revolution' of an educated democracy with a socialist consciousness and the Anderson/*New Left Review* attempt to create an elite of marxist theoreticians who could act as the storm troopers of the cultural struggle in the long march through the institutions. Hall was struck in particular by Gramsci's conception of the 'organic intellectual'. Even though they were not sure what it would mean, 'there is no doubt in my mind that we were trying to find an institutional practice in cultural studies that might produce an organic intellectual' (Hall, 1996: 267).

For him, the crucial aspect of this kind of intellectual was her or his alignment with an emerging historical movement. But where was it to be found?
After over a century, the 'working class' or 'labour' movement was hardly
emergent any longer and seemed to have fossilised into a set of bureaucratic institutions concerned with what Gramsci would have called defensive economico-corporate positions, whereas what the Centre was looking
for were the building blocks of Gramsci's ethico-political.

Despite the absence of an obvious social movement with which he or
she should be aligned, the organic intellectual must work on two fronts
simultaneously. It was essential both to be at the forefront of intellectual
theoretical work and to engage in educational work. The organic intellectual had the responsibility of transmitting those leading ideas to those who
did not belong to the professional class of intellectuals. Without those
fronts operating at the same time, Hall argued, the project of cultural studies was fatally flawed, because you might get enormous advances on the
theoretical front without any engagement at the level of the political project. Hall confessed that the intellectuals of the Centre never connected
with 'that rising historic movement' and had to content themselves with
operating with it as a metaphor and 'as if'.

For Hall, the second major irruption into the cultural struggle and cultural studies was the women's movement and feminism. But was this not
precisely the connection between the organic intellectuals (of feminism)
and the rising historic movement (of women), Hall was seeking? The history of women's studies in Britain demonstrates great debts to the educational activity of women in self-help groups and in adult education where
the connections between theoretical understanding and political practice
could at times be close and effective (Rowbotham, 1989: xiv). The boys'
club of the New Left suddenly came under sustained assault and 'a thief in
the night, it (feminism) broke in; interrupted, made an unseemly noise,
seized the time, crapped on the table of cultural studies' (Hall, 1996: 269).
Hall had no doubts about the impact of this turn: it demanded the politics
of the personal; expanded the notion of power to the non-public sphere;
centred gender and sexuality alongside, or instead of, class; opened up the
question of the subject and the subjective; and reopened the closed frontier
between social theory and psychoanalysis. Thus while Gramsci had effectively displaced orthodox marxism from cultural analysis, feminism all but
dispensed with conventional constructions of class, power and the subject.
Cultural politics therefore took a quantum leap from the modest proposals
of the CPGB of the early 1950s to reinvent a national identity and the
old New Left of the late 1950s to recreate a common culture. Hall's third

irruption, that of ethnicity and race, effectively opened the cultural struggle on the front previously occupied largely by the right. Here too theory could connect swiftly with a social movement and organic intellectuals might find themselves with a political function beyond the academy. Significantly, the initial energy for both feminists and black consciousness came from the United States, where both the women's and black movements were more angry and more assertive than in Britain and Europe. Yet the ultimate connection between theoretical work and social movements seem not to have happened in the way that Hall wanted. Why not? Hall implies that the crucial tension between textual or theoretical practices and social affiliations was either broken or never fully established. Despite the dazzling theoretical contributions made by cultural studies, no corresponding advance was made in cultural politics. In America cultural studies appears to have broken completely free from social movements and become both fully institutionalised and isolated within the academy. In Britain the tension still exists but the moment of profound danger which for Hall is represented by institutionalisation has been recognised by those, like Angie McRobbie, who have striven to become 'organic intellectuals', as a crisis in cultural studies (McRobbie, 1991). McGuigan insists that cultural studies has lost touch with political economy (McGuigan, 1992) and has instead tended to bifurcate between, at one extreme, a celebratory populism in which anything goes, so long as it comes from the people and, at the other, mandarin (or should we say Martian) theoretical discourses which make no concessions to the intelligent layperson.

Recognising this, Hall makes the point that, although they might abut and even overlap at times, academic work is not the same as intellectual work. The movement for cultural politics has not achieved an 'organic intellectual political work' 'which does not try to inscribe itself in the overarching meta-narrative of achieved knowledges, within the institutions' (Hall, 1996: 274–5) – and language like that perhaps explains why. In other words, in Gramsci's terms, the new knowledge has not translated itself into the new common sense, but has been content to remain trapped in the political economy of academic institutions. Whole careers have been made from it.

How much is Hall's pessimism conditioned, despite his best intentions, by a metropolitan outlook? Do the marginal spaces hold out any hope? Hall's colleague at the Open University, Angus Calder, has argued consistently that Scottish cultural politics and intellectual work cannot simply be incorporated into the English hegemony and has subtly resisted the more arcane elements of current cultural theory. Calder annoyed many of his colleagues in the early 1980s by suggesting that many of the new Emperors of Theory were not in fact wearing any clothes and that the debate over popular culture in English left-wing circles represented 'a compound of displacements' (Calder, 1994: 238). In the first place many of the translations from French cultural theory simply failed to resonate in English and carried little specific purchase. Secondly, the very heavy theoretical superstructures which were deployed to deal with elements of popular culture such as James Bond films or Coronation Street were frequently comic. Perhaps the worst indictment Calder makes, however, was the displacement by many academics of genuine political practice by theoretical argument. Some colleagues managed to convince themselves and their students that doing cultural theory was, somehow, politics. On the whole, Calder argues, precisely because of Scotland's marginality, even provinciality, the discussion of fashionable French thinkers has been severely limited.

In England, certainly, the dislocation during the last two decades, between academics and social movements, has been such that Raymond Williams could argue that the project of cultural studies no longer recognised the social formation to which it belonged (Williams, 1989). Despite the undoubted fecundity of contemporary Cultural Studies, what began in the late 1950s as a movement for a new left politics and a popular democratic education, threatens to become, in the 1990s, deeply pessimistic of rational political intervention, obsessed with style and frankly conservative in its aspirations. Fewer practitioners engage with social movements or even accept their existence, even to what might have been the hope of the new politics, the women's and ecological movements. Instead, as Rowbotham notes, 'The women's studies courses which emerged out of argument and struggle have now begun to grow into a little knowledge industry of their own' (Rowbotham, 1989: xiv).

The role of public intellectuals has of course changed significantly. While Debray noted the rise of the intellectual as smooth television commentator, Bauman has argued the drift from the nineteenth century of the intellectual as legislator to that of interpreter. Intellectuals in effect have been mostly reduced to the role of supervisory academics overseeing a multiplying plethora of paper qualifications within a system whose drastically declining unit of resource threatens to deprive them of even the most cursory contact with their students, let alone a wider public. The decline in academics' pay relative to other professional groups graphically states their fall in status and the new vocationalism of qualifications recognises the deep suspicion of liberal and humanistic learning in governing circles.

WORK, PLACE, PEOPLE AND PLAY

In 1996 I moved from Leeds '24-hour City' to Glasgow 'City of Culture'. While Leeds seemed to be taking off culturally, Glasgow already seemed to be in decline. 1997 saw the last Mayfest, Scottish Opera losing its orchestra, museums shut one day weekly and widespread accusations of city corruption. Leeds on the contrary, under its squeaky clean New Labour administration, now has Opera North, a vibrant West Yorkshire Playhouse under Jude Kelly, the Henry Moore Sculpture Centre, several excellent dance companies, a great club scene, street cafés and a postmodern lighting scheme in the shopping centre. I used to think that the strength of Leeds's cultural scene was really its underground as in the avant-garde Nietzschean group the Leeds Arts Club and subsequent societies (Steele, 1990), the punk and Gothic art house bands of the 1970s and 1980s and alternative presses. With the greater visibility of official culture this may have changed but clearly many more people can simply enjoy living in the city than ever before.

Even in decline, however, Glasgow is much richer culturally. It's not just the six theatres offering a brilliant range of productions, Scottish Opera, the Scottish National Symphony Orchestra, avant-garde chamber music at the Royal Scottish Academy of Music and Drama (RSAMD), the Glasgow Film Theatre, the Celtic Connections Festival, the wealth of art galleries and museums including the Burrell Collection, Mackintosh's School of Art, the People's Palace, etc., etc. though they mark an institutional valuation of culture few other cities of comparable size could match. But there is something about the life of the town itself in its multitude of clubs, bars and cafés where talk and music are endless. Even contemporary bands sing songs about Glasgow in a way that rarely happens elsewhere and there seems to be a powerful commitment in the vibrant musical and literary scene of musicians, writers and singers to the place itself. Yes, this is provinciality, but it is an extraordinarily productive and resonant provinciality which makes metropolitan culture seem limp and regressive. It respects Patrick Geddes's mantra: 'Work, Place, People' to which Pat Kane, the cultural commentator, might add 'Play'.

I don't know whether this is to do with a resurgent Scottish nationalism and an instinctive anti-metropolitanism or a shrewd political intervention by a now discredited city boss, but it is surely the product of a still-serious attitude towards learning and living, intense enjoyment of a sense of place, and feel for social justice and historic struggle, which is a form of cultural politics. All this is powerful and persuasive and produces a fine quality of life for all those with disposable income. However, as in Leeds, the inhabitants of the windswept 1960s council estates and unfashionable tenements get little value from it. Cultural politics has left them without a politics. Calder notes that a Glasgow colleague found the pronunciation of 'hegemony' that came easiest off the tongue was 'Hey Jimmy!' – and Gramsci, of course, had to be Gramsky.

The cultural turn in politics has been vital and has produced incisive critiques of the dominant culture (its own invention) which left an older Marxism and socialism tongue-tied. So successfully has it opposed the base and superstructure metaphor, however, that it has all but disconnected from political economy and loosed culture theory into the stratosphere. Abandoned by New Labour and the culture of labour all but destroyed, the inhabitants of the estates and the tenements have discovered other diversions, which have required them to be heavily policed (see 'Trainspotting' and the TV drama series 'Jo Jo'). Intellectuals and cultural theorists will be positioned once more in the nineteenth-century role of colonial missionary and explorer in order to gain the consent of the oppressed to new forms of governance. Alternatively, they could begin to build a new educational movement and offer their collective services, free, to whatever groups are seeking humane, democratic and socialist solutions for their situations. Fifty years of 'Gramsky' has to have its uses.

REFERENCES

Anderson, P. (1966), 'Socialism and Pseudo Empiricism', *New Left Review*, 35, pp. 2–42.
Anderson, P. (1991), 'Components of the National Culture', *English Questions*, Verso.
Calder, A. (1994), *Revolving Culture, Notes from the Scottish Republic*, I.B. Tauris.
Corner, J. (1991), 'Studying culture: reflections and assessments. An interview with Richard Hoggart', *Media Culture and Society*, Vol. 13, 1991, pp. 137–51.
Croft, A. (1995), 'Authors Take Sides: Writers in the Communist Party, 1920–1956' in *Opening the Books: New Perspectives in the History of British Communism*, Kevin Morgan, Nina Fishman, Geoff Andrews (eds), Pluto Press.
Dworkin, D. (1997), *Cultural Marxism in Postwar Britain*, Duke University Press.
Eliot, T.S. (1948), *Notes Towards a Definition of Culture*, Faberand Faber.
Goode, J. (1990), 'Thompson and the Significance of Literature', Harvey J. Kaye and Keith McClelland (eds), *E.P. Thompson, Critical Perspectives*, Polity Press, pp. 183–203, p. 190.
Gramsci, A. (1971), *Prison Notebooks* (eds) Q. Hoare and G. Nowell Smith, Lawrence and Wishart.
Hall, S. (1996), 'Cultural Studies and its Theoretical legacies' in (eds) David Morley, Kuan-Hsing Chen and Stuart Hall *Critical Dialogues in Cultural Studies*, Routledge.

Hall, S. (1990), 'The Emergence of Cultural Studies and the Crisis of the Humanities, October, 53, 1990, pp. 11–23.

Henderson, H. (1997), *The Armstrong Nose, Selected Letters of Hamish Henderson* (ed.) Alec Finlay, Polygon Press.

Hoggart, R. (1957), *The Uses of Literacy*, Pelican.

Hoggart, R. and Williams, R. (1960), 'Working-Class Attitudes', *New Left Review*, No. 1, Jan/Feb 1960, pp. 26–30.

Kaye, H.J. and McClelland, K. (1990), (eds), *E.P. Thompson, Critical Perspectives*, Polity Press.

Kenny, M. (1995), *The First New Left British Intellectuals After Stalin*, Lawrence and Wishart.

Kilminster, R. (1993), 'Norbert Elias and Karl Mannheim; Closeness and Distance, *Theory, Culture and Society* Vol. 10, No. 3, August 1993, pp. 81–114.

McGuigan, J. (1992), *Cultural Populism*, Routledge.

McRobbie, A. (1991), 'New Times in Cultural Studies', *New Formations*, 13, Spring.

Pels, D. (1993), 'Missionary Sociology between Left and Right: A Critical Introduction to Mannheim', *Theory, Culture and Society*, Vol. 10, No. 3, August 1993, pp. 45–68.

Rée, J. (1984), *Proletarian Philosophers*, Clarendon Press.

Rowbotham, S. (1989), *The Past is Before Us, Feminism in Action since the 1960s*, Penguin.

Steele, T. (1990), *Alfred Orage and the Leeds Arts Club, 1893–1923*, Scolar Press.

Steele, T. (1997), *The Emergence of Cultural Studies 1945–65: Adult Education, Cultural Politics and the English Question*, Lawrence and Wishart.

Swindells, J. and Jardine, L. (1990), *What's Left, Women in Culture and the Labour Movement*, Routledge.

Thompson, E.P. (1951), 'William Morris and the Moral Issues Today' in *The American Threat to British Culture*, Arena Publications, pp. 25–30, p. 30.

Thomson, E.P. (1955), *Romantic to Revolutionary*, Lawrence and Wishart.

Thompson, E.P. (1968), *The Making of the English Working Class*, Pelican.

Thompson, E.P. (1977), 'Caudwell' in Socialist Register 1977, J. Saville and R. Miliband (eds), Merlin Press, pp. 228–76, p. 244.

Thompson, E.P. (1978), 'The Peculiarities of the English' in *The Poverty of Theory and Other Essays*, Merlin Press, p. 35.

Watnick, M. (1962), 'Relativism and Class Consciousness: Georg Lukács' in Leopold Labedz (ed.), *Revisionism Essays on the History of Marxist Ideas*, pp. 142–65.

Williams, R. (1958), *Culture and Society 1780–1950*, Penguin.

Williams, R. (1961), *The Long Revolution*, Pelican.

Williams, R. (1979), *Politics and Letters*, Verso.

Williams, R. (1989), 'The Future of Cultural Studies', in *The Politics of Modernism*, Verso.

3 Stars and Moons: Desire and the Limits of Marketisation
Wendy Wheeler

KISSING THE WORLD BETTER

Sometime in the 1960s, my mother – advocate of the unlikely mix of Freudianism and astrology which produced the intense sixties interest in the work of Carl Jung – took me, excitedly (because here was evidence of a new, popular and marketable, interest in the esoteric ideas which she considered important), to a new bookshop in Camden Town. This bookshop – Compendium – sold and thus released upon the market *ephemerides* (plural of *ephemeris* – the annual book of tables detailing the movements of the planets which are used by astrologers to erect astrological charts) which had, previously, only been available via very limited specialist outlets.

Compendium bookshop is still there – astrology and alternative everything at the back; heavy critical theory downstairs. In the sixties, its exterior – including the whole house above it – was covered in a sort of hippy, flower-power, mural. By the mid to late sixties, the whole of north Camden Town, focusing on the open-air market by Camden Lock, and the Roundhouse at Chalk Farm, was a celebration of alternative sub-culture and entertainment. People living alternative life-styles made what they could by selling (gorgeous) second-hand clothes, or home-made hippy candles, or stuff brought over from India in the wake of the obligatory guru-pilgrimage of the period. Stars and moons and fairies were everywhere. Almost everyone read Tolkien's *Lord of the Rings*.

Twenty-five or so years later, in 1993, I went down to Compendium for some books I needed (downstairs department) and, afterwards, wandering around Camden Town in the leisurely way that is only possible for an academic on sabbatical, I realised that the shops (Camden Lock market having been replaced by a bricks and mortar version) were full of stars and moons again. The old hippy candles were back, supplemented this time by candles and candle-stands of a more frankly medieval and ecclesiastical sort, of the kind once only available from church outfitters in Victoria. India was well represented again also – in jewellery, incense, and clothes.

The difference was that what we had once thought of as the stuff of an alternative culture – alternative to capitalism, you understand – was now very obviously commodity. What, I asked myself, was going on?

For a brief while – exemplified in the golden summer of 1967 when anyone wearing a kaftan and beads was your friend, man – me and kids like me really believed that we would be able to love the despised world of the adults, of the 'straights' in their suburbs and suits, and of the West with its wars and murderous nuclear hatreds. Joannie Mitchell sang 'By the time we got to Woodstock, we were half a million strong'; the British contribution to the first global TV link-up was the Beatles, with a studio crammed full of friends, singing 'All You Need is Love'; and, a little later, if memory serves, John and Yoko would have bed-ins and bag-ins, and all the other forms of love-in through which we flower children pursued our liberatory credo.

In 1993, and subsequently, it seemed to me that the commodification of the sixties marked the desire to retrieve that brief and youthful hope when we went about trying to kiss everything, and everyone, better. It is often said these days that the young are depoliticised, or that they express their 'politics' in different ways – single-issue campaigns, rebellious celebrations of drug culture, green politics, and so on. But, in the main, we were no different. Party politics were where the 'straights' were; going on CND marches did not, for most, lead to joining the Labour Party; taking illegal drugs (it was in the sixties that Release – an alternative culture law service for people who had been 'busted' – was set up in a rundown area of Notting Hill) was for personal enlightenment and to put two fingers up to the Establishment; tree-hugging (usually when stoned) affirmed both different ways of experiencing living things, and also an alternative way of valuing life on earth.

ESCAPING COMMODIFICATION

The stars and moons in Camden in 1993 (and, still in 1997, more or less everywhere, with the late addition of kitschy Christian iconography, and decorated utility articles such as calculators with multi-coloured plastic jewels for buttons) speak to a desire for symbolic enrichment and a rejection of the dominant utilitarian and neo-economic-liberal culture of the post-1979 period. The predominant gesture of the mid to late 1960s was the search for spiritual and cultural authenticity, for a place that capital couldn't reach. The commodification of the 1960s which began in the early 1990s, implicitly makes that gesture again – rather sadly, this time, by commodifying an earlier site of attempted resistance. All that the commodification of hippiedom in the 1990s can do is to express, via the obscure desires of the market, the fact of a hopeless desire for that earlier moment, and especially for what it signified; it cannot be made real again, but it can be made, and then sold.

The problem, as Marx foretold, is that the inexorable logic of capitalism is to commodify – that is to marketise – everything. As became very evident on the night of May 1st/2nd 1997, very many people believed that something in what Tony Blair said, and stood for, might allow us to escape – even if only a little – from the debasing worship of the market, and from its accompanying devaluation and degradation of ethical life; that is to say that, in the 1997 General Election, what was expressed was some form of desire for a way of living in which the good life is not reducible to possessions, greedy getting, or simple self-interest, but in which other, not strictly accountable, things might also be seen to have value. For clearly, it is in non-accountable things – things which cannot be priced – that resistance to the ethically enfeebling rule of money is to be found. Political commentary, criticism and gossip since the election has really revolved around the question of authenticity and principles. Does the Blair government have integrity at its core (pictures of Tony and Cherie on their knees at church on Labour Party Conference, Sunday 1997), or has Blair simply understood, much more clearly than Margaret Thatcher even, that politics is a commodity too – to be packaged and sold (New Labour, endlessly spun to the punters)?

But, of course, commodification is always caught up in desire. The lure of the commodity does not lie simply in its utility (although very often that it a part of its attractiveness), but in the way in which it stands in for something that seems perpetually to elude us. Where there was once danger and magic in the world, or something magically transforming in our direct and labouring engagement with the world, with modernity there has been disenchantment and reason. The commodity, like any fetish, has an auratic quality; in it we glimpse, all unknowingly, the power of an identity which seemed once to be in the world, and which now seems estranged from it and hopelessly fragile.

An earlier generation of Freudians had believed that the expression of desire in non-violent forms – full and natural self expression (including, of course, sexual self-expression), existential freedom, and so on – would be the undoing of the world of bourgeois repressions, and all the other forms of psychical and physical violence associated with capitalism. Thirty years on from the 'liberation movements' of the 1960s, the manifest untruth of this seems incontestable. Bourgeois society may have

classically produced neurotics, but various critics, and many psycho-
analysts, have noticed a steady increase this century in patients suffering
from the unresolved narcissisms of the so-called 'borderline' personality
(the borderline is between normality and psychosis) in whom desire is dis-
organised, and affective life deadened. The classic background to borderline personalities is not too much repression and too much (irrepressible)
affect, but too much affectlessness; the borderline personality has suffered
from a lack of relatedness and an emotional deadness in early (usually
maternal) care. In other words, desire must be organised. That means pro-
voked, enjoined and constrained. Desire is not desire unless it is organised.
Just as much as gravity and topography make possible the great force of
a mighty river, so desire is nothing without the forces which contain
and channel it, no matter how much it is in continual 'conflict' with them.
The great question about desire for twentieth-century critics (Adorno, for
example) sceptical of 'liberation of desire' theories such as those associated with the work of Marcuse or R.D. Laing, was that of describing a
form of constraint, or 'mastery', which is not experienced as a violent
objectification.

The most compelling answers – psychoanalyst D.W. Winnicott's, for
example – take us directly back to one of the things which was also
directly articulated in sixties flower-power: the matter of love. For
Winnicott, the non-violent excitation/containment of desire is found in
what he called 'holding': holding is a form of emotional containment
which is endlessly reciprocal and adaptive. It certainly implies one who
holds and one who is held, but it also includes the idea of mutual
exchange and learning, and mutual transformation. As all good enough
parents know, the emotional space which is marked out by the child–
parent relation is not simply about the authority of the one who holds;
it is about authority as responsibility; that is: continually readjustive
responsiveness. Typically this relationship also marks the space – what
Winnicott called the 'transitional' space which is filled with 'transitional
objects' – where the infant first creatively invents his or her own forms of
symbolic life. Note that meaning is not 'violently' imposed here; there is
negotiation, eccentricity, waywardness, and a to and froing of the labour
upon the symbols being created, bartered, and exchanged. Containment –
or 'holding' – is achieved through a mixture of anarchic devotion to the
miracle of human creativity and development, and an understanding
of the importance of limits as the recognition of safety and trust in the
reliability of others. It is quite clear that, for Winnicott, these creative
transitional spaces of holding and making are the model of the conditions
of the good life.

THE LIMITS OF MODERN RATIONALISATION AS MARKETISATION

What does this have to do with the question of the politics of desire as that was widely and popularly raised during the 1960s? Then, bourgeois life was seen as deadeningly oppressive to human creativity and relationship. One of the results of the intervening 30 years has been a significant lessening of stifling conventionality. Nonetheless, the unbinding forces of capital – increasing and intensifying marketisation – have taken over the disciplining effects of convention; where once we were subject to the disciplines of moral convention, now we are subject to the disciplines of the market. What is still lacking – and what born-again Christians, new agers, cultists of various sorts, and purchasers of stars and moons still seek – is a space for an experience (call it what you will: spirituality; creativity; love) which cannot be bought. This cannot be a fantasised space of absolute freedom of desire. As I have suggested above, desire is precisely what is called into being and channelled; 'free' desire is not desire at all, but rather its opposite: affective deadness and psychotic-like amorality. If a playful and creative space – something like Winnicott's transitional space – offers a model of possible sites of resistance to the claustrophobic grip of the commodification of all human experience, what would the implication of this understanding of desire be for politics, political action, and policy?

Tony Blair's call to modernisation remains problematic. Markets do not provide for all human needs: there can be no market of true affections, no market of the inexplicable things that move us and which make life worth living. If modernisation means more investment in the production of skills, and in education, then it is still the case that, there too, not everything in the relationship between a teacher and a learner can be reduced to a simple checklist of aims and objectives. Mysterious things happen in relationships between individuals whose minds and abilities are bent on the same task. Such things effect transformations upon all those involved – and these transformations, by which new things can come about, and in which cultural life and knowledge are truly renewed, are not susceptible to strict calculation. The Oxbridge colleges wish to preserve the economic privileges which make the one-to-one tutorial possible because they understand very well the transformative and educational power of close human contacts. Modernisation as rationalisation has its limits. Rational conduct – simply understood – is neither creative, nor productive, nor, actually, how our most pressing personal and political problems are solved. Here, for example, is Thomas Powers, describing the transcripts when reviewing *The Kennedy Tapes: Inside the White House During the Cuban Missile Crisis* (eds Ernest May and Philip Zelikow) in the *London Review of Books* (Powers, 1997, p. 18ff):

> This exchange is elusive; its exact meaning seems to hover just out of reach. Other passages are simply incomprehensible as Kennedy's advisers converse with each other in a semi-coherent shorthand of sentence fragments, truncated questions, vague allusions, swallowed words, repetitions, deferential nods and shrugs and miscellaneous noises of objection, assent, qualification, emphasis. There are pages so opaque and unrecoverable that it seems one could evolve a whole new perspective on spoken language as depending less on grammar and syntax than on a kind of emotional semaphore.
>
> What becomes clear in the course of these often tedious discussions is that men in groups don't so much try to figure things out – an intellectual process depending heavily on articulation – as feel things out: to weigh what they are planning to do, and their reasons for doing it, by consulting their gut.

Here we see, in the most critical and pragmatic situation of the postwar period imaginable – when World War 3 seemed imminent – just how very much some of the most central actors were not, thank God, constrained by some idiotic and limited idea of rationality. And here is the lesson for Blair's continuing commitment to Thatcher's market neo-liberalism: the absolutely managed life-world – the life-world in which everyone jumps to the supposedly 'rational' tune of markets and commodification – is dangerous because inhuman. Fully human processes and negotiations – such as those recorded at the White House during the Cuban missile crisis in which a third world war was averted – are rather like, as Powers notes, the human negotiations within a good marriage:

> Such crises, routine at home, are rare among nations. Kennedy did not live to write his account of the lessons learned from the Cuban missile crisis, but it would probably have sounded very much like the sort of thing marriage counsellors say every day to marriage partners at the breaking point: 'leave your anger in the office, decide what you want, if you want to make up say so; if it's over, say that; draw the line and make it clear, set your limits, stick to your guns'.

Powers's drawing of the affective domestic parallels to political relations seems right. If you want to raise a good society, it is necessary to make spaces for affective, 'gut', work; over-rationalisation and over-management are deadly to creative problem-solving and real progress; toleration of the creative messiness of emotional semaphore is essential. What the

Kennedy Tapes expose is the extent to which good political judgements rely upon the apparent incoherences of transitional spaces where people can feel their way to creative solutions.

ECOLOGIES OF MIND

All this may seem a hundred light year's away from the pragmatic concerns of politicians and policy, yet Geoff Mulgan, since May 1997 installed in the Policy Unit at Number 10, has – in his 1997 book *Connexity* – made an extended version of the argument offered here (Mulgan, 1997). 'Soft' knowledges, emotional literacy, and all the forms of human relationship skills which are, strictly speaking, non-calculable, are increasingly important in contemporary societies. In a chapter entitled 'Ecologies of Mind', Mulgan concludes by saying:

> In a modern liberal society we see ecologies of mind as somehow outside the realm of politics and of conscious choice. The choosing individual is sovereign. But in densely populated societies, this is not a sustainable perspective. We depend on the minds of others, on their being healthy and well-intentioned. The implication of taking these ecologies seriously is that every institution is open to judgements: it becomes legitimate to ask what mentalities they tend to create, whether they leave those who come into contact with them stronger or weaker, more able to bear responsibilities or less so, ethically fluent or ethically stunted. If they drain, suppress, destroy the human spirit then it is legitimate to ask them to make up the cost they impose on everyone else. (Mulgan, 1997: 144)

For Mulgan, such ecological 'mentalities' (understood in the broadest sense) constitute 'social capital'; but the term may be misleading since such 'social capital' cannot in fact be bought, only acquired through time and affection. Significantly, Mulgan himself turns to the parent–child relation as the model of good or bad 'mentalities': 'The starting-point for understanding mentalities is childhood. It is at an early age that we learn to make connections with others.' (Mulgan, 1997: 132)

Tony Blair has said that people expect too much of governments; yet it is clear – eighteen years of Thatcherism made it obvious, and New Labour's 1997 Election Campaign made it central – that one thing which governments can do is to set a certain tone which then spreads out into all aspects of society at large. Thatcherism elevated individualism and markets above all else; Blair campaigned on anti-corruption and integrity (which is why the November 1997 Formula One tobacco advertising exemption, following upon a million pound donation to the Labour Party by the Formula One Chief Executive Bernie Ecclestone, caused such a furore). The idea that a government could promote the importance of emotional competence, and the importance of the non-calculable things which nurture such competence, is not far-fetched.

THE LEGACY OF THE 1960s AT THE END OF THE TWENTIETH CENTURY – RE-ENCHANTMENT

We have come a long way since the 1960s. Then, the question of human desire and self-expression was first widely raised as a political question. Hippiedom sought to resist the most dehumanising aspects of bourgeois commodity culture and the disenchanted world. It didn't succeed, but it did put in train, and popularise, a way of thinking about the world which has not only not disappeared but which, thirty years later, is being expressed with even greater force – albeit, very often, in commodified forms. Alongside this, perfectly serious and realistic people (in the humanities and in the sciences) have begun the processes of thought, research and publication which feed into what is increasingly a mainstream, and perfectly level-headed body of work which returns us to the roots of counter-cultural concerns. These roots lie in the perception that what is most valuable about human beings – their creative communicative souls – can never be a commodity upon the market because the labour of love and relatedness that makes it is absolutely incalculable.

In talking about the cultural importance of protected 'held' creative spaces, I mean, of course, both science and art; not all research or thought must be money-profit or ends directed. But in these market-god times, perhaps a special plea needs to be made for the humanities – for the liberal arts. Only totalitarian regimes seem fully to appreciate the subtle effects of the arts; democracies often seem inclined to think them peripheral, or at least, not as sources of real knowledge (which position, it is popularly believed, only science can attain). Yet when we think about the most profound social and cultural changes of the second half of the twentieth century, a substantial part of these – the gender revolution and the black and gay consciousness movements – have neither come from the 'hard' sciences nor, barely, been articulated by them at all. It has been from the social sciences and from the arts – not from the hard sciences and business – that a substantial part of our changing self-perceptions in the contemporary world have arisen.

What the 1960s put in train on a wide and popular scale was the possibility of thinking human goods differently. What this meant was that enchantment and love were 'in the air', as something resistant to the affective violences of bourgeois life, because uncommodifiable. Capitalism will try to commodify the soul – witness the presence in the shops of kitsch Catholic iconography on candles, keyrings, and so on – and the wisest among us will try to resist it. This is not because the cash nexus is simply evil – capital is immensely inventive and creative in its own ways – but because, as with Louisa Gradgrind and James Harthouse in Dickens's *Hard Times*, it turns the heart to ice. The coup de grâce of capitalist commodification will lie in obliging it to recognise non-Faustian space – the unpurchaseable place – and thus in obliging it to recognise the unquantifiable, that is, the priceless, value of its absolute 'other': the spaces which escape commodification. Here, the logic of commodification would reach its limits, and would reach something like Hegel's attained community of mutual recognition in which the absolute other cannot be mastered, but can only be – must be – simply acknowledged as absolutely other – and absolutely valuable on that account.

REFERENCES

Mulgan, G. (1997), *Connexity*, Chatto & Windus.
Powers, T. (1997), 'And after we've struck Cuba?', *London Review of Books*, Vol. 19, No. 22, November 13, 1997.

4 We Didn't Know It Would Be So Hard: the Short, Sad, Instructive History of the US New Left

Marvin Gettleman

Of all the western countries in which something like a new left appeared during the 1960s, probably that in the United States exhibited the most stunted sense of historical continuity with earlier movements both in the US and abroad (Caute, 1988; McDermott, 1997). Part of the reason was cultural, rooted in the romantic American illusion of having escaped from history into a realm of pure voluntarism. But the virtual disappearance in the preceding decade of a viable Communist old left did deprive the New Left of a generation of elders who might have passed along some much-needed political wisdom and historico-internationalist perspective. But by the beginning of the 1960s, the CP/USA had become a moribund dogmatic sect, its once-extensive praxis destroyed by government repression during what has been called the McCarthy era (Schrecker, 1983, 1993, 1998). New leftists saw little to admire in what was left of American communism, ideologically tethered to its increasingly unattractive Stalinist political orientation. The Port Huron Statement, the New Left's major early ideological manifesto flatly stated that 'we are in basic opposition to the communist system' (Miller, 1987, p. 350; cf. Weinstein, 1970, Ch. 7). For their part the Communists contemptuously dismissed the new leftists as troublesome anarchists, while the independent Marxists around *Monthly Review* magazine ignored them (Green, 1971; Miller, 1987, p. 162).

Yet subtle organic ties linked these two generations of American leftists. For one thing many new leftists were 'red diaper babies' with parents who were, or who had been, in the CP/USA. Whatever doctrinal and tactical disputes separated these generations, the young folk sometimes prodded their discouraged relatives back into political action (Isserman, 1987, Ch. 5; Gitlin, 1987, pp. 67–77; Breines, 1982, Ch. 4) and to fruitful inter-generational political discussions. Another less wholesome and even more complex link derives from the Communist old left's uncritical admiration of the Soviet Union, which the New Left justifiably repudiated. But in a few short years, significant portions of the American New Left would come to embrace strategies drawn from third world liberation movements of no less dubious relevance to circumstances in the US. (Here the difference between the British New Left, which included a number of distinguished former Communist intellectuals, as well as an active Ban The Bomb movement, whose praxis had considerable impact, is instructive.)

Some early new left activists did seek political guidance as they began to plan their assault on the all-too-evident faults in American society, and although a few individual old leftists played an advisory role, that whole generation of trusted, experienced elders from whom these activists might have learned more, was no longer available. Pacifists contributed as much as any group, especially on the level of demonstration tactics (DeBeneditti, 1990, *passim*). Of the old left groupings, the Trotskyist Socialist Workers Party (SWP) probably had the best working relationship with the New Left, because of its occasionally acrimonious but generally responsible work in the Vietnam era anti-war movement – bringing needed good sense into a movement that was constantly in danger of breaking out into ultra-left fantasies (Halstead, 1978). Progressive Labor (PL), although it only emerged in the 1960s, was definitely old left in orientation, ideology and agenda. Its aim was to replace the CP/USA as the keeper of the flame of Stalinist orthodoxy, and also to infiltrate and take over the major New Left youth organisation – Students for a Democratic Society (SDS). As we shall see, by 1968 PL had succeeded in this aim, revealing what was by then the New Left's volatile vulnerability, and its already precipitous decline.

Could the collapse of the New Left have been averted? Or to pose the counterfactual question in a narrower form: what lessons might the New Left have drawn if it had available a more respected and credible set of political ancestors? For one thing New Left radicals might have been diverted from the naive but tempting analysis that the major problem of the era was America's moral failure to live up to its ideals. A more nuanced and realistic approach, less parochial, focusing instead on Marxist categories of economic interests that had to be overcome in the hoped-for transformation to a brave new world. Such a perspective could have helped counter the debilitating despair (and its attendant tactical consequences) when the inevitable discovery came – that neither the US nor any other country invariably lives up to its announced ideals. Contact with trusted elders might also have militated against the romantic fascination about revolutions elsewhere (and their dashing heroes) that impeded sober appraisals of actual conditions in the US.[1] Nor, as will be mentioned later, was the potentially useful wisdom of Antonio Gramsci yet available to American radicals.

Even so, the US New Left, undeterred by hostility from old left spokespersons, and not yet stalked by PL, managed to produce a movement of great vitality in the early and mid 1960s. A Civil Rights movement, a student movement, an anti-war movement and a women's movement were considerable achievements, even if not all of these can be credited solely to the new left. Furthermore, these radical projects at first developed with the characteristic North American sense of near-limitless possibility. This illusion that these students and other young people could remake the world reflected a giddily optimistic mood American of the 1960s that many of us later came to look back upon with wonder – and some shame. Why didn't we know it wouldn't be so easy? What attenuated our realism and tragic sensibilities?

The New Left's initial improvisational and non-ideological approach derived in great measure from the example of young black protestors in the upper south who courageously challenged segregation. The spark was struck at Greensboro, North Carolina, in early 1960 when students at the local Agricultural and Technical College refused to leave a segregated Woolworth's lunch counter and immediately inspired imitators all through the region. Out of this wave of lunch counter sit-ins would eventually emerge the main New Left civil rights organisation – the Student Non Violent-Coordinating Committee (SNCC), which, along with the Congress of Racial Equality (CORE), galvanized young people white and black all over the country.

When white college radicals in the north began demanding an end to segregation and racial oppression, and themselves joined SNCC or SNCC-support groups, the New Left was born. Racial injustice, along with the threat of nuclear annihilation and the prevalence of bureaucratic insensitivity to injustice (and later, when it became possible to utter the words, imperialism and sexism too), became the perceived by-products of a debased American liberalism. The University of Wisconsin-based journal, *Studies on the Left* (1959–1967), which along with SDS's *New Left Notes*, became the closest approximations of theoretical journals of the New Left, also helped focus the nascent movement's ideological energies on 'Cold War Liberalism', deemed the New Left's main ideological enemy (Weinstein and Eakins, 1970; Buhle, 1990, Ch. 10). The colleges became the initial incubators for the upsurges of both black militancy and the closely linked white struggle that comprised much of the early New Left, as well as for the anti-war and the women's liberation struggle that eventually emerged, but whose outlines were taking shape earlier (Matusow, 1984, pp. 321–5; Evans, 1979; Echols, 1989).

The *ur*-text of the New Left, containing some of its most compelling ideas, as well as its unresolved dilemmas (the woman question is totally absent from its pages) was Tom Hayden's 1962 SDS manifesto, the Port Huron Statement. The Students for a Democratic Society had its roots in the obscure, moderate leftist Student League for Industrial Democracy, which in order to reinvigorate itself, in 1960 hired University of Michigan graduate student Al Haber as Field Secretary. Haber's vision was of a radical organisation that seeks the 'root causes' of the 'inadequate society of today' and pursues solutions 'with vigor, idealism and urgency, supporting our words with picket lines, demonstrations and even our own bodies...'. The conservative older LID leadership fired Haber, but then reluctantly re-engaged him in chastened recognition that only his new youthful enthusiasm (or that of someone like him) would enliven the near-moribund parent organisation and its student offshoot. Haber hired Tom Hayden, a recent Michigan graduate, who had studied the writings of dissident Columbia University sociologist C. Wright Mills, and then travelled around the country (making contact with SNCC activists in the South). Debating with critics who attacked the vague utopianism of his draft manifesto and retaining much of Mills's influence, Hayden revised the position paper he was planning to present at the SDS convention scheduled for June, 1962, at Port Huron, Michigan (Sale, 1973).[2]

The final version of the Statement adopted at Port Huron was, as the historian of SDS put it, 'unabashedly middle class' (Sale, 1973, p. 50). Although sympathy for the poor and suffering pervaded the document, it spoke not primarily for the downtrodden masses but for 'university people... bred at least in modest comfort', who were uneasy about the world they were about to inherit. Two immediate situations shaped that unease: the struggle against racial bigotry, which 'compelled most of us from silence to activism'; and the 'common peril' of nuclear annihilation, which similarly challenged us to take active personal responsibility 'for encounter and resolution'. To Hayden, who on this matter voiced the common views of an entire political generation, the threshold for effective action comes with the escape from 'subjective apathy' into active citizenship, a sundering of 'shell of moral call[o]us' that deadens sensitivity to human suffering, even our own. The prevalence of such apathy within the American population allows the dominant business community to eviscerate democracy, while hypocritically rhetorically upholding its tenets. The notion of active democratic citizenship along with its correlate, 'participatory democracy', was the main theme of Port Huron. And it soon became the core idea of a vast reborn student movement that did not long remain only on campus.[3]

Interspersed with its hard, analytical passages (on overseas investment, trade unions, nuclear deterrence strategies, automation and military–industrial politics), SDS's new-minted ideological manifesto also contained naive quasi-anarchist visions of 'inherently good men and women liberated from hierarchic institutions and living in decentralized communities where the individual counted' (Breines, 1982; Sale, 1973, Chs. 7–9). What is remarkable is that in its early years the New Left actually created approximations of such communities, one of which even took shape at SDS's bureaucratic centre – the National Office in New York City. Dedicated teams of new leftists elsewhere, especially in the segregated south, in northern ghettos, and at anti-war coffee houses set up around US military bases, were able for a time to create little 'beloved communities' of radical activists which, in their internal relations, prefigured the good society they were attempting, but never quite managed, to build.

Before the final, partially self-inflicted total defeat of the new left, there were also interim defeats (as well as occasional victories). 1963–64 saw the advent of SDS's Economic Research and Action Project (ERAP), which dispatched mostly white students to such northern and upper south cities as Philadelphia, Louisville, Boston, Cleveland, Trenton and Newark. A tactical shift away from campus organising, ERAP seemed like white, missionary social work ('romantic Narodnikism', the historian of SDS put it), paternalistic in its very striving to avoid paternalism. Years later Todd Gitlin conceded that ERAP 'was based on [white] guilt' (Sale, 1973, pp. 143, 161). By 1965, its cadres unsure of what they were supposed to do in these mostly black communities, and under attack from advocates of what would come to be called 'black power', ERAP disbanded.

Alongside the failure of ERAP there were victories, none more spectacular than Berkeley in 1964–1965. When University of California students (some of whom had spent the previous 'Freedom Summer' working in the south with SNCC and other civil rights' organisations) returned to the Berkeley campus in the fall, they found that university administrators had banned political activity and fund-raising on a strip of the campus where it had previously been allowed. SDS did not play a prominent organisational role in the struggle that followed. Campus civil rights groups took the initiative in contesting a ban they felt (with considerable justification) was directed against them. Just as they had battled oppression in racist Mississippi they did so again right on the Berkeley campus. When a CORE member was arrested for setting up a table and soliciting funds on the proscribed strip, students surrounded the police vehicle and in effect held the arresting officers captive. Within a short time thousands of students joined what had become a spontaneous sit-in and an open forum against what Mario Savio, a leader of the Free Speech Movement, termed 'the greatest problem of our nation – depersonalized, unresponsive bureaucracy'. When fraternities threatened violence, the crowd sang to bolster its confidence. This experience of a community that had instantly come into being, and was shaping its own collective life, became a classic new left epiphany. The scenario might have come right out of the Port Huron Statement, as could Savio's famous speech in early December, before the Berkeley administration capitulated:

> There is a time when the operation of the machine becomes so odious, makes you so sick at heart, that you can't take part: you can't even passively take part, and you've got to put your bodies upon the gears and upon the wheels, upon the levers, upon all the apparatus and you've got to make it stop. And you've got to indicate to the people who run it, to the people who own it, that unless you're free, the machine will be prevented from working at all.

Police arrests on campus rallied moderates, and the faculty 'roused itself to endorse the demands of the students' (Matusow, 1984, pp. 317–18; Rorbagh, 1989; Kitchell, 1990). Victory over the Berkeley administration and trustees energised the new left there (and all throughout the country) for the next obvious crusade: to end the war in Vietnam.[4]

African-Americans and white new leftists, willing to fight domestic oppression in the name of racial justice and democracy, also came to see the war in Vietnam as a conflict in which the US was supporting the wrong side. At first, few would follow the logic of this position and come right out and say they were in favour of victory of the Communist-led forces. Even Martin Luther King Jr., who, a year before his murder, ascended the pulpit in New York's Riverside Church with apologies for not having spoken out earlier and more forcefully against that war, would not go that far. But in his 1967 sermon King offered a far more truthful position on the conflict in Indochina than had a series of US presidents and governmental spokespersons.[5] King saw the Americans as 'strange liberators' in Vietnam, supporting the post-war restoration of French colonialism there, and later blocking unification of the country, land reform and genuine independence. Still striving to preserve the image of a legitimate American aims in Vietnam, he pointed to the 'cruel irony of watching Negro and white boys on TV screens as they "kill and die together for a nation that has been unable to seat them together in the same schools".' In Vietnam, the US was 'wrong from the beginning', exhibiting 'the deadly Western arrogance' that undermines the stated goals of 'revolution, freedom and democracy'. King lamented the racial oppression at home and 'violence and militarism' abroad as poisoning America's soul (King's 1967 Sermon, in Gettleman, 1995, Reading 46). Even earlier, SNCC had reached a similar, if not so eloquently stated, position on the war (SNCC,

1966; Carson, 1981, pp. 183–90), while the National Liberation Front for South Vietnam (NLFSV) was clever enough to post notices on Vietnam battle fields specifically directed to 'Negro army men', who were told that they were 'committing the ignominious crimes in South Vietnam that the KKK [Ku Klux Klan] is perpetrating against your family at home' (Young, 1991, illustration facing p. 242).

Appeals like these eventually undermined morale in the American armed forces among both black and white troops. Many soldiers who originally supported or went along with their country's war changed their perspective once they arrived 'in country'. The new leftists, who led the early opposition to the war, planned their campaigns mainly for the civilian home front, and only sporadically connected with these largely working class 'grunts' in 'Nam (Appy, 1993). By the late 1960s largely spontaneous opposition to the war among US armed forces, along with the continued unpopularity among growing numbers of Vietnamese for the US-backed military governments there, became serious problems for Washington war managers (Gettleman, 1995, Readings 30, 48, 49; Gibson, 1986). The image of antiwar protest taking place only among pampered youth seeking to escape conscription was one of the most persistent myths of the Vietnam war era. At first, before the draft calls increased but with the war greatly intensifying, students and old pacifist activists from the War Resisters' League and other organisations sponsored major 'actions', the seasonal demonstrations – a spring March in Washington, then another in the fall – more or less coordinated with local events of a similar kind. SDS's planned demonstration on April 17, 1965 attracted over 20 000 people to Washington DC, the largest peace march in American history (Sale, 1973, Ch. 11). No one dreamed that it would go on for yet another decade, extend into the Nixon years, and include invasions of Laos and Cambodia. A complex political and social choreography ensued in which US government escalation prompted shifts to ever more radical (but not necessarily more realistic) oppositional strategies within the US – all played out against the apparent backdrop (but really the main arena of struggle) of Vietnam and the neighbouring countries of southeast Asia.[6] US escalation of the war prompted ever more bold and daring Vietnamese military responses, they also seemed to demand escalation of efforts in the US to end it – moves from mere protest to militant, even ultra-militant, resistance.

Charting in proper sequence the major steps of this three-sided escalation cannot be attempted here, but as the war dragged on the domestic American advance from mere demonstration and protest to active resistance came to include burning draft cards, refusing induction, attempting to halt troop trains, breaking away from legal demonstrations to engage in illegal actions.[7] Beyond what these civilian antiwar militants did were the steps of resistance taken by US military personnel – sometimes spontaneous acts (fragging, i.e. killing their own officers by means of a grenade), or refusals to go into action, or outright desertion. Some of these were undertaken collectively, and may have reached some outer boundary when the soldiers in and around the Marxist group Workers' World attempted to organise a Servicemen's Union (Cortright, 1975). The ambiguous heading under which many of these actions took place was 'bringing the war home'. Some antiwar and black power militants, along with guilt-drenched white radicals, interpreted this to mean the obligation to reproduce the Vietnam war on the streets of such American cities as Berkeley and Chicago, with them playing the heroic role of the Vietnamese insurgents (Farber, 1988). Gone was the 'speak truth to power' sentiment that animated the earlier, peaceful 'teach-in' phase of anti-war protest.[8] As it turnedout, what was hard to accept both by new leftists and right-wing American defenders of the war in Vietnam, was that the conflict in Indochina might be resolved in the way it eventually was – by the successful military and political efforts of the Vietnamese themselves at long last to liberate their country, which they did by 1975.

Despite their consistent opposition to US aggression in Vietnam, the main task of leftists in the US were domestic – combating racial oppression, gender discrimination and poverty. But internal fissures, some with deep historical, cultural and political roots, rendered unified action, and eventually any effective action, on these matters increasingly difficult. The civil rights movement, once the common interracial commitment of the entire New Left, by mid-decade became contested political terrain. Former allies (white and black civil rights activists) divided sharply on both tactics and strategies. On one level it was a replay of SDS's failed ERAP programme – sending white volunteers into the black ghettos of northern cities to facilitate community action. Similar problems came up as Freedom Summer 1964 approached.

The Freedom Summer Project brought 700 white college students to Mississippi. Segregationists greeted the Freedom Summer pilgrims with the same savage hostility that had shown to local black civil rights militants. Three civil rights workers – James Chaney, a black Mississippian, Michael Schwerner a white CORE member from New York City, and Andrew Goodman, a student at New York's Queens College – were brutally murdered near the town of Philadelphia (Carson, 1981, pp. 114–15). Working under harrowing danger, the Project volunteers also experienced tensions internal to the movement, especially what was perceived as the contradiction within an effort to empower poor southern blacks that also needed to call upon whites to carry out their plans. Another was the delicate problem of interracial sex, especially between white women and black men, which became a divisive one among the beleaguered civil rights communities under constant assault.

The effort that summer to organise a Mississippi Freedom Democratic Party (MFDP) that would unseat the segregationist delegation at the Democratic Party's national convention in that tense election year was blocked, and the disenchantment of blacks with what they considered, with considerable justification, as a betrayal, contributed to the growth of black separatism (Carson, 1981, Ch. 9). By the end of the summer the racial coalition had begun to unravel; despair, discouragement and pessimism soon led to the appearance of the divisive programme of 'black power'.

The complicated roots of the black power tendency cannot be extensively explored in this chapter, but it had profound effects on the New Left, greatly hastening its dissolution. A 1966 SNCC paper argued that after '400 years of oppression and slavery', blacks in America had good reason to feel intimidated by whites 'no matter what their liberal leanings are'. Therefore, since the racial problem in the US is far more a white problem – even a colonial problem – whites should battle racism where it mainly exists, in white communities. To help preserve the group identity and organisational integrity of black communities, the work that hitherto was done by interracial teams, would be handled by blacks alone (Carmichael and Hamilton, 1967; Carson, 1981, Ch. 14). Soon it was made clear to whites in SNCC and CORE that their presence was no longer wanted. Also contributing to this separatist trend was the growth of the Nation of Islam and the Black Panther Party, which on the basis of its revolutionary programme, demanded leadership over the entire New Left (Matusow, 1984, Ch. 12).

Partially independent of these developments in the black movement, and in the white New Left, but affecting both, was the amorphous set of Dionysian impulses that are collectively termed the counterculture of the 1960s. Loosely uniting rock 'n' roll enthusiasts with advocates of sexual freedom, drug use and 'far out' gestures, a segment of the counterculture became allied with a segments of the anti-war and black power movements that celebrated and even practised revolutionary violence. This was the movement's anarchist fringe, followers (most unknowingly) of Mikhail Bakunin and practitioners of 'propaganda of the deed' (Carr, 1961). Many in the counter-culture remained non-violent flower children, pacific distributors of free food, macrobiotic vegetarians and erotic experimenters.

But in such locales as San Francisco's Haight-Ashbury, an unstable, 'far out', drug-crazed fringe 'became willing cannon fodder for the increasingly violent demonstrations' planned by New Left leaders (Gitlin, 1987, Ch. 13; Matusow, 1984, Ch. 10). Having abandoned rationalism and embraced mindless ultra-radicalism, these final new leftists (Weathermen and the other splinter groups thrown up when PL took over SDS in 1968–69) were ready to bring about the violent end of a vulnerable 'Amerika' of their imagination. One such group in early March 1970 were preparing explosives in an elegant borrowed house in New York's Greenwich Village when it blew up, killing three of them (Sale, 1973, pp. 3–5). Since the Vietnamese were actively and successfully challenging the US by armed defence of their country, it seemed that the only way for Americans to be 'true revolutionaries' was to emulate the Vietnamese by picking up a gun, or making bombs – to bring the US closer to its deserved and destined apocalyptic extinction.[9]

Contributing to this embrace of violence in the New Left was a heightened sensitivity to the media, and the temptation offered by media coverage to stage spectacular but ephemeral spectacles instead of pursuing serious political strategies. The laid-back counter-culture contributed greatly to the impatience with serious activity of any kind, political or otherwise. Former SDS leader Todd Gitlin has analysed the temptation to become 'celebrity leaders' before TV cameras, and to conform to the gaudy image of what the news media assumed radicals 'had to be'. Humdrum work of non-charismatic rank and filers was not 'news' (Gitlin, 1980). While internal forces in the movement and in the surrounding society undoubtedly did more than media distortions to shape the New Left's downward trajectory, it is a factor that must be acknowledged.

As both antiwar and civil rights wings of New Left collapsed, another movement arose, phoenix-like, out of the political ruins of the late 1960s – the woman's movement. Its intellectual and political core took shape around the recognition of male oppression of female comrades, and it broadened to a general theory of patriarchy. Going far beyond Betty Friedan's poignant critique of the oppressive domesticity that affected white middle-class women (Friedan, 1963), movement women began tentatively, and then more forcefully, to protest not only against imperialism and racism, but against sexism as well – including the attitudes and behaviour of male comrades. As early as 1964 a SNCC position paper credited women as being the crucial cohort 'that keeps the movement running on a day-to-day basis', but are excluded from policy-making (SNCC, 1964). The following year two white women working in SNCC raised the question within SDS (Hayden and King, 1965). The New Left's male 'heavies' did not like to hear of this new internal protest in the ranks, and fought against it as a 'diversion' from more important matters, like ending the Vietnam war. Eventually, in ways that Sara Evans and Alice Echols have made fairly clear (Evans, 1979; Echols, 1989; cf. Gitlin, 1987, Ch. 16), an independent women's movement did grow out of the New Left, forming at first those 'beloved communities' that neither SDS or SNCC were able to sustain. But even this new movement was not able to escape some of the splits and internecine feuds similar to those that affected the New Left itself – and a few original ones as well. Few of the other New Left organisations and publications survived the 1970s, and thus the New Left's major institutional creation within civil society is the woman's movement.

The importance of the creation of such institutions to contest oppressive social hegemonies is of course a central part of the legacy of Antonio Gramsci, which unfortunately was not available to American new leftists in their brief and troubled history.[10] Had his 'Lettere dal Carcere' been translated earlier into English or had his ideas been given wider, earlier currency by the US Communist movement, there might have been a stronger collective voice raised against several of the more bizarre and unfortunate forms of sectarianism that marked the American New Left's precipitous decline, and its almost total subsequent effacement from the US political scene. Some pockets of 1960s radicalism still survive under the leaky umbrella provided by a few academic institutions in the US. And as has been noted, there still exists a woman's movement of sorts. Few of the great battles the New Left entered were won, and some of them (race relations, poverty, just to name two arenas of struggle), despite a decorative veneer of reform, remain in as critical a state and as far from satisfactory solution as ever.

What newer historians of the New Left are now stressing is that, even as leftists were waging their battles of the 1960s, there was forming beneath the surface of American life a deep popular current of anti-revolutionary sentiment and a resurgent hegemonic value system virtually deifying 'the market' (Farber, 1994c). Proponents of triumphant post-cold war global capitalism have met some of their most vehement opponents on the loony fringes of the American right, people who are also the left's enemies. Clearly if a 'newer' American left were to emerge, there are many lessons about sectarianism, about political unity, about clear-sighted political realism, about media distortions and about the use of tact in trying to win people over, that will have to be pondered. When the present doldrums experienced by the left have ended, when appropriate praxis is developed, there will be many texts – not the least of them Gramsci's writings – to be studied and discussed. Historical amnesia will then be, as it was in the 1960s, a costly error that must be overcome.

NOTES

1. Of all the third world radicals revered by the New Left, probably the most universally admired was Che Guevara, but as Allen Matusow has observed, few of his American disciples heeded the wisdom in his 1961 book, *Guerrilla Warfare*: 'Where a government has come into power through some form of popular vote, fraudulent or not, and maintains at least an appearance of constitutional legality, the guerrilla outbreak cannot be promoted, since possibility of peaceful struggle have not yet been exhausted.' (Quoted in Matusow, 1984, p. 326).

2. Beside Mills, another academic loner whose ideas influenced the New Left was University of Wisconsin historian William Appleman Williams. See Buhle, 1990, Ch. 28 and Abelove, 1983, pp. 123–46.

3. There had been a vibrant earlier student movement that terminated when the 1939 Nazi-Soviet Pact broke up the Socialist-Communist alliance that underlay it (Cohen, 1993).

4. By no means the last student uprising of the 1960s, or of the new left era, Berkeley had a sequel four years later, when the Columbia University campus erupted over the decision to build a University gymnasium on public parkland in the adjoining black Harlem community. The gym was never built (Sale, 1973, pp. 430–41; Avorn, 1969).

5. Compare, for example, President Ronald Reagan's ludicrously inaccurate 1982 account of the genesis of the Vietnam conflict (Reagan, 1982) with King's sermon in Gettleman, 1995, Reading 46.

6. During the Nixon years, in a strange response to and inversion of the new left fantasy of 'bringing the war in Vietnam home', the President's advisers acted out a counter-fantasy, setting up spring and fall 'war rooms' in the White House to direct the battles against anti-war protesters, as if it were a real war. This fantasy became something of a self-fulfilling prophecy. The behaviour of Nixon and his entourage is well-brought out in an otherwise undistinguished volume (Wells, 1994), far inferior to the best book on the antiwar movement: DeBenedetti, 1990. Another bizarre distortion (not totally unrelated to the behaviour in the Nixonite White House) crept into the American discourse on Vietnam, in which the shadow conflict in the US became inflated and the indigenous Asian nature of the war tended to downplayed. In Gettleman 1991, I call this Cartesian imperialism ('we invade you, therefore you are').

7. Women had no draft cards, since they were not (and are not) subject to conscription. Thus, as the antiwar movement progressed new left women, who were asserting themselves against sexism throughout

the movement, felt they were being reduced to subordinate roles in the antiwar struggle as well. This was one of the factors that gave rise to the women's liberation movement (Echols, 1989, Ch. 1).

8. To 'speak truth to power' constituted the motivation for much of the intellectual antiwar activity. The naivete of this notion was clearly revealed in 1970 when Daniel Ellsberg and Anthony Russo, antiwar militants within the US government, 'liberated' and publicized the Defense Department's twelve-volume history of the war known as The Pentagon Papers (for bibliographical data on the three published versions of The Pentagon Papers, see Gettleman, 1995, p. 541). Although confirming the main points that antiwar scholarship was striving to establish at the time (that Vietnam was one nation, not two; that the Communist leader Ho Chi Minh was a justly revered Vietnamese patriot; and that the US bore major responsibility for supporting post-World War 2 French colonialism, and primary responsibility for the post-1954 phase of the conflict), The Pentagon Papers also showed that Washington's war managers knew everything we did, but discounted it!

9. The belief that 'Amerika' was on the verge of extinction reflected the ultra-militant New Left's inability to distinguish its own desires from actual real-world possibilities. Having abandoned rationalism, rejected the peace movement, this group that became dominant just as the New Left disappeared of course repudiated anything that could be construed as conventional 'bourgeois' thinking. Hence it could not recognise that the greatest of all apocalyptic threats, nuclear war, was being held in abeyance by a tacit US–Soviet Cold War agreement.

10. This is not the place for any extended discussion of Gramsci's ideas, or their impact in America. One of the earliest books on Gramsci is still perhaps the best guide (Cammett, 1967, and the follow-up, Cammett, 1991).

REFERENCES

Abelove, H., ed. (1983), *Visions of History* [a publication of MARHO – the Radical History Organization], Pantheon Books.
Appy, C. G. (1993), *Working-Class War: American Combat Soldiers & Vietnam*, University of North Carolina Press.
Avorn, J.L. and members of the *Columbia Daily Spectator* staff (1969), *Up Against the Ivy Wall*, Atheneum.

Belfrage, S. (1965), *Freedom Summer*, Fawcett Crest.
Bloom, A. and Wini Breines, eds (1995), *'Takin' it to the Streets': a Sixties Reader*, Oxford University Press.
Breines, W. (1982), *Community and Organization in the New Left, 1962–1968: the Great Refusal*, Praeger.
Brown, M., R. Martin, F. Rosengarten and G. Snedeker, eds (1993), *New Studies in the Politics and Culture of U.S. Communism*, Monthly Review Press.
Buhle, M.J., P. Buhle and D. Georgakis, eds (1990), *Encyclopedia of the American Left*, Garland Publishing Co.
Buhle, P., ed. (1990), *History and the New Left: Madison, Wisconsin, 1950–1970*, Temple University Press.
Cammett, J. (1967), *Antonio Gramsci and the Origins of Italian Communism*, Stanford University Press.
—— (1991), *Bibliografia Gramsciana, 1922–1988*, Fondazione Istituto Gramsci [an ongoing series of annotated bibliographies].
Carmichael, S. and Hamilton, C.V. (1967), *Black Power*, Penguin.
Carr, E.H. (1961), *Bakunin*, Vintage Books [first published, 1937].
Carson, C. (1981), *In Struggle: SNCC and the Black Awakening of the 1960s*, Harvard University Press.
Caute, D. (1988), *The Year of the Barricades: a Journey Through 1968*, Harper & Row.
Cohen, R. (1993), *When the Old Left Was Young: Student Radicals and America's First Mass Student Movement, 1929–1941*, Oxford University Press.
Cortright, D. (1975), *Soldiers in Revolt: the American Military Today*, Doubleday Anchor.
DeBenedetti, C. and Chatfield, C. (1990), *An American Ordeal: the Antiwar Movement of the Vietnam Era*, Syracuse University Press.
Echols, A. (1989), *Daring to be Bad: Radical Feminism in America*, University of Minnesota Press.
Evans, S. (1979), *Personal Politics: The Roots of Women's Liberation in the Civil Rights Movement and the New Left*, Vintage Books.
Farber, D. (1988), *Chicago '68*, University of Chicago Press.
—— (1994a), *The Age of Great Dreams: America in the 1960s*, Hill and Wang.
—— ed. (1994b). *The Sixties: From Memory to History*, University of North Carolina Press.
—— (1994c), 'The Silent Majority and Talk About Revolution', in Farber (1994b), pp. 291–316.
Freidan, B. (1963), *The Feminine Mystique*, W.W. Norton.
Gettleman, M.E., ed. (1965), *Vietnam: History, Documents and Opinions…*, Fawcett Books.
—— (1991), 'Against Cartesianism: Three Generations of Vietnam Scholarship', in D. Allen and N.V. Long, eds, *Coming to Terms: Indochina, the United States, and the War*, Westview Press, Ch. 11.
—— J. Franklia, B. Franklin and M. Young, eds (1995), *Vietnam and America*, Grove Press.
Gibson , J.W. (1986), *The Perfect War: Technowar in Vietnam*, Atlantic Monthly Press.
Gitlin, T. (1980), *The Whole Word is Watching: Mass Media in the Making and Unmaking of the New Left*, University of California Press.

Gitlin, T. (1987), *The Sixties: Years of Hope, Days of Rage*, Bantam.

Grant, J., ed. (1968), *Black Protest: History, Documents, and Analyses 1916 to the Present*, Fawcett Books.

Green, G. (1971), *The New Radicalism: Anarchist or Marxist?* International Publishers.

Halstead, F. (1978), *Out Now! A Participant's Account of the American Movement Against the Vietnam War*, Monad Press.

Hayden, C. and King, M. (1965), 'Sex and Caste: A Kind of Memo', in *'Takin 'it to the Streets': a Sixties Reader* (A. Bloom and W. Breines, eds), Oxford University Press, New York, 1995, pp. 47–51.

Horowitz, D. (1996), 'Rethinking Betty Friedan…', *American Quarterly*, 48 (March).

Isserman, Maurice (1987), *'If I had a Hammer…': The Death of the Old Left and the Birth of the New Left*, Basic Books.

Kitchell, M., producer & director (1990), *Berkeley in the 1960s*, First Run Films.

Lipset, S.M. and Wolin, S. eds (1965), *The Berkeley Student Revolt: Facts and Interpretations*, Doubleday Anchor.

Matusow, A.J. (1984), *The Unraveling of America: A History of Liberalism in the 1960s*, Harper & Row.

McDermott, J. (1997), 'On the Origin of the Present World in the Defeat of "the 60s"', *Socialism and Democracy*, XI (Fall).

Miller, J. (1987), *'Democracy is in the Streets': From Port Huron to the Siege of Chicago*, Simon and Schuster.

Moody, A. (1968), *Coming of Age in Mississippi*, Dell Laurel.

Port Huron Statement (1962), See Miller, James (1987), Appendix.

Race, J. (1972), *War Comes to Long An: Revolutionary Conflict in a Vietnamese Province,* University of California Press.

Raskin. M.G. and B.B. Fall, eds (1965), *The Viet-Nam Reader*, Random House.

Reagan, R. (1982), *Statement on the Vietnam Conflict* (1982), Public Papers of the Presidents of the United States: Ronald Reagan, 1982, Washington DC, 1983), I, pp. 184–5.

Rorbagh, W.J. (1989), *Berkeley at War: the 1960s*, Oxford University Press.

Sale, K. (1973), *SDS*, Random House.

Schrecker, E. (1983), 'The Missing Generation', *Humanities in Society*, VI (Spring/Summer).

—— (1993), 'McCarthyism and the Decline of American Communism, 1945–1960', in *New Studies in the Politics and Culture of U.S. Communism* (eds M. Brown, R. Martin, F. Rosengarten and G. Snedeker).

—— (1998), *Many Are the Crimes: McCarthyism in America*, Little Brown.

SNCC (1964), 'Women in the Movement', in *'Takin' it to the Streets': a Sixties Reader* (eds A. Bloom and W. Breines) pp. 45–7.

—— (1966), 'Statement on Vietnam', in Grant (1986), pp. 416–18.

Weinstein, J. and Eakins, D.W., eds (1970), *For a New America: Essays in History and Politics from Studies on the Left*, Random House.

—— (1975), *Ambiguous Legacy: the Left in American Politics*, New Viewpoints/ Franklin Watts.

Wells, T. (1994), *The War Within: America's Battle over Vietnam*, University of California Press.

Young, M.B. (1991), *The Vietnam Wars, 1945–1990*, HarperCollins.

5 The Three New Lefts and their Legacies

Geoff Andrews

'We were all still on the escalator Progress, the whole world ascending towards prosperity. Did anyone challenge this happy optimism? I don't remember it. At the end of a century of grand revolutionary romanticism; frightful sacrifices for the sake of paradises and heavens on earth and the withering away of the state; passionate dreams of utopias and wonderlands and perfect cities; attempts at communes and commonwealths, at co-operatives and kibbutzes and kolhozes – after all this, would any of us have believed that most people in the world settle gratefully for a little honesty, a little competence in government?' So writes Doris Lessing in *Volume Two of My Autobiography 1949–1962* (Harper Collins, 1997: 368).

If it wasn't apparent before then the 'revolutionary' year 1989 seemed to mark the final end of the dreams of the New Left. Other moments, such as the failure of the left to benefit from the economic crisis of the mid-1970s and the rise of the New Right were already down as markers. The significance of 1989 however was far-reaching. Wrongly seen by many on the left as a mere escape from Stalinism, it signified the emergence of a quite new global politics which threatened to undermine traditional left–right polarities that had been consolidated around the capitalism–socialism divide in the framework of the Cold War and under the shadow of which the New Left developed. The different utopias of the New Left which attempted to revive the socialist idea such as 'libertarian socialism', 'creative Marxism', Althusserian structuralism, 'Socialist Internationalism', 'Marxist–feminism', 'Eurocommunism', appeared themselves as almost relics from another age. Together they became incorporated as the 'old socialism' – or indeed, paradoxically 'Old Left' – whose end projects were now thought unachievable. If further confirmation of the demise of the New Left were needed, then it seems one only has to look at the contemporary fortunes of some of its leading protagonists; those who helped to shape the aspirations, reading groups and demos of the period have either long departed the scene or else have been reincarnated as media pundits, born-again liberals or (arguably worst of all) career academics.

However to see the sixties and indeed the wider influence of the New Left as either irrelevant or its protagonists merely political fall guys for the New

Right is to misunderstand the contribution the ideas of this 'movement' continue to pose for contemporary politics. Moreover to see all the ideas, aspirations and cultural concerns of the New Left as having been replaced by the harsh realities of global capitalism or having no purchase on the contemporary shifts in economies, cultures and politics of western societies merely gives credence to postmodern cynicism as well as preventing us from learning from history in a reflective, non-dogmatic way.

It is certainly important to recognise the crisis of the grand narratives, that is the inability of those emancipatory projects of the western enlightenment – liberalism, social democracy and Marxism – to organise people's belief systems in the conditions of late modernity. In the wake of the 'post-isms' which increasingly shape the debate about the future of politics, the 'big issues' related to the emancipatory projects of the grand narratives are, rightly, interrogated; what remains from them, what still holds good in the reinvention of politics, gets much less attention. Yet if we look more carefully we find that the reinterpretation and application of older currents in new configurations will continue to inform political debate.

My main argument here therefore is that while the New Left, in what I see as its three moments, is no longer around to organise a new utopia, or bring about a new mass politics, or provide a global alternative to capitalism, released from its totalising ideological frameworks, it contains, in different ways, important comments on the direction of contemporary societies. Specifically what is common to the New Left which relates closely to current dilemmas are the projects of what I would call 'radical modernisation'. Radical modernisation included the need to democratise culture, a particular concern of the first New Left; to confront in different ways the new forms of power, strategy and control and the rise of new social movements that were taken up by the second New Left, and an engagement with the 'new times', the main concern of what I see as a third New Left.

Common defining features which united and distinguished the New Left can be summarised as follows. Firstly, the New Left developed as an alternative 'third way' between Stalinism and social democracy. Although never an organised movement, it sought political space outside orthodox political structures. Indeed in doing so it helped to redefine politics itself, providing a broader understanding of culture, and the importance of the autonomy of political movements. Secondly, it took as a starting-point the need to analyse and confront new forms of capitalism, which included at different times, the mass consumer society and technocratic managerialism, imperialism and latterly post-fordism. Thirdly, there was a need to move away from the state and to turn towards the sphere of civil society for solutions. Fourthly, the New Left rejected vanguardism and democratic centralism; indeed it rejected most forms of centralised political organisation. 'Only connect', a phrase used as a criticism of the first New Left, could now be seen in a more positive light to prefigure the looser political structures that were becoming characteristic of contemporary societies.

Thus the history of the New Left in many ways illuminates some of the major cultural, political and economic dilemmas of the 'long 1960's' as a whole. This engagement with modernity I will argue should be seen as a major organising theme that ran through the different projects of the New Left. The underlying principle which gave expression to this was agency. This was conceived in quite different ways. In the first New Left, for example, which takes as its defining moment the period of 1956 and the break with Stalinism as well as the onset of mass consumerism, it was the cultural terrain which was seen as providing a new focus for emancipation. For the second New Left, whose moment was '1968', the belief in agency was emphasised by the concern with analysing new forms of state and economic power and the need for the autonomy of the new social movements that grew in civil society. It was this sphere, independent of the state, which was thought to be decisive for those movements such as CND, the anti-Vietnam War movement, the feminist and workers control movements of the 1970s and given theoretical justification in the works of Marcuse, Althusser, Gramsci and Foucault for whom in different ways the manufacturing of consent, and the 'relative autonomy' of ideological struggles were the decisive areas of politics. For the third New Left, which takes 1979 as its starting-point as a recognition of the crisis of the left and the rise of the right in the late 1970s, the focus was on the 're-making of the political', a broader concept of politics rooted in the multiple identities of individuals and the need to 'reconnect' the left with the diverse aspirations and activities of the people that were characteristic of 'New Times'.

These then are the themes which will organise my argument. I accept that the New Left was a movement with a strong international flavour and that the focus here will be limited to the British traditions. I also realise in making this argument that some of the interesting complexities and ruptures between the different elements of the New Left may be underplayed; this is not to deny them or to assume a coherence and continuity that didn't exist, but to draw out what I believe to be the lasting legacies, written from a position of hope and optimism.

THE FIRST NEW LEFT

The first New Left was characterised by an eclectic range of influences. It combined the labour movement ethos of the dissident communists who left in 1956, such as E.P. Thompson and John Saville, based in the North of England, with a more cosmopolitan and metropolitan chic of writers and university students (including Stuart Hall and Raphael Samuel) who met in places such as the Partisan Coffee House and Jimmy's Restaurant in Soho or student houses in Oxford. Its journals, *Universities and Left Review* (later *New Left Review*) and *The New Reasoner*, brought together a creative, humanist brand of Marxism, which distinguished their objectives from both the statist ideologies of orthodox Leninism and social democracy. As Peter Sedgewick, a left critic of the first New Left suggested, they 'brought... an explicit commitment to class struggle, an iteration of the role of human agency as against impersonal historical process, be it gradual or cataclysmic, a devotion to relatively punctilious work' (Sedgewick, 1976: 135).

This emphasis on agency was apparent in many of the key texts of the time. In *Out of Apathy*, written in 1960, E.P. Thompson felt that the new consumer-driven affluence of contemporary capitalism, while maintaining the old inequalities, had encouraged new forms of apathy, resignation and political expediency. This needed to be met by a moral revolution which would release the capacity for 'democratic self-activity', a greater participation in decision-making and popular democratic control of the economy. He explicitly rejected forms of state monopoly, in the form of either the bureaucratic or technocratic features of social democracy or the dictatorship of the proletariat, while advocating the decentralisation of political power to the locality, abolition of the House of Lords, and reform of the House of Commons. His humanism extended to international affairs where he argued for the democratic self-determination of the third world. (Thompson, 1960; Chun, 1992: 47–51). The campaign for Nuclear Disarmament which had recently formed was to Thompson, in *The New Reasoner*, an 'assault against fatalism' (p. 5, quoted in Archer *et al.,* 1989: 7).

The necessity for working people to take control over their lives was further expanded by Thompson in 1963 in his *The Making of the English Working Class* in which agency rather than structure was recognised as being at the root of working class formation and development. In his Workers' Educational Association classes, which provided the backdrop to his work, Thompson challenged the empiricism and economism of orthodox scientific socialism which said nothing about the human and moral aspects of working-class experience. Thompson's interest in the work of William Morris reinforced the view that the ethical critique of capitalism should be at the heart of socialist values. This preference for the moral critique of capitalism over a more developed analysis of the economic system was recognised as a distinguishing feature by other members of the first New Left in retrospect as well as the basis for conflict with their immediate successors (Samuel, 1989: 46).

In a much publicised dispute with the theoreticists of the second New Left, who took over the editorship of *New Left Review* from 1962 – notably Perry Anderson – Thompson's work was regarded as a provincial and untheoretical contribution which made no attempt to interrogate contemporary forms of British capitalism. Anderson did not share Thompson's view of a native Marxist tradition and was not enthused by the traditions of the English labour movement. Thompson was involved in a 'moral protest' rather than a theoretical engagement, guilty of a 'messianic nationalism' in his attempts to redefine a progressive concept of Englishness. The battle here became one of structure and agency. Thompson, it was argued, had not addressed the structural questions that needed to be at the heart of any analysis of British society. In particular this included the backward and deferential political culture that had prevented the development of the political maturity of the working class. Anderson and his colleagues on the other hand, according to Thompson, had shifted towards theoretical abstraction and dogma and had separated theory from practice. While there were clear theoretical differences between the two that were taken further throughout the 1960s, following the growing influence of Althuserian structuralism, there was also a question of the difference in political allegiance and culture of the protagonists. The socialisation of Thompson *et al.* by the Communist Party of Great Britain (CPGB), as well as their links with the labour movement, were quite distinct from the more aloof and elitist postures of Anderson. On the other hand, the latter's interest in theories of power helped to provide a context for the later theoretical debates between Marxists in the 1970s, between for example Poulantzas and Miliband (Chun, 1992: 61–4).

The importance given to agency by the first New Left was further reflected in the political role attributed to intellectuals and as the basis for renewing the left at different moments. The first New Left was crucial in delivering a new concept of the intellectual, one closely resembling the organic, public, critical type associated with Gramsci (even though the latter's work was yet to become fully available). This was closely related to the 'organic' links between first New Left intellectuals and adult education. It was an explicit recognition of the new opportunities available to working people to achieve personal fulfilment. This encouragement of self-realisation and autonomy was rooted in an alternative philosophy of education, exemplified by the particular commitment to adult education made by members of the first New Left. Indeed as Tom Steele has argued the creation of the new discipline of cultural studies which reflected many of the academic concerns of New Left thinkers – most obvious in the Centre for Contemporary Cultural Studies, set up by Richard Hoggart – was a result of the struggles and alternative philosophy that had taken place in adult education; it was the outcome, Steele argues, of a 'political project of popular education amongst adults'. (Steele, 1997: 15). In addition to Saville and Thompson's work for the Workers' Educational Association, Raphael Samuel embarked on a 30-year association with Ruskin College, the college of the labour movement, and helped set up the History Workshop; Raymond Williams spent his early teaching time in extra-mural departments and took much of his inspiration for his work on culture from this and Richard Hoggart was succeeded by Stuart Hall as Director of the Centre for Contemporary Cultural Studies. Hall, a figure who appears in all the phases of the New Left, went on to become Professor of Sociology at the Open University. The importance then of being a committed and organic intellectual, linking intellectual work to popular movements, a phenomenon almost anathema to contemporary academic life, was a defining feature of the first New Left.

What this illustrated was the importance given by the first New Left to the way in which history was made by working people through their own experiences and contributions. The interrogation of popular culture was a further example of this and given much prominence as the route for emancipation. Indeed this sphere produced a pioneering and exceptional contribution from the first New Left thinkers. This approach found its way into a far-reaching analysis of the changing nature of post-war British society, the dangers as well as opportunities that modernity was bringing, the breaking down of the barriers between 'high' and 'low' culture; ultimately an interrogation and redefinition of the concept of culture itself. Michael Kenny identifies three reasons for this new attention given to culture. These were firstly the need to respond to the narrowness of Stalinism and Labourism when it came to cultural questions. Culture was inevitably reduced to the economic sphere, 'either as an appendage to more important considerations or as a purely epiphenomenal entity'. The second reason, according to Kenny, was the 'novelty' and 'specificity' of what was a period of tremendous cultural change. The third reason were the changes in popular culture which were transforming the landscape of societies (Kenny, 1995: 87).

This new emphasis on culture was taken up in the work of Richard Hoggart in *The Uses of Literacy* and Raymond Williams in his seminal works *Culture and Society* and *The Long Revolution*. Their concerns were with the implications of the major cultural transformations underway in western societies in what Eric Hobsbawm has termed the 'golden decades'.

For Hobsbawm working class consciousness had reached its peak by the end of the second world war yet by the 'golden years' of the 1960s and 1970s had been 'undermined' by 'the combination of secular boom, full employment and a society of genuine mass consumption (which) utterly transformed the lives of working class people in the developed countries and continued to transform it' (Hobsbawm, 1995: 306).

Hoggart's work is an attempt to come to terms with the effect of cultural changes on the lives of working-class people, the dilemmas brought by this onset of mass culture, such as the 'danger of reducing the larger part of the population to a condition of obediently receptive passivity, their eyes glued to television sets, pin-ups and cinema screens' (Hoggart, 1957: 316). He saw contradictory tendencies emerging. On the one hand, the breaking down of old class barriers had provided new opportunities, while on the other new types of conformity and degeneration were produced by the shift towards the commercialisation and standardisation of mass culture. Hoggart perceived a conflict between an 'earnest minority' who sought a critical engagement with the new mass culture, and a cynical working class majority.

Raymond Williams was also worried about the 'visible moral decline of the labour movement' (1983: 32). However, Williams remained optimistic about the prospects of change that cultural transformation could deliver. According to Williams we were engaged in a long-term struggle against the alienation of a consumer society from which the possibilities of a more democratic culture needed to emerge. Cultural expansion could enable not only the fulfilment of individual aspirations and talents, as an 'empowered learning community' but it also reinforced the need for democratic control of cultural institutions (Rustin, 1989: 118–28).

This particular engagement of the first New Left led them into a wide ranging debate on socio-cultural questions, including the debate with the Croslandite revisionists over the implications of changes in the post-war class structure, where it was argued crucially that the working class should not always be seen as on the 'receiving end of transmissions from an alien agency, whether as the objects of survey research, the beneficiaries of welfare and planning proposals, or the consumers of shoddy cultural goods' (Sedgewick, 1976: 137–8). The 'new classlessness in culture' therefore had brought positive and negative aspects. These were the negative aspects; however there was also evidence of what Hoggart referred to as a 'good classlessness' (Hoggart, 1957: 137) and the possibility of a common culture breaking down traditional divisions and forms of elitism, a situation made possible by more access to cultural forms such as the cinema, the extension of educational opportunity and more consumer power.

The legacy of the first New Left then remains the way in which aspects of modernity encouraged the ability of working people to intervene and extend control over their lives. They left many forms of power and control untouched and their concept of culture while addressing the 'personal' and 'subjective' in very specific ways (such as working class 'lived experience'), did not for example account for the significance of gender. Indeed Hoggart's concepts of community while containing a strong emphasis on the role of working class women, did not question in any depth the extent of inequality and patriarchy. With the exception of isolated examples such as Doris Lessing's *The Golden Notebook* the position of women got scant attention in the first New Left, nor even in 'The May Day Manifesto', a political intervention from a reunion of first New Leftists published in 1967. It was one example of an absence of theories of power, an omission developed by the second New Left.

THE SECOND NEW LEFT

The second New Left differed sharply in its view of the impact of capitalist modernisation. Indeed its approach grew out of the critique of the historical, 'populist', 'moralist' and 'culturalist' (as it saw it) perceptions of Thompson and others. The second New Left, which was initially characterised by the new generation of intellectuals who took control of *New Left Review*, was quite a different grouping; younger, more privileged backgrounds, less assimilated into – indeed, at times openly hostile to – the political culture of British socialism and less connected to the organic movements that had helped shape the priorities of their predecessors. Their inspiration was from theory rather than history and more European rather than 'native' English. The second New Left, however, was much broader in scope and it is difficult to establish close points of contact; it is better to see them as a looser set of groups who had some defining features. These derived from the new analyses of capitalism and in particular the renaissance in new forms of western Marxism – notably the works of Althusser, Marcuse, Gramsci and Foucault. Although there was a rise of Trotskyist groups during this period, with the exception of the International Socialists (particularly at its most productive and creative period around 1967–68), these reverted to more orthodox Leninist forms of organisation. The movements that were inspired by these thinkers included the second wave feminism, the students' movement, the workers' control movement and Eurocommunism and it is these that I will consider.

These movements' view of radical modernisation stemmed from their analysis of the power structures of modern capitalism, which in different ways threw up important 'contradictions'; for example the extension of liberal rights and social democratic welfare reform had failed to address the position of women, let alone alleviate poverty and social inequality, while the rise of consumerism had brought new cultural and technocratic forms of control and alienation. The state itself had become bureaucratised and its legitimacy increasingly open to question. What was the nature of power relations in contemporary (or 'late') capitalism? Was the state still the instrument of a particular class or did it operate with 'relative autonomy'? How, in a society characterised by mass culture and an extension of civil society, was consent 'manufactured'? What other forms of power do modern capitalist societies produce and what are the terrains and positions, in which this power is to be exercised? And, fundamentally, what social forces and movements exist to be organised as a challenge to these power structures? These were the questions that dominated this part of the New Left, given of course greater focus and optimism by the 'moment' of 1968, in which 'revolution' was once more on the agenda. There were many different responses to these questions which reflected different sections of the second New Left and which often found themselves in conflict with each other, for example, between the group around *New Left Review* (such as Blackburn, Ali, Anderson and Nairn) and others such as the younger generation of communists in the CPGB.

The important analysis which pre-occupied the group around *New Left Review* was the deep-seated conservative culture of Britain's class society. According to this 'Nairn–Anderson thesis', the lack of a hegemonic bourgeoisie (and specifically a bourgeois revolution) had sustained deference and forms of social hierarchy that preserved a backward and antiquarian political system and culture. In addition the lack of an effective British Marxism had meant that the working class, despite having been 'made' earlier than in other European countries, was unable to accede to its historical mission. Instead it was shaped by a variety of reformist ideologies compatible with the development of capitalism and given credibility, it was argued, by E.P. Thompson's romanticism. The working class had shown all the signs of a deferential culture, with no motivation for revolution, a condition reinforced by the reformist, parliamentarist, labourist and corporatist ideologies of the left which Tom Nairn and others spent much time analysing. As Anderson put it: 'a supine bourgeoisie produced a subordinate proletariat' (Anderson, 1964: 39).

As is evident from the conflict between Thompson and Anderson alluded to above the differences between the approaches of the two New

Lefts in this context is quite clear. The somewhat elitist and obscurantist (and certainly less engaged) approach of the second New Leftists around *New Left Review* took it away from the humanist, activist elements of the first New Left. This shouldn't suggest that it was completely isolated from movements; indeed in the aftermath of 1968 the analysis shifted towards what were becoming 'new social forces'. Tariq Ali's autobiographical reflections, *Street Fighting Years*, reads as a left-wing adventure story of the times. What changed things of course were the events of 1968. 'Be realistic; demand the impossible', may not have been on the lips of all student activists and political movements of the time, but it illustrates the change of mood. Students in particular were at the forefront of activities at the LSE – as they were to a higher degree in France in the same year and Italy a year later – while the Prague Spring was the defining moment for an emerging generation of (Euro) communists (Andrews, 1995).

New analyses of 'student power' saw students as a new social group that had benefited from the expansion of higher education and who had not been conditioned to the same extent by the mass culture. It was not only the militancy of the student movement (and its Red Bases, occupations and demos) it was a wider self-confidence of an emergence in the political generation. The era of the 'counter course' provided a theoretical critique of the nature of power in higher education, taking further some of the concerns of Hoggart's 'earnest minority'. Reading groups brought dynamism and an overlap of study and politics, a development extended to a much higher degree in the Communist University of London which met from 1969 until 1981. The Eurocommunist-led Broad Left took control of the National Union of Students, and delivered a new form of pluralism and an alternative to careerist Labour students.

The new spirit of optimism and activism was reflected in other 'new social movements' such as feminism. The revival of feminism in its more militant and creative forms in the late sixties was a consequence of changes in the socio-economic structure and in particular the greater freedom that had come from the pill, abortion and the rise in women's employment. The theoretical input of Marxist thinkers like Althusser who provided a 'structuralist' analysis of women's position, or Gramsci who gave specific attention to non-class forms of oppression within ruling hegemony, gave feminism new frameworks for challenging power inequalities. More grassroots movements, including that of the History Workshop, gave a voice to women, the first women's liberation movement conference being held at Ruskin College in 1969. The transformation that was taking place within the left itself offered new opportunities for women. As Sassoon has argued, feminism posed a real challenge to the left to modernise and transform its structures, 'to recast its own ideological framework, abandoning the unspoken axiom that the socialist movement was a movement of men which women could join on men's terms and, in exchange, receive men's support. This new movement of universal emancipation required a demasculinised politics; a socialism for women and men' (Sassoon, 1996: 422). The publication of Juliet Mitchell's 'Women: The Longest Revolution', in *New Left Review* (*NLR* 40, Nov–Dec 1966) probably the first defining second-wave feminist text, was important in taking the project of the second New Left forward.

The Institute For Workers Control provided the focus for another social movement concerned with strategies for power. It had some roots in the first New Left where democratic control of industry, based on alternatives to bureaucratic nationalisation, was put forward in the debate over Harold Wilson's plans for modernisation. The Workers Control Movement identified a new route to power and a way of challenging capital by labour. It took on a new significance with the greater bargaining power of the trade unions and the victory of the left within the biggest unions from the late sixties, aided by movements such as the Liaison Committee for Defence of Trade Unions. The sit-ins at the Upper Clyde Shipbuilders in the early 1970s and at Lucas Aerospace in the late 1970s gave it more impetus and helped create the conditions for the Bullock Report on Industrial Democracy (1977), though ultimately little came of this. It would be naive to link these developments with later interest in stakeholding, except to say that there was a continuity in the belief in workers' ability to participate in decision-making as a way of exercising control over their working lives.

There was greater emphasis on strategy in the latter period of the second New Left, yet it continued the New Left tradition of poor collective organisation. Perhaps the nearest expression of any perceived coming together of class and social forces was the adoption of the 'broad democratic alliance' strategy of the CPGB at its 1977 Congress, a partial recognition of the influence of Gramsci in seeking a coalition between the working class and its allies. Yet this was too little too late; the CPGB itself was showing signs of terminal decline and division while the rest of the Left was starting to fragment.

The decline of the second New Left became clear around the late 1970s when it become evident – if it wasn't already – that the left would not be the beneficiaries of the economic crisis. The Eurocommunist input which had brought some changes to the CPGB's politics fell away with the defeat of the 'historic compromise' in 1978 which had brought the Italian Communist Party close to power in Italy. Leading feminists meanwhile showed their impatience with the rest of the left and attempted to 'go beyond the fragments', which merely confirmed that the divisions within the feminist movement reflected the rest of the left. And, of course, there was Thatcherism.

THE THIRD NEW LEFT

The failure to go 'beyond the fragments' was not merely a problem for feminism, it was at the heart of the left's overall dilemmas. Moreover, the continuing changes associated with late modernity: for example, the decline of class as an organising principle of beliefs and identity, indicated the wider problem of marrying socialism with an increasingly diverse set of aspirations and concerns. Black politics, along with other movements associated with identity, was becoming by the mid-to-late seventies disconnected from the left; the dispute over 'black sections' in the Labour Party in the mid-eighties being one example of this. The working class itself, seeing its conditions being transformed in a variety of ways, was beginning to show much weaker alignment to its traditional political base. In what should be seen as the defining analysis of the third New Left, Eric Hobsbawm in his seminal Marx Memorial Lecture – 'The Forward March of Labour Halted' – argued that the achievements of the labour movement had come to a halt 30 years previously (ie in the late 1940s/early 1950s), echoing perhaps Raymond Williams' argument about the 'visible moral decline of the labour movement' twenty years earlier. Since this time the character of the working class had undergone major transformation, becoming more heterogeneous, more feminised, with greater demarcation between different trades. This led to greater sectionalism among workers. Despite the rise of militancy in the late 1960s and early 1970s, Hobsbawm argued, this shouldn't be interpreted as an indication of political radicalism. Indeed, he argued that many of the disputes had been 'economistic' in nature – confined mainly to wage struggles – and reflected a growth in sectionalism between different workers on an unprecedented scale, resulting in decreased class consciousness and solidarity. Hobsbawm ended his argument with the following stark warning to the left and labour movement:

> If the labour and socialist movement is to recover its soul, its dynamism and its historical initiative, we as Marxists, must do what Marx would certainly have done; to recognise the novel situation in which we find ourselves, to analyse it realistically and concretely, to analyse the

reasons, historical and otherwise, for the failures as well as the successes of the labour movement and to formulate not only what we would want to do, but what can be done. We should have done this even while we were waiting for British capitalism to enter its period of dramatic crisis. We cannot afford not to do it now that it has. (Hobsbawm, 1981: 19)

Hobsbawm's argument of course appeared initially before the 1979 election, the result of which took him into a deeper analysis of the predicament of the left and 'Labour's Lost Millions' (Hobsbawm, 1983). It follows then that the second defining feature of the third New Left was the significance it attached to Thatcherism and the long-term implications this brought for the future of the left. It was here in the pages of *Marxism Today* that the Gramscian analysis of Thatcherism as a 'hegemonic project' was formulated. With its roots in the organic crisis of British society, its ability to challenge the unresolved contradictions of social democracy, to form a historic block out of the conjunctural opportunities of the moment, Thatcherism had been able to create a new common sense around anti-collectivism and anti-statism, resulting in what Stuart Hall called 'authoritarian populism' (Hall, 1983). Not only was this an indication of the success of the right as a new form of conservative rule, it indicated that a major schism between the left and its traditional constituencies had taken place. The tasks set by the third New Left in the group which had consolidated around Martin Jacques's editorship of *Marxism Today* from 1977 could be described in this way: how can the left reconnect with changing values and popular aspirations? This took them into a deeper analysis of British society and culture eventually leading to the much talked of 'New Times' analysis.

At the heart of this argument was the view that the left was out of touch with the grain of cultural and social change. The third New Left followed its earlier predecessors in emphasising the importance of culture. Here the 'cultural is political approach' defined by Chun (1992: 26), took on a more concrete level. Gone were the more romantic interpretations of the working class as labour movement heroes; here the workers had taken on a variety of identities, as consumers, partners, as individuals. The concerns about the impact of consumerism were not as evident in the third New Left. Although the view of capitalist consumerism was not uncritical, it saw the improvements in living standards such as greater choice and mobility as providing new forms of positive identity. The focus of *Marxism Today* became increasingly cultural, the boundaries between 'the political' and 'the cultural' breaking down all the time, in the style and format of the journal as well as in the nature of its analysis. *Marxism Today* took on an appraisal of trends in consumption, sport, fashion, sexuality and soap operas as well as the more traditional political topics. It even became part of the consumption cycle itself offering 'MT credit cards', mugs, T-shirts and even suggesting, in the late 1980s, a passion for 'designer Marxism'. At times it toyed with the older lefts (including the first and second New Lefts, although its main target was labourism) illustrating perhaps what it perceived to be the massive divide between the culture of the left and that of the people it claimed to represent. This brought much resentment from others on the left, including from those of the first New Left. John Saville, in his survey of the 1988 issues, found *Marxism Today* to be full of 'shallow and superficial trivia', and its general preference – as he saw it – for culture over politics and economics he found 'an exceedingly dispiriting experience' (Saville, 1990: 35–59).

There was, however, a serious political point being made. The left, if you like, had failed to come to terms with the extent of 'the long revolution'. According to Stuart Hall in *The Culture Gap*, while negative aspects of the new consumerism remained, there were positive, even emancipatory sides to the cultural changes which the left needed to address:

A labour movement which cannot identify with what is concrete and material in those popular aspirations and expropriate them from identification with the private market and private appropriation will look, increasingly, as if it's trapped nostalgically in ancient cultural modes, failing to imagine socialism in twentieth century terms and images, and increasingly out of touch with where people are at. (Hall, 1984)

But it was the pioneering 'New Times' analysis that gave the third New Left its most critical engagement with modernity. First developed between 1988–1989 it was an attempt to analyse the new 'settlements' and then to propose a radical view of modernisation in opposition to that offered by the New Right. Thatcherism according to Hall had pursued a form of 'regressive modernisation': that is it situated its politics in what it perceived (rightly) to be fundamental socio-economic, global and cultural trends of, if not a new epoch, then a very distinctive moment in late modernity. Thatcherism, through its engagement with these 'New Times', or post-fordist economies based on the flexible specialisation of work and the international division of labour, information technology and the rise of consumptions proclaimed the inevitability of the market, the realities of individualism and the end of collective ideologies. Yet, there was an alternative scenario if the left were to engage with the new times: a chance to pursue a radical rather than regressive modernisation.

Essentially this was to be located in a new radical and pluralist politics which took as its theoretical starting-point the new social subject. The experience of the GLC in the mid-eighties gave it a political legitimacy, while the extending myriad of activities going on within civil society gave momentum to an idea of radical pluralism or radical democracy. Here the emphasis on agency is paramount; the decentring of the individual into more fragmented and unstable multiple selves came into sharp conflict with the earlier subjects of the individual-as-worker. As Hall says, 'New Times are both "out there", changing our conditions of life, and "in here", working on us. In part it is "us" who are being "re-made".' But such a conceptual shift presents particular problems for the Left. The conventional culture and discourses of the left, with its stress on 'objective contradictions', 'impersonal structures' and processes that work 'behind men's (sic) backs', have disabled us from confronting the subject dimension in politics in any very coherent way' (Hall, 1989: 120).

The end of *Marxism Today* in 1991 meant that many of these influences fragmented. It had not succeeded in providing a strategy for the revival of the left, only the critique that explained its predicament. Yet in retrospect the traditions of the third New Left have had more of a bearing on contemporary politics than was first apparent. Their own contribution towards modernisation had some impact on the Blair transformation in the Labour Party, particularly in the need to break out of labourism, to modernise the party and to situate it in the wider culture. Blair [himself a contributor to *Marxism Today* in its later years], often speaks a similar language of 'projects' and 'moods' and 'civil society' and, at least in some areas such as welfare reform, is not afraid of heresy; he was, after all, the '*Marxism Today* candidate' (Jacques/Hall, 1997). Like *Marxism Today*, Blair took as his defining moment the defeats of the left in the early 1980s and comes across strongly as a strategic politician (Andrews, 1997).

This has led to a common assumption that the 'new times' analysis paved the way for the emergence and success of New Labour: that the modernisers of *Marxism Today*, in effect, had a parental responsibility for the modernising positions of the 'Blair Project' (Freedland, 1998). Indeed one of *Marxism Today*'s later luminaries, Geoff Mulgan, is now a key adviser in the Downing Street Policy Unit, while another, Charlie Leadbeater, was one of the first to theorise New Labour's idea of the 'Third Way'. However, while there may be some close continuities – notably the critique of aspects of the traditional left – key differences can be detected, between the MT'ers and New Labour. These primarily concern the scope of modernisation. For Martin Jacques writing nine months before the election of 1997, Blair clearly had a 'project for the party'; what he lacked however was a 'project for the country': in other words, according to Jacques, there was no vision of how Britain would be a different place or of how the Labour government intended to engage with cultural, social and economic change (Jacques, 1996).

In October 1998 a one-off issue of *Marxism Today* returned to offer its analysis of the first 18 months of the Blair government. The collection of articles from Hobsbawm, Hall and Tom Nairn among others highlighted a deeper, more significant difference between New Labour and the traditions of the New Left as a whole. This was the contrast between the New Left's emphasis on the constraints of 'meta–politics', in which the global economy and its ideological and cultural frameworks remains the barometer for constraining social policy and the possibility of political invention and that of New Labour's 'Third Way', in which the emphasis shifts away from the 'bigger picture' of left versus right and economic conflict to 'modernising' initiatives at the 'micro' level, where pragmatism looks set to replace ideology (Giddens, 1998: Mouffe, 1998).

WHAT'S LEFT OF THE NEW LEFT?

Donald Sassoon in 1996 has argued that it is too early to judge the impact of the 1960s. If we try to analyse the impact of that decade we find contradictory modernising trends, which suggest both a consolidation of New Left traditions as well as a vacuum that could be filled by looking again at the different New Left legacies. The election of the Blair government in 1997 has shown a commitment to modernisation in many areas, notably the move away from the state towards civil society for solutions, a determination to modernise forms of governance and to decentralise power. Here the constitutional agenda of Charter 88, a pressure-group set up by members of the New Left under the influence of the 'Nairn–Anderson' thesis has come to fruition. It is some irony that the more theoreticist leanings of the second New Left should result 30 years later in one of the more practical forms of political modernisation. The Blair government has tried to construct an alternative notion of Britishness, particularly in the wake of the death of Princess Diana, but it has been limited. If *Marxism Today* still had still been around at this time, there would no doubt have been a 'special issue' on the death of Princess Diana, as an indication of the contradictory cultural, national and political themes it raised.

However, while there may be some close links between the modernising projects of the third New Left and the Blair government, there are many differences. Blair's concept of modernisation has accepted much of the neo-liberal framework including a populist endorsement of meritocracy, expressed at a cultural level by the Millennium Dome, 'BritPop' and 'Cool Britannia'. It remains conservative in its view of community, preferring the safety of Middle England as its cultural yardstick by which to measure the possibility of change, and is yet to articulate a convincing vision of a more fluid, culturally diverse, society.

In the spheres of education – particularly higher education – we see more evidence of the 'long revolution' envisaged by Raymond Williams, as we move from an 'elite' to a 'mass' system, with the right to university education now becoming almost a hallmark of citizenship. Yet the institutions of higher education – together with other cultural institutions – are 'over-ripe' for democratic reform. The bureaucratic and technocratic trends taking place within universities are characteristic in many ways of Wilsonite modernisation. For those inspired by the traditions of the New Left much scope exists here for the kind of participative ideals and philosophy of education that characterised the commitment of members of the first New Left to Adult Education in order to challenge the shallow ethos and priorities of the new managerialism.

A combination of demographic, economic and educational factors suggest that it will be women who will shape the social agenda of the next decades. The transformation in the role of women has been one of the most significant social changes of the last 30 years. More evidence has also been produced to indicate greater egalitarianism between men and women of a new generation (Wilkinson and Mulgan, 1997). However, the 'longest revolution', as Mitchell described it over 30 years ago has a long way to go, something made clear by the emergence of communitarian thinking – itself a reaction to the 1960s – and the reassertion of traditional notions of the family.

Globalisation must present the most significant dilemma for the project of 'radical modernisation'. The benefits of a more global culture have brought greater pluralism along the lines suggested by the third New Left and have confirmed perhaps that one legacy of the sixties is the decline of the liberal enlightenment subject, rather than its extension. On the other hand the relentless shifts towards globalisation and the assimilation of politics into economics, confirming in many ways the validity of New Left Marxist critiques of contemporary capitalism, continue to create real problems of democratic control. It is this question of how to rediscover the importance of agency, perhaps the New Left's most recurrent political ideal, which remains central to the project of radical modernisation.

REFERENCES

Anderson, P. (1964), 'Origins of the Present Crisis', *New Left Review* 23 Jan/Feb 1964.

Anderson, P. (1980), *Arguments Within English Marxism*, Verso.

Andrews, G. (1995), 'Young Turks and Old Guard' in *Opening the Books* (eds G. Andrews, N. Fishman and K. Morgan), Pluto.

Andrews, G. (1997), 'Curiosity Free Learning', *New Statesman* August 29.

Andrews, G. (1997), 'Breaking Free: Tomorrow's Intellectuals and New Labour', *Renewal* Vol. 5, No. 1 February.

Archer, R., Bubeck, D., Glock, H. *et al.* (eds) (1989), *Out of Apathy: Voices of the New Left Thirty Years On*, Verso.

Chun, L. (1992), *The British New Left*, Edinburgh University Press.

Freedland, J. (1998), 'The Marxists Return to Pronounce on the Fruit of Their Ideas: Blairism', *The Guardian* September 9.

Giddens, A. (1994), *Beyond Left and Right*, Polity Press.

Gidders, A. (1998), *The Third Way: Renewing Social Democracy*, Polity Press.

Gray, J. (1995), *Enlightenment's Wake*, Routledge.

Gray, J. (1997), *Endgames*, Polity Press.

Hall, S. (1984), 'The Culture Gap', *Marxism Today*, January.

Hall, S. (1989), 'The Meaning of New Times' in *New Times* (eds S. Hall and M. Jacques), Lawrence and Wishart.

Hall, S. (1996), 'New Ethnicities', in *Stuart Hall: Critical Dialogues in Cultural Studies* (eds D. Morley and K.H. Chen), Routledge.

Hall, S. and Jacques, M. (1989), *New Times*, Lawrence and Wishart.

Hall, S. and Jacques, M. (1983), *The Politics of Thatcherism*, Lawrence and Wishart.

Hobsbawm, E.J. (1995), *Age of Extremes*, Michael Joseph.

Hobsbawm, E.J., Jacques, M. and Muthearn, F. (eds) (1981), *The Forward March of Labour Halted*, Verso.

Hobsbawm, E.J. (1983), 'Labour's Lost Millions', *Marxism Today*, October.

Hoggart, R. (1957), *The Uses of Literacy*, Chatto and Windus.

Jacques, M. (1996), 'His Project for the party is a triumph, but what about his project for the country?' *The Guardian* September 26.

Jacques, M. and Hall, S. (1997), 'Cultural Revolutions', *New Statesman* December 5.

Kenny, M. (1995), *The First New Left: British Intellectuals After Stalin*, Lawrence and Wishart.

Kenny, M. (1996), 'After the Deluge', *Soundings* Autumn.

Laclau, E. (1996), *Emancipations*, Verso.

Mitchell, J. (1966), 'Women: the Longest Revolution', *New Left Review*, 40, Nov–Dec 1966.

Mouffe, C. (1998), 'The Radical Centre', *Soundings*, Issue 9, Summer 1998.

Mulgan, G. (ed.) (1997), *Life After Politics,* Fontana.

Rustin, M. (1989), 'The New Left as a Social Movement' in *Out of Apathy* (eds R. Archer, D. Bubeck, H. Glock, *et al.*), Verso.

Samuel, R. (1989), 'Born-Again Socialism', in *Out of Apathy* (eds R. Archer, D. Bubeck, H. Glock, *et al.*), Verso, pp. 41–57.

Sassoon, D. (1996), *One Hundred Years of Socialism*, I.B. Tauris.

Saville, J. (1990), 'Marxism Today: An Anatomy' Socialist Register, *Merlin Press*, pp. 35–59.

Sedgewick, P. (1976), 'The Two New Lefts' in *The Left in Britain 1956–1968* (ed. D. Widgery), Penguin.

Segal, L. (1989), 'The Silence of Women in the New Left' in *Out of Apathy* (eds R. Archer, D. Bubeck, H. Glock, *et al.*), Verso, pp. 114–16.

Steele, T. (1997), *The Emergence of Cultural Studies*, Lawrence and Wishart.

Thompson, E.P. (1960), *Out of Apathy*, New Left Books.

Thompson, E.P. (1963), *The Making of the English Working Class*, Victor Gollancz.

Wilkinson, H. and Mulgan, G. (1997), 'Freedom's Children and the rise of generational politics' in *Life After Politics* (ed. G. Mulgan), Fontana, pp. 213–21.

Williams, R. (1983), *Towards 2000*, Chatto and Windus.

Williams, R. (1958), *Culture and Society*, Chatto and Windus.

Williams, R. (1968), *May Day Manifesto*, Penguin.

Williams, R. (1965), *The Long Revolution*, Penguin.

6 The New Right and the 1960s: the Dialectics of Liberation
Richard Cockett

Like every other decade, there were several stories to the 1960s and those who lived through it emerged with their own narratives, their own singular version of events. What is so striking about the 1960s, however, which marks it out from any comparable era in modern British history, is just how different those narratives proved to be, as if there were two or more tribes living together, side by side, who spent ten years barely noticing each other. On the one hand, the most persuasive and recognisable narrative which has survived through to the 1990s is what I shall call the 'populist' narrative, of the 1960s – as the decade was transfigured into the generic term 'sixties', the age of Carnaby Street, Woodstock, the Beatles, drugs, hippies and the transformation in sexual and moral manners. In so far as the sixties means anything today, it is the populist narrative that matters, particularly to the young – our contemporary pop culture is suffused with elaborate references to the iconic pop stars and songs of that era. For them, as for most people, the sixties has gently subsided into popular imagination as a collage of revolting students, permissiveness and personal freedom.

However, to most people who lived through the 1960s, the above picture would be scarcely recognisable as an account of their ordinary lives. There has always been a debate as to whether 'the sixties' as 'populist' narrative was not in fact, confined to a bedsit in Hampstead and as far as the political classes were concerned, it certainly was. You can trawl all the memoirs and biographies of the politicians of all parties for the 1960s in vain for any reference to the 'populist' narrative; there is sometimes a genuflection towards the Beatles, but that's about it. The 'high political' narrative, as I shall call it, is an unremitting and depressing story of balance of payments crises, devaluation, economic stringency and the twists and turns of the embattled Wilson governments. As for the 'sixties' of modern memory, it might just as well never have happened. Aaron Copland once advised that if you want to know about the sixties, listen to the Beatles. But that will clearly only give you a very partial account as the nearest that the denizens of Whitehall and Westminster ever got to a psychedelic experience was watching the reserves melt away in 1967. Never did a generation of political leaders understand or know so little about the times that they lived through.

Of course, the two narratives occasionally intersected, but usually as broad comedy. In his diaries the comparatively youthful Minister for Technology, Tony Benn, proudly records how he even removed his jacket to observe a student 'debate' at the LSE, only to sound like a diligent anthropologist analysing a newly discovered species of ape.[1] Very few realised that there was a gap to be bridged, let alone attempted to do anything about it. Benn was one on the left who sought to do so, his diaries chronicling his steady dissillusionment with Whitehall-minded, technocratic ethos of Wilsonianism and from 1970 he became increasingly eager to embrace the counter-culture politics of the 1960s to re-invigorate British Socialism in the 1970s and early 1980s. Enoch Powell attempted to do the same for the right, channelling the anger felt by many traditionalists and conservatives (with big and little Cs) at the onward march of multiculturism and the dreaded permissiveness into a new kind of Toryism. 'Powellism', of which more later, was the right-wing mirror of Bennism and both doctrines, if that isn't to dignify two political arguments that were often incoherent, owed much to their authors' different reactions to the sixties. But they were the exception. Parliamentarians could hardly escape registering the anti-Vietnam protests even if they had wanted to, but on the whole their attitude was one of ignorance and hostility, especially on the Conservative benches. Neither is this very surprising; the political mindset of the ruling political class of the 1960s had been forged in the ideological struggles and debates of the 1930s and 1940s, and they merely carried the intellectual battlelines of the so-called 'Devil's Decade' into the 1960s with them. Like the eponymous general, they were busy fighting the battles of previous generations, which is why there is such a clear sense of disjuncture between the politics of desire and the politics of Westminster. It is remarkable that Britain had to wait until 1997 for a Prime Minister, Tony Blair, who was happy to carry the legacy of the 1960s (including the regulation guitar) into high office with him. Mrs Thatcher yearned for the certainties of the 1920s, or even the Victorian era, while John Major harked back to the 1950s Britain of the corner shop and the Great Western Railway. Most politicians fix their political bearings at an early age and seldom change much; a high degree of intellectual inflexibility is a prerequisite for party politics. In this respect, the 1960s was little different from any other decade.

Most politicians and their apparatchiks who were to emerge as the leaders of the New Right by the end of the 1970s (and Powell was never, politically, one of them) shared this political tin ear for the cultural and moral texture of the sixties. In this sense, the sixties had very little impact on them at all. Mrs Thatcher's first marital home was in a flat off the King's Road in the 1950s, and after a suburban interlude the family moved back to a more substantial house in Flood Street, a block away from their old flat, in 1970. The new Minister for Education was obviously appalled by what had happened in the interim, as the prim, middle-class Chelsea of her youth had transformed itself into the epicentre of the cultural revolution. She records in her memoirs: 'Eastern mysticism, bizarre clothing and indulgence in hallucinatory drugs emerged. I found Chelsea a very different place. ... I had mixed feelings about what was happening. There was a vibrancy and talent, but this was also in large degree a world of make-believe. A perverse pride was taken in Britain about our contribution to these trends. Carnaby Street in Soho, the Beatles, the mini-skirt and the maxi-skirt were the new symbols of "Swinging Britain". And they did indeed prove good export earners. The trouble was that they concealed the real economic weaknesses. ...'[2] In this way the sixties could be reduced to the balance sheets of political economy, dismissing any inherent meaning of these events as merely 'perverse'. The criteria for judging the sixties were fixed firmly in another age, another place; 1920s Grantham. Norman Tebbit, another putative member of the New Right, was attempting to get into national politics in the late 1960s, and was finally selected for Epping in 1969. His adoption speech only dealt with the 1960s at one point when, towards the end, he came to the subject of 'Law and Order and the so-called permissive society'. (It is instructive that, even then, the politics of the 'liberation of desire' was seen as a 'problem of law and order'.) Tebbit said: 'Some parts of this permissiveness – I suspect those of sexual morals, particularly – are part of a cycle of fashion, and will turn back before long. Pornography, I think, will become a bore. Exhibitionist and erotic shows will become as passé as the Dancing Years – and Shakespeare will still fill the theatres.'[3] He reflected the view of many Conservatives that the natural hierarchy of values would remain intact, as the natural order of things; the discovery that one of the artistic legacies of the 1960s was that Shakespeare could just be updated and even, in the hands of a new generation of theatre directors, still fill the theatres by becoming sexy was to keep Tebbit in paid employ as the most visible opponent of what he perceived to be the corrupting values of the 1960s for the next 30 years. Like many Tories, he is still wishing the 1960s would just go away, and that society could thus be allowed to revert to the 1950s nirvana of monogamy and hot cocoa. Most New Right Conservative politicians of Tebbit's generation either pretended that the sixties had never happened or that it was just a temporary aberration – to their cost, as they found out in the 1990s.

Essentially, then, the New Right – that cluster of politicians, economists, journalists, businessman and writers who gathered round Mrs Thatcher in the 1980s[4] – conformed to the general political ignorance of the 1960s. They were chiefly concerned with reversing what they saw as the historic and misguided electoral verdict in favour of economic collectivism of 1945 – their intellectual crusade was already well advanced by the 1960s. The New Right that emerged in the late 1970s could claim a long prove-nance; even by the beginning of the 1960s the sacred texts had already been written, the high priests identified and the foot-soldiers for freedom (as Hayek had dubbed them) had been slogging it out in the academic and political trenches for years. The New Right might only have received its journalistic sobriquet in 1968, but by that time it was already a fully formed intellectual, if not quite political, force. The 'Austrian School' of economists, notably Ludwig Von Mises, had provided the crucial critique of Socialism in the 1920s, Hayek had penned his biblical denunciation of Keynesianism and the 'middle way' in 1944 and Popper's attack on his-toricism had been published in *The Open Society and its Enemies in 1945.* Hayek's international liberal debating society, the Mont Pelerin Society, had been formed in 1947 and the Institute of Economic Affairs, the fount of so much that was to make up 'Thatcherism', had been going since 1955. By the 1960s, under the evangelical stewardship of messrs. Fisher, Seldon and Harris, the IEA was churning out pamphlets in favour of privatisation and Trades Union reform, the basic gruel of New Right poli-tics. Keith Joseph had begun writing in *The Times* and the *Financial Times,* helped by the impish intellectual dissident Alfred Sherman, on the need for a more 'free-market' approach in government. And in December 1967, Milton Friedman of the 'Chicago School' propounded the ideas of Monetarism, backed by decades of empirical research on the US money supply, to the 80th annual meeting of the American Economic Association. Most of the intellectual ammunition used against the collaps-ing social democratic consensus in the 1970s was, by then, getting on for 20 or 30 years old – and just as out of date, according to the critics. To the New Right as it was then constituted, the 1960s was important in affirming the follies of economic mismanagement by planning and Keynesianism, but the same could be said of the 1940s and 1950s and would be said of the 1970s. In this sense, the 1960s was no more than another decade's indictment of the ruling politico-economic wisdoms, merely adding further empirical proof against the reigning 'post-war consensus' which neither major political party particularly wanted, but which both found themselves forced to live with, boxed in as they were by the intractable trinity of the Cold War, Britain's post-war impoverishment and the electoral popularity of a burgeoning Welfare State.

So, in an important sense, at the high 'political' level, the sixties was relatively unimportant to the New Right, merely confirming all their gloomiest economic forebodings. In as far as the New Right engaged with the sixties at a 'populist', or cultural level, it was, as we shall see, as a reaction *against* most of what the sixties came to stand for. This was to give Thatcherism its high moral tone, its Gladstonian sense of political earnestness. If she had ever had the time or the inclination to step out of her Jaguar to wander down the King's Road by the late 1980s she would doubtless have been pleased to note her old stamping ground filled with retail outlets like Next and Gap to dress the new *working* class rather than the hippy boutiques of an earlier era. Although the Thatcherite *kulturkampf* took second place to its economics, it was still an important element. In the long run the sixties was certainly to be of considerable importance to both the success, in the 1980s, of Thatcherism, and to its failure in the 1990s. The sixties unleashed various forces which aided and sustained the revolution in political economy in the 1980s, but it also unlocked attitudes and movements which New Right conservatism was antithetical to and would struggle to, and eventually fail, to contain. These subterranean forces at work were little understood at the time and were to take several decades to work their way through society. For the New Right the aberrant decade of the sixties would become both an unintended blessing and a curse.

In short, the contradictory legacy of the sixties of the New Right was a function of the contradictory nature of New Right conservatism, epitomised by Mrs Thatcher; an economic liberal but a social and moral conservative. Such an ideology could work with the grain of the 1960s when it came to the economic aspirations of self-determinism epitomised by the self-made fashion designers and pop-moguls of that era (displaying laudable amounts of 'vibrancy and talent'), but found itself completely at odds with the aspirations to sexual, moral and political self-determinism which usually went hand in hand with the economic liberalism. If there was a single idea, leitmotif, to the sixties generation, it was personal emancipation, or liberation – but this encompassed the entire variety of human life, economic, social, physical and moral. Theirs was an à la carte liberalism, whilst liberalism for the New Right was strictly a set menu. New Right conservatism tended to view the only valid area for unregulated activity as the economic sphere, but for the rest most of them remained statists, or, at least, entirely static in their opinions. This is, of course, a contradiction that has often been remarked upon. Even before the 1960s was barely over, Samuel Brittain wrote in the *Financial Times* that 'The Non-Muscovite left favours freedom in everything but economics ... the right is sympathetic to freedom only in the economic sphere.'[5] If his formula seems rather exaggerated, that is only because so many on either side seemed to go out of their way to live up to the caricature. This contradictory discourse, economic liberalism and social authoritarianism, has characterised much of twentieth-century conservatism, and the New Right were little different; the St John the Baptist of Thatcherism, Enoch Powell, being a supreme example of a man combining the theology of the economic free-trader with that of the unbending social and moral statist in the same body. The Tories had always promised to 'Set the People Free' after the socialism of 1945–51; Eden had famously declared that conservatism, unlike its rival doctrine, stood for 'liberty of the individual, his right to ... respect for his own distinctive personality'. However, as Martin Francis has written in an essay on the 'Conservatives and the State', 'the Tories were not going to tolerate individualism and diversity if these led to deviance and a challenge to traditional moral authority'.[6] There was never going to be pluralist, post-modern politics under the New Right, despite, as we shall see later, the obvious affinities between a lot of New Right thinking and post-modernism. But in this, the New Right was little different from every other conservative strand.

The New Right were essentially reductionists, wedded to what one critic has described as 'market-fetishism'.[7] Their interest in explaining how society worked in terms of micro-economics led to a micro-focus. This gave the thinkers and politicians of the New Right a wonderful clarity, an unusually clear intellectual cutting-edge, but also rendered them almost totally blind to any other way of thinking about society, and in particular any other framework for thinking about human 'freedom', a lot of which, like the feminist movement or multiculturalism, came directly out of the sixties. In as far as Mrs Thatcher and her acolytes even acknowledged the existence of any of these movements, they were usually hostile to them for the sound conservative reasons enumerated above.

But to take the question of economic liberalism first, how did the sixties help, and even sustain the New Right? The answer has been given in its most extreme and even bitter form by the writer and former record producer Ian Macdonald in his definitive account of the Beatles and the sixties, *Revolution in the Head*. Sam Beer has also given some more refined answers to the same question in his book *Britain Against Itself*[8] in which he characterises the 'populist' 1960s as the 'romantic revolt'. Macdonald's principal thesis about the sixties is that it was a 'reaction of free essence against the restraints of outmoded form … a flood of youthful energy bursting through the psychic dam of the fifites'. Macdonald is surely right in his judgement that the popular culture of the sixties, all stoically ignored by Mrs Thatcher as it washed up on her doorstep in Flood Street, for the first time since the war legitimated individual self-expression and aspirations against the collective restraints of a society that had grown increasingly restrictive, censorious and thus hypocritical since the 1930s. The sixties seemed to make possible a more meritocratic and 'classless' society; whatever the statistics showed, this was the rhetoric and it was repeated so often that the words virtually became cultural artefacts in their own right. With this more meritocratic society went the belief that the individual was responsible enough to make their own choices about the lifestyles that they wanted to lead, and when obstructed in this by the state, the personal, for the first time, became the political. And integral to these beliefs was the growth of affluence and consumerism which have been so well documented and the feeling that the newly wealthy – and in particular, the young, newly wealthy – should be able to keep as much of their money as possible, even (or especially) when they mocked the inherited wealth of the old conservative order with it, an example being John Lennon's psychedelic Rolls-Royce.

Macdonald writes: 'The irony of right-wing antipathy to the sixties is that this much-misunderstood decade was, in all but the most superficial senses, the creation of the very people who voted for Thatcher and Reagan in the Eighties. It is, to put it mildly, curious to hear Thatcherites condemn a decade in which ordinary folk for the first time aspired to individual self-determination and a life of material security within an economy of high employment and low inflation. The social fragmentation of the Nineties which rightly alarms Conservatives was created neither by the hippies (who wanted to "be together") nor by the New Left radicals (all of whom were socialists of some description). So far as anything in the sixties can be blamed for the demise of the compound entity of society it was the natural desire of the "masses" to lead easier, pleasanter lives, own their own homes, follow their own fancies and, as far as possible, move out of the communal collective altogether.'[9]

Thus, although it was the mass hysteria, the screaming girls and fashion-conscious student Maoists who tended to catch the eye of the casual, or hostile, observer, all of which seemed to presage the nervous breakdown of capitalist democracy altogether, to anyone who cared to look just beneath the surface, the economic and aspirational politics of the sixties generation dovetailed perfectly with the older economic liberal traditions of what would become Thatcherism. One such person who was allowed a closer glimpse of rebellious youth than most was William Rees-Mogg, then the fogeyish editor of the *The Times*, complete with establishment lisp, and later journalistic cheerleader for Thatcherism. He was one of the usual suspects from the 'Establishment' (together with, in the tireless search for novelty, a bishop) picked by the young television producer John Birt to interview Mick Jagger on the lawn of a country house for *World in Action* in July 1967. It was one of the more bizarre 'happenings' of the decade, particularly so for Rees-Mogg as, doubtless to the intense disappointment of John Birt, he found himself in surprising agreement with the living icon of the supposed 'counter-culture'. As he later recalled, he was astonished to discover in Jagger a 'right-wing libertarian – straight John Stuart Mill.' For all their posturing and Jagger's own (brief but much publicised) flirtation with revolutionary politics, in essence the Rolling Stones much preferred material accumulation to any sort of politics, and in this they reflected much of their generation. Jagger himself went along with the march on the American Embassy in Grosvenor Square in 1968, but the extent of his radicalism was clearly stated by his own musical response to the turmoil of 1968 in the song 'Street Fighting Man'. The title alone was enough to have it banned by a paranoid BBC, but the lyrics told a different story, which was to lead inexorably to the Rolling Stones corporate rock of the 1990s with the Hell's Angels employed erecting the hospitality suites rather than clubbing members of the audience to death 1969-style:

> 'Everywhere I hear the sound of marching, charging feet / cause summer's here and the time is right for fighting in the street, boy.
>
> So what can a poor boy do, 'cept sing for a rock n'roll band, cause in sleepy London town / there's no place for a street fighting man.
>
> They said the time is right for a palace revolution / but where I live the game to play is compromise … .'

The millionaire 'glimmer twins' were still playing the anthemic 'I can't get no satisfaction' at the end of their mammoth stadium tours in the 1990s, as, at one level, the apparent radicalism of the 1960s submerged into the harmless mainstream of contemporary pop. When it came to the crunch, the heroes of the 'populist' 1960s would always prefer to play by the rules of the acquisitive society rather than risk the rewards for their creativity by embracing any one of the varieties of extremist collectivist politics then on offer. By the time that the Stones recorded 'Exile on Main Street' in 1974, they had also been tax exiles for several years.

Tariq Ali quotes 'Street Fighting Man' in his memoir of the 1960s. 'Street Fighting Man' was in many ways a comical account of trying to bring the rock elite of the sixties to a state of revolutionary consciousness, and failing every time. The Beatles were no better from this point of view. George Harrison recorded 'Taxman' in 1966 as the first pop protest against the high levels of Wilsonian taxation and in 1968 John Lennon wrote his own commentary about the quasi-revolutionary situation, 'RevolutionOne'. Written at the Maharashi Mahesh Yogi's Himalayan meditation retreat, the actual writing of the song anticipated 'les événements' of that year by several months but still explicitly condemned the different student politics of the day as 'Minds that hate', and blandly assured his listeners that everything would be 'alright'. His ambivalence towards the whole revolutionary situation was encapsulated in his famous refrain 'You can count me in/out'.

By the time that the Beatles re-recorded the song as the B-side of 'Hey Jude' in July 1968, the ambivalence had disappeared and the line was now firmly 'Count me out', much to the disgust of the radical left. Lennon himself briefly succumbed to Ali's blandishments before settling down to an apathetic millionaire's lifestyle amidst the false security of the Dakota building in New York. As Macdonald wryly remarks, 'Tiananmen Square, the ignominious collapse of Soviet Communism, and the fact that most of [Lennon's] radical persecutors of 1968–70 now work in advertising have belatedly served to confirm his original instincts.'[10] Paul McCartney and George Martin, the Beatles record producer, were both knighted by the Conservative government of John Major, thus belatedly authenticating the inherent conservatism of much of what passed at the time for sixties radicalism. This represented one of the main confusions of the era, as originality was often mistaken for 'radicalism', form for substance.

The sixties brand of economic liberalism occasionally teetered on the brink of something more subversive, but never quite went over the edge. Many of the most prominent entrepreneurs of late-twentieth-century capitalism in Britain were products of the 1960s, such as Richard Branson (who started out in that quintessential sixties industry the music business), Anita Roddick, Clive Hollick or Greg Dyke of the media company Pearson. Ted Turner of CNN provides an example from the United States. They are all capitalists, but what marks them out as different from capitalists of any previous era is that they are all sixties capitalists in that they all have non-economic agendas inherited from the radicalism of the sixties. One commentator had observed of this generation that '... old capitalism ventured into social affairs to protect its business agenda; new capitalism runs business in order to advance its social agenda .... Listen to them talking, and you hear men and women who regard profit and loss not as ends in themselves, but as tools to realise a world vision."[10] These people used economic liberalism for different purposes than their predecessors; Thatcherism allowed them, and indeed encouraged them, to become capitalist entrepreneurs, but they also brought their own agendas from the sixties with them. 'Pure' capitalism, of profit and loss, was no longer priveleged above everything else, and, as in the Body Shop, the 'hidden hand' gave way to very direct propaganda. These people, together with the pop 'aristocracy' of Mickie Most, Elton John *et al.* represented the sixties vision of a new meritocracy of self-made men and sometimes women which the New Right advocated and promoted into a social crusade.

In this respect, the sixties pointed the way towards Thatcherism and helped to sustain it electorally in the 1980s. Even if much of the 'populist' 1960s refused categorisation along a straight left/right spectrum, it was united by a radical brand of anti-authoritarianism and, more particularly, a radical anti-establishmentarianism which also informed Thatcherism. Indeed, a lot of the Thatcherites of the 1980s were radicalised by their attacks on the established order in the 1980s, even if their targets then were slightly different. But the mindset remained extremely consistent. Many of the Thatcherites viewed their politics as a crusade against the pettiness, restrictiveness, traditionalism and inertia that characterised the post-war settlement and first started mobilising against it in the early 1960s. This was very much a politics of generational change; it was an analysis that the radical left shared with the radical right in equal measure, articulated by the satire of Peter Cook subverting the cherished myths of wartime endeavour that was in danger of numbing a generation brought up on the 'Dambusters' and the Battle of Britain. If any single moment could be said to have breached the 'psychic dam' of the 1950s, it was Cook's sketch with Jonathan Miller in the 'Beyond the Fringe' show in which Cook, as an RAF officer, invites Miller to go on a suicide mission as a 'futile gesture' to raise morale. In an instant, the high seriousness of stiff-upper-lip military endeavour which everyone had been dragooned into endorsing since 1945 fell away. This was the intellectual landscape of John Osborne's 'The Entertainer'. Indeed, it was the failure of Wilson's governments of 1964–70 to do much about breaking down the social, class and gender barriers to self-advancement that drove many who were ostensibly on the left in the 1960s over to the New Right in the 1970s, including some of Mrs Thatcher's cabinet ministers such as Lord Young.

There they found that Mrs Thatcher, the lower-middle class shopkeeper, was much more eager to upset the cosy assumptions of the haute bourgeoisie than either the Oxford technocrat Harold Wilson or the naval patriot Jim Callaghan. The source of their discontent was summed up in the one word, 'Establishment': the word itself coined in the right-wing *Spectator* magazine in 1954 by Henry Fairlie. Baiting the Establishment became the chief sport of this generation of writers and intellectuals, and the assault burst into full bloom in the early 1960s, brought to a mass television audience by the unlikely figure of David Frost in 'That Was The Week That Was'. (Incidentally, among the scriptwriters on TW3 was Ian Lang, later one of John Major's cabinet ministers.)

In this respect, the skirmishes with the Establishment in the early 1960s established a diagnosis that was to be translated into a more full-blooded political assault in the 1980s. It was a diagnosis pioneered by people who were perceived to be, broadly, on the left in the 1960s – a testimony to the eclectic radicalism of the New Right. There is little that a Thatcherite would have found to disagree with in the old-Etonian Perry Anderson's complaints about British society in his famous essay on 'The Origins of the Present Crisis' in the *New Left Review* in 1964: 'The lasting contours of British society were already visible before the rise of the military–industrial imperialism of the 1880s. Yet it was this ostensible apotheosis of British capitalism which gave its characteristic style to that society, conserving it and fossilising to this day its internal space, its ideological horizons, its intimate sensibility. It is, above all, from this period that the suffocating "traditionalism" of English life dates ... traditionalism and empiricism henceforward fuse as a single legitimating system; traditionalism sanctions the present by deriving it from the past, empiricism binds the future by fastening it to the present. ... A comprehensive conservatism is the result, covering society with a pall of simultaneous philistinism (towards ideas) and mytogogy (towards institutions).'[12] All this would become familiar to the New Right through the pages of Martin Weiner, Correlli Barnett, Bernard Levin, Paul Johnson and others in the 1980s, just as the 'Angry Young Men' of the 1950s, tilting at the same windmills, would join the ranks of the Thatcherite *kulturkampf* for the same reasons. At the same time as E.P. Thompson was organising a group of his colleagues to lead Britain out of its torpor through socialism in the book of essays 'Out of Apathy', so another young historian, Hugh Thomas, was doing the same with his own collection of firebrands in his 1959 edited collection of essays called, simply and pointedly, 'The Establishment.'[13] This is an instructive collection, because many of the authors who thundered against the faceless bureaucrats and time-serving fixers of their day were the same men attacking the same targets in the 1980s. Hugh Thomas, then a historian recently escaped from the establishment clutch at the Foreign Office, later became Chairman of the Centre for Policy Studies and Mrs Thatcher's chief unofficial adviser on foreign policy – and eventually Lord Thomas of Swynnerton. In his preface, he wrote that: 'It is this Victorian England, with all its prejudices, ignorances and inhibitions, that the Establishment sets out to defend. The Establishment is the present-day institutional museum of Britain's past greatness. ... To those who desire to see the resources and talents of Britain fully developed and extended, there is no doubt that the fusty Establishment with its Victorian views and standards of judgements, must be destroyed.'[14]

In the pages that followed, Thomas's authors dutifully showed how to take a sledgehammer to the Establishment: John Vaizey to the Public Schools, Henry Fairlie to the BBC, Hugh Raven to the Army and Tommy Balogh to the Civil Service. John Vaizey was an economist who converted to Thatcherism in the late 1970s and who wrote at length as to why his generation became so disenchanted with the social democracy – or just socialism – of their youth.[15] By the 1980s they had added some new targets to their usual list, principally the Trade Unions – absent from any consideration of the Establishment in the 1960s, but which would later be condemned as an archaic, fusty, Victorian institution in the same way as the BBC, the Civil Service or the Judiciary – for powdered wigs read cloth caps. However, once again this dual assault on both sides of the Establishment (the Middle/Upper Class and Working Class Establishments) which characterised at least the rhetoric of Thatcherism also formed part of the appeal of Wilson's new-look Labourism of 1963/4, with his promises to apply the 'white heat of technology' to sweep away the 'restrictive practices' of 'both sides of industry'. The perceived failure of Wilson ushered many into the radical Tory camp as early as the late 1960s.

Although this generation of radicals shared the same diagnosis of an ailing, backward Britain in the early 1960s, those who identified with what became known as the 'New Left' and the putative New Right eventually came to radically different conclusions about what was to be done about the problem. The instruments of redemption were, of course, very different. The left wanted to use the powers of a strong state to bring about a more equal, democratic society, while the right looked to the liberating potential of the free market. The New Left stressed the virtues of 'democracy' as the righteous path to an open society; 'industrial democracy' as much as electoral democracy. Robin Blackburn, one of the most important New Left critics of the 1960s, later acknowledged that both sides were in pursuit of the same goal of personal freedom, and shared the same enemies of Tory paternalism or social feudalism; 'The idea of controlling one's own life, which in 1968 was subsumed into hopes of a complete change of society, showed its negative side. ... Mrs Thatcher was able to give a neo-Conservative twist to this radical individual appeal: instead of controlling your own place of work, it became a question of owning your own home. Common to both was anti-statism.'[16] Except that when it came down to the bottom line of policy-making, it was the New Left which proved as out of touch with the economic aspirations of the sixties as the New Right proved to be with the social and moral aspirations. Just as the New Right were, essentially, playing out the economic battles of the 1940s, so the New Left remained rooted in the political confrontations of the 1950s – and, in particular, 1956. In the end, the egalitarian society of the New Left could only be implemented by effectively insulating Britain from the global economy. A workers democracy would only come about, as the New Left authors of the 'May Day Manifesto' of 1968 admitted, by 'nationalising British privately-held foreign shares and securities. But this implies ... extensive intervention in the banking system and in the capital market ... for import quotas would be established and a total control instituted over foreign exchange'.[17] Thus, at the very moment when Britain was becoming an entrepôt state of fashion, culture, technology and service industries (such as advertising as well as banking), the New Left wanted to condemn the country to the parochial insularity of a siege economy. These ideas eventually ended up as the Bennite 'Alternative Economic Strategy' of 1976, finally defeated as a practical possibility by a Labour Cabinet determined to maintain Britain's role as an outward-looking, internationalist trading nation, even if this meant accepting much of the economic logic of the New Right.

It was out of his concern for the New Left disappearing up the cul-de-sac of economic statism, which seemed to be so out of step with the spirit of the age, that David Collard wrote his seminal pamphlet, 'The New Right; a Critique', for the Fabians in October 1968. He sounded a warning-bell that, in economic thinking, the left, although associated with most of the progressive causes of the 1960s, was being successfully out-flanked by the Right. He was no sympathiser with the economic liberals, but in surveying the work of bodies like the Institute of Economic Affairs, nonetheless argued that 'The New Right must be respected for the quality, consistency and rigour of its approach to the treatment of private industry. In this sense it is rather unfair to lump it together with organisations such as Aims of Industry. The economic vision of the New Right is the economist's model of perfect competition in which rational consumers indicate their preferences to profit-seeking producers by means of prices under conditions of perfect information. This is very far removed from a crude approach on the vested interest of capitalists.'[18] Indeed, at the same time as the May Day Manifesto appeared under the aegis of the New Left, several key figures of Collard's New Right gathered at Swinton College, the Conservative Party's college of the North, to prepare a similarly utopian manifesto for the future. Instead of Raymond Williams, a young journalist called John O'Sullivan took the chair. He was a tutor at Swinton, editor of the *Swinton Journal* and later worked in Mrs Thatcher's policy unit at Downing Street and added the much-needed jokes to her memoirs.

There is no doubt that the young generation of tutors there were all influenced by the heady blend of idealism and optimism that infused the sixties generation. Besides John O'Sullivan, both Stephen Eyres and David Alexander played important roles in converting key sections of the Conservative Party to Thatcherism in the 1970s. The symposium that O'Sullivan organised in the summer of 1968 was entitled 'Intellectuals and Conservatism' and involved several who were to become the leading lights of Thatcherism – Arthur Seldon, Geoffrey Howe, John Biffen, Russell Lewis, David Howell and Michael Spicer. In his editorial in the *Swinton Journal* introducing the symposium, O'Sullivan proclaimed 'the liberal hour' with all the fervour that his fellow activists of the left were contemporaneously ripping up the flagstones in Paris. He wrote of the '... sheer intellectual vitality of economic liberalism. It is scarcely an exaggeration to say that liberalism claims to cure more ills than patent medicine. Are you worried about the world monetary crisis? Flexible exchange rates will ease your mind. Is urban congestion a problem in your town? Enquire about road pricing today. ... Now is the time for the Conservative Party to commit itself to this liberal tradition in clear and unequivocal terms.'[19] It would take another 15 years for the party to do so, and even then the scepticism expressed at the symposium about the compatibility of conservatism and such a radical ideology as economic liberalism was never really overcome. However, in the context of the 1960s, it was John O'Sullivan *et al.* who proved to be better attuned to the changing times than their doppelgängers on the New Left.

So the rhetoric of self-determinism, classlessness and meritocracy that permeated Thatcherism was, to a significant degree, a legacy of the generational politics of the 1960s. In this sense, the New Right worked with the grain of the 1960s, with electoral dividends when that generation translated its somewhat inchoate youthful idealism into the hard-headed political action of the 1970s and 1980s. However, in another and equally important sense, Thatcherism was also heavily influenced by a strong counter-revolutionary ethos, directed against what was perceived to be the pathological aberrations of the 1960s – but which many of that same generation who were natural economic liberals regarded as the most hard-won freedoms in social and moral attitudes. As has been noted, the New Right differed little from mainstream Conservatives in regarding most of the social developments of the 1960s as, at worst, reprehensible, or, at best, merely faddish. Thus the New Right was as much a reaction against the 1960s as an embodiment of it. They were, after all, fiscal liberals and conservative moralists, and they could not understand how the one could go quite naturally with the other. Or, to put it another way, they could not allow that the individual was capable of behaving with the same level of self-responsibility in the conduct of their 'private' life as they might be able to exercise in the conduct of their economic life.

In the numerous bibliographies of freedom issued by the New Right from the 1970s onwards, the 'freedoms' insisted upon are overwhelmingly economic. As Chris Tame, one of the most prominent self-proclaimed 'libertarians' of the 1960s, wrote in the forward to a Centre for Policy Studies version of such a bibliography, 'The largest section ... is on economics, because of both that subject's importance and that fact that the revival of libertarian scholarship has been most extensively developed (or at least published) in that field.'[20] To the New Right, personal liberty was never really conceived of in any other way, thus ignoring the enormous body of work, principally from the sixties, associated with the post-modernist school, the new sociology, the feminist writers from the late 1960s onwards who all argued for completely different freedoms, freedoms which seemed just as relevant and even more urgent to the 1960s generation as economic liberalism. All this work was usually dismissed by the New Right as being inherently 'collectivist', written, as most of it was, by people identified with the political left. But to the consumers of such thought, these different schools of thought on the left in fact frequently argued for the same sort of autonomy, toleration and responsibility that the New Right could only accept in the economic sphere. Thus most of them never really challenge the notion of a paternalistic state, subscribing to a Victorian ethic of religious, racial and sexual conformity.

The vast majority of Conservatives in Parliament, including those who were to be prominent in the New Right, either voted against the Home Office 'social reforms' of the 1960s, or voted for them on sufferance. Mrs Thatcher, for instance, certainly did not vote for any of Roy Jenkins's reforms to create a new, more humane society. As she records in her memoirs: 'As regards abortion, homosexuality, and divorce reform it is easy to see that matters did not turn out as was intended. For most of us in Parliament – and certainly for me – the thinking underlying these changes was that they dealt with anomalies or unfairness which occurred in a minority of instances, or that they removed uncertainties in the law itself. Or else they were intended to recognize in law what was in any case occurring in fact. Instead, it could be argued that they have paved the way toward a more callous, selfish and irresponsible society.' What she certainly did not intend by voting for them was to provide 'a radically new framework within which the younger generation would be expected to behave'.[21] If the sixties was an era of rapid transformation in sexual behaviour, social attitudes and lifestyles, none of these transformations were ever accepted by the leaders of the New Right. It was, after all, Enoch Powell who sounded the clarion-call against a multi-ethnic, multicultural society, and who became the most unyielding defender of moral and racial intolerance. Even before the end of the sixties, people from the New Right had already become involved in the backlash against what was labelled 'permissiveness'; Mary Whitehouse launched the National Viewers and Listeners Association, and the Black Papers were published to protest against the 'liberalisation' and 'comprehensivisation' of education by the likes of Rhodes Boyson, Dr Dyson and Professor Cox. The Black Papers were of particular relevance, as they were first published as a direct response to the student revolution of 1968 and their authors would go on to have a direct impact on the 'great debate' about education that was launched by Jim Callaghan in his 1977 Ruskin College speech. Thus the discourses of the New Right and most of those radicalised by the sixties remained peculiarly compartmentalised; for the New Right, the feminist movement, environmentalism, the campaign for homosexual and lesbian rights, anti-colonialism and much else just passed them by, or was studiously ignored. Here was the 'liberation of desire', and it became, almost by default, the political preserve of the left – the anti-statist project of the left. But the New Right were, after all, not only economic liberals, they were also Cold War Warriors, nationalists and frequently Christian and for all their interest in the benefits of flexibility that a free-market would bring to working people, they remained remarkably inflexible in their thinking on almost everything else.

There is a profound irony here. The import of much of the rejection of the manners and morals of bourgeois society that characterised the 1960s was essentially post-modern, in the sense that in place of the meta-narratives of the state that the New Right still wanted to uphold (church, family, patriarchy, etc.) the sixties generation, and many on the left, wanted to replace with their own autonomous brand of lifestyle, proclaiming along the way the 'emancipation' of the individual from the constraints of bourgeois culture sanctioned by the state. Yet it was the New

Right that promoted the equivalent agenda in economic terms, which was broadly resisted by the left. What Hayek, for instance, proposed was really a style of 'post-modern economics', rejecting any notion of a grand 'narrative' of economic aggregates, or macro-economics, in favour of what he called a catallaxy. Andrew Gamble has described this notion as follows: 'the most general kind of spontaneous order for Hayek is the market order, which he describes as catallaxy, rather than an economy. The word "economy", derived from the Greek word for household, suggests planning and conscious control. In a catallaxy, no single person is responsible for planning the whole because knowledge is imperfect, fragmented and total.'[22] This is the post-modern economics of the fragmented, atomistic 'Blade-Runner' society, the essence of which had so much in common with the cultural and sociological explorations and 'happenings' of the 1960s, from art to pop music. At its most radical and avant-garde, the 1960s substituted a new mentality of a spontaneous/simultaneous aesthetic, for instance on the Beatles 'White Album', for the older mentality of coherence/development, and for the first time, spread this new aesthetic to the new mass forms of communications such as pop, television, advertising and the press (the *Sun*, for example), all new forms of re-invigorated late-twentieth-century styles of consumer capitalism pioneering a new form of economic aesthetic. However, because the New Right, pop artists, post-modernists and the New Left all existed in their own insulated, self-sustaining universes, with their own grammar, iconography and lifestyles, few ever attempted to make any political or cultural connections. Michel Foucault was one who did, albeit much later. In 1979, in his annual lectures at the College de France, this protean thinker of the French radical left, who had literally been on the barricades in 1968, urged his students to read the collected works of Hayek and Von Mises in order for them to think about 'the will not to be governed'. It was a belated recognition of the way that the Austrian school could be used to describe and further the liberalism of the 1960s, but it remains almost a unique example – and I shouldn't imagine that any of his students took his advice.[23]

This is, eventually, where the New Right fell foul of the 1960s. Even if the new politics of the 1960s described above, where the personal very insistently became the political, was confined to a small minority of people in the 1960s – even if not quite the proverbial bedsit in Hampstead – by the 1980s and 1990s they had virtually become the normal way of thinking for most people under the age of forty – as was brilliantly demonstrated by the success of the BBC drama series 'This Life' in 1996/7. In 1982, Sam Beer, updating his classic, *Modern British Politics* (first published in 1965), wrote in *Britain Against Itself* of the changed social environment which he beheld at the beginning of the Thatcher decade: 'Today, in Britain as in the US, the fighting causes of the counterculture have in great degree been absorbed into the fabric of everyday life for a large part of the society. Consider, for example, how readily people put up with, accept, and where appropriate, practise cohabitation, abortion, homosexuality, pornography, protesters ... undergraduates sitting on University committees, woman doing day jobs traditionally considered men's work, blacks in jobs formerly performed by whites, and, most impressive to the returning foreigner, very little "Sir" and "Ma'm". Shorn of some of its wilder fantasies, the new populism has been institutionalised in political debate ... .' The New Right, by trying to insist on the ethical, moral and sexual code of pre-sixties Britain, was, even before the end of the 1980s, looking tired and irrelevant. And when John Major tried to translate this old morality into a political campaign in the early 1990s with 'Back to Basics', his government merely looked silly, probably the most dangerous adjectival description of all to evoke among voters. What research that has been done, mainly in the United States, shows that the 'baby boom generation' of the 1960s are both economically and socially liberal. An analysis studying young corporate executives in the US concludes that '... baby boom business leaders are taking a fresh look at politics. Neither consistent liberals or Conservatives, they oppose government intervention in both the economy and their personal lives'. To this generation, the politics of Thatcherism, and even more so of John Major, seemed one-dimensional; handing out knighthoods to ageing sixties pop stars could not disguise the fact that the New Right ran into a social and moral cul-de-sac just as the left had run into an economic cul-de-sac a generation before.

Timothy Evans, a young activist of the libertarian New Right, in his book *Conservative Radicalism*, makes a persuasive case for a post-modernist conservatism. 'Unlike the young Conservatives of the 1960s or their forebears, the Libertarian right reflects the diffuse patriotic politics of traditional Conservatism. They have little feeling for the nation, the Monarchy and the established order of society. They are post-modern radicals with world-view that attempts to cut across boundaries of geography and ethnicity, class and nationality, religion and ideology ... but freedom does not mean that individuals can impose their will on others.'[25]

This might constitute a post-modern conservatism, but in fact it has so little to do with traditional conservatism, much of which the New Right tried to uphold, that it might as well not be conservatism at all. And in that intellectual conundrum rests the main political dilemma of the New Right and the Conservative Party today. The election of the 37-year-old William Hague as leader is a rather banal attempt to address precisely this issue.

Trying to preserve a traditional state-sanctioned morality within the context of a rapidly changing post-modern catallaxy was always bound to put an unbearable stress on the political programme of the New Right, and so it proved by the early 1990s. The logical consequences of technological, electronic and economic deregulation in the 1980s was always going to be the 'Gaytime TV' and 'This Life' of the 1990s rather than re-runs of the 'Onedin Line'. The ideas and attitudes associated with the populist narrative of the sixties did not go away, as Norman Tebbit hoped they would, but stayed, fructified and, shorn of the hedonsitic excesses of that era, became the mainstream culture of the next generation but two. For them, multi-culturalism, homosexuality, women's equality and consumerism come as naturally as did Queen and Country to earlier generations.[26] The failure of the New Right to acknowledge this eventually made them look as remote and implausible as the left became in the 1970s.

In the end it was the left that put the post-modern jigsaw together, marrying the social and moral legacy of the sixties to the economic liberalism of the post-war era, and New Labour have been the successful and astute beneficiaries of this process. Just as the left was out-flanked by the late 1960s, so a revived and transformed left eventually out-flanked the New Right in the 1990s, or rather leap-frogged over a political generation. The intellectual weaving together of these disparate elements took place largely in the pages of *Marxism Today* in the 1980s under the guidance of Martin Jacques and Stuart Hall. It was in the pages of *Marxism Today* that the remainders of the left which had been radicalised by the 1960s and 1970s dropped the insistence on a collectivist economy, acknowledging that that argument had been lost. The way was thus left open for this New (or Newer) left to bring what had been an often obscure debate about 'rights', 'inclusiveness', 'empowerment' and 'democracy' in the dreary concrete halls of the polytechnics of the 1970s into the mainstream of political thinking, where it found a ready audience among those who no longer shared an automatic deference to or interest in the crown, church, monarchy, and nation – especially after the revolutions of 1989. As Jacques has admitted, *Marxism Today* was long on theory and analysis and very short on policy proposals, and it had to wait for the think-tank DEMOS, founded by Jacques and the sometime *Marxism Today* essayist Geoff Mulgan in 1993, to translate a lot of this new thinking into policy proposals specific enough to be used by a government. Just as Timothy Evans's 'post-modern' conservatism cannot actually be described as 'Conservative' in any sense, even of that most elastic of political terms, to the new politics of 'New' Labour, and DEMOS cannot really be characterised as anything to do with Socialism, or even in the interests of

'Labour' – the old working class. That this is true, and the fact that both parties are now grappling for new definitions and new directions, is to a large extent the social and cultural legacy of the 1960s combined with the legacy of the revanchist capitalism of the 1980s. Tony Blair likes to describe such a new direction as 'the Third Way'. Many scoff that this is too amorphous to be taken seriously, but it at least shows a determination to grapple with the intellectual consequence of those two revolutionary decades, something that Conservatives have failed to do.

The New Right underestimated the legacy of the 1960s, and failed to come to terms with the changes in society that occurred during that much-maligned decade. Theirs was primarily an economic vision of society, a vision which was reinforced during the decade, but the primary importance of the decade for most people was to show how limited a vision that might actually be, and, in the long run it was to undo the New Right.

NOTES

1. See Benn diaries, Vol. 2.
2. Margaret Thatcher (1995), *The Path to Power*, Harper Collins, p. 153.
3. Norman Tebbit (1988), *Upwardly Mobile*, Wedenfeld and Nicolson, p. 80.
4. See my book *Thinking the Unthinkable* (1994), Harper Collins, for a precise definition of the personnel and, where appropriate, principles of the New Right.
5. Samuel Brittan, *The Role and Limits of Government; Essays in Political Economy* (1984), Temple Smith, p. 50.
6. *The Conservatives and British Society, 1880–1990* (1996), ed. Martin Francis and Ina Zweininger-Bargielowski University of Wales Press.
7. Mandela and Polanyi-Levitt, quoted by Radhika Dasai in her excellent analysis of the origins of the New Right in 'Thinking Up Thatcherism', the *New Left Review* (1994), p. 203.
8. Sam Beer, *Britain Against Itself* (1982), W.W. Norton.
9. Ian Macdonald, *Revolution in the Head – The Beatles Records and the Sixties* (1994), Fourth Estate, p. 29.
10. See Macdonald, pp. 223–9 for a full analysis of the social and political background to the Beatles songs of 1968, and Tariq Ail, *Street Fighting Years* (1987), Collins.
11. Trevor Phillips in the *Independent on Saturday*, 8 November 1997.

12. Perry Anderson, *English Questions* (1992), Verso.
13. E.P. Thompson, *Out of Apathy* (1960), Stevens and Sons. and Hugh Thomas, *The Establishment* (1962).
14. Hugh Thomas (ed.), *The Establishment* (1962).
15. See his article in *The Cambridge Review*, 27 April 1981.
16. Quoted by Lin Chun in *The British New Left* (1993), Edinburgh University Press, p. 194.
17. *May Day Manifesto* (1968), ed. Raymond Williams, Penguin.
18. See *Thinking the Unthinkable* for a longer discussion of this pamphlet, p. 157.
19. See the *Swinton Journal*, Summer 1968, and for the background *Thinking the Unthinkable*, pp. 191–4.
20. *Bibliography of Freedom* (1981), CPS.
21. *Path to Power*, pp. 152–3.
22. Andrew Gamble, *Hayek; The Iron Cage of Liberty* (1996), Polity Press, p. 38.
23. See James Miller, *The Passion of Michel Foucault* (1993), Harper Collins, p. 310.
24. Sam Beer, *Modern British Politics* (1965), Faber & Faber.
25. Timothy Evans, *Conservative Radicalism* (1996), Berghahn Books, p. 130.
26. See, for example, 'The Social Survey on Youth' in the *Independent*, 20–21 November 1997.

7 The New Right, New Labour and the Problem of Social Cohesion
Peter Saunders

We are used to thinking about political ideologies in terms of a continuum from 'left' (socialism) to 'right' (conservatism). Such imagery is misleading, however, for there is a third core political ideology of modernity – liberalism – which cannot be located on this continuum. In Britain, classical liberalism withered at around the same time (the late nineteenth century) as modern socialism emerged. Socialism thus displaced liberalism as the antithesis to conservatism, and this probably explains why we have retained the misleading image of politics as a simple continuum between two opposing positions. Since the 1970s, however, there has been a revival of classical liberal thought, both in Britain and in the United States, and this makes it impossible any longer to map the contours of contemporary political debate using a simple left–right continuum. Today, politics are structured around three distinct positions – not a continuum, but a triangle (Figure 7.1).

The defining feature of the classical liberal tradition is its concern to defend individual liberty and its corresponding distrust of the use of state power to bring about collective goals. Any growth in state power tends to

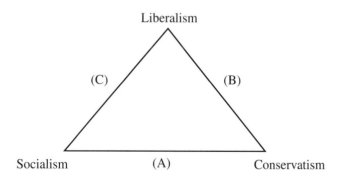

Figure 7.1   The three core political ideologies of modernity

be resisted, even where it commands widespread support and is intended to bring about beneficial improvements in social conditions, for extension of state responsibility necessarily implies a reduction in individual freedom. This concern was clearly expressed in the sociology of Herbert Spencer who spent many years warning his Victorian contemporaries of the dangers posed by their gradual acceptance of increased state intervention in social affairs. Where others saw benign and overdue reform, Spencer saw the looming shadow of state coercion: 'Dictatorial measures, rapidly multiplied, have tended continually to narrow the liberties of individuals' (Spencer, 1982, p. 3). Similarly, Friedrich Hayek warned of the dangers inherent in the renewed enthusiasm for social reform in the 1940s when he suggested at the start of *The Road to Serfdom* that: '... in our endeavour consciously to shape our future in accordance with high ideals, we ... in fact unwittingly produce the very opposite of what we have been striving for' (1944, p. 4). For writers such as Spencer and Hayek, good intentions pave the road to a coercive Hell.

This fear of growing state power sharply differentiates liberalism from both socialism (which seeks to use state power to bring about goals such as greater equality) and conservatism (which seeks to use state power to achieve such goals as the maintenance of a traditional social order). While liberals and conservatives share a common position against socialists on issues to do with private property and wealth distribution, socialists and conservatives take up a common position against liberals on issues to do with individual liberty and the rights of the collectivity. Conservatives and socialists alike talk of the duties and responsibilities which individuals owe to the collectivity, and they justify policies on the grounds that they contribute to the 'common good', even if some individuals lose out. Liberals, by contrast, see the freedom of the individual as paramount and are sceptical of any claim by governments to know better than their own citizens what is and is not in their own best interests.

In practice, of course, governments rarely pursue strategies which consistently operationalise any one of these ideals. Nevertheless, it is only when we clarify the distinctions between them (and in particular, when we recognise that contemporary politics are structured around three distinct positions rather than two), that it is possible to understand the key shifts which have occurred in Britain, and to some extent in other western countries as well, since the Second World War.

For thirty years after the war, British politics was grounded in a broad political consensus. Conservative and Labour governments alike were committed to the basic principles of the comprehensive welfare state, Keynesian economic management designed to maintain full employment, and a 'mixed economy' in which government owned and ran key sectors of industry. Seen in terms of the triangle of ideologies, this period was dominated by a compromise between socialism and conservatism (position 'A' in Figure 7.1, above).

During the 1970s, this compromise fell apart. Keynesian economics led to stagflation with rising unemployment and state-owned enterprises became increasingly sclerotic; attempts by government to govern in co-operation with the powerful trade union movement ended in a wave of industrial unrest and political chaos. Chastened by its failures in government between 1970 and 1974, the Conservative Party in opposition began to search for new ideas and initiatives, and it found them in a return to classical liberal free market principles (see Cockett, 1994).

For twenty years from the mid-seventies onwards, the Conservative Party in Britain pursued a radically new programme which abandoned the old post-war compromise between conservatism and socialism, and which instead sought to link conservatism to the long-neglected principles of classical liberalism (position 'B' in Figure 7.1, above). This self-consciously ideological 'New Right' programme was economically liberal but socially conservative. Its liberalism could be seen in its commitment to reducing the role of government in managing and regulating the economy (eg by abandoning Keynesian demand management, by ending the drift to corporatism, and by privatising the nationalised industries), as well as in its determination to break the monopoly power of the unions. All of this was intended to reawaken a culture of enterprise and individual initiative among the British people (something which conspicuously failed to happen – see Jowell *et al.* 1996).

Alongside this liberal economic agenda, the 1979–97 governments pursued a rigorously conservative social and cultural programme. The powers of government were centralised. Police powers were increased. Uniform national standards of education were imposed across all state schools and universities. Alternative lifestyles were discouraged (eg by banning 'raves', legislating against the promotion of homosexuality, and acting against 'travellers'). Emphasis was placed on the importance of strengthening traditional social institutions including marriage and the nuclear family. National unity and distinctiveness was fiercely defended through opposition to European federalism, Scottish nationalism and Northern Irish republicanism as well as rigorous defence of the Falklands at the time of the Argentine invasion in 1982. These governments also recognised the importance of political tradition through their firm commitment to the monarchy, the established Church and the hereditary Upper House. It was this strongly conservative element in the agenda of Thatcherism (and, across the Atlantic, of Reaganism) which led critics such as Stuart Hall (1983) to define the programme of the 'New Right' as 'authoritarian populism'.

It is one of the paradoxes of the Thatcher/Major years, however, that for all the emphasis placed on national unity, solidarity and continuity, these governments actually presided over a remarkable erosion of social cohesion and traditional morality. On most indicators, the 1980s and 1990s witnessed an increase in social fragmentation and a decrease in social order. In the view of some critics, this was an inevitable result of the pursuit of their liberal economic agenda.

One obvious indicator of growing social fragmentation was the rising crime rate. Despite the increased emphasis on 'law and order', the total number of criminal offences notified to the police doubled between 1979 and 1993. According to the *British Crime Survey*, more than one in ten adolescent males has a criminal record for a non-motoring offence by the age of eighteen, and a staggering 40 per cent of British males have such a record by the time they reach the age of 40. England and Wales today have the highest recorded crime rate in the western world – higher than any other country in Western Europe, and higher even than the United States. The 1997 *International Crime Victimisation Survey* shows not only that England and Wales have more burglaries and more car thefts per head of population than the USA, but also that they have more assaults, robberies and sexual attacks. Only the homicide rate is lower than in America.

Another indicator of the erosion of social cohesion and collective morality can be found in the family statistics (see, for example, Land and Lewis, 1997). Again, despite their official support for the traditional family, the Thatcher and Major governments saw divorce rates escalate to the second highest in Europe (behind Denmark). By the early 1990s one couple was getting divorced in England and Wales for every two getting married, and one in ten marriages was ending within just two years. Meanwhile, the rate of births outside marriage exploded from one in twelve in 1971 to one in three by the mid-nineties. No fewer than 84 per cent of mothers under 20 today are unmarried. Although some illegitimate births are to cohabiting couples, one-quarter are registered in only one name, and half of the remainder are to parents living ats different addresses. Two and a quarter million children are now being raised by just one parent. Of 7.2 million mothers in England and Wales, 1.2 million are raising their child/ren without their father, and one million of these rely on state income support.

The escalation in crime rates and the dramatic increase in the rate of family disintegration both point to the failure of the Thatcher and Major governments to maintain social cohesion. But was social fragmentation an inevitable by-product of New Right policies?

Defenders of the New Right believe not. Rather like defenders of communism who long argued that the theory was right even though the practice kept going wrong, 'New Right' analysts like Charles Murray (1994) believe that the failure to ensure social cohesion should not be blamed on the policies pursued in the 1980s. Murray argues that the rise in criminality can largely be explained by the collapse of the traditional family, and that the collapse of the traditional family is the result of growing state intervention since the 1950s. The problem, in other words, pre-dates Thatcherism by at least two decades.

Critics of the New Right disagree. Writers like Will Hutton (1995) trace the cause of social fragmentation to the emphasis placed in the Thatcher years on values of individualism and competitiveness. It is Hutton's thesis that the Conservative governments of the 1980s and 1990s allowed the market to 'rip through' all aspects of British society, widening inequalities and deepening social deprivation while simultaneously emphasising a 'get-rich-quick' mentality which was relatively unconstrained by any ethic of social responsibility. In his view, it was the growth of inequality and poverty, coupled with the encouragement of greed and selfishness, that was eroding social cohesion (as well as hindering long-term economic efficiency and modernisation), and what was needed to put it right was a renewed commitment to the principles of collective responsibility which the Conservatives had neglected.

It is certainly true that inequality increased in Britain between 1979 and 1997, and that the Thatcher governments in particular emphasised values of individualism and competitiveness, but is this an adequate explanation for why crime rates, divorce rates and other indicators of social fragmentation rose so dramatically during this period?

Hutton's analysis was extremely influential (his book, *The State We're In*, became one of the most unlikely best-sellers of the 1990s), yet in some respects, his critique was misplaced. It was not true, for example, that the poor in Britain became poorer during the Thatcher and Major years, and it is at least debatable whether the number of people in poverty grew as Hutton and others assume. While the income gap between top and bottom certainly widened, expenditure data show clearly that the living standards of the poorest 10 per cent of the population rose in real terms over this period. Indeed, defining the 'poverty line' as an income below 50 per cent of average income, the proportion of the population in poverty fell from

8 per cent in 1979 to 5 per cent in 1995 (Green, 1998; Dennis, 1997). It is still possible, of course, to argue that widening inequalities somehow contributed to social breakdown, but it is difficult to see how social deprivation in and of itself could be said to have caused the increase in social fragmentation which took place during this period.

A further problem with the Hutton thesis is that most indicators of social fragmentation were rising long before Thatcher took office; both crime rates and divorce rates, for example, had been rising since the late 1950s, and both were already at record levels by 1979. Murray's emphasis on the pernicious effects of growing welfare provision seems to fit this chronology rather better than Hutton's emphasis on the pernicious effects of the new economic individualism, for whatever started the ball rolling must have been present from the 1940s/50s, and the welfare state clearly presents itself as an obvious potential factor.

It should also be remembered that the Thatcher and Major governments were nowhere near as indifferent to the question of social cohesion and social responsibility as their critics sometimes implied. Both Thatcher (in her call for a return to 'Victorian values') and Major (in his ill-fated 'Back to Basics' campaign) hoped to balance their emphasis on economic individualism by encouraging a renaissance in the traditional values of charity, compassion and social duty. As liberals, they sought to extend economic freedoms, but as conservatives they were also alive to the need to maintain or restore the old virtues of personal responsibility, emphasising duty over self-indulgence and moral conscience over the pursuit of narrow self-interest. That the boys in red braces in the City of London wine bars paid little heed to this message only demonstrates how difficult it is for any government to direct cultural change, and how unlikely it always was that the values of one century could be dusted down and reinserted into the material conditions of another.

It is by no means clear, therefore, that the neo-liberal economics of the Thatcher/Major years can be blamed for the deleterious social trends of that period. What is clear, however, is that these governments seemed powerless to halt or even slow down developments of which they disapproved. Both Thatcher and Major were undoubtedly concerned by the drift to social fragmentation, but they conspicuously failed to do anything effective about it. The critics may not be correct in locating the fundamental causes of the problem in New Right policies, but they are surely justified in pointing to the impotence of New Right governments in the face of these developments. British society did become more atomised during these 20 years, and 'conservative liberalism' offered few realistic solutions to the problem.

It was the failure of New Right governments to ensure social cohesion and stability which left open to the Labour Party the possibility of forging a new and distinctive politics.

The success of Thatcherite economic reforms (overseas as well as in Britain), coupled with the final collapse of socialism in eastern Europe, had forced the British Labour Party during its long exile from government to come to terms with the legitimacy of large-scale private enterprise and of relatively unregulated and open commodity, financial and labour markets. However, the evident need for a social programme designed to combat the growing disintegration of British society allowed the party to combine its new-found economic liberalism with its more traditional roots in social democratic values emphasising 'social justice' and common citizenship. What emerged was a new politics of 'social liberalism' (position 'C' in Figure 7.1, above).

Like Clinton's 'New Democrats' in the USA, Blair's 'New Labour' Party believed that it should be possible to harvest the benefits of a dynamic global system of capitalism while avoiding the costs of social deprivation and social pathology which have hitherto gone along with it. The strategy for accomplishing this balancing act is two-fold. First, ensure that everybody has a role to play within the social system and that nobody is allowed to abdicate their social responsibility. Central to this first part of the strategy is an attack on 'social exclusion' through fundamental reform of state welfare and an emphasis on the importance of work. Second, ensure that everybody can see that rewards are distributed 'fairly'. This second part of the strategy entails active pursuit of the goal of 'meritocracy' including an emphasis on education as the key means by which individuals can be offered the opportunity to realise their full potential, and a willingness to attack those (such as the much-maligned 'fat cats' of the privatised utilities) whose wealth appears not to be the product of hard work and enterprise. As we shall see, this combined strategy of maximising 'social inclusion' and support for 'meritocracy' is largely consistent with the prescriptions for social cohesion set out by Emile Durkheim over 100 years ago.

To understand the New Labour project for social reconstruction, we have to begin by clarifying why the Thatcher/Major governments failed in their attempts to encourage a stronger sense of social responsibility as a complement to the extension of economic freedoms. The basic reason for this failure was that they thought, wrongly, that they could run history backwards.

Looking back several generations, these Conservative governments saw how economic liberalism had once coexisted with a culture of mutual co-operation and self-help. Believing that this culture had been undermined by the growth of state welfare, they deduced that it could be revived by 'rolling back' the growth of the state. Get government off people's backs, and this generation will develop the sort of self-reliance and social responsibility which earlier generations had exhibited. The reasoning, however, was fallacious.

Dramatic social changes, such as the sudden escalation in divorce rates and illegitimacy rates since the 1960s, clearly have multiple causes. Whether the expansion of state welfare is one of these causes is contentious and debatable, but what cannot be disputed is that welfare provisions have *enabled* these changes to occur (a point made forcibly by many conservatives including Charles Murray and Lawrence Mead). Without welfare support, single parenthood would be economically non-viable for most people, which is precisely why unmarried pregnancy and marital breakdown carried such fears and attracted so much stigma and opprobrium in most social strata in both Britain and America until the 1950s. The extension of state benefits since then has made it easier for men to desert their families (for their wives and children will still be looked after), just as it has made it easier for young women to raise babies without ensuring they have a committed male partner to help them. The economic fear has been lifted, and the stigma associated with divorce and illegitimacy has in consequence all but disappeared. If the deserted family can still get by, why shouldn't the erstwhile father/husband seek to maximise his gratification elsewhere? If the babies can be fed and clothed, why shouldn't young teenage mothers have children on their own if that is what they want? With the state there to pick up the pieces, why shouldn't we all indulge our selfish needs and desires?

What is true of divorce and illegitimacy is also true of other areas of personal and collective morality. It is not that state provision *induces* people to change their behaviour (few young women are tempted to get pregnant with a view to receiving state benefits or even a council flat). It is rather that such provision *enables* people to pursue courses of action which would otherwise have incurred high personal costs. By reducing or even eliminating these costs, state provision makes irresponsible behaviour viable and thereby weakens the traditional norms and sanctions which have hitherto regulated it.

New Right theorists have long recognised this problem. For them, the fundamental problem with state welfare provision is that it 'crowds out' precisely those forms of behaviour which we 'should' seek to encourage and it enables those forms of behaviour which we 'should' seek to deter. It is not just that individuals cease to take responsibility for the consequences of their own actions and come to rely increasingly upon the non-judgemental largesse of the state. It is also that state provision renders pointless those forms of voluntary and communal self-help which foster the bonds of solidarity and cohesion which today seem to be fraying so badly.

David Green (1985) has given one example of how state provision tends to undermine self-provisioning in his work on the history of the Friendly Societies. He shows how the introduction of compulsory state unemployment and sickness insurance in Britain in 1911 led directly to the collapse of the working class friendly society movement. With the introduction of compulsory state contributions, the need for voluntary saving was reduced, and the stimulus for working people to organise together for their common welfare was removed. As a result, the friendly societies, which had evolved as institutions of communal solidarity and support without any prompting from above, simply withered away. As Murray (1988) says, if we want individuals to act responsibly, then we must give them something to be responsible for, and if we want people to come together in thriving communal activities, they must be left with something to do for themselves (see also Berger and Neuhaus, 1977).

New Right analysts and politicians have always understood this. Where they went wrong, however, was in thinking that historical causation could simply be rolled backwards. If state provision had contributed to the erosion of personal responsibility and social cohesion, then, they reasoned, a reduction in state provision would surely begin to re-establish it. Take away the provisions which had stunted communal activity and such activity will spontaneously re-emerge.

The logic, however, was faulty. The culture which sustained and educated ordinary people in the virtues of mutual self-help and social responsibility was the product of an era when nobody expected help from government. The morality governing the behaviour of the respectable working class from the Victorian era through to the inter-war years reflected the common sense of the time, for if people did not assume the responsibility for improving themselves and looking after those close to them, nobody else would. Today, by contrast, common sense tells us that there is no need to live by the irksome rules which governed the behaviour of our grandparents. For fifty years, we have been living by a very different message – one that promises unconditional support whenever we need it, 'from cradle to grave'. In this changed cultural environment, the old virtues have fallen into disuse, and in some cases have even been inverted (see Himmelfarb, 1995 for examples).

It is extremely doubtful whether this could now be reversed. The growth of state provision during the twentieth century undermined a culture based on personal responsibility and communal self-help and replaced it with a 'claimant culture' emphasising political 'rights' to social support. Taking away the state provision will not recreate the old culture, but is more likely to leave people beached in their dependency, thereby provoking festering resentment and social withdrawal. To call, as Thatcher and Major did, for a return to old values is in this sense to misunderstand how culture is reproduced and changed.

The Marxist literature of the 1970s and 1980s probably had a better grasp of this problem than the New Right literature did. In his 1976 work, *Legitimation Crisis*, for example, Juergen Habermas saw that, in the period before extensive state intervention, people had nobody to blame when they fell upon hard times. In the era of the modern welfare state, however, people *expect* government to come to their aid. The welfare state has, he says, undermined the idea of 'natural fate' and has stimulated and sustained 'the demands *that it has placed on itself*' (1976, p. 69, emphasis in original). He goes on to argue that, if the state ceases to meet these demands, the eventual result is likely to be a 'crisis of motivation' as people withdraw from active participation in mainstream society. Rolling back the state, in other words, produces not revitalisation but demoralisation. The emergence of an underclass 'dependency culture' in recent years has begun to look very like this 'crisis of motivation', for it seems that increasing numbers of people have lost the impulse to find work and no longer understand the need to take responsibility for their own lives (see Buckingham, forthcoming).

New Labour seems to have grasped this in a way that the New Right never did. Like Thatcher, Blair is committed to the classical liberal values of enterprise, individual effort and reward for risk and effort. Unlike her, however, he understands that social responsibility will not simply re-emerge once the weight of state dependency is lifted. It has to be encouraged, cajoled and if necessary coerced, for the conditions which originally sustained it have long since been destroyed.

New Labour recognises that a re-imposition of market principles cannot by itself recreate the conditions of social cohesion. Equally, however, New Labour also recognises that simply continuing to expand state welfare is no solution either. Just as the political right has wanted to believe that social cohesion can be achieved by reducing state welfare, so the traditional left has long believed that it can only be achieved by strengthening it, but *both* positions are now understood by New Labour to be fallacious. For 50 years, the Party was convinced that society is held together by giving people handouts. What we are seeing today is the long-delayed realisation that people are held together, not passively by receiving, but actively, by working.

The idea that the post-war comprehensive welfare state functioned as a source of social cohesion was most clearly expressed in Marshall's arguments about the principle of universality grounded in the notion of a common citizenship. In his celebrated essay, Marshall (1964) argued that modern citizens must share equal 'social rights' as well as equal legal and political rights. In the modern welfare state society, in other words, we all have the right to claim social support. Everyone gets treated when they fall ill, everybody's children can go to state schools, and everyone gets cash benefits when they fall on hard times and state pensions when they retire from work. Because we all share in the benefits of the system, the assumption has been that we all owe allegiance to it (or, in Hutton's terminology, that we are all 'stakeholders'). Social cohesion derives from the fact of our shared rights as consumers of state largesse. It is for this reason that writers in this tradition tend to resist mean testing, and are willing to accept a situation where huge amounts of money go to middle-class households which do not need it, for this is seen as the price that has to be paid to keep everybody tied into the system (see Goodin and LeGrand, 1987).

The whole emphasis of this model is on *rights*. The principle of universality does not extend to *responsibilities*, for the model does not expect everybody to contribute. It is true that National Insurance as originally conceived was a system in which individuals established rights to benefits on the basis of earned entitlements, but the National Insurance budget was never ring-fenced from general state revenues and individual contributions were used to pay out current claimants rather than to establish a proper insurance fund. Unlike the old friendly society insurance schemes, therefore, state welfare has generally failed to link contributions to benefits, responsibilities to rights. Far from creating a unified society in which all citizens feel and express a sense of common identity, this system has ended up creating a bifurcated society in which one group pays into the common pool while another group simply draws out.

As I have argued in more detail elsewhere (Saunders, 1993), a system like this is more likely to generate fragmentation than cohesion. There are two reasons for this. The first is that those who are obliged to pay in will feel resentment against those who persistently draw out. In a commercial or truly mutual system of insurance, such resentment is muted because (a) everybody establishes entitlement by paying contributions; (b) benefits are normally paid out only following some calamity which is not the fault of the claimant; and (c) continuing membership is voluntary and 'exit' is readily possible for those who become dissatisfied with the way the fund is being managed. None of these conditions holds in the case of state welfare. Not only is it possible for claimants to have paid little or nothing into the system, but the mere fact of being 'in need' is generally sufficient to establish their claim without further investigation into the circumstances through which the need has arisen. As the old morality of personal responsibility has been eroded, so too has the old distinction between a 'deserving' and an 'undeserving' poor. Inevitably, therefore, the suspicion arises among contributors that funds are being paid out to people who do not really need or deserve support, but the principle of compulsory contributions means that they can do nothing about this. Denied the option of exiting the system, people simply grow increasingly disenchanted and resentful (see Saunders and Harris, 1989).

The second reason why state welfare fosters fragmentation rather than cohesion is that (paradoxically) it encourages individual self-interest. A system of universal benefits is inherently prone to what has been called the 'tragedy of the commons' (Hardin, 1977). In any situation where a large number of people share access to a common resource, the rational, self-maximising individual will seek to make the fullest possible use of the resource in question. Self-restraint will do little to maintain the common resource unless one can be assured that all other individuals are exercising similar restraint, but maximal exploitation of the resource will bring major benefits to oneself while making little impact on the size of the common resource provided others do not follow suit. The consequence is that rational individuals will try to milk the system lest others end up getting more than they do, and the common assets will be over-exploited as a result. State welfare, in other words, encourages egoism rather than altruism and is inherently prone to over-exploitation and cheating.

In the language of rational choice game theory, the welfare state is a particularly intractable 'Prisoner's Dilemma' game in which rational individuals are encouraged to cheat even though this is not in their collective long-term best interests. In the 'prisoner's dilemma game', I stand to gain most if I defect (cheat) and you do not. The result is that we are both likely to cheat, yet this is a worse outcome for both of us than if we both play by the rules. In smaller groups (such as the nineteenth-century friendly societies) this problem can be overcome, for all members know each other and are therefore likely to be more willing to moderate their own self-maximising behaviour. As Olson explains, 'Social pressure and social incentives operate only in groups of smaller size, in the groups so small that the members can have face-to-face contact with one another' (1971, p. 62). In larger-scale contexts, however, the dilemma may be irresolvable without imposition of strong rules and surveillance or creation of strong individual incentives to co-operate. Neither condition seems to have applied in the post-war welfare state.

All of this is richly ironic, for socialists have long argued that capitalist free market systems foster widespread resentment and encourage the pursuit of narrow self-interest. We now see that the development of the post-war welfare state has tended to have much the same effect. A system of state welfare which was explicitly set up with the intention of countering the fragmentation of the market by bonding society together has in fact generated conditions which almost inevitably contribute to further fragmentation – a classic example of how unintended (and perverse) consequences can flow from actions intended to bring about quite different results (see Giddens, 1984).

New Labour has come to understand all this. It sees that a free and comprehensive system of state welfare is not the answer to the problem of ensuring social cohesion. Instead, it has begun to search for an answer in solutions which were first put forward over 100 years ago by the French sociologist, Emile Durkheim.

More than any other single social theorist, Durkheim was concerned with the problem of social cohesion in modern societies. In *The Division of Labour in Society* (1933), he identified two main causes of what he saw as the modern malaise of social disorganisation and moral deregulation (what he called 'anomie'). The first was the lack or weakness of any institutional framework expressing to people the importance of the ties of functional interdependence which bind them together. In a modern society with a complex division of labour, we all necessarily depend upon each other for our own welfare for we each perform specialised tasks which allow us to prosper only through extended co-operation with others. Too often, however, we fail to realise how much we depend on others and they in turn depend on us, and like the players in the tragedy of the commons, we focus on how we can maximise returns to ourselves with little regard for how this is likely to affect the whole social order on which we ultimately depend.

In the medieval period, according to Durkheim, the crucial social significance of the occupational division of labour was expressed in the guild system. Individuals belonged to occupational guilds and it was through the interrelation of the guilds that they found a wider common interest and membership in the city and the corporation. In the modern period, however, occupational forms of membership and representation are much weaker and political representation is organised on the basis of relatively meaningless territorial units rather than more meaningful occupational ones. The solution, for Durkheim, is clear – we need to recreate on a national level the sorts of occupationally-based corporations which used to thrive at a smaller scale in medieval times, for only in this way will individuals come once again to realise the importance of co-operation to their own survival.

This is not enough, however, to ensure a properly functioning and relatively harmonious social order. Durkheim argues that a second major source of the anomic conditions characteristic of modernity is the existence of institutional arrangements which prevent the realisation of natural talent. A society need not be equal in order to be harmonious, but it is important that such inequalities that exist are widely felt to be fair and legitimate. This will be the case, in Durkheim's view, only when 'natural inequalities' between people come to be reflected in social inequalities. For this to happen, individuals must all have the opportunity to develop and realise their talents (eg through education), and unearned privileges, such as the inheritance of property, must be reduced or broken down altogether.

Durkheim was writing in the late-nineteenth century, and the prescriptions which seemed sensible then may not necessarily seem sensible or desirable now. We can accept his analysis of the causes of the problem, therefore, without necessarily accepting his identification of the solutions.

The first problem identified by Durkheim is how to guard against excessive self-interest by reinforcing an awareness of functional interdependency. Durkheim was surely right to emphasise the importance of *work* or employment as the source of this interdependence, but his emphasis on corporatist solutions now seems inappropriate. Not only were corporatist forms of organising national solidarity tarnished by the experience of Italian fascism under Mussolini, but weaker forms of corporatism were tried and failed in Britain during the latter years of the period of social conservatism. Between 1962, when the government established the National Economic Development Council, and 1979, when the final attempt at an agreed wages compact with the unions collapsed in the chaos of the 'winter of discontent', government, big business and trade union leaders tried and failed to come to binding agreements which they could impose on their various constituencies (for a review, see Dearlove and Saunders, 1991).

Corporatism thus failed decisively and disastrously in Britain, but its abandonment during the Thatcher years resulted precisely in the sort of moral vacuum which Durkheim had identified. The 1980s was a decade when individuals were seemingly pursuing affluence with little regard to others, and what was lacking was any strong institutional expression of interdependence and social inclusion.

The second problem identified by Durkheim is how to ensure the legitimacy of inequalities. His answer was that an institutional framework was needed which would enable individuals to realise their full potential. Durkheim emphasised that it is not enough that I should recognise how much I depend on others and they depend on me. It is also necessary that I should recognise that others have a right to occupy the positions they hold and that I too occupy an appropriate position given my 'natural' talents and capacities. Both Thatcher (the daughter of a Grantham grocer) and Major (the son of a Brixton circus performer) seemed to understand the importance of this, for both emphasised their view of Britain as an 'open society' in which effort and ability were rewarded. This was not, however, a view widely shared among ordinary people, for as the 1996 *British Social Attitudes Survey* made clear, public opinion through the Thatcher and Major years became increasingly opposed to existing income inequalities, and these governments never succeeded in convincing the electorate that the rich (derided increasingly by opponents as 'fat cats') deserved their good fortune.

To summarise: If Durkheim was right, what is needed for social cohesion, and what the period of liberal conservatism failed sufficiently to provide, is first, a system of social 'inclusivity' based in some way on the occupational system, and second, a system of meritocracy in which social placement depends solely on individual ability and effort. It is these two principles which lie at the heart of New Labour's social liberalism.

One of the sharpest contrasts between the liberal conservatism of the New Right and the social liberalism of New Labour is the latter's concern with social inclusion – a concern that everybody should participate in, and feel part of, a single, cohesive society. This concern has been manifested institutionally in the formation of a new inter-departmental 'social exclusion unit' reporting directly to the Prime Minister. It has also been manifested symbolically in the populism of New Labour rhetoric (notably the tendency to present itself as 'the People's Party'). But most significantly of all, it has been manifested politically in New Labour's commitment to reforming the post-war welfare state.

The core idea of social inclusion is that nobody should be allowed to drift apart from mainstream society. This can mean that escape hatches at the top have to be battened down (one of the new government's first actions, for example, was to abolish the assisted places scheme which allowed bright children from less affluent backgrounds to escape from the state system of comprehensive schooling into the private sector). More often, however, it means that trapdoors at the bottom have to be secured. In particular, people must not be allowed to drop out of employment and live their lives on state benefits. Whether they be the young unemployed, single mothers or able-bodied people claiming disability benefits, those who can work should work.

The Labour Party has traditionally opposed the American principle of 'workfare', in which able-bodied claimants are expected to work in return for benefits, and it has always been deeply distrustful of any attempt to erode the principle of entitlement on the basis of need. New Labour has therefore had to move cautiously, and its policy of 'Welfare to Work' has been couched in the language of enablement rather than coercion. The rhetoric has it that claimants want to work and that the government is simply helping them to do so, although the 'new deal' for the young unemployed has removed any option of remaining on benefit (a move reflecting Lawrence Mead's plea for a strategy of 'help plus hassle'). In reality, New Labour appears to be pursuing a strategy in which work is emphasised as a responsibility which individuals should be obliged to recognise and discharge.

The significance of this switch from old-style citizenship to new-style social inclusion cannot be overstated. Citizenship emphasised rights; social inclusion emphasises duties. Citizenship sought to ensure social cohesion by giving to anyone in need; social inclusion seeks to ensure social cohesion by encouraging everybody to work. Citizenship was passive; social inclusion is active. New Labour's reform of the welfare state is driven partly, it is true, by economic considerations, for the social security budget now accounts for one-third of government spending, and the cost of benefits has increased eight-fold in real terms in fifty years. But more pressing than this economic agenda is a moral one, for the new emphasis on the responsibility to work is part of Labour's answer to the problem of social fragmentation. Like Durkheim, New Labour has come to recognise that social cohesion is grounded in the division of labour, and that moral bonds between people are forged, not through receipt of largesse, but through work. Only when everybody contributes can everybody feel a common sense of membership and interdependence.

Coupled with this new emphasis on the responsibility to work has been a renewed commitment to the principle of meritocracy. In the 1997 election campaign, Tony Blair identified his three priorities as 'education, education and education', and in his speech to the Commonwealth Heads of Government conference shortly after taking office, he proclaimed that, 'The Britain of the elite is over. The new Britain is a meritocracy where we break down the barriers of class, religion, race and culture' (quoted in the *Daily Telegraph*, 25 October 1997, p. 6). The emphasis on education is a recognition that individual opportunity depends increasingly on access to training and the achievement of paper qualifications. The corresponding emphasis on meritocracy reflects a belief that 'social justice' consists not in the achievement of end-state equality, but rather in a system where individuals fill social positions solely on the basis of their ability and their hard work.

As in its commitment to the responsibility to work, so too in its commitment to the principle of meritocracy, New Labour is following a Durkheimian agenda which represents a radical break with old Labour thinking. Old-style social justice emphasised the distribution of resources; new-style social justice emphasises the distribution of opportunities. Old-style social justice was concerned to achieve greater equality of results; new-style social justice is concerned only to ensure that inequalities between individuals have been fairly 'earned'. The emphasis on meritocracy is, in fact, much closer to the sentiments expressed by the previous Conservative administration than those associated with traditional Labour thinking, for John Major too made clear his commitment to the principles of meritocracy early on in his Premiership. The only difference between them is that the Conservatives saw as fair and just certain high earnings (eg those in the City) which New Labour still sees as illegitimate.

Here, then, is social liberalism's answer to the problem which liberal conservatism never managed to solve, the problem of ensuring social cohesion. Where Thatcher and Major believed that a culture of social responsibility would renew itself simply as a result of a shift away from state paternalism, New Labour understands that the problem cannot spontaneously solve itself. Unwittingly taking its cue from the profound insights of Emile Durkheim over a century ago, New Labour seeks to bond us together by emphasising the commitments which we owe each other through our work and by ensuring that hard work and ability are rewarded, thereby minimising the grounds for widespread resentment. The question, of course, is whether this two-pronged strategy will work.

Both parts of this strategy represent a major break with Labour's past, and together they represent much that is distinctive in the new social liberalism. The emphasis on social cohesion through work has displaced the old emphasis on cohesion through welfare, and the emphasis on cohesion through meritocracy has displaced the old emphasis on cohesion through equality of outcomes. The old strategy of welfare-based citizenship and egalitarianism failed because it created resentment and encouraged self-interest. So will the new strategy fare any better?

There are at least two reasons why we might remain sceptical. One is that the United States is on many measures a deeply fractured society, yet this is a country where unemployment is low, where state welfare has always been much less extensive than in Britain, and where the commitment to principles of meritocracy is built into the 'American dream'. If widespread work and a belief in individual opportunity have failed to create cohesion in the USA, why should they be any more successful in Britain?

A second problem is that there may be good grounds for believing that even a genuine meritocracy may encounter severe problems of social cohesion. It is worth remembering that Michael Young's original fable of the rise and fall of a meritocracy ended with a popular revolt against the elitism of intelligence (Young, 1958), for those at the bottom of the heap may be no more inclined to accept the legitimacy of intellectual privilege than the legitimacy of inherited privilege. Indeed, I have suggested elsewhere that a meritocratic system can be self-defeating, for the greater the opportunities available to individuals, the harder it is for failures to accept their fate, and the less likely it is that those who succeed will feel any great benefit or privilege as a result (Saunders, 1996). Meritocracies can breed just as much resentment as any other systems of social inequality.

New Labour's Durkheimian social strategy may well fail to rebuild social cohesion, but it is difficult at the present time to think of a realistic alternative strategy for social renewal. If the triangle in Figure 7.1 really does represent a comprehensive map of modern political ideologies, then it is clear that New Labour has moved to fill the last position that has not yet been tried. Social conservatism's development of a welfare system where resources were allocated purely on the basis of need is today discredited, for in practice welfare dependency and the pursuit of egalitarianism produced not a cohesive society of citizens but a fragmented society of resentful payers and dependent recipients. Equally, liberal conservatism's dream of a return to the small-scale mutualism and market-based co-operation of the nineteenth century must also now be rejected, for the culture that sustained that system of communal self-help has disappeared and cannot be recreated. This leaves only the social liberalism of New Labour with its emphasis on the social duty to work and the individual opportunity to succeed. If this fails to work, then it is difficult to see whence any fourth alternative could arise. As Margaret Thatcher might have put it, it really does seem now that there is no alternative.

REFERENCES

Berger, P. and Neuhaus, R. (1977), *To Empower People*, American Enterprise Institute for Public Policy Research.

Buckingham, A. (forthcoming). 'Is there an underclass in Britain?' *British Journal of Sociology*

Cockett, R. (1994), *Thinking the Unthinkable*, Harper Collins.

Dearlove, J. and Saunders, P. (1991), *An Introduction to British Politics*, Polity Press.

Dennis, N. (1997), *The Invention of Permanent Poverty*, London: Institute of Economic Affairs.

Durkheim, E. (1933), *The Division of Labor in Society*, Macmillan.

Giddens, A. (1984), *The Constitution of Society*, Polity Press.

Goodin, R. and LeGrand, J. (1987), 'Not only the poor' in their *Not Only the Poor: the Middle Classes and the Welfare State*, Allen & Unwin.

Green, D. (1985), *Working Class Patients and the Medical Establishment*, Gower.

Green, D. (1998), *Benefit Dependency*, Institute of Economic Affairs.

Habermas, J. (1976), *Legitimation Crisis*, Heinemann.

Hall, S. (1983), 'The great moving right show' in Hall, S. and Jacques, M. (eds) *The Politics of Thatcherism*, Lawrence & Wishart.

Hardin, G. (1977), 'The tragedy of the commons' in G. Hardin and J. Baden (eds) *Managing the Commons*, W.H. Freeman.

Hayek, F. (1974), *The Road of Serfdom*, Routledge.

Himmelfarb, G. (1995), *The Demoralization of Society*, Knopp.

Hutton, W. (1995), *The State We're In*, Jonathon Cape.

Jowell, R., Curtice, J., Park, A., Brook, L. and Thomson, K. (1996), *British Social Attitudes: the 13th Report*, Dartmouth.

Land, H. and Lewis, J. (1997) 'The emergence of loan motherhood as a problem in late twentieth century Britain' *Welfare State Programme Discussion Paper* No. 134, London School of Economics.

Marshall, T. (1964), 'Citizenship and social class' in T. Marshall (ed.) *Class, Citizenship and Social Development*, Doubleday.

Mead, L. (1992), *The New Politics of Poverty*, Basic Books.

Mead. L. (1997), *From Welfare to Work*, Institute of Economic Affairs.

Murray, C. (1988), *In Pursuit of Happiness and Good Government*, Simon & Schuster.

Murray, C. (1994), *Underclass: the Crisis Deepens*, Institute of Economic Affairs.

Office for National Statistics (1997), *Social Focus on Families*, The Stationery Office.

Olson, M. (1971), *The Logic of Collective Action*, Harvard University Press.

Saunders, P. (1993), 'Citizenship in a liberal society' in B. Turner (ed.) *Citizenship and Social Theory*, Sage.

Saunders, P. (1996), *Unequal But Fair?*, Institute of Economic Affairs.

Saunders, P. and Harris, C. (1989), *Popular Attitudes to State Welfare Services*, Social Affairs Unit (Research Report No. 11).

Spencer, H. (1982), *The Man versus the State*, Liberty Classics.

Young, M. (1958), *The Rise of the Meritocracy*, Thames & Hudson.

8 1968's Unfinished Business – Cultural Equality and the Renewal of the Left

Hilary Wainwright

The spirit of 1968 sometimes seems like an exotic bird: predators seek to kill it and steal the plumage to enhance their own appearance. A shared political characteristic of Margaret Thatcher and Tony Blair is their relish in condemning the legacies of the sixties while selectively deploying its rhetoric for their own ends. Mrs Thatcher destroyed the radical Greater London Council (which put resources and political clout behind ideas seeded by the social movements of the late 1960s and early 1970s). Her policies devasted trade union strength and confidence, another continuity from the sixties. She attacked the democratic, 'progressive' teaching methods that had flourished in the aftermath of 1968. With her mock Victorian family values she sought to contain feminism and stigmatise gay liberation – both gaining new impetus from the cultural firment of this derided decade. Yet at the same time she paraded the plumage of 'liberation', 'empowerment' and 'individual fulfilment'. Similarly, Tony Blair talks 1960's language about 'the third way', 'participation', 'openness', 'new politics' while at the same time presuming private ownership to be a God-given fixture, drastically centralising party power into the hands of his own coteries, closing down debate on controversial issues like the legalisation of cannabis, and receiving business barons in a manner reminiscent of a feudal court.

It is time then, to rescue some integrity for the legacy of 1968. This does not mean a nostalgic dig for treasure buried beneath the detritus of the last 30 years. Rather it requires identifying the possibilities that were opened up. For 1968 was a moment when a repressive culture, already hollowed out, visibly collapsed; before a new cultural order could establish itself, unthinkable alternatives suddenly seemed feasible. State and corporate authority re-stabilised itself but the vulnerability of apparently invincible regimes left powerful impressions on younger generations who witnessed the way that the powerful tottered. Through this process, a genie of cultural confidence had grown among people who had previously accepted a subordinate status; an assertion of cultural equality which could not easily be rebottled.

Which, if any, of the seeds of revolt and of utopia that were sown in the fertile years of 1968 and 1969 have taken root and produced lasting traditions? Which have been distorted by defeat? What innovations and openings have emerged recently that carry on and develop these traditions in new ways?

There is a particular question on which I want to focus. It may be only of personal value but I'll chance it just the same. I believe that a distinctive left, a libertarian left, was born, perhaps reborn, out of the late 1960s. It had roots in the 'new left' that came out of the traumas of 1956 and was associated with E.P. Thompson and also had continuities with earlier non-statist socialist traditions from William Morris to G.D.H. Cole and with the short-lived traditions of cultural equality associated with the French revolution and Thomas Paine. Indeed the continuity that links these varied political phenomena and justifies reference to a distinctive tradition is a shared belief not only in programmes of political and economic equality but also in the need to do away with paternalism and presumptions of cultural superiority by would-be ruling elites – whether political or economic – and to devise methods of democratic self-government. This left has not been morally and intellectually defeated by either the collapse of the Soviet Union or the pressures of the global market. Or to put it more cautiously, the challenges posed by the political bankruptcy of the Soviet bloc and by the increasingly global organisation of capitalist production have been central to its politics from 1968 itself; developments in the past 30 years intensify these challenges but do not put the libertarian left on the intellectual or moral defensive. Its ways of organising have been influenced by the insights of social movements of the last three decades, most notably the women's liberation movement and the radical shop stewards movement of the late sixties and seventies. The experience of the liberated areas in struggles against imperialism, in Africa and Asia, the European peace movement's challenge to the mentality and reality of the Cold War and the doubt cast by the green movement on the uncritically progressive claims for the advance of science, have all shaped its eclectic politics. My question is, what explains the resilience of this libertarian left and is it well founded?

Along with the rest of the left, this diffuse tradition has been severely battered in the past 30 years, beginning with the defeat of radical forces that had gained influence in Labour's shadow cabinet in the final, strike-torn years of the 1970–74 Conservative government of Edward Heath. The sidelining of the left was followed by the ignominious defeat of the Callaghan Labour Government and the victory of Mrs Thatcher with all that followed from it: the erosion of union strength, the virtual destruction of local government, the straight-jacketing of education, the inculcation of fear and insecurity, the destruction of any base for opposition or plural politics. The repercussions of the Thatcher years for the libertarian left were so profound that perhaps they have not fully sunk-in. On an international scale too, this left has been weakened by the impact of de-regulation and globalisation on labour and social movements North and South. Its libertarianism is, after all, based on a belief in democratic collectivities and their importance as a basis of social co-operation; if popular democratic organisations are weakened the libertarian left appears utopian, lacking feasible forms of agency.

The libertarian left's belief, however, in the possibility of a social order based on social co-operation, equality and democracy has retained its moral confidence. Socialists from this tradition do not find their foundations to be shaken in the way that many on both the communist and social democratic left feel theirs to have disappeared. Many from these ruling left traditions believed they had no option but to abandon a commitment to socialism or to redefine it as a humanised capitalism. The socialist vision of many leftish western social democrats as well as Communists was closely associated with the model of the command economy. Jack Straw's description of his youthful vision being 'the command economy plus parliamentary democracy'[1] summed up a view shared by many, and shattered by increasing evidence of the failings of economies run by a centralised state. The criticisms made by this kind of socialist of the Soviet model were not primarily of the economic system (the lack of decentralised common and co-operative ownership, accountable economic co-ordination and workplace democracy, for instance) but of the undemocratic, unparliamentary character of the state which ran it. For them, the only alternative to the centralised state, as far as economics was concerned, was private property and the market or some mix of state and private market.

For the libertarian left, the rejection of the Soviet model was more fundamental. The political spirit of 1968 was in opposition to the authoritarianism of Moscow and Peking as much as the imperialism of Washington and London. Our socialism was, from its foundations, shaped as much by our reflections as we protested at the Soviet invasion of Czechoslovakia as by our thoughts as we marched to stop the Americans bombing Vietnam. As a generation frustrated by the bluntness of parliamentary democracy we were both inspired by the original Soviet ideal of participatory democracy and sobered by its fate when the popular participation in local as well as national soviets was subordinated to centralised planning and single party monopoly. The need to combine participatory forms of economic democracy with rules for political pluralism was consequently fundamental to our thinking. But we also learnt directly from our own fraught experiences of participatory decision making, our knowledge of the democratic – and problematic – co-operative models in the areas liberated by guerrilla movements in Vietnam and Mozambique and our involvement or observation of the shopfloor democracy – potential and real – evident in the militant trade unionism of the late sixties and early seventies.

Initially our vision and with it our timetable was somewhat over-optimistic about the power of direct forms of democracy. Harold Wilson's puppet-like stance – whether the strings were pulled by Lyndon Johnson or the City of London – had discredited parliamentary democracy. Events in Paris, along with activity in our own streets, campuses and factories, had given us hope that in some ill-thought-out way, we could bypass this mirage of democratic government with institutions more direct, alert and innovative in meeting the needs of the people.

As quasi insurrectionary hopes gave way to a radical gradualism and as we moved from the flexibility of student life to work in institutions whose bureaucratic routines persisted through lack of a credible alternative, we honed our vague belief in participatory democracy into detailed ideas for the democratisation of every area of public administration from primary, secondary and higher education through to mental health. Through the Institute For Workers Control, some of us collaborated with an earlier generation of radical and free-spirited socialists like Steve Boddington, Ken Coates and Michael Barratt-Brown and a network of left-wing trade unionists who believed in industrial democracy and knew that the creativity and power to bring it about was to be found among workers and their communities. This network of workers and intellectuals led to numerous plans and proposals for democratising nationalised industries, turning medium size companies into co-ops and combining the bargaining power of government and workers to impose some social responsibility on the footloose multinationals.

The women's liberation movement, especially the socialist feminists like Sheila Rowbotham who were part of its origins, made a notable contribution to the feasibly utopian character of the new left in the seventies.[2] As feminists we refused to postpone womens liberation until after the revolution or until a socialist government was elected to office. For women to have even the autonomy necessary to play an active part in working for social change, the conditions of their lives had to improve in the present: women abused by men needed refuge now; mothers trapped in the home by the responsibilities of children needed shared or public childcare now and of a sort over which they had some control. As women gained confidence and a strong collective sense of their needs they took the initiative to make public services such as health, education and transport responsive to women.

Throughout the first half of the seventies these practical schemes, a renewal of the feasibility of democratic socialism, had real popular resonance. The positive alternatives that sprang from these diverse sources were not just academic pipe dreams but the basis of campaigning demands on local government, education and health authorities across the country; they were a radical presence in debates about the future of television and radio; they influenced bargaining strategies and demands on government in industries such as engineering, building, coal and telecommunications.

What we lacked was political representation. When extra-parliamentary activity was at its height this did not seem to matter. The radical left seemed to have its own momentum, even if this was in fact more the product of converging movements with their own concerns rather than being the sign of a single movement with a coherent direction. As Tory cutbacks and company downsizing began to pose new problems for which direct action was not sufficient, and as the impact of radical social and industrial movements began to reverberate through the Labour Party, the libertarian left began to take a wary interest in party politics. Often, they did so in a new way, keeping their social movement or trade union base and attempting to bend the Labour Party to its concerns.

Two moments of political innovation and conflict were the outcome of this collision of extra-parliamentary radicalism and a Labour Left open to new directions. First, the efforts, associated with Tony Benn, to democratise industry and the party itself; secondly, the attempts by Labour Parties, long out of national office, to carry out radical change through the municipality – most famously in London but also in different ways in Sheffield, Walsall and Manchester.

Innovation was inspired by creative convergencies between radical leftists influenced by 1968 and the 1970s and genuine social democrats like Tony Benn and Stuart Holland, radicalised by their government experience under Harold Wilson. The latter group had entered this government as egalitarian and democratic modernisers (not as Clause 4 socialists) and had come up against the hostility of civil service mandarins and City moguls alike, and often in concert. Such politicians, committed as they were to their radical, modernising manifesto commitments turned, sometimes reluctantly, to the organisations of the people in whose interests the policies were intended to be.

In particular, given their concern for industrial modernisation, Benn and Holland turned to the shop stewards movement to make common cause in calling management to account. Tony Benn had long been a critic of old-style nationalisation, quipping that 'Alf Robens plus the Coal Board doesn't equal socialism' (a reference to the chair of the nationalised coal industry when it began a major programme of pit closure and redundancies). His experiences of the energy and intelligence evident among shop floor workers during the work-in to save the Upper Clyde Shipbuilders in sharp contrast to the conservative vested interests at the heart of government, led him enthusiastically to espouse the cause of industrial democracy. He broke away from traditional corporatist relations between government, management and trade union leaders and worked with shop floor representatives on detailed plans for job creation and industrial democracy. The most vivid example was the plan drawn up by the shop stewards committee in Lucas Aerospace, a plan not only for saving jobs but also for converting from the production of missile components to the production of innovative transport equipment, the latest medical technology and innovative energy saving equipment – as the Lucas stewards put it, 'an alternative corporate plan for socially useful production'.

The Lucas workers' plan was one of many but its coherence, technical credibility and the strength of the organisation behind it made it exemplary. It was exemplary of a new approach – in practice if not in theory – to relations between the state, popular organisations and the markets (including the financial markets, in that the Lucas workers prepared plans for democratising pension funds, which make up a major part of the market for capital). The idea of 'a workers' plan' came out of a shared experience of the limits of nationalisation: 'we can't look at it through the eyes of nationalisation 1945 or the eyes of nationalisation in the past ten years. We need to draw up a completely new concept' said one of the shop stewards in the early first discussion of the idea. The 'new concept' built on the old social democratic goal of 'common ownership of the means of production, distribution and exchange' but in the light of experience it involved rejecting the assumption that this necessarily meant 'nationalisation' that is: government ownership, management and administration. No one denied that nationalisation was as another steward put it, 'far, far better than the old set-up – under private ownership. The miners will tell you that. But we have to build on it. It's up to us to look for new forms. If we are going to sit back and leave it to the politicians to carry on, then, well we deserve everything we get'. This self-confidence born of ten years of shop floor strength together with a pride in their combined skills, was the impetus to their innovation: 'to draw up a plan without management. Let us start here from this Combine Committee; after all over the years it has grown and grown', urged a shop steward from the Lucas Aerospace factory near Liverpool. 'The Combine (shop stewards) Committee has the ability not only in industrial disputes but also to tackle wider problems. Let's get down to working on how we'd draw up a plan, on our terms rather than management's to meet the needs of our community'. Which is what they did, drawing on ideas put forward, discussed, and evaluated at Lucas Aerospace factories from Burnley in Lancashire down to Neasden in West London.[3]

Their proposals had implications for government, which was already the company's major customer, as well as for management. Government or at any rate the public sector, would still under the workers' plan be a major customer, but it would be buying products to improve transport services, NHS facilities and energy conservation, rather than military equipment. Their campaigns for the plan involved nurses and doctors, local councillors and an extensive network of people with an interest both in the needs they were responding to and the innovative methods they used. Their plan was resisted by management, some trade union leaders and most of the government, not because of the substantive engineering content – many of its product proposals have since been taken up by other companies – but because of its challenge to established relations of power.

I describe the Lucas workers' initiative in detail because it illustrates in practice distinctive principles which the libertarian left sought to develop and promote, and it illustrates the existence of the spirit of this left in Labour's heartlands. On the one hand it defended, built on and tried to extend the basic principles, and practical achievements of social democratic government (achievements that were already under steady erosion): public provision of welfare, education, health infrastructure, public intervention including conditional subsidies and actual ownership of key parts of the economy, employment protection and a degree of redistribution of wealth. Hence it presumed a legislative framework for success and engagement with the parliamentary process to achieve it. It was not simply a latter day syndicalism. On the other hand, the shop stewards drew on their own practical and technical knowledge – on which after all the company depended – the democratic organisation they had built up over the years and their wider social involvement, from the local council and the health service through CND to projects supporting the Third World, to show a way of democratising this public intervention, making it more effective in meeting social needs.

Thus several years before Margaret Thatcher launched her free market campaign against public services and nationalised industries, exploiting and exaggerating all their inefficiencies and paternalism, there were elements of an alternative embedded in the practice of those who had witnessed in their daily lives both the benefits and the failing of the social democratic state. The Lucas case is just one of the more coherent, well worked out examples of an alternative direction – not yet a model – based on democratising rather than privatising public resources.

The Labour government was impervious to the potential of these shop floor experiments to refresh with a massive dose of democracy the ideal of public industries and provision. But at a local level, a minority of Labour councillors were more responsive. Many of them had indeed been involved in similar experiments over housing, urban planning and community provision. From 1982–86 the Greater London Council managed to confront Mrs Thatcher's mix of freedom rhetoric and centralising reality with a genuinely liberating alternative. With the resources of a small nation state, a large workforce and a wide range of responsibilities, the GLC was able actually to implement ideas campaigned for by the libertarian left in the seventies. The principle drawn from these ideas and partially theorised in an important but undervalued book *In and Against the State*[4] was to defend and extend public resources but democratise their means of management and administration. Many methods of democratising public provision were tried at the GLC. Especially important was the delegation of policy implementation to civic organisations working in close liaison with the Council staff.

A good example would be the planning and development of inner city areas like Coin Street in Waterloo, the hinterland of King's Cross and many parts of London's Docklands: in the 1970s and early 1980s there were forceful and imaginative community campaigns in these areas pressing the needs of local people against the vulture-like interests of property developers. The London Labour Party's GLC manifesto committed the new administration to inner city development to meet the needs of the local communities. It implemented this commitment in a new way. The GLC used its statutory planning powers to ward off the property developers but then, instead of its highly prestigious, expert Planning Department taking over the planning of these areas, the Planning Committee gave grants to coalitions of local community organisations to draw up their own plans, using GLC staff as a resource and source of advice. The plans were then the basis, after negotiation and discussion with interested parties and the GLC's Planning Committee, for the areas' development. The same principles were put into practice in relation to child care, police monitoring, many aspects of economic policy, and policy towards ethnic minorities and women. The logic was not always thought through but it went like this: these are new areas of policy on which local government professionals have very little knowledge. Those with the knowledge and the sense of direction are the democratic community or workplace organisations of the people directly affected. The GLC should support these organisations, including financially, and work with them to elaborate and implement the policy commitments on which the Council was elected. It was an approach which was pragmatic and radical at the same time and productive of results which won the GLC widespread popular support, way beyond traditional Labour constituencies. No wonder the Conservative government felt more worried by what was happening across the river than across the floor of the House of Commons. 'This is modern socialism', said Norman Tebbit at the time, 'and we will kill it'.[5]

And they nearly did. 'They' being not just the Thatcherite Conservatives but also New Labour's children of Thatcher. What they nearly killed was not 'modern socialism' as a complete model, no such thing was, or indeed could have been, fully developed. What they almost put an end to was a messy process by which the egalitarian foundations of the post-war settlement were being built on by a generation with the self confidence and expectations to think that the people could run things themselves in a democratic and co-operative manner with the state as the back up and the publically accountable source of resources. Their liberation of public provision from the mechanical constraints of a social engineering sort of socialism was hijacked mid-journey. It was taken over by people who spoke the language of freedom but in reality provided only the false freedom of money.

Without its own political voice the ideas of the libertarian left were drowned in the cacophony of inner Labour Party conflict. The popularity that built up around the GLC (from an initial low point during which its radicalism was the object of mockery and abuse) provided a brief and incomplete illustration of the potential of the general approach of the libertarian left to provide an answer to the growing appeal of the free market right. Indeed in countries where some variant of a libertarian left had its own voice, Denmark, Germany, Sweden and Norway, for example, the radical right never gained an ideological hold. (Of course there are many other reasons for this including the distinctive strength of Christian Democracy on the right of the political spectrum in these countries and the fact that social democratic principles were entrenched in their written constitutions but the fact that a left alternative to social democracy has had real political legitimacy is undoubtedly an important factor.) In Britain this potential was stymied by peculiarities of both the electoral system and Labour's history as the singular political expression of a unified trade union movement. In the absence of an electoral competitor to its left, the Labour Party as first and foremost an electoral machine, looks over its right shoulder and takes the left for granted. It always gravitates to the centre. And never more so than after four consecutive election defeats.

The result has been a situation in which the left has been locked into a permanently subordinate position within the Labour Party without any other political outlet. In this situation there was little opportunity for new ideas from the left – usually generated or at least influenced by social forces outside the party – to be nourished and promoted in a sustained way. When such ideas did surface in the party, as in the early and mid 1970s as we have just seen, influenced by the radical movements of the time, they become mangled by the inner party power struggle. A vicious spiral of caricature ('loony left', etc), blame (for causing Labour to lose elections), leading to beleaguerment and causing defensive and sectarian tendencies to gain the upperhand. This was one way in which the radical libertarian left lost its momentum in the latter half of the 1980s after the abolition of the GLC and the defeat of the miners' strike.

The defeat of the miners was symbolic of a wider problem for the libertarian left: its ideas depended in good part on the strength and confidence of democratic social movements in the workplace and the community. In the 1970s and early 1980s, the scope and creativity of trade union and other social movements were inter-related. Consider the issue of public housing: self-confident and socialist shop stewards committees in the Direct Labour Organisations of local councils were increasingly open to making common cause with tenants' committees on council house estates in an effort to improve the quality and democratic control over council housing; in some cities, Birmingham, for instance, building workers took up environmental issues, arguing for 'Green Bans' – vetoing by direct action building on certain environmentally precious parts of the town. Such vistas of democratisation opened up partly because of a weakening of the old state and corporate hold on power and partly because of the pressure of a new generation of activists in the unions and the community influenced by the confident, democratic spirit of 68.

New possibilities also depended on there being within mainstream politics a strong commitment to social regulation and intervention. For example, ideas about democratising and materially improving public housing gained momentum, albeit limited, because the ideas of tenants, DLO shop stewards and sympathetic researchers were taken up positively by radical or open-minded Labour councillors. Usually, though, these were in a minority and in the end could achieve very little. A rare example of a formalised relationship between the distinctive power and knowledge of workplace organisations and the legal framework laid down by representative government is provided by the health and safety legislation that was part of the 1974 Labour government's Social Contract. Instead of presuming that state inspectors could police this relatively tough legislation on their own, the legislation delegated powers to Health and Safety Committees based on the workplace shop stewards committees. This way the workers with all their practical knowledge of the risks of the workplace would be able to trigger off the implementation of the legislation. It illustrates principles of delegation and de-centralisation of powers to democratic civic organisations that could be adapted to implement tough and effective regulation on for example, the environment, low pay, sex and race discrimination. In other words strong social intervention in the market does not necessarily mean a greater concentration of power in the state.

The application of this principle in the 1974 Health and Safety legislation was not the result of a thought-through commitment to such a new approach to social regulation. Rather, it was the outcome of the strength of the shop stewards movement and some innovative thinking in the trade union movement. Such creative thinking has tended to wane as shop floor organisations have lost their strength and the self-confidence that it generates. One of the reasons why democratic popular movements are so important for libertarian socialism is the confidence that people gain through the power of their collective resistance and the creativity that can be released as a consequence. The radical republican Tom Paine put this point dramatically in the *Rights of Man* written in the late 18th Century:

> It appears to general observation, that revolutions create genius and talents; but those events do no more than bring them forward. There is existing in man, a mass of sense lying in a dormant state, and which unless something excites it to action, will descend with him in that condition to the grave. As it is to the advantage of society that the whole of its facilities should be employed, the construction of government ought to be such as to bring forward, by quiet and regular operation, all that extent of capacity which never fails to appear in revolution.

Tom Paine was arguing against monarchy for representative democracy, which he thought would enable that 'extent of capacity' to be brought forward by 'quiet and regular operation'. But now his appeal points to a damning limit of representative government: while it might, depending on the pluralism and accountability of its structures, ensure the representation of the general opinions of the people, it does not bring forward that full extent of human capacity from which society would benefit. Another way of expressing this is that while representative, parliamentary, democracy presumes formal political equality – universal suffrage, equality before the law, for instance – it can co-exist not only with economic inequality but also cultural subordination. The cultural subordination implied by, for instance, the paternalism of professional social reformers, who presume a cultural superiority to those on whose behalf they are devising reforms; or the benign employer who presumes to know what is in the best interest of their employees. Paine was arguing for cultural equality alongside political equality. Such an intertwining of the two is a part of the radical tradition that has been marginalised in the first 60 or so years of the 20th century. Its revival, connecting it firmly with the socialist goal of economic democracy, is one of the consequences of 1968 – which has indeed been followed by a revival of interest in the late 18th or early 19th century radicals: Paine, Shelley, Wolstencraft, for instance, for whom political égalité and cultural emancipation were inseparable.[7]

The way that this radically democratic tradition was swept aside during the 19th and 20th century by left traditions which turned economic and political equality into goals independent of the cultural capacities of the people, is a pressing study in itself. There is one aspect of the explanation which I would suggest now because it is relevant to understanding the significance of 1968 in reviving the importance of cultural equality for a feasible vision of democratic socialism. It is this: that the marginality of cultural equality in the dominant, and often ruling socialist traditions of the 20th century, is associated with approaches to science, method and knowledge that came to guide the organisations of state and economy during and following the industrial revolution. The struggle associated with the Enlightenment to rid society of the fog of superstition and religious dogma also laid the basis for another kind of domination, in the name of progress: the rule of the all-knowing expert, whether that be the professional politician, civil servant, army general, corporate manage or party general secretary.

A vital element in the new forms of domination which came with the development of science, was the particular philosophy of science that became the orthodoxy of the day, first in the theorisation of natural science and then in the methodology of social science and its application to economic management, technological development, and state administration. It was based on the model of natural sciences which aspired to formulate general laws describing regular conjunctions of events or phenomena. This provided the premises from which science, social as well as natural, was thought to be able to make certain predictions and gain ever more perfect knowledge as discovery of generalisations progressed. Initially this positivistic model had a progressive impact, undermining as it did the influence of religious faith and superstition. However, by the mid-twentieth century it had come to underpin an unduly optimistic faith in scientific production, manipulation and control, and in the capacity of science to move forward, morally, socially and intellectually. When applied to the study and reform of society, it presumed that general (in positivist terms, 'scientific') laws were the only valid form of knowledge. This created the cultural conditions for a separation of the goal of purposeful social change from democratic self-government (in Paine's terms, forms of government that 'bring forward, by quie and regular operation, all that extent of capacity which never fails to appear in revolution'). The people could protest, rebel, cry in pain, but the diagnoses and the solutions were the task of the experts – the professionals schooled in science. As Beatrice Webb, the exemplary social reformer in this school of benevolent experts put it, 'the average sensual man can describe his problem but is unable to prescribe a solution'.[8] Such a presumption stemmed not from prejudice but from a view of knowledge which relegated the knowledge that stems from experience simply to the level of raw material for scientific laws; a source of evidence, in other words, for the constant conjunctures on which scientific laws, according to positivism, are built. Such a minimal, passive role for the social knowledge of the mass of people, tended towards a social engineering model for processes of social reform. A model, in other words, which presumes that the most effective operators of social change, whether a social democratic state or a Leninist party, are acting on society from the outside, without any self-consciousness of the social relations connecting them and the subject of their study. To varying degrees, society was understood as the material, the raw steel. State institutions, in the hands of social reformers, or new state institutions, operated by the revolutionary party, were the engineers working the political machinery to transform the material. They were guided by what they presumed to be a scientific understanding of the material, based on past observance of the recurring patterns of its behaviour, gained through statistical surveys.

A postivistic method also reached into the organisation of labour, first in manufacturing, though latter applied to state administration. F.W. Taylor developed his 'principles of scientific management' in the 1890s and 1900s but they were elaborated in theory and practice for the following half century or, until the workers revolts of the late 1960s made them unworkable. Fundamental to his principles is the assumption that the practical knowledge uitilised by workers in the course of their labour is so simple that there is no obstacle to its codification and centralisation: 'Every single act of the workman can be reduced to a science', he asserts in *The Principles of Scientific Management*.[9] Under his system, 'the workman is told minutely just what he is to do and how he is to do it; any improvement which he makes upon the order given is fatal to success'. His ideas inspired Henry Ford to give mechanised reality in the assembly line to the precise division of labour and machine-like workmanship that his science inspired. In Britain, Fabian notions of planning and Herbert Morrison's model of the public corporation both drew heavily on Taylor in their measures of efficiency and their centralising methods of administration. Moreover in the development of social services, the idea of the standard product was put to social democratic purposes in building the welfare state.

East and West, the late 1960s witnessed a crisis in the practice of social engineering and scientific management just at the same time as philosophy of science and social science was in a state of momentous flux.[10] The confidence that scientific knowledge would show the way reached its political apotheosis in the West in the early to mid 1960s, with the technocratic confidence surrounding both the Wilson government and the Kennedy regime in the United States. In the East a related faith, focused on the command economy, reached its zenith in the mobilisation of Soviet resources to defeat the Nazis in 1944 and complete the country's industrialisation. Significantly, history dealt blows to the confidence of the ruling élites on both sides of the Iron Curtain in quick succession. In the East, the sources were Krushchev's revelations of the crimes of Stalin, followed by the repressed uprisings of Hungary, Poland and then, 12 years later, Czechoslavakia; in the West it was Vietnam, and the defeat by a peasant army and campus revolts of the technologically mightiest army in the world which showed that the methods of the industrial, military and political élites were not only morally flawed but practically fallible.

The movements originating in the late sixties of students, workers, tenants and women were also pressing alternatives to the more everyday legacies of social engineering: the univeristy campuses in bleak parklands, designed with little practical knowledge of students' needs and desires; medical training and hospital organisation developed without knowledge of the particular needs and concerns of women; transport systems worked out as if children and old people did not exist; council housing that gave tenants no power over the colour of their door let alone the efficiency of their repairs; work routines that timed workers' absence in the toilet, and so on.

The movements resisting these and similar indignities and seeking to initiate, not just demand, alternatives echo Tom Paine. They (and the sustained struggles of later years such as the examples mentioned earlier like the Lucas Workers Combine Committee or others like 1984/85 miners' strike) were like a low intensity revolution in the sense that time and time again new groups of people would become involved in struggles through which they found talents and strengths that were surprising even to themselves. This was most dramatic in the case of women – the thousands who became active in the women's movement whether middle-class housewives or night cleaners; the Asian women who created Southall Black Sisters; the women of the mining communities who formed Women Against Pit Closure, these are just better-known examples. In these struggles women both transformed their own lives, became speakers, organisers, writers, poets and in the process created new social forms, some of which have lasted and become focal points of change and support.

The problem, at the nub of Tom Paine's statement, is how the conditions producing this creativity and stretched capacity can be sustained beyond the inevitably limited moments of revolution, resistance or social upheaval. How can the forms of co-operation, mutual encouragement and effective participation produced by such events, enhancing people's self-confidence and bringing out their capacities, become central to everyday economic and political decision making? How could popular participation become endemic to different social organisations rather than exceptional? What are the necessary economic, educational and institutional structures for such regular participation to be possible, realistic and effective? What forms of democratic discipline and social cohesion are necessary for participative organisations to be sustainable, beyond moments of obvious enthusiasm and unproblematic common purpose? Answers to questions such as these would begin to unite once again ideals of political and economic equality with cultural equality.

The libertarian left, in a variety of practical projects, some examples of which I discussed earlier in the chapter, aspired to unite these ideas and in doing so to bring together economic and social reform with democratic self-government, throughout society. It has begun in practice, if not yet in theory, to answer these questions. In a sense its ability to do so was cut short by Thatcherism and the global influence of free market capitalism. This chapter therefore has to have an open-ended conclusion. All I want to do to conclude is to argue that the practical challenge of the libertarian left to the social engineering tradition of social democracy and the command economy, provides at least some tools for an egalitarian and democratic alternative to neo-liberalism. This is important because the hegemony of neo-liberal theory lives on, in Britain and the USA, even though its practice is ripping itself apart.

I have suggested at length in my book *Arguments for a New Left, Answering the Free Market Right*, how the left that was shaped by the social movements that exploded in 1968 holds out the basis for a new left that can answer the appeal of neo-liberalism in the way that the traditional left cannot.[11]

I will summarise these arguments here because doing so demonstrates the innovative character of the left that has been shaped by the social movements of the last 30 years – what I have called 'the libertarian left'. The way in which this left has tools to answer the free market right also helps to explain its resilience in the face of two decades of neo-liberal government.

At the foundations of neo-liberalism's free-market ideology is a theory of knowledge, based on the work of Frederick Hayek which the traditional left has not adequately answered. It is a theory of the limits of social scientific knowledge and the importance of practical knowledge to which I would argue the libertarian left has a distinctive and convincing answer.

The object of Hayek's attack was the social engineering state and the positivistic orthodoxy which I have just analysed (though not in Hayekian terms). The students' and workers' movements of the late 1960s and even more so in consequent movements – most notably the women's, green and peace movements and more recent direct action movements – implicitly challenged this methodology from several angles. They questioned the inevitably progressive character of science and its application, without turning their back on science itself. Also, in their practice and to some extent in their theory, they both valued practical/tacit knowledge and demonstrated the social character of all forms of knowledge, everyday and theoretical. It is this that provides the left influenced by these movements with the tools to answer the neo-liberal justification of its free-market policies.

Underlying the neo-liberal worship of the market is the critique made by Frederick Hayek of both classical economic theory and both social democratic and USSR style socialism (the only kinds of socialism he could imagine). He argued that much essential economic knowledge is not of the law-like, quantifiable or at least codifiable kind that can be easily centralised; millions of economic decisions depend on practical knowledge. This knowledge is frequently tacit, 'things we know but cannot tell',[12] in the words of the original theorist of such knowledge, Michael Polanyi; it is often ephemeral and developmental. It cannot be captured or anticipated by a central brain, however computerised such a centre might be. The connection between social purpose and intention and outcome is broken; we cannot design the social order and it is a 'fatal deceit' to think we can. The only legitimate social order is one, i.e. the unregulated market, arrived at without human design, the haphazard outcome of millions of individual decisions miraculously co-ordinated through the workings of the price mechanism. Not only is this order achieved without conscious intervention but so delicate is its balance, goes the neo-liberal logic, that it would be destroyed by such intervention – however well intentioned its purpose.[13]

In response to these arguments the libertarian left – judging by its practice – would agree about the importance of practical knowledge, though in rather different terms, but strongly reject the idea that the free market is the mechanism that can best make use of the wealth of such practical knowledge. There is an illegitimate leap in Hayek's logic – a leap which provides the libertarian left with the opportunity to trip up the neo-liberals. The leap involves assuming that practical knowledge, as if by definition, is individual. Hayek maintains that, 'all the possible differences in men's moral attitudes amount to little, so far as their significance for social organisation is concerned, compared with the fact that all man's mind can effectively comprehend are the facts of the narrow circle of which he is the centre'.[14] What is significant about this statement is not its recognition of limits on human reason but the dogmatically individual nature of these limits, closing off not only the idea of total rationality and complete knowledge (rightly) but also (wrongly) the possibility of social action to share information and extend the knowledge of individuals beyond their immediate circle.

Hayek's theory of knowledge, the foundation stone of the neo-liberal belief in the unfettered market, completely excludes the possibility that practical knowledge might be shared or socialised. The social organisation of knowledge can take many forms; it does not have to be centralised or even fully codified. Once it is acknowledged that practical knowledge could be social, though in different ways from other, for example, statistical, forms of knowledge, then the possibility exists that the social organisations through which such sharing takes place could influence the character of the market, framing, regulating, constraining it and intervening in it, including in partnership with an elected political authority.

It is in the development of this socialisation of practical knowledge that the vital innovation of recent social movements lies. The theme common to the social movements which shaped this left was a rebellion against authority, both public and private; against the paternalism of those who presumed to know what is good for people: professors of students; men with power of women without it; managers of workers; the state of the people. In their ways of organising and thinking they held out the value of practical and tacit knowledge, testing its insights with those of theoretical knowledge. Their practice is backed up by recent developments in the philosophy of science which have shown the importance of practical knowledge, a central form of knowledge which has tended, in the positivist orthodoxy of most of this century, to be part of 'the empirical' and subsumed under general laws.[15]

A recognition of the distinct importance of practical knowledge and its interaction with theoretical understanding, has immense political implications. It provides a vital foundation stone for thinking through feasible forms of participatory democracy. I explore some of these implications in *Arguments for a New Left*, with the *caveat* that much work still needs to be done: the research agenda of the libertarian left is ambitious though there is much rich practice on which to draw. Whether learning lessons from work with the liberation movements of Asia and Africa in 1968 or from linking with the movements of peasants and casualised workers across the world to resist the Multilateral Agreement on Investment in 1998, the libertarian left has a special contribution to make towards democratic governance in the face of the deregulated global economy. Its alertness to the limits of parliamentary democracy has been sharpened by witnessing both the flaws of even the most meritocratic, representative ruling élites and by directly experiencing the capacities of the people for democratic self-government with all the messy uncertainty which that entails.

NOTES

1. Answer to a warm-up question on 'Any Questions', October 1997.
2. See Rowbotham, Sheila. *The Past is Before Us: Feminism in Action Since the 1960's* (1989), Penguin.
3. See Hilary Wainwright and David Elliott *The Lucas Plan; a new Trade Unionism in the Making* (1982), Alison & Busby.
4. *In and Against the State* The London Edinburgh Weekend Return Group. A working group of the Conference of Socialist Economists (1980), Pluto.
5. Documents from the GLC's Economic Policy Group, including 'The London Industrial Strategy' are available from the Centre for Local Economic Strategies, Whitworth Street, Manchester. See also *A Taste of Power, the Politics of Local Economics* eds Maureen Macintosh and Hilary Wainwright (1987), Verso.
6. 'The Rights of Man', in *The Thomas Paine Reader* (1987), Penguin, p. 277.
7. See E.P. Thompson *The Romantics, England in Revolutionary Age* (1997), Merlin, for a rare and brilliant analysis of these and other themes through the work of Wordsworth, Coleridge and Thelwell.
8. For a discussion of this tradition in the context of British socialism see Fred Whitmore 'British Socialism and Democracy in Retrospect' in *Socialism and Democracy* eds Sean Sayers and David McLellan (1991), Macmillan.

9. *Principles of Scientific Management* (1911), New York, p. 34.
10. Roy Bhaskar's entry on 'Knowledge, Theory of' in 'The Blackwell Dictionary of Twentieth-Century Thought' (1993), Blackwell (eds) William Outhwaite and Tom Bottomore provides a useful summary. Especially important was Thomas Kuhn's *The Structure of Scientific Revolutions* (2nd edn) (1970), University of Chicago Press.
11. *Arguments for a New Left; Answering the Free Market Right* (1994), Blackwell.
12. F. Hayek. 'The Use of Knowledge in Society' in *Individualism and Economic Order* (1949), Routledge.
13. The potential agents of such intervention are understood to be either particularistic interests such as trades unions or an over-bearing, social engineering state; over-bearing private corporations using unequal market power to capture further market power somehow seem to escape scrutiny.
14. F. Hayek. *Individualism and Economic Order* (1949), Routledge, p. 14.
15. See William Outhwaite, *New Philosophies of Social Science* (1987), Routledge, Roy Bhaskar, *A Realist Theory of Science* (1978), Harvester.

9 The Long Sixties in the Short Twentieth Century

Michael Williams

Waiting for the end, boys, waiting for the end.
What is there to be or do?
What's become of me or you?
Are we kind or are we true?
Sitting two and two, boys, waiting for the end.

'Waiting for the end, boys, waiting for the end': such is the refrain of
William Empson's hilarious parody 'Just a Smack at Auden' published in
1937 (Skelton, 1964: 64). His direct target was Auden's 'A Communist to
Others' (published in 1933) but that refrain highlighted the sense of
impending apocalypse that dominated the tone of so much of the literature
of the 1930s and raised Empson's own poem above the transient value of
mere parody.

The end envisaged in the 1930s was, of course, the impending climactic
struggle between reaction and democracy, fascism and communism,
modernity and tradition that all could predict and which threatened the
survival of civilisation. The same kind of atmosphere surrounded at least
the first couple of decades of Cold War and can be sensed in such works as
George Orwell's *Nineteen Eighty-Four* (1949) and his friend Arthur
Koestler's *The Age of Longing* (1951) which anticipated a Soviet takeover
of Western Europe. Only in the early 1960s, with Stanley Kubrick's
Dr Strangelove – or how I learned to stop worrying and love the bomb,
did we begin to shrug off our fears. By 1965, when Barry Maguire topped
the US charts with 'Eve of Destruction', that sense of impending apocalypse was fit material for a hit single.

Now that long-impending end seems to have arrived – not exactly with
a whimper but certainly not with the bang which so many predicted and
feared. The last decade has been dominated by a sense of the end: we are
no longer waiting for the end; the end has arrived. This sense of an ending
is implicit in the notion of the post-modern which has been present at least
since the 1960s but has gathered increasing currency in recent years. The
very calendar as the end of the second millennium approaches seems to
proclaim it. And it has dominated political debate since the publication of

Francis Fukuyama's seminal article 'The End of History?' published in the American periodical *The National Interest* in 1989 (Fukuyama, 1989), later expanded to book length in *The End of History and the Last Man* (Fukuyama, 1992). Fukuyama was writing as a former US State Department policy analyst turned political philosopher but the very titles of his article and book constituted a challenge to historians to offer their own interpretations of the century – and indeed of the modern age.

I have chosen to focus on the interpretations offered in recent surveys of the century by two British historians – Eric Hobsbawm's *Age of Extremes: the Short Twentieth Century 1914–1991* (Hobsbawm, 1994a) and Robert Skidelsky's *The World After Communism: a Polemic For Our Times* (Skidelsky, 1995). Both are historians of undoubted distinction (Hobsbawm was made a Companion of Honour in the 1998 New Year Honours for services to history) and both also have played an important political role. My title borrows Alan Hooper's notion of the Long Sixties – from 1956 to 1976 – developed elsewhere in this volume – and, of course, the subtitle of Hobsbawm's work. The notion of the Short Twentieth Century has become associated with him since the publication of *Age of Extremes* but, as he acknowledges in an essay published in *Marxism Today* in 1990, it is not his own (Hobsbawm, 1990: 123). He borrowed it from his friend, Ivan Berend, former President of the Hungarian Academy of Sciences and now Professor at the University of California, Los Angeles (personal communication).

The first part of this chapter compares and contrasts the background and intellectual development of Hobsbawm and Skidelsky. For Hobsbawm I have been able to draw on several published interviews as well as frequent autobiographical interpellations and reflections in essays and books written since the 1960s. Skidelsky's presence in his work has been more muted than Hobsbawm's but I was fortunate to have the opportunity to talk to him at some length about his intellectual development as well as the lasting significance of the sixties. The second section turns from the men to their work and looks at their interpretations of the twentieth century and the significance of the sixties. I then argue that political and social changes linking the 1960s and the 1990s can best be understood as moments in a process of democratisation – in what de Tocqueville described in the 1830s as the 'great democratic revolution' that characterised the modern age (Tocqueville, 1835: 9). I conclude with some personal reflections.

Hobsbawm and Skidelsky have both been kind enough to comment on this chapter in draft. I am very grateful for their help. The views are, of course, my own – as are any remaining errors, misunderstandings, or infelicities in tone or expression.

The lives and work of Hobsbawm and Skidelsky are full of fascinating contrasts and parallels. Both are survivors of cultures that were destroyed by the two great cataclysms of this century – of 'the Jewish middle-class culture of central Europe' (Hobsbawm, 1971: 250) destroyed by Nazism, and of the Imperial Russian bourgeoisie destroyed by Bolshevism.

Hobsbawm, as he tells in the opening pages of *The Age of Empire* (Hobsbawm, 1987a: 1–2), was born in 1917 in Alexandria of Jewish parents, his father a British citizen (of Russian/Polish descent) and his mother an Austrian. His parents left for Vienna shortly after the war ended and the young Hobsbawm joined his uncle (also a British citizen) in Berlin after his parents' death (personal communication). It was here in 1931 that he first encountered the Communist movement (Walker, 1994). More than once he has recalled the moment when, as a schoolboy, he saw the newspaper headline announcing Hitler's appointment as Chancellor (Hobsbawm, 1993: 230; 1994a: 4). Not long afterwards Hobsbawm travelled with his uncle to Britain where he studied history with distinction at Cambridge and joined the Communist Party. His fellow-student Noel Annan recalled him as one of two 'formidable marxists': 'astonishingly mature, armed cap-a-pie [sic] with the Party's interpretation of current politics, as erudite as he was fluent, and equipped to have a view on whatever obscure topic one of his contemporaries might have chosen to write a paper' (the other, an Indian, was killed in an air crash while serving as a minister under Indira Gandhi) (Annan, 1991: 254–5). In 1939 he was elected to that most elitist of secret societies – the Cambridge Apostles (personal communication).

For Hobsbawm, the Popular Front of the 1930s was the defining moment in his political evolution. It is the constant touchstone of his political journalism of the 1980s (collected in Hobsbawm, 1989) in which he called, again and again, for 'some way of uniting the majority of the British people which is opposed to Thatcherism' (Hobsbawm, 1983: 67). He gloried in criticisms that he was a 'simple, unvarnished Popular Frontist' (Callinicos, 1985: 155; Hobsbawm, 1984: 81–2). The Spanish Civil War which pitted the Popular Front against fascism was for him 'the only political cause which, even in retrospect, appears as pure and compelling as it did in 1936' (Hobsbawm, 1994a: 160). His lifelong commitment to communism, as he admitted in an interview in 1994, 'wasn't rational. The commitment was … I would almost say religious' (Tyler, 1994). I am reminded of the commitment to communism of Georg Lukács, the greatest representative of the central European Jewish Marxist tradition to which Hobsbawm belongs. At the end of his life Lukács saw his political development (in terms borrowed from Kierkegaard) as one of transition from an aesthetic, through an ethical to an ultimately religious position (Lukács, 1983: 49, 53–4, 151–9). I don't suppose Hobsbawm (who met Lukács while writing *The Age of Revolution*) would be displeased by the comparison (Kadarkay, 1991: 455–6). The whole of his scholarly work – from the early studies in British labour history to the tetralogy concluded by *Age of Extremes* – bears the mark of his political commitment. As he put it himself in an interview in 1978, all are studies in 'the development of capitalism' and 'the nature of popular movements' in response to capitalist development (Abelove *et al.*, 1983: 37).

Skidelsky was born politically and geographically almost at the opposite extreme from Hobsbawm: in 1939 in Manchuria of White Russian exiles. His father was Jewish but took no interest in his Jewish background until late in life when he became interested in Israel. The family had not suffered from the anti-semitism so prevalent in Tsarist Russia; indeed they 'did extremely well and became very wealthy'. Family legend had it that Skidelsky's great-grandfather travelled eastwards across Siberia and was involved in building the Trans-Siberian railway which terminated in Vladivostok where Skidelsky's father was born in 1907. His mother's family supported Kolchak during the Civil War and escaped afterwards to Manchuria whence his father too had fled. The young Skidelsky was interned for some months by the Japanese before coming to England with his parents in an exchange of prisoners in 1942. The rest of the family disappeared into the Gulag when the Red Army marched into Manchuria in the last days of the Second World War. So, as Skidelsky put it – and in striking contrast to Hobsbawm – 'in so far my family were victims of twentieth-century cataclysm we were victims of what took place in Russia and not what took place in Germany'; they were 'victims of Bolshevism' rather than of Nazism. Intellectually Skidelsky understood the horror of Nazi anti-semitism and the whole history of anti-semitism that led to it, but neither formed part of his own cultural experience – which might help to explain the 'detachment and sympathy' which he brought to his biography of Oswald Mosley (Skidelsky, 1975a: 12).

If Hobsbawm may be regarded (like Isaac Deutscher, George Lichtheim, Karl Polanyi and Piero Sraffa – mutual friend of Gramsci and Keynes (Skidelsky, 1992b: 289)) as part of a relatively small 'Red' emigration of the 1930s, then Skidelsky may be regarded as a belated and youthful member of the much more numerous 'White' emigration which, according to Perry Anderson's classic account (Anderson, 1968: 60–5), dominated English intellectual life in the post-war period. Like older members of this 'White' emigration (such as Isaiah Berlin, Karl Popper and Lewis Namier), Skidelsky has sought to reinforce a characteristically

English liberalism and empiricism – in his case, that of Keynes, searching for a middle way – a 'liberal socialism' in his words (cited Moggridge, 1976: 44) – between the ideological extremes of Lenin and Hayek. Skidelsky conceded that his personal background must have had an influence in shaping his views – 'you identify perhaps with eventually a more right-wing view of things' – but he insisted that he had always tried to 'hold some middle ground'. Just as Hobsbawm's work has been marked by an engagement with the Marxist critique of capitalism, so has Skidelsky been preoccupied with Keynes' attempt to save capitalism from itself, from his account of the 1929–31 Labour Government (Skidelsky, 1970), through his biography of that maverick Keynesian Mosley, to the life of the great man himself on which he is still engaged (Skidelsky, 1992a, b).

Hobsbawm and Skidelsky have both played an increasing role as political intellectuals in recent years. Hobsbawm first made a political impact on the wider Left beyond the Communist Party through his famous (and prophetic) Marx Memorial Lecture of March 1978 on 'The Forward March of Labour Halted?' and then through a series of articles in *Marxism Today* during the 1980s (Hobsbawm, 1989). At the time, Hobsbawm was claimed to have had a great influence upon Neil Kinnock's reshaping of the Labour Party. Robert Harris described him as 'Kinnock's favourite Marxist' (Harris, 1984: 236). Reading these articles today, the extent to which they can be seen to prefigure the strategy and themes of Tony Blair's New Labour is much more striking. After Labour's third successive defeat in 1987 Hobsbawm stressed the need for the party to have 'a positive project for the future – a mission for the nation' (Hobsbawm, 1988: 237). What that project might involve was set out more fully in an earlier article: 'Labour will return to office only a party that offers ... a New Deal: modernisation – and in a humane and responsible manner'. Labour would have to accept that not everything done since 1979 should be rejected – 'the British economy ... *needed a kick in the pants*' (original italics). A modernising Labour government would have to be just as ruthless in its own way as Thatcher. The 'most vital' part of its project would be ensure a better educated workforce (Hobsbawm, 1987b: 209–12).

The resemblance to the Blair project is obvious. Blair's attempts to appeal to 'the nation', to build links with the Liberal Democrats and even Europhile Conservatives, echo Hobsbawm's call for a popular front against Thatcherism. Some of Blair's closest advisers, like Geoff Mulgan, David Miliband and Peter Mandelson, as well as intellectual outriders such as Anthony Barnett, John Lloyd and Charles Leadbeater, and the sympathetic academics organised through the Internet as Nexus, have emerged from a Marxist background, often from within the Communist Party. In a recent interview, Martin Jacques, erstwhile editor of the journal, recalled how Stuart Hall described Blair in 1994 as 'the *Marxism Today* candidate' (Jacques and Hall, 1997). Alex Callinicos was not far short of the mark in characterising Hobsbawm and his fellow contributors to *Marxism Today* as furthering the rightwards evolution of a generation of socialist activists (Callinicos, 1985: 165). But, then, others might reply: what did the Socialist Workers' Party do to end Conservative rule?

Skidelsky has also taken an increasingly prominent role in politics since the early 1980s – though from a very different starting point. If Hobsbawm's politics are rooted in the anti-fascist struggles of the 1930s, Skidelsky's are rooted in the internal Labour Party conflict between the Gaitskellites and the Left of the 1960s. Skidelsky told me that he had little interest in politics when he arrived at Oxford in 1958 but joined the Labour Club and the Gaitskellite Campaign for Social Democracy in his final year in 1960–61. He was 'very excited' to hear Gaitskell – 'a marvellous man' – address the Labour Club. As a research student at Nuffield his thesis (published as *Politicians and the Slump*) was supervised by Anthony Crosland's friend (and Gaitskell's future biographer) Philip Williams. The atmosphere at Nuffield was, he recalled, 'very social democratic; they hoped to be the brains behind the new Labour Government – in which ambition they didn't entirely succeed'. During this time he was close to William Rodgers (Labour Cabinet Minister in the late 1970s and one of the original 'gang of four') and David Marquand (Labour MP from 1966 until 1977 when he followed Roy Jenkins to the European Commission) (Marquand, 1997: 12–20).

By the late 1960s, after trying half-heartedly and unsuccessfully to secure a Parliamentary seat, disillusionment had set in. Richard Cockett describes how in 1968 Skidelsky was involved with Arthur Seldon and Ralph Harris of the Institute of Economic Affairs in attempting to rally support for the dissident Labour MP Desmond Donnelly who, expelled from the Labour Party, fought and lost his seat as a Democrat in 1970 (Cockett, 1995: 179–80). An article in *Encounter* in 1969 lamented a 'general disillusionment with politics' and called for a government of the strong centre capable of rising above party disputes in the service of a wider national interest (Skidelsky, 1969: 25, 34). Skidelsky drifted out of the Labour Party in the 1970s as it approached a 'looming crisis of social democracy'. By 1975 – perhaps under the influence of Mosley whose biography he completed in that year – he was arguing that 'the Keynesian state will be, is already being, replaced by the Corporate State' (Skidelsky, 1975a). A couple of years later he was still anticipating a 'post-Keynesian' rather than a 'pre-Keynesian' resolution to the current economic crisis (Skidelsky, 1977: 40). The turn of the decade found Skidelsky 'looking for a middle way of toughness and tenderness' which the Labour Party under Michael Foot could not provide. Old friendships brought him into the SDP as a founder member in 1981, and admiration for David Owen (who described Skidelsky as 'a close friend' in his memoirs (Owen, 1991: 802)) kept him there until the bitter end. In 1991 he was elevated to the House of Lords where he sat with the SDP until just before the 1992 election when the party lost its last two seats.

Since then Skidelsky has taken the Conservative whip in the House of Lords. He had already admired much of what Thatcher had been doing but 'still believed that an omelette could be made without breaking eggs': in that sense, intellectual conviction was at odds with emotion; he still wished to stand well with people he respected. 'Once the SDP collapsed I was free. Whether I would have gone back to the Labour Party if it had been a Blairite party I can't answer with absolute assurance. When the SDP collapsed it was still a Kinnockite party and I disagreed with too much of what it stood for.' But Skidelsky remains an independent-minded figure – more drawn to tough-minded mavericks ('bold men' as he described them in *Politicians and the Slump* (Skidelsky, 1970: 424)) like Owen – or, dare one say it, Mosley – than to particular parties. He describes himself as 'a Thatcherite Keynesian – although Margaret herself would be appalled by that particular linkage'. *The World After Communism* contains a respectful account of the Marxist analysis of the economic crisis of the 1970s and his biography of Keynes acknowledges the acuteness of the 1930s Marxist Dimitri Mirsky's analysis of the Bloomsbury Group as an intellectual aristocracy which, not being directly involved in the production process, could consider itself as above or outside class (Skidelsky, 1992b: 233–4; 1995: 118–9). In occasional essays and political journalism he sometimes deploys Marxist categories with a facility that might embarrass many socialists. In one place he describes the welfare state as 'designed in the 1940s to protect weakened capitalist economies against the assault of revolutionary socialism' (Skidelsky, 1996a: 38). In another he refers to Britain and the US as adopting 'the Keynesian policy of full employment ... in order to put capitalism in a stronger position to withstand revolutionary assaults, both domestic and international', and to 1960s 'growthmanship' as 'reflecting the view of virtually the whole of the British ruling class that Britain was "falling behind" the more successful capitalist economies like Germany and France' (Skidelsky, 1996b: 48, 57).

As a political figure rather than a historian and biographer he has become best known as Chairman of the Social Market Foundation. Founded originally as a think tank for the SDP in 1989 it was relaunched in 1992 with an orientation towards the social agenda of the Major government. Lewis Baston in his account of the SMF shrewdly remarks that it was well-placed in the early 1990s to occupy ground lost by the more unambiguously right-wing think tanks such as the Centre for Policy Studies and the Adam Smith Institute following the fall of Thatcher and that its turn towards Major largely reflected the fact the Conservatives were in government. He predicted that it might prove to be a rare case of a think tank that would be able to retain its influence with a new government (Baston, 1996: 69–71). Such indeed seems to have been the case. The *Financial Times*'s 'Observer' column reported in September 1997 that the SMF had been included with the Institute of Public Policy Research and Demos in consultations on the revamped Citizen's Charter while the Institute of Economic Affairs and the ASI were left out in the cold. 'Observer' commented that the SMF had 'sashayed effortlessly from SDP to Tory to New Labour' (*Financial Times*, 19.9.97). Recent SMF publications such as Fukuyama's *The End of Order* (Fukuyama, 1997), Frank Field's *Reforming Welfare* (Field, 1997) and Skidelsky's own *Beyond the Welfare State* (Skidelsky, 1997a) have all been directed to the Blair government's key objectives of curbing public expenditure, reforming welfare and remoralising society.

We have seen that Hobsbawm and Skidelsky started out almost from opposite poles in the political spectrum. Both began and have remained political outsiders. Hobsbawm has never abandoned his commitment to communism as a political cause despite its eclipse as a significant social and political movement. Skidelsky remains an unusual (and, I suspect, for some) an uncomfortable figure in the Conservative Party. His biography of Mosley still excites controversy. Unlike many of his friends and former associates in the SDP such as Marquand or Rodgers he has not found his way back into the national coalition that Blair has been trying to assemble. He has little patience with Marquand's ideas for modernising the British state which have aroused such resonance on the left (Skidelsky, 1997b). As Skidelsky put it, he (unlike Marquand) was 'not cradled in the Labour Party'. Nor too, of course, is Blair: 'he's not a Labour boy'. Perhaps that is why Blair has been able to draw on a political strategy and themes mapped out during the worst travails of the Labour Party in the 1980s by a lifelong Communist rooted in a lost central European culture – and why he is prepared to draw on ideas for government from a source headed by a Conservative peer. Hobsbawm stressed the need for Labour to be ready to make hard choices; Skidelsky and the SMF have been mapping out some of the directions in which that those hard choices might take them. From opposing political and ideological positions Hobsbawm and Skidelsky have converged in providing a strategy and themes and then an agenda for New Labour.

So far I have looked at the intellectual and political development of Hobsbawm and Skidelsky and noted the way their trajectories had converged in the contributions each has made to the emergence of New Labour. I now look beyond the personal and the political to their contrasting visions of the twentieth century and the place of the sixties.

Hobsbawm describes the 'structure of the Short Twentieth Century' in striking if uncharacteristically inelegant terms as resembling 'a sort of triptych or historical sandwich'. The First World War marked the breakdown of liberal, capitalist civilisation and the beginning of 40 years of calamity – an Age of Catastrophe in which capitalism 'was shaken by two world wars, followed by two waves of global rebellion and revolution, which brought to power a system that claimed to be the historically predestined alternative to bourgeois and capitalist society, first over one sixth of the world's land surface, and after the Second World War over one third of the globe's population'. During the 1930s the capitalist system faced breakdown and by 1940 liberal democracy had been confined to 'all but a fringe of Europe and parts of North America and Australasia'. So far, all had happened as a Marxist might have predicted.

This Age of Catastrophe which lasted until the aftermath of the Second World War was followed by some 25 or 30 years of exceptional economic growth and social transformation which could be seen in retrospect 'as a sort of Golden Age' which came to an end in the early 1970s. According to Hobsbawm, this Golden Age has been succeeded by 'a new era of decomposition, uncertainty and crisis – and indeed, for large parts of the world such as Africa, the former USSR and the formerly socialist parts of Europe, of catastrophe'. This third period, which he calls the Landslide, showed no sign of ending as he wrote: 'As the 1980s gave way to the 1990s, the mood of those who reflected on the century's past and future was a growing *fin-de-siècle* gloom. From the vantage-point of the 1990s, the Short Twentieth Century passed through a brief Golden Age, on the way from one era of crisis to another, into an unknown and problematic but not necessarily apocalyptic future' (Hobsbawm, 1994a: 6–7). Thus Hobsbawm's vision of the twentieth century, as one would expect from a life-long Communist, is essentially one of disappointment; his vision of the twenty-first clouded yet pessimistic. Elsewhere he has described the twentieth century as a continuing descent into barbarism (Hobsbawm, 1994b). Skidelsky describes *The World After Communism* as a polemic, and at times it reads as an extended response to *Age of Extremes* although he told me that he did not read the book until some time after he had written his own. Whereas Hobsbawm focuses on the internal dynamics of capitalism, especially when describing the impact of the Landslide, Skidelsky focuses on ideas, taking his cue from what he calls, perhaps rightly, Keynes's 'too often quoted passage' (at the end of *The General Theory of Employment, Interest and Money*) that 'the ideas of economists and political philosophers, both when they are right and when they are wrong, are more powerful than is commonly understood. Indeed the world is ruled by little else' (Skidelsky, 1992b: 570). Skidelsky therefore sees the twentieth century in terms of 'the rise and fall of collectivism', which he defines as 'the belief that the state knows better than the market, and can improve on the spontaneous tendencies of civil society, if necessary by suppressing them' and which he condemns as 'the most egregious error of the twentieth century', affecting with varying degrees of severity the liberal democracies of the West as well as Fascist and Communist states (Skidelsky, 1995: xiii). At one point he stresses that 'the collectivist belief system existed independently of the facts of modern life' (67). Elsewhere he devotes a dozen pages to the ideas of mid-century liberal opponents of collectivism – Keynes (heading the list), Beveridge, Popper, Hayek and Schumpeter (70–82).

Within that broad explanatory framework of the rise and fall of collectivism Skidelsky largely adopts the same tripartite periodisation as Hobsbawm. Like Hobsbawm he sees the First World War and the Great Depression as the great watersheds of the early part of the century, to be followed by 'the so-called "golden age" of the 1950s and 1960s – the twentieth-century equivalent of the nineteenth century's "age of equipoise" ' (46, 52, xiv). However, he sees the third period (Hobsbawm's Landslide) in terms of the 'shock therapy' needed to correct the 'unbalanced macro-economies' dependent on 'ever heavier state subsidies', a collectivist drift developing during the Golden Age. 'These subsidies were carried to extremes in the wholly state-owned Communist economies, which is why they led to a crisis not in the system but of the system. But they were present in most economies by the end of the 1970s' (140). Skidelsky, unlike Hobsbawm, is bullish about the future: 'The pessimists are a wearying lot. … I am an optimist. I regard the end of Communism, the rolling back of the frontiers of the state, the globalisation of economic intercourse, as the most hopeful turn of the historical screw which has happened since 1914' (xiii).

Whatever their differing perspectives on the century, Hobsbawm and Skidelsky are agreed upon the centrality of the dialectic between

Communism and the capitalist West. For Hobsbawm, the century has been 'dominated by the confrontation between the anti-capitalist communism of the October revolution, represented by the USSR and anti-communist capitalism, of which the USA was the champion and exemplar' (Hobsbawm, 1994a: 143). Only a 'temporary and bizarre alliance' with the Soviet Union enabled the West to defeat Hitler, and the renewal of hostility in the Cold War was an essential stimulus to welfare capitalism. 'It is one of the ironies of this strange century that the most lasting result of the October revolution, whose object was the global overthrow of capitalism, was to save its antagonist, both in war and in peace – that it is to say, by providing it with the incentive, fear, to reform itself after the Second World War, and, by establishing the popularity of economic planning, furnishing it with some of the procedures for its reform' (7–8). Hobsbawm stresses the importance of the Cold War in the economic revival of Western Europe and Japan (239, 275–6). The vogue for planning in the Western economies reflected the impact of the Soviet example (274).

Skidelsky rightly points to the malign role of Stalin in facilitating the rise of Nazism (Skidelsky, 1995: 55) but, as we have seen, he has conceded Hobsbawm's argument about the essential stimulus of the Soviet example in reforming post-war capitalism. In *The World After Communism* he argues that the perceived economic challenge from the Soviet Union in the 1950s and 1960s was crucial in fostering 'the vogue for growthmanship' in the capitalist economies which contributed to the economic problems of the 1970s (Skidelsky, 1995: 11–13). In one of his most eloquent passages, Skidelsky sums up the impact of the Soviet Union: 'The economic imagination of the West has been profoundly influenced by the seeming success and eventual failure of the Soviet model. In the 1930s the gargantuan power of the Soviet industrial machine … provided an irresistible contrast to the idle factories and dole queues in the industrial West. In the Second World War it was the huge Soviet tanks which hurled back the invading Germans in the great tank battles of 1943 that impressed. In the 1950s it was the prodigious growth rates being chalked up by the Soviet economy which … helped frighten industrial nations into "planning for growth". Conversely, the stagnation of the Soviet system after 1970 helped turn the non-Communist imagination against collectivism … . The revival of the free market in the West was built on the decrepitude of Soviet planning' (103). One might add that the decay and eventual collapse of Communism created the opportunity for Reagan and Thatcher to overturn the consensus established in the 1940s and to begin dismantling the Keynesian welfare state. As Hobsbawm remarks: 'the absence of a credible threat to the [capitalist] system, such as communism and the existence of the USSR [has] diminished the incentive to reform' (Hobsbawm, 1994a: 574). Even by its absence the fate of the Soviet Union has had an impact on the West.

So much for Hobsbawm's and Skidelsky's interpretation of the century and the central dialectic between the capitalist West and the Soviet Union. How do they interpret the position of the sixties in this story? Only Hobsbawm has written at length about the social and cultural revolutions of the post-war period (Hobsbawm, 1994a: Chapters 10 and 11). He sets the global student rebellion of 1968 against the background of the unprecedented social and economic transformations of the Golden Age. Key factors were the dramatic movement from countryside to cities throughout the world – 'the death of the peasantry' (289) – and the equally unprecedented increase in student numbers as a result of the growth of occupations requiring secondary and higher education (295). Both of these factors contributed to an unprecedented gulf in experience and expectations between people born before around 1920 and since around 1950 – the so-called generation gap about which so much was written in the 1960s and which must seem incomprehensible to generations born since then (301). The generation gap between parents born around 1920 and children born around 1950 was all the greater for the fact that many political leaders of the time (such as de Gaulle, Macmillan, Eisenhower, Adenauer and Khrushchev) had been born before the century began (325). All of these factors contributed to the global youth culture and the explosion of 1968.

What is unusual about that explosion is that, at least in the capitalist heartland of Western Europe and the US, it involved mainly the beneficiaries rather than the victims of the social and economic transformations of the preceding decades and was directed against the symbols of mass consumption that either had not existed in the 1930s or 1940s or had been available only to a privileged minority. In a sense, therefore, this was a revolt by the generation of whom Keynes wrote in his famous paper on 'Economic Possibilities for our Grandchildren' (Keynes, 1930) when he speculated that the economic problem of scarcity would be solved. The 'strenuous purposeful money-makers' would have carried us all 'into the lap of economic abundance', to be enjoyed by 'those peoples, who can keep alive, and cultivate into a fuller perfection, the art of life itself and do not sell themselves for the means of life'. Then, 'we shall be able to rid ourselves of many of the pseudo-moral principles which have hag-ridden us for two hundred years, by which we have exalted some of the most distasteful of human qualities into the position of the highest virtues'. 'The love of money as a possession' would be 'recognised for what it is,

a somewhat disgusting morbidity', once it was no longer needed to promote the accumulation of capital. Keynes thought that the economic problem would be with us for at least another hundred years (Keynes, 1930:
326–31). Skidelsky was not alone in believing in the 1960s that 'the day
of Keynes' grandchildren had arrived' as a result of the Golden Age combination of steadily rising living standards and increasing welfare provision
with full employment and modest personal taxation.

Skidelsky would be the first to point to the irony that the conviction that
the economic problem had been solved became current just at the moment
when the Golden Age was about to end. In an eloquent passage,
Hobsbawm describes the student rebellion as 'a warning, a sort of *memento
mori* to a generation that half-believed it had solved the problems of western society for good' (Hobsbawm, 1994a: 285–6). Skidelsky, writing
in the immediate aftermath of 1968, saw 'the arrival of youth on the political stage' as 'the beginning of the end' of the consensus of the 1950s
(Bogdanor and Skidelsky, 1970: 13). Far more significant in bringing the
Golden Age to an end was a 'shift in labour's mood', a 'worldwide wage
explosion' triggered by rising inflation which was in turn a product of
declining profitability and declining growth in real wages resulting from a
slowing in the rate of productivity growth. The student rebellion was
important mainly through the stimulus given to working class demands for
higher wages and better conditions (Hobsbawm, 1994a: 301). Skidelsky
would agree. For him too the main reason for the end of the Golden Age
was a slowdown in productivity which contributed to an emerging fiscal
crisis as welfare spending continued to grow faster than the economy itself
(Skidelsky, 1995: 93–4). The crisis of ungovernability of the 1970s was,
in his words, 'labour movement-led', as workers sought to increase real
wages while resisting technological changes necessary to restore profitability. Skidelsky, as we have seen, thought that it heralded the Corporate
State. Hobsbawm, addressing Birkbeck students in January 1975, pointed
to a real prospect for an advance to socialism as a way of resolving what
he described as 'the most serious crisis of this country ... since the post-
Napoleonic period' (Hobsbawm, 1975: 11, 16 – I owe this reference to
Alan Hooper).

A second irony is that the stress on personal liberation that we associate
with the sixties, and which was associated at the time with political radicalism, has turned out to have more in common with the assumptions of
neo-liberal defenders of consumer capitalism than with those of its critics
on the left. Skidelsky reminded me that Samuel Brittan had pointed to this
connection in *Left or Right: the Bogus Dilemma* (Brittan, 1968). Hobsbawm
made a similar point in a famous article on 'Revolution and Sex' which

argued that there was no consistent relationship between sexual permissiveness and political liberation. 'The belief that a narrow sexual morality
is an essential bulwark of the capitalist system is no longer tenable'. On
the contrary, 'rulers find it convenient to encourage sexual permissiveness
or laxity among their subjects if only to keep their minds off their subjection'. Past revolutions may have included libertarian and antinomian elements but far more significant was 'a persistent affinity between
revolution and puritanism ... . The Robespierres always win out over the
Dantons' (Hobsbawm, 1969: 216–9). The link between sexual freedom
and economic freedom in the neo-liberal sense is much more obvious now
than it appeared in the late 1960s. After all, Sonny Bono ended up as a
Republican Congressman. Richard Branson sold copies of his first paper
among the crowds at an anti-Vietnam War demonstration in London.
Skidelsky has described Bill Gates as a kind of hippie in the 1960s.
Arguably the moral and cultural changes of the 1960s conflicted with the
socialism of many of their adherents on the New Left and contributed to
the rise of the New Right and the capitalist revival of the 1980s. Perhaps
some of the origins of the animal spirits of the boardrooms of the 1980s
can be found in the animal spirits of the bedrooms of the 1960s.

   In this respect Hobsbawm was quite right to warn in 1971 that the left-
wing radicalism of the late 1960s might prove to be temporary and that the
radical right might be the main beneficiary of another lengthy period of
economic crisis (Hobsbawm, 1971: 256). The comparison he drew was
with the wave of revolt which preceded and followed the First World War.
The Italian anarchist Errico Malatesta warned about the dangers of unsuccessful attempts to overthrow the bourgeoisie: 'If we do not go on to the
end, we shall have to pay with tears of blood for the fear that we are now
causing the bourgeoisie' (cited in Stone, 1983: 388). *Age of Extremes*
acknowledges that the rise of the radical right between the wars was 'a
response to the danger, indeed to the reality, of social revolution and working-class power in general, to the October revolution and Leninism in particular'. In those years, the real danger to democracy came from the right
(Hobsbawm, 1994: 124, 112). The same could be said of the decades after
1848: the beneficiaries of left-wing failure were Louis Napoleon
Bonaparte, Camillo di Cavour and Otto von Bismarck. As Marx remarked:
'Unless the radicals unite Germany by revolutionary means Bismarck will
unite it by reactionary Junker means' (cited in Taylor, 1950: 123).

   Hobsbawm has described 1968 as 'the single moment', if there were
any, 'in the golden years after 1945 which corresponds to the world simultaneous upheaval of which the revolutionaries had dreamed after 1917'
(Hobsbawm, 1994a: 298). The failure of the Left, not only in 1968 but

also during the 1970s, opened the way to the rise of the New Right. In 1975 Hobsbawm could argue that 'the capitalists have no ready made solution' to 'the present crisis of capitalism' (Hobsbawm, 1975: 8) and Skidelsky foretold the arrival of the Corporate State. Neither foresaw that Reagan and Thatcher would solve by neo-liberal means the economic problems that a divided and demoralised Left had failed to solve by collectivist means. And freedom was the slogan under which they advanced. As Skidelsky pointed out, the working class was no longer satisfied with 'the utilitarian, standardised social services that were established during the Second World War' when a much wider range of choice had been opened up in other parts of their lives. The climax of the Long Sixties between 1968 and 1976 can thus be seen as a watershed between two epochs in the Short Twentieth Century and, like 1848, as a turning point at which the world failed to turn in the expected direction.

So far this chapter has looked, first, at the intellectual and political development of Eric Hobsbawm and Robert Skidelsky, pointing to a degree of convergence in the strategy, themes and programme of New Labour and then, secondly, at their complementary rather than contrasting perspectives on the century and the place of the sixties within it. We have seen how, as in the decades after 1848 and 1917, the dreams of the Left turned into nightmares as the Right advanced under stolen banners – of nationalism in the 1850s and 1860s, of radical collectivism in the 1920s and 1930s, and personal freedom in the 1970s and 1980s. I now go on to argue that the apparently paradoxical developments of the last third of the century, in which Thatcher and Reagan seemed to benefit from the cultural changes of the sixties, can best be seen as different moments in a continuing process of democratisation.

This notion of democratisation is, of course, derived from Alexis de Tocqueville's notion, advanced in the first volume of *Democracy in America* published in 1835, of a 'great democratic revolution' of which America represented the 'extreme limits' to which Europe was advancing (Tocqueville, 1835: 9). Tocqueville was not the first to see America in this light as the pattern of the future. Hegel in his *Lectures on the Philosophy of History* (first delivered at the University of Berlin in 1818) described the United States as 'the land of the future, where, in the ages that lie before us, the burden of the World's History shall reveal itself'. In his *Aesthetics* he remarked: 'If one wants to have an idea of what may be the epic poems of the future, one has only to think of the possible victory of

American rationalism, living and universal, over the European peoples.' Both of these passages are cited by Paul Berman, in his recent perceptive assessment of the sixties, as examples of what he wittily calls 'Yankee Hegelianism' (Berman, 1996: 309–10). Something of the notion can be found in Gramsci's notion of fordism as 'an organic extension and intensification of European civilisation' (Gramsci, 1971: 318) – and, of course, in Alexandre Kojève and his disciple Fukuyama, with his vision of the United States as the destination to which all nations are travelling, like wagons crossing hostile territory (Fukuyama, 1992: 203, 291, 338–9).

When, in the second volume of *Democracy in America* published in 1840, Tocqueville contrasted 'democratic society' and 'democratic man' with 'aristocratic society' and 'aristocratic man', he had in mind far more than different systems of political power (Aron, 1968: 187; Siedentop, 1994: 45). Tocqueville's notions of democratic society and the democratic revolution are best understood as a process of 'levelling' involving the gradual elimination of civil inequalities and the creation of a common system of values which can be described in terms of a mass society or a classless society. Tocqueville saw this as a process extending over centuries. Moreover, there is in his account of the rise of industry and the dangers of a 'business aristocracy' the implication that the process might be put, at least temporarily, into reverse by the rise of new divisions between workers and manufacturers (Tocqueville, 1840: 557). However, Tocqueville's notion of a persistent tendency towards equality did not entail the elimination of inequalities of wealth, although he did anticipate an elimination of gross extremes of wealth and poverty and a gradual spread of property ownership. The notion of a 'property-owning democracy' has a strong flavour of Tocqueville about it.

For Tocqueville the democratic revolution involving a gradual elimination of legal and social distinctions and the spread of common values also entailed growing individualism. Democratic society was a society of competitive individuals: 'equality ... tends to isolate men from each other so that each thinks only of himself. It lays the soul open to an inordinate love of material gain' (444). Violent revolution on the French model might be needed to establish civil and political equality but the resulting spread of property-ownership and growing individualism would have a profoundly conservative effect. 'I know nothing', he wrote, 'more opposed to revolutionary morality than the moral standards of traders. Trade is the natural enemy of all violent passions. Trade loves moderation, delights in compromise, and is most careful to avoid anger. ... Trade makes men independent of one another and gives them an idea of their own importance; it leads them to want to manage their own affairs and teaches them how to succeed therein. Hence it makes them inclined to liberty but disinclined to revolution' (637).

Moreover, the democratic society of isolated, competitive individuals, constantly striving against one another to better their positions, is not a happy one. 'In America', wrote Tocqueville, 'I have seen the freest and best educated of men in circumstances the happiest to be found in the world; yet it seemed to me that a cloud habitually hung on their brow, and they seemed serious and almost sad in their pleasures' (536). He explained this chronic dissatisfaction in terms of a formal equality which aroused great ambitions in many people while at the same time frustrating those ambitions because, inevitably, such ambitions could be realised only by a minority, exciting constant envy in the rest. 'That is the reason', he wrote, 'for the strange melancholy often haunting the inhabitants of democracies in the midst of abundance, and of that disgust with life sometimes gripping them in calm and easy circumstances' (537–8). This is the society portrayed by Fred Hirsch (Hirsch, 1977), in constant pursuit of positional goods that, by their nature, can be enjoyed only by a minority, the 'nation of wannabes' portrayed more recently by popular psychologist Oliver James, 'permanently dissatisfied, always yearning for what we have not got' (James, 1997: 27).

This process of democratisation has long been evident to students of popular culture in this country. Richard Hoggart's seminal study of working-class culture in the 1950s, *The Uses of Literacy* published in 1957, is peppered with quotations from Tocqueville. His main argument is that the new commercial culture of mass entertainment has 'unbent the springs of action' (the words are Tocqueville's) among the working class; now, in the 1950s, 'we are becoming culturally classless' (Hoggart, 1958: 169, 342). Differences between the working class and the lower middle class had become 'largely superficial' (343). The new mass entertainment culture tended towards 'a view of the world in which progress is conceived as a seeking of material pleasures, equality as moral levelling, and freedom as the ground for endless irresponsible pleasure' (340). For Hoggart, 'working people' were in danger of being induced 'to accept a mean form of materialism as a social philosophy' that would undermine the achievements of the working class movement and the reality of democracy (ibid: 323). His was essentially a pessimistic vision of the consequences of a democratic society for the traditional socialist values of the Left.

Raymond Williams, writing a few years later in *The Long Revolution* (first published in 1961 and revised in 1965) was more sanguine about the implications for the Left of what he described as 'the democratic revolution' (Williams, 1965: 10). He found comfort in 'a determination not to be regimented' (321). He anticipated hopefully that this resistence to regimentation would find expression in the rejection of an economic system that denied to most of the population the autonomy that they enjoyed in other areas of life and which was inconsistent with the ideals of political democracy. 'The aspiration to control the general directions of our economic life is an essential element of democratic growth. ... It is difficult to feel that we are really governing ourselves if in so central a part of our living as our work most of us have no share in decisions that immediately affect us' (332). Williams looked forward to growing pressure for 'industrial democracy', for a real 'participating democracy', which was bound to raise issues of ownership that lay at the heart of the socialist vision (339, 343). While he was too acute an observer not to notice the 'visible moral decline of the labour movement' and the way in which socialism 'has almost wholly lost any contemporary meaning' (328), he nevertheless failed to recognise the way in which the resistance to regimentation which he detected and which was such a hallmark of the 1960s could be turned by the resurgent Right against the achievements of the labour movement such as the trade unions and the institutions of the welfare state.

Hobsbawm's main intervention in this debate was, of course, the lecture published as 'The Forward March of Labour Halted?' (Hobsbawm, 1978). Tocqueville had pointed to the homogeneous nature of the separate classes and estates of aristocratic society which would disappear in the course of the long process which he described as the democratic revolution. Hobsbawm argued in his seminal lecture that the traditional industrial working class had lost much of its former homogeneity and sense of class solidarity since the 1950s. He pointed to 'a growing division of workers into sections and groups, each pursuing its own economic interest irrespective of the rest'. Under conditions of what he described as 'state-monopoly capitalism' (which others might have described as corporatism) the bargaining strength of striking workers depended on their ability to bring pressure to bear on the public and thus to break the political will of the government. The effect, according to Hobsbawm, was not only to 'create potential friction between groups of workers, but also [to] risk weakening the hold of the labour movement as a whole' (18). The consequences of this behaviour which, it might be argued, reflected the process of democratisation analysed by Tocqueville and perceived by the likes of Hoggart and Williams, were to become all too clear in the next few years, when Thatcher was able to mobilise sections of the working class in a struggle against 'the enemy within'.

Another aspect of this process of democratisation can be seen in the downwards spread of moral values associated with a social elite epitomised by Bloomsbury in the earlier part of the century. Looking back on his youth, Keynes described his Cambridge and later Bloomsbury friends as being 'amongst the first of our generation ... to escape the Benthamite tradition. ... We entirely repudiated a personal liability on us to obey general rules. ... We repudiated entirely customary morals, conventions and general wisdom. We were, that is to say, in the strict sense of the term, immoralists'. Theirs was essentially a doctrine of an elite. The mature Keynes recognised that the rules and conventions scorned by him and his friends were the foundation of the civilisation of which they were among the main beneficiaries. He was quite aware of the danger for that civilisation of a juncture between their 'libertinism and comprehensive irreverence' and the 'vulgar passions' (Keynes, 1938: 447–50). It might be argued that what has been described as the Keynesian welfare state depended upon customary conventions among the working classes that began to break down in the 1960s.

Skidelsky remarked in conversation upon the coincidence between a democratisation of Bloomsbury hedonism (or immoralism) and the weakening of the British economy in the 1960s. His friend Michael Holroyd's seminal biography of Lytton Strachey, published in 1967, played an important role in revealing the sexual behaviour of Bloomsbury to a wide audience (and in so doing revolutionised the art of biography). I well recall the impression it made, when serialised in the *Sunday Times*, upon a sixth-form friend of mine. Skidelsky thought that the relaxation of moral constraints in the 1960s could indeed be seen as a kind of democratisation of Bloomsbury ideals. As he observed, 'The one thing that really offends a lot of old Bloomsburies nowadays is the idea that their ideas are the common property of the masses – and they really don't like it, because the Bloomsbury idea was really a variant of the old aristocratic idea. The bounds of the permissible for them were just drawn more widely than for others'. However, the consequences of the relaxation of moral constraints upon the working class are much more serious for the rest of society – and for the welfare state devised in the 1940s – than for a tiny elite. One of Skidelsky's (and the SMF's) main concerns today – a concern shared by the Blair Government – is with the consequences of this relaxation of moral constraints for the family and for society as a whole in terms of increased demands upon the public purse. Thus the democratisation of Bloomsbury hedonism in the sixties and after may be seen to have contributed to a growing moral authoritarianism exhibited by New Labour.

This notion of democratisation as a kind of masterkey in understanding the transition from the radicalism of the 1960s to the conservatism of recent decades is not confined to this country. It may be significant that the

American New Left emerged from the Civil Rights movement of the late 1950s and the early 1960s which sought to consummate the process of democratisation in the United States by extending full civil rights to African Americans. Tocqueville himself had commented in 1840 that 'If ever there are great revolutions [in the United States], they will be caused by the presence of the blacks upon American soil. That is to say, it will not be the equality of social conditions but rather their inequality which may give rise thereto' (Tocqueville, 1840: 639). The subsequent transmutation of the American New Left into the so-called 'identity politics' of the Women's Movement and the Gay Movement can be seen as another stage in extending equality.

In Europe the New Left turned to terrorism only in countries like Germany and Italy where liberal democracy had shallower roots than in Britain and France (with the significant exception of Ulster, where the refounded IRA was as much a product of the sixties as were the Red Army Fraction and the Red Brigades). The student rebellion in the streets of Paris in 1968 can be seen as complementing in the social and cultural sphere the process of economic modernisation begun by Jean Monnet and de Gaulle. Perhaps that was why it proved so much more evanescent than in Italy and Germany (and Ulster) where the New Left transmuted into formidable terrorist movements. The process of democratisation found expression in southern Europe in the overthrow of the Greek Colonels and the termination of fascism in Spain and Portugal. The democratic impulse behind the overthrow of soviet power in eastern Europe and the Soviet Union itself needs no underlining. Farther afield the same process of democratisation can be seen in the end of Apartheid in South Africa and the rise of market relations in China.

My purpose in this chapter has been to examine the work of Eric Hobsbawm and Robert Skidelsky as interpreters of their age and as significant influences upon a new political formation – Tony Blair's New Labour. I have suggested that, despite differing backgrounds, their interpretations of the century bear significant resemblances and differences in their perspectives are largely complementary rather than contradictory. Finally I have sought to argue that the apparent paradoxes and ironies of the transition from the political radicalism and moral antinomianism of the sixties to the conservatism and moral authoritarianism of the 1980s and 1990s can best be understood as moments in a process of democratisation charted with exceptional foresight and acuteness by Alexis de Tocqueville.

An earlier version of this chapter ended at this point but Skidelsky challenged me – very tentatively he insisted – to give my own opinion of whether one should start the twenty first century as a bull or a bear. How could I resist the challenge?

Like Tocqueville I am torn between two views of this whole process. His other great work *The Ancien Régime and the French Revolution* describes how '[t]he eighteenth-century Frenchman was ... both better and worse than ourselves'. He had 'nothing of that discreet, well-regulated sensualism which prevails today ... . Even the bourgeoisie did not devote themselves exclusively to the pursuit of material comforts; they often aspired to loftier, more refined satisfactions and were far from regarding money as the sole good' (Tocqueville, 1856: 141–2).

In some ways I regret the passing of the heroic illusions of modernity rather as Tocqueville did 'the outstanding personalities' of eighteenth-century France, 'those men of genius, proud and daring, who made the Revolution what it was: at once the admiration and the terror of succeeding generations' (143). As a boy in the 1950s I regretted having been born too late to fly a Spitfire; as a student in the late 1960s I regretted not having had the chance to fight on the barricades of Madrid or Petrograd. But as a young man in the 1970s I joined the civil service where I stayed for 20 years. And I know that the grandchildren of the militiamen who fought and lost in Madrid are better off – in all conceivable ways – than the great-grandchildren of the Red Guards who fought and won in Petrograd.

Yet today I find something banal in images of heroism drawn mainly from the sports field – televised exclusively on satellite TV and garnished with commercial logos. I was dispirited to read in the *Observer* (22 February 1998) about diminishing numbers of young people volunteering for service overseas in the developing world (even though in all honesty I would not have cared to do so myself). I was saddened to read in the *Economist* (17 January 1998) that 75 per cent of American freshmen consider financial success to be an essential or very important goal of education compared with 41 per cent seeking a meaningful philosophy of life – an almost complete reversal of answers given by students in the 1960s.

Looking back, the generation of the sixties seems to stand on the cusp of history – born and bred in the Golden Age but growing up in the afterglow of the heroic illusions of the Age of Catastrophe and destined to grow to middle age through the Landslide of those illusions, enduring their own sentimental education like Flaubert's protagonists in that greatest of all novels of disillusionment. Now the heroic illusions of modernity have faded and we aspire only to 'a kind of decent materialism' (Tocqueville,

1840: 534) dignified as the post-modern condition. At least in the heart-lands of capitalism, and by no means for everyone, we seem to be advancing ever closer to the destination sketched by Tocqueville in 1840, to a world in which '[t]here is little energy of soul, but mores are gentle and laws humane. Though heroic devotion and any other very exalted, brilliant and pure virtues may be rare, habits are orderly, violence rare, and cruelty almost unknown ... Life is not very glamorous, but extremely comfortable and peaceful. Almost all salient characteristics are obliterated to make room for something average, less high and less low, less brilliant and less dim, than what the world had before' (703–4).

In some moods, one is tempted, like Tocqueville, to feel saddened and chilled by the prospect, but perhaps, like him, one should find comfort in the fact that, within what he described as vast limits, humankind is 'strong and free' to fashion a more just society. One should also recall that the French Revolution which excited his 'admiration and terror' may have lain behind him but that the heroic illusions of modernity, with all their unimagined terrors, lay ahead. Who knows what new illusions might succeed the 'decent materialism' of our present sceptical age? Who knows what terrors a new age of faith might bring?

REFERENCES

Abelove, H., Blackmar, B., Dimock, P. and Schneer, J. (eds), *Visions of History*, Manchester University Press, nd (but probably 1983).

Anderson, P. (1968), 'Components of the National Culture', in *English Questions* (ed. P. Anderson) Verso, 1992.

Annan, N. (1991), *Our Age: the Generation That Made Post-war Britain*, Fontana.

Aron, R. (1968), *Main Currents in Sociological Thought* 1, Penguin.

Baston, L. (1996), 'The Social Market Foundation', in *Ideas and Think Tanks in Contemporary Britain: Volume I* (eds M.D. Kandiah and A. Seldon, Frank Cass).

Berman, P. (1996), *A Tale of Two Utopias: the Political Journey of the Generation of 1968*, W. W. Norton & Co.

Bogdanor, V. and Skidelsky, R. (eds) (1970), *The Age of Affluence 1951–1964*, Macmillan.

Brittan, S. (1968), *Left or Right: the Bogus Dilemma*, Secker & Warburg.

Callinicos, A. (1985), 'The Politics of *Marxism Today*', *International Socialism*, 29.

Cockett, R. (1995), *Thinking the Unthinkable: Think-Tanks and the Economic Counter-Revolution, 1931–1983*, Fontana.

Field, F. (1997), *Reforming Welfare*, Social Market Foundation.

Fukuyama, F. (1989), 'The End of History?', *The National Interest*, 16.

Fukuyama, F. (1992), *The End of History and the Last Man*, Hamish Hamilton.

Fukuyama, F. (1997), *The End of Order*, Social Market Foundation.

Gramsci, A. (1971), *Selections from the Prison Notebooks*, Lawrence & Wishart.

Harris, R. (1984), *The Making of Neil Kinnock*, Faber and Faber.

Hirsch, F. (1977), *Social Limits to Growth*, Routledge & Kegan Paul.

Hobsbawm, E.J. (1969), 'Revolution and Sex', reprinted in *Revolutionaries*, Hobsbawm, 1973.

Hobsbawm, E.J. (1971), 'Intellectuals and the Class Struggle', reprinted in *Revolutionaries*, Hobsbawm, 1973.

Hobsbawm, E.J. (1973), *Revolutionaries*, Weidenfeld & Nicolson.

Hobsbawm, E.J. (1975), *The Crisis and the Outlook*, Birkbeck College Socialist Society.

Hobsbawm, E.J. (1978), 'The Forward March of Labour Halted?', reprinted in *Politics for a Rational Left*, Hobsbawm, 1989.

Hobsbawm, E.J. (1983), 'Labour's Lost Millions', reprinted in *Politics for a Rational Left*, Hobsbawm, 1989.

Hobsbawm, E.J. (1984), 'Labour: Rump or Rebirth?', reprinted in *Politics for a Rational Left*, Hobsbawm, 1989.

Hobsbawm, E.J. (1987a), *The Age of Empire 1875–1914*, Weidenfeld.

Hobsbawm, E.J. (1987b), 'Out of the Wilderness', reprinted in *Politics for a Rational Left*, Hobsbawm, 1989.

Hobsbawm, E.J. (1988), 'The Signs of a Recovery', reprinted in *Politics for a Rational Left*, Hobsbawm, 1989.

Hobsbawm, E.J. (1989), *Politics for a Rational Left: Political Writings 1977–1988*, Verso.

Hobsbawm, E.J. (1990), 'Goodbye to All That', in *After the Fall: the Failure of Communism and the Future of Socialism* (ed. R. Blackburn, Verso, 1991).

Hobsbawm, E.J. (1993), 'The Present as History', reprinted in *On History*, Hobsbawm, 1997.

Hobsbawm, E.J. (1994a), *Age of Extremes: The Short Twentieth Century 1914–1991*, Michael Joseph.

Hobsbawm, E.J. (1994b), 'Barbarism: A User's Guide', reprinted in *On History*, Hobsbawm, 1997.

Hobsbawm, E.J. (1997), *On History*, Weidenfeld & Nicolson.

Hoggart, R. (1958), *The Uses of Literacy*, Penguin.

Holroyd, M. (1967), *Lytton Strachey: A Critical Biography*, William Heinemann Ltd.

Jacques, M. and Hall, S. (1997), 'The great moving centre show', *New Statesman*, 21 November.

James, O. (1997), 'Curse of comparison', *Prospect*, October.

Kadarkay, A. (1991), *Georg Lukács: Life, Thought, and Politics*, Basil Blackwell.

Keynes, J.M. (1930), 'Economic Possibilities for our Grandchildren', in *The Collected Writings of John Maynard Keynes: Volume IX, Essays in Persuasion*, Macmillan, 1972.

Keynes, J.M. (1938), 'My Early Beliefs', *The Collected Writings of John Maynard Keynes: Volume X, Essays in Biography*, Macmillan, 1972.

Lukács, G. (1983), *Record of a Life: An Autobiographical Sketch*, Verso.

Marquand, D. (1997), 'Journey to an Unknown Destination', in *The New Reckoning*, Polity Press, 1997.

Moggridge, D.E. (1976), *Keynes*, Fontana.

Owen, D. (1991), *Time to Declare*, Michael Joseph.

Siedentop, L. (1994), *Tocqueville*, Oxford University Press.

Skelton, R. (ed.) (1964), *Poetry of the Thirties*, Penguin.

Skidelsky, R. (1969), 'Politics is not Enough', *Encounter*, January.

Skidelsky, R. (1970), *Politicians and the Slump: The Labour Government of 1929–31*, Penguin.

Skidelsky, R. (1975a), *Oswald Mosley*, Macmillan.

Skidelsky, R. (1975b), 'The future of the state', *New Society*, 2 October.

Skidelsky, R. (ed.) (1977), *The End of the Keynesian Era: Essays on the Disintegration of the Keynesian Political Economy*, Macmillan.

Skidelsky, R. (1992a), *John Maynard Keynes: Hopes Betrayed 1883–1920*, Macmillan (first edition 1983).

Skidelsky, R. (1992b), *John Maynard Keynes: The Economist as Saviour 1920–1937*, Macmillan.

Skidelsky, R. (1995), *The World After Communism: A Polemic For Our Times*, Macmillan.

Skidelsky, R. (1996a), 'Welfare without the state', *Prospect*, January.

Skidelsky, R. (1996b), 'The Fall of Keynesianism', in *The Ideas That Shaped Post-war Britain* (eds D. Marquand and A. Seldon, Fontana).

Skidelsky, R. (1997a), *Beyond the Welfare State*, Social Market Foundation.

Skidelsky, R. (1997b), 'Marquand's missing link', *Prospect*, December.

Stone, N. (1983), *Europe Transformed 1878–1919*, Fontana.

Taylor, A.J.P. (1950), 'German Unity', in *Europe: Grandeur and Decline*, Penguin, 1967.

Tocqueville, A. de (1835, 1840), *Democracy in America: Volumes I & II*, ed. J.P. Mayer, Harper & Rowe, 1966.

Tocqueville, A. de (1856), *The Ancien Régime and the French Revolution*, Fontana, 1966.

Tyler, C. (1994), 'Post-mortem on a bloody century', *Financial Times*, 8/9 October.

Walker, M. (1994), 'Old comrades never say die', *The Guardian*, 15 October.

Williams, R. (1965), *The Long Revolution*, Penguin.

10 The Rise and Fall of an Anti-Racism: from Political Blackness to Ethnic Pluralism

Tariq Modood

INTRODUCTION

Looking back at the issue of 'race' in Britain as it emerged in the 1960s and as it is today the most fundamental question is whether 'race relations' can be understood in terms of a black–white racial dualism. From the 1960s onwards a growing body of political activists, social researchers and equality professionals have answered this question with a 'yes', till by the mid to late 1980s the idea was a racial equality orthodoxy. It is perhaps most succinctly expressed in a sentence from Salman Rushdie:

> Britain is now two entirely different worlds and the one you inherit is determined by the colour of your skin. (Rushdie, 1982)

It has been argued that this recognition of a common racism led in the 1960s and 1970s for Afro-Caribbean and Asian people to come together in common political struggles, to transcend their ethnicities and to forge the anti-racist concept of blackness, the unity in resistance of all those who in not being white suffered racism (Sivanandan, 1987). A major consequence of this act of creating a new political 'black' identity was that as Stuart Hall puts it:

> politically speaking, 'The Black Experience', as a singular and unifying framework based on the building up of identity across ethnic and cultural difference between the different communities, became 'hegemonic' over other ethnic/racial identities – though the latter did not, of course, disappear. (Hall, 1988: 27)

No, they certainly did not. For, as is now increasingly recognised, the ethnicities have struck back; to such an extent that not only has political blackness lost its once dominant position, its hegemony (Ali, 1991: 195), but, as Hall argues, we have seen the end of the essential black subject

(Hall, 1992). Indeed, putting it with his usual bluntness, Sivanandan has declared that 'there is no longer a Black struggle in Britain which embraces all the non-white communities' (Sivanandan, 1995).

By uniting all those who suffer from white racism into a single category of *blackness* the race egalitarians of the 1970s and 1980s did provide a sharper political focus and achieved a partial mobilisation of the oppressed groups. But they failed to appreciate that the ethnic pride of various groups, necessary for a confident and assertive participation in a society from which the groups had been excluded and held as inferior, could not be built out of the mere fact of common inequality. Excluded groups seek respect for themselves as they are or aspire to be, not simply a solidarity on the basis of a recognition of themselves as victims; they resist being defined by their *mode of oppression* and seek space and dignity for their *mode of being* (Modood, 1992). Hence, however disappointing it has been to the Left, it is not all that surprising that most Asians have not positively embraced the idea of themselves as 'black' (Modood, 1988, 1994a) and that many Muslims have mobilised around a Muslim rather than a 'black' identity (Modood, 1990, 1992). The narrow focus on colour – racism and the development of a unitary non-white political identity has not only been politically short-sighted but, as will be argued below, has obscured important dimensions of racism.

If you will accept a crude distinction between an 'inside left' (the left inside the Labour Party) and an 'outside left' (the left beyond the Labour Party), it would be fair to say that the idea of political blackness, whatever its specific origins, was very much developed by the 'outside left' in the 1970s, but came to be part of the vocabulary and politics of the 'inside left' in the 1980s, especially in London, in Black sections, and in metropolitan local authorities, a combination perhaps best exemplified in Ken Livingstone's GLC (Shukra, 1993). It is therefore perhaps not surprising that criticism of this later form of political blackness should first appear among the 'outside left' (Sivanandan, 1985; Gilroy, 1987, 1992). To be sure it was not a criticism of political blackness *per se*, and nor was the criticism all of a piece. It was a criticism of what was taken to be a spoilt form of political blackness. Spoilt because it was, variously, a politics of careerists jumping onto a bandwagon, overly bureaucratised and professionalised, with little appreciation of the historical and global liberation struggles, out of touch with the communities it claimed to represent and collaborating with state structures it ought to be opposing, while at the same time steeped in dangerous appeals to culture and ethnicity (Sivanandan, 1985; Gilroy, 1987, 1992). At about the same point in time I too began to develop a critique of this form of political blackness. The central idea was that political blackness cannot do justice to the oppression and aspirations of Asian people (Modood, 1988, 1994). What I would like to do here is to point to some developments since the 1960s which I think help to explain why racial dualism no longer fits the facts, if it ever did.

ECONOMIC DIVERSITY

Despite the persistence of racial discrimination, the ethnic minorities in Britain are reversing the initial downward mobility produced by migration and racial discrimination.[1] All ethnic minority groups, however, continue to be employed and to earn below the level appropriate to their educational qualifications and continue to be grossly under-represented as managers in large firms and institutions. Moreover, while the Chinese and African Asians have achieved broad parity with whites, the Indians and Caribbeans are relatively disadvantaged, and the Pakistanis and Bangladeshis continue to be severely disadvantaged. The qualifications, job-levels and earnings spread in 1994 are roughly what one would have predicted from the spread of qualifications in 1974, if racial exclusion was relaxed but not absent. Those groups that had an above-average middle-class professional and business profile before migration seem to have been able to re-create that profile despite the occupational downgrading that all minority groups initially experienced. The progress of ethnic minorities has also depended on their studying harder and longer than their white peers, and their working harder and longer in their jobs. The high representation of most of the Asian groups in self-employment may represent the same phenomenon. Certainly, self-employment has been critical to the economic survival and advancement of some groups, and to narrowing the earnings gap with whites. There is severe and widespread poverty amongst Pakistani and Bangladeshi households, with more than four out of five having an income below half the national average – four times as many as white non-pensioners. This is related to their poor qualification levels, collapse of the Northern manufacturing industries in which they were employed, large families, poor facility in English amongst women, and the very low levels of economic activity among women.

While many Caribbean people seem to have escaped from disadvantage, others are probably worse off in some ways than their equivalents 20 years ago. Young black men are disproportionately without qualifications, without work, without a stable family life, disproportionately in trouble with the police and in prison. Many young black women are in work, with earnings higher than white women's; but others are disproportionately likely to be lone parents, unemployed and in social housing – with all that implies for poverty. While for most groups disadvantage may be diminishing across the generations, this is less clearly the case for Caribbeans.

In the 1960s, it just about made sense to portray all non-white groups as uniformly disadvantaged in terms of educational, economic and professional opportunities. Today, with some minority groups, such as the African Asians and the Chinese, being among the highest academic achievers, and others, such as the Pakistanis and the Bangladeshis, continuing to be in intergenerational poverty, the idea that British racism would produce a common class position for all non-whites is unsalvageable. Race and class continue to interact but as much in making possible various forms of social mobility as in creating underclass formations. All non-white groups for the time being are still under-represented in the top jobs, but some of them have successfully re-created their pre-migration middle-class character. Moreover, not all those in poverty have given up their middle-class aspirations, as evidenced for example in the number of Caribbean women and South Asian men and women university students from working class homes (Modood and Acland, 1998).

DECLINE OF AN ATLANTOCENTRIC PERSPECTIVE

One of the most important developments has been to do not with class but with what we mean by 'race'. Here, Britain has been moving away from an Atlantocentric perspective. What I mean by an Atlantocentric model is the conceptualisation of the black–white relationship in the Atlantic rim as the paradigm of race relations (Modood,1993). The historical core of this model is the slave trade triangle, and the modern political core consists of the US civil rights movement, anti-apartheid, the urban and equal opportunities programmes that arose in response to riots and the prospect of social breakdown in the inner cities. In this way the Atlantic triangle could be said to be widened from Liverpool to West Africa – Virginia to London – Soweto to Los Angeles. As such it represents, of course, a valuable political force with much to its credit. Yet the conceptualisation of British race relations in Atlantocentric terms, even if it once seemed plausible, is currently faced with three problems. The first is the non-Atlantic character of the majority of non-white Britons. According to the 1991 census two of the three million people in Britain of non-European origins have origins from outside the Atlantic triangle, above all from the Indian sub-continent. They bring with them cultures, solidarities, communal authorities, aspirations, emnities, memories, including a colonial relationship of subordination, which is quite different from the Atlantic pattern.

The second flows from the first. Events outside the Atlantic world, outside of its intellectual and political frame, are now impinging on domestic British race relations – in fact more so than the race relations events within other parts of the Atlantic area are affecting Britain. Khalistan, Kashmir, and Khomeni; the Gulf War, the destruction of the mosque at Ayodha and the fate of multiculturalism in Bosnia; all have a greater influence on British race relations than the fortunes of the ANC in South Africa, Jesse Jackson or the riots of Los Angeles. In 1989 the chairman of the influential US congressional black caucus brought a large delegation to London to support the launch of a parallel organisation at Westminster; it has sunk without a trace. The Ayatollah Khomeni, without leaving Teheran, was able to inspire and possibly fund the creation of a 'Muslim Parliament' in London launched in 1992, which has repeatedly been able to capture the media headlines and, for better or for ill, colours majority–minority relations in the UK.

The third reason for the declining relevance of the Atlantocentric model is Britain's increasing integration into European political structures. If the principal Atlantic racial line is that of black–white, in Europe the fault-line Europa–Islam is equally if not of more importance in understanding contemporary prejudice and racism. I think it is already the case in Britain now, as it has been in Europe for some time, that the extra-European origin group that suffers the worst prejudice and exclusion are working-class 'visible' Muslims. As about two-thirds of all non-white people in the European Union are Muslims, Islamophobia and the integration of Muslims have rightly emerged as key race relations issues.

ETHNICITY UNPRIVATISED

Minority ethnicity, albeit white ethnicity, has traditionally been regarded in Britain as acceptable if it was confined to the privacy of family and community, and did not make any political demands. Earlier groups of migrants and refugees, such as the Irish or the Jews in the nineteenth and the first half of the twentieth century, found that peace and prosperity came easier the less public one made one's minority practices or identity. Perhaps for non-European origin groups, whose physical appearance gave them a visibility that made them permanently vulnerable to racial discrimination, the model of a privatised group identity was never viable. Yet, additionally, one has to acknowledge the existence of a climate of opinion quite different from that experienced by the earlier Irish or Jewish incomers.

In the last couple of decades the bases of identity-formation have undergone important changes and there has come to be a minority assertiveness as described in the Introduction, above. Identity has moved from that which might be unconscious and taken-for-granted because implicit in distinctive cultural practices to conscious and public projections of identity and the explicit creation and assertion of politicised ethnicities. This is part of a wider socio-political climate which is not confined to race and culture or non-white minorities. Feminism, gay pride, Quebeçois nationalism and the revival of Scottishness are some prominent examples of these new identity movements which have come to be an important feature in many countries in which class-politics has declined. Identities in this political climate are not implicit and private but are shaped through intellectual, cultural and political debates and become a feature of public discourse and policies, especially at the level of local government. The identities formed in such processes are fluid and susceptible to change with the political climate, but to think of them as weak is to overlook the pride with which they may be asserted, the intensity with which they may be debated and their capacity to generate community activism and political campaigns.

CULTURAL RACISM

British race relations policies and anti-racisms have been premised on the assumption that the problem is of an exclusionism typified by the notice that some landladies in the 1950s and 1960s put in their front windows: 'No Coloureds'. The imagined solution to this exclusionary tendency is symbolised by the black and white handshake that serves as the logo of the Commission for Racial Equality. But neither the problem nor the solution were ever quite so simple. The 'No-Coloureds' racism was not unitary: racists always distinguished among the groups they rejected, and while the likelihood of someone who discriminated against one group discriminating against other groups probably was high, the culturally constructed grounds of rejection varied depending upon the immigrant group.

The latter have over time developed to a point where colour-racism may continue to be a constant but the different brands of racism have separated out from each other. For example, white people who are racists towards some ethnic groups can yet admire other ethnic groups because of, for example, aspects of their subcultural styles:

Most typically, of course, many White working-class boys discriminate positively in favour of Afro-Caribbean subcultures as exhibiting a macho, proletarian style, and against Asian cultures as being 'effemi-nate' and 'middle-class'. Such boys experience no sense of contradic-tion in wearing dreadlocks, smoking ganja and going to reggae concerts whilst continuing to assert that 'Pakis Stink'. (Cohen, 1988: 83)

Les Back found these insights confirmed in his ethnographic study of a large South London council estate in 1985–87 (Back, 1993). He observed among the young Whites on the estate a 'neighbourhood nationalism', side-by-side and in tension with a British nationalism. While the latter was understood as a preserve of Whites, the former was based on racially mixed groups of friends and the prestigious position of black youth cul-tures and styles in the area, and embraced blacks as well as whites. The Vietnamese on the estate were, however, excluded from both these local patriotisms and therefore incurred 'the full wrath of the new racism which defines "outsiders" in terms of "cultural" difference' (228).

Cultural-racism is likely to be particularly aggressive against those minority communities that want to maintain, and not just defensively, some of the basic elements of their culture or religion; if, far from denying their difference (beyond the colour of their skin), they want to assert this difference in public and demand that they be respected just as they are. Some of the early researchers on racial discrimination in England were quite clear about the existence of a colour and cultural component in racial discrimination, and yet thought the former much the more important. A leading study in the 1960s by W.W. Daniel, for example, concluded:

> The experiences of white immigrants, such as Hungarians and Cypriots, compared to black or brown immigrants, such as West Indians and Asians, leaves no doubt that the major component in the discrimination is colour. (Daniel 1968: 209)

This was further confirmed for Daniel by the finding that West Indians experienced more discrimination than Asians, and he takes the view that people who physically differ most from the white population were dis-criminated against most and therefore, he argues, 'prejudice against Negroes is most deep-rooted and widespread' (209). In contrast, he thought that lighter-skinned Asians suffered from some discrimination for cultural reasons, but that this would tend to decrease for British-educated second generation Asians. While his prediction appears, on the surface, reasonable, it overlooked the increasing significance that cultural-racism was to play in determining attitudes to ethnic minorities.

The annual Social Attitudes Survey, which began in 1982, has consis-tently recorded, as have other surveys, that the English think there is more extreme prejudice against Asians than against Afro-Caribbeans. The differences, initially minor, have tended to widen. The most recent evidence shows that young white people are half as likely again to express prejudice against Asians as Caribbeans (Modood *et al.*, 1997: 352). It was also found that all ethnic groups believe that prejudice against Asians and/or Muslims is much the highest of all ethnic, racial or religious prejudices (Modood *et al.*, 1997: 133–4). Part of the explanation for the failure of Daniel's prediction may be found in Michael Banton's observation that:

> the English seemed to display more hostility towards the West Indians because they sought a greater degree of acceptance than the English wished to accord; in more recent times there seemed to have been more hostility towards Asians because they are insufficiently inclined to adopt English ways. (Banton, 1979: 242)

Since that time there has been a significant growth in black–white sociability and cultural synthesis, especially among young people. This is evident in the high esteem in which black cultural styles are held in high prestige, in the hero-worship of successful Black 'stars' in football and sport, music and entertainment (Boulton and Smith, 1992), and in how black–white marriage and cohabitation has become quite common in a way that has not occurred in the United States. Of those born in Britain, half of Caribbean men, and a third of women have a white partner at any time (compared to about 10 per cent of South Asians) (Modood *et al.*, 1997). It is particularly important to note that this sociability is not necessarily in a colour-blind assimilationist, 'passing for white' context in which racism is ignored. For some young people it can take place in ways in which black ethnicity and anti-racism are emphasised – or, indeed, are the point. Black persons can be admired not in spite of, but because of, their blackness, for their aesthetics, style and creativity as well as for their anti-racist resistance: for example, at a typical performance of the controversial black nationalist rap band, Public Enemy, more than half the audience will be white.

COMPETITION BETWEEN IDENTITIES

There have been attempts to form a single 'black' constituency out of the non-white settlers and their British-born descendants. Such attempts have sometimes seemed promising. But they have yet to succeed and it is not obvious that they will ever do so. For example, only a fifth of South Asians, with no significant age or class differences, ever think of themselves as 'black' (Modood *et al.*, 1997: 295). This is not an Asian repudiation of 'the essential black subject' (Hall, 1992) in favour of a more nuanced and more pluralised blackness, but a failure to identify with blackness at all. Hence, the last few years have seen the growing use of a plurality of identities to form pressure groups and coalitions to win public resources and influence and the emergence of open competition between them.

While some groups assert a racial identity based on the experience of having suffered racism, others choose to emphasise their family origins and homeland, others group around a caste or a religious sect as do Hindus such as the Patels or Lohanas, while yet others promote a trans-ethnic identity like Islam. Yet the competition between identities is not simply a competition between groups: it is within communities and within individuals. It is quite possible for someone to be torn between the claims of being, for example, 'black', Asian, Pakistani and Muslim, and also having to choose between them and the solidarities they represent or having to rank them, synthesise them or distribute them between different areas of one's life – and then possibly having to reconcile them with the claims of gender, class and Britishness.

The important contrast between groups was that religion is prominent in the self-descriptions of South Asians, and skin colour in that of Caribbeans. Although younger people are generally less connected to a religion than their elders, they still think religion is important to how they lead their lives. This is changing the character of religion in Britain, not just by diversifying religion but by giving it a greater public policy significance. Interestingly, the minority faiths are beginning to side with the Church of England against those who say multiculturalism requires a severing of the ties between religion and the state (Modood (ed.), 1997).

THE FUTURE OF ANTI-RACISM

In the three decades from the 1960s to the end of the 1980s there have in fact been two different anti-racisms, an earlier and later version. The early response, for example, in the shape of Campaign Against Racial Discrimination (CARD) in the 1960s, influenced by the US Civil Right Movement and the leadership of Martin Luther King Jr, was to deny the significance of the black–white dualism by arguing that we are all the same under the skin. This colour-blind humanism gave way, again first in the United States and more slowly in Britain where it only became prominent in the 1980s, to two forms of colour-consciousness. One form consisted in the recognition that the socio-economic disadvantage of non-whites and structural bias against them in all the institutions of a white society meant that monitoring by colour was essential to identify discrimination and measure inequalities and whether any progress in their elimination was being made.

The second form of anti-racism consisted in raising black consciousness, in getting black people to emphasise their blackness and pride in their roots, in solidarity with other black people and their struggles and in organising as black people in mutual self-help and collective empowerment (Malcolm X, 1966; Cleaver, 1968; Blauner, 1972). This movement was, in effect, to create a black identity or a black political ethnicity. The result was that the racists' dualism of people into black–white was accepted, even sharpened by racism-awareness, but reinterpreted. When this American anti-racist movement was pursued in Britain, there was a problem. For in Britain there was also a second dualism, a West Indian–Asian dualism. Despite the different political and cultural histories that this cleavage represented, British anti-racism, having accepted the first opposition between black and white, continued to deny any political or anti-racist significance to this second division (Modood, 1997).

The growing calls to revise and update anti-racism by pluralising the concept of political blackness are to be welcomed (eg Hall, 1988: 28; Jasper, 1993; Parekh, 1994: 102). An element of this project depends on the argument that a 'black' political identity does not compete with or replace other identities, for example, 'Asian', for, it is argued, different identities refer to different aspects of a person's social being or are emphasised in different situations, say, one in politics, the other to do with culture. As no one has yet given this idea any content, I am unsure as to what is being proposed. Who, for example, is to decide what is a political situation and what a cultural one? As a matter of fact, most of the minority of Asians who think of themselves as 'black' do not think so in relation to specific contexts but to what they perceive as a pervading fact of social existence (Modood *et al.*, 1997: 295–7). Moreover, is 'blackness' really available to Asians when some of the most thoughtful and acclaimed contributions to the development of 'blackness' are not about downgrading the cultural content but increasing the reference to African roots and the Atlantic experience (eg Gilroy, 1987, 1993)? Can political blackness, emotionally and intellectually, really hope to replace an ethnic blackness, with all its powerful resonances and appeals to self-pride, with a notion that is supposed to unite in certain limited contexts for pragmatic purposes? It is because I think that 'blackness' has so much of the history, sorrow, hopes and energy of descendants of African enslavement in the Atlantic world that I do not think that it can be turned into a politics that is neutral between different non-white groups. It cannot have the same meaning or equally give strength to those who can identify with that history and those who cannot.

There is in racial discrimination and colour-racism quite clearly a commonality of circumstance among people who are not white. It is partly what gives sense to the term 'ethnic minorities' and to suggestions for a 'rainbow coalition' (Modood, 1988: 402). The question is not whether coalitional anti-racism is desirable, but of what kind. My personal preference and commitment is for a plural politics that does not privilege colour-identities. We must accept what is important to people, and *we must be even-handed between the different identity formations*. Political blackness is an important constituent of this pluralism, but it can't be *the* over-arching basis of unity. The end of its hegemony is not without its problems and dangers, but is not to be regretted. A precondition of creating/recreating a coalitional pluralism is the giving up of the corrupting ideal of a solidaristic monism.

Indeed, one has to go further and have a sense of society that is more than just a coalition of non-whites, or, even, a coalition of the oppressed. One such sense of society is the idea of multicultural Britishness. The 1980s saw the promotion of a chauvinistic and ungenerous form of Britishness, for example, in some of the coverage of the Falklands War, in the Christian nationalism of the Education Reform Act of 1988, and in Norman Tebbit's 'cricket test'. Consequently, some anti-racists and social theorists wrote off nationalism as an inherently monistic, 'essentialist' and quasi-racist idea (for example, Gilroy, 1987; Anthias and Yuval-Davis, 1992). This was an over-reaction, and I am pleased too see that pluralistic notions of nationality and citizenship are now being elaborated (Parekh, 1990, 1998; Kymlicka, 1995; Miller, 1995).

It is clear that what is often claimed today in the name of racial equality is more than would have been recognised as such in the 1960s. The shift is from an understanding of equality in terms of individualism and cultural assimilation to a politics of recognition, to equality as encompassing public ethnicity. Equality is no longer simply about access to the dominant culture but also not having to hide or apologise for one's origins, family or community but expecting others to respect them and adapt public attitudes and arrangements so that the heritage they represent is encouraged rather than contemptuously expected to wither away. The challenge today is twofold. Firstly, to devise and pursue a pluralised concept of racial equality that focuses policy on the variously disadvantaged circumstances of some minority groups without assuming that all the ethnic monorities are worse off than the white population (Modood *et al.*, 1997). Secondly, to reach out for a multicultural Britishness that is sensitive to ethnic difference and incorporates a respect for persons as individuals and for the collectivities to which people have a sense of belonging. That means a multiculturalism that is happy with hybridity but has space for religious identities (Modood, 1998). Both hybridity and ethno-religious communities have legitimate claims to be accommodated in political multiculturalism; they should not be pitted against each other in an either-or fashion as is done all too frequently (by for example, Rushdie, 1991; Waldron, 1992). The emphasis on a new Britishness is particularly worth emphasising because there are people today who want not just to be black or Indian in Britain, but positively want to be black British or British Indians. They are not so much seeking civic rights against a hegemonic nationality as attempting to politically negotiate a place in an all-inclusive nationality.

Such political demands create argument and debate and unsettle identities, sentiments, symbols, stereotypes, etc., especially amongst the 'old' British. Yet, despite some wild rhetoric, it should be clear that the politics of ethnic identity is a movement of inclusion (at least from the side of those excluded) and social cohesion, not fragmentation. Translated into policy it could be a contribution to a renewal of British nationality or national-rebuilding of the sort exhorted by Prime Minister Blair, especially in his Labour Party conference speech of September 1997 (Jacques, 1997). The idea, as mistakenly once supposed by Salman Rushdie and quoted at the start of this chapter, that Britain is 'two worlds' of black and white, has rightly given way to a more sensitive awareness of plurality. But it is a plurality that aspires to be not just 'in' Britain but 'of' Britain.

NOTES

1.   The evidence for the factual claims in this and the next four paragraphs is to be found in Modood *et al.*, 1997.

REFERENCES

Ali, Y. (1991), 'Echoes of Empire: Towards A Politics of Representation', in *Enterprise and Heritage: Cross Currents of National Culture* (eds J. Cromer and S. Harvey), Routledge.

Anthias, F. and Yuval-Davis, N. (1992), *Racialised Boundaries*, Routledge.

Back, L. (1993), '"Race" Identity and Nation Within An Adolescent Community in South London', *New Community*, 19: 217–33.

Ballard, R. and Kalra, V.S. (1994), *The Ethnic Dimension of the 1991 Census*, University of Manchester.

Blauner, R. (1972), *Racial Oppression in America: Essays in Search of a Theory*, Harper and Row.

Boulton, M.J. and Smith, P. (1992), 'Ethnic Preferences and Perceptions Among Asian and White British Middle School Children', *Social Development*, 1(1): 55–66.

Cleaver, E. (1968), *Soul on Ice*, McGraw Hill.

Cohen, P. (1988) 'The Perversions of Inheritance: Studies In The Making Of Multi-Racist Britain', in *Multi-Racist Britain* (eds P. Cohen and S. Bains), Macmillan.

Commission for Racial Equality (1990), *Britain: A Plural Society*.

Daniel, W.W. (1968), *Racial Discrimination in England: a Penguin Special based on the PEP Report*, Penguin.

Donald, J. and Rattansi, A. (eds) (1992), *'Race', Culture and Difference*, Sage.

Gilroy, P. (1987), *There Ain't no Black in the Union Jack*, Routledge.

Gilroy, P. (1992), 'The End of Anti-Racism' in *'Race', Calture and Difference* (eds J. Donald and A. Rattansi), Sage, originally published as a Runnymede Trust lecture in 1987.

Gilroy, P. (1993), *The Black Atlantic: Modernity and Double Consciousness*, Verso.

Hall, S. (1988), 'New Ethnicities', in *Black Film, British Cinema* (ed. K. Mercer), also in *'Race', Culture and Difference* (eds J. Donald and A. Rattansi), Sage, 1992.

Hall, S. (1992), 'The Question of Cultural Identity' in *Modernity and its Futures*, (eds S. Hall and T. McGrew), Polity Press.

Jacques, M. (1997), 'The Melting Pot That Is Born-Again Britannia', The *Observer*, 28 December, pp. 14–15.

Jasper, L. (1993), 'Shades of Blackness!', *Black To Black*, Issue No. 2, 1990 Trust.

Jones, T. (1993), *Britain's Ethnic Minorities*, Policy Studies Institute.

Kymlicka, W. (1995), *Multicultural Citizenship*, Oxford University Press.

Malcolm X. (1966), *The Autobiography of Malcolm X*, written with Alex Hailey, Hutchinson and Collins.

Miller, D. (1995), *On Nationality*, Oxford University Press.

Modood, T. (1988), '"Black", Racial Equality and Asian Identity', *New Community*, 14(2).

Modood, T. (1990), 'British Asian Muslims and The Rushdie Affair' *The Political Quarterly*, 61(2), 143–60; also in *'Race', Culture and Difference* (eds J. Donald and A. Rattansi), Sage, 1992.

Modood, T. (1991), 'The Indian Economic Success: A Challenge To Some Race Relations Assumptions', *Policy and Politics*, 19(3); also in Modood, T. (1992), *Not Easy Being British: Colour, Culture and Citizenship*, Runnymede Trust and Trentham Books.

Modood, T. (1992), *Not Easy Being British: Colour, Culture and Citizenship*, Runnymede Trust and Trentham Books.

Modood, T. (1993), 'The Limits of America: Re-thinking Equality in the Changing Context of British Race Relations', in *The Making of Martin Luther King and the Civil Rights Movement* (eds B. Ward and T. Badger), Macmillan.

Modood, T. (1994), 'Political Blackness and British Asians', *Sociology*, 28(4).

Modood, T. (1997), '"Difference", Cultural Racism and Anti-Racism' in *Debating Cultural Hybridity* (eds P. Werbner and T. Modood), Zed Books.

Modood, T. (ed.) (1997), *Church, State and Religious Minorities*, Policy Studies Institute, 1997.

Modood, T. (1998), 'Anti-Essentialism, Multiculturalism and the "Recognition" of Religious Minorities', *Journal of Political Philosophy*.

Modood, T. and Acland, T. (eds) *Race and Higher Education*, Policy Studies Institute, 1998.

Modood, T., Beishon, S. and Virdee, S. (1994), *Changing Ethnic Identities*, Policy Studies Institute.

Parekh, B. (1990), 'Britain and the Social Logic of Pluralism' in Commission for Racial Equality, *Britain: A Plural Society*, London.

Parekh, B. (1994), 'Minority Rights, Majority Values', in *Reinventing The Left*, (ed. D. Milliband), Polity Press.

Parekh, B. (1998), 'National Identity', The Kapila Lecture.

Rushdie, S. (1982), 'The New Empire Within Britain', *New Society*, 9 December.

Rushdie, S. (1991), 'In Good Faith' in S. Rushdie *Imaginary Homelands*.

Shukra, K. (1993), 'Black Politics and Ethnicity in Britain', British Sociological Association Conference on 'Research Imaginations', University of Essex, April.

Sivanandan, A. (1985), 'RAT and the Degradation of the Black Struggle', *Race and Class*, XXVI(4).

Sivanandan, A. (1987), *A Different Hunger: Writings on Black Resistance*, Pluto Press.

Sivanandan, A. (1995), 'Interview', *CARF*, February/March.

Waldron, J. (1992), 'Minority Cultures and The Cosmopolitan Alternative', *University of Michigan Journal of Law Reform*, (25), 3 & 4.

11 From Berkeley to Blair: a Dialogue of the Deaf?
Anne Showstack Sassoon

TRAJECTORIES PERSONAL AND POLITICAL

Thinking about the past provides the occasion, for those of us who have lived it, not only to analyse political, social, and economic developments, or cultural trends, but our own growth and development, or lack of it. Noticeably absent, however, from most political or intellectual discussions is self-interrogation. This is not surprising given the vulnerablity that this can expose. There is a strange pretence that we have always been what we are now. Convincing intellectual and political argument, whatever the content, wears the clothes of infallibility. By convention academic and political legitimacy and authority are rooted in certainty, which is required both of those in leading roles, and, it is expected, of those who accept such leadership. A parent–child relationship is constituted in which little if any change and development is expected of either part.

Reflective modes of debate run the risk, of course, of self-indulgent narcissism. Such narcissism is neither useful nor attractive and only rarely interesting. There should be a place, however, for reflecting on personal trajectories as one, even if a small, contribution to producing some of the questions which can inform wider discussions. Private trajectories, of course, are not representative or even pre-figurative of wider truths, but they can provide insights into wider phenomena. What follow are some explorations and conjectures, no more than that, which grow out of trying to learn from rather than take for granted the widespread opposition to Blair and New Labour of the generation of the left whose political culture is rooted in the 1960s. Those of us who, while not endorsing every aspect, feel comfortable with Blair's political project because we see it as expressing many of the aspirations and criticisms of mainstream politics going back to the 1960s, are few and far between. We are oddballs, or at the very least non-conformists.

DISSENT FROM THE POLITICS OF DESPAIR

The fact that some of us have gone in another direction from this 1960's left 'mainstream' does not feel, at least, like movement to the 'right' or weary accommodation to a supposed neo-liberal hegemony. How is it possible that some of us dissent and look to the future if not with confidence at least with hope? A new political generation is in power which has both been influenced by and rejects its elders. Those elders, my contemporaries, in turn, lacking recognition, refuse to believe that any of their ideals can become reality. This is in part because a lifetime of oppositional politics is deeply conditioning. It is also because the collapse of communism, the challenge of globalisation, and nearly 20 years of neo-liberal hegemony in the US and Britain have contributed to undermining the real capacities and the political legitimacy of state intervention and much of the expertise and professional practice associated with it. It needs to be reiterated that New Left criticism and the contradictory effects of welfare state provision have also played their role in undermining the postwar consensus. This alienation, particularly evident in demoralised state sector professionals, has lead to no little political despair as the symbols and much of the content of the left politics of decades gone by have been relegated to the scrapheap. A still younger generation in their teens and twenties were delighted to be rid of the Tories. Rebranding Britain without any need for exhortations from above, they are engaged in their own opposition to parental figures. They are probably only interested in political relics from the past as artefacts.

REFLECTIONS, EXPLORATIONS, CONJECTURES

I grew up in the United States before coming to this country in 1966. The 1960s were the period of my secondary and university education. From a political perspective, my life spanned joining the Young Democrats at 16 and helping to elect John F. Kennedy in 1960, when that was a radical thing to do in Orange County, California, to attending the University of California, Berkeley from 1962–66 during the period of mobilisation around civil rights, the free speech movement, and the Vietnam War, and coming to the LSE just before it erupted at the end of the decade. There I studied the work of Antonio Gramsci and Marxist theory more generally, the history of the working-class movement in Europe, the Russian Revolution, and Italian fascism. Along with new-found friends from the British student left, I shared anti-Americanism, dismissed Labour politics because the British government supported American intervention in Vietnam, and was inspired by a heroic image of the working class. Recently I re-read some of my own work from a decade later, and I was struck by how the easy use of leftist language, for example, reference to 'the masses', conveys the impression of certainties long gone. However, this represents only one aspect of how many of us felt. Inspired by many different sources, for example, not only Gramsci but Trotsky and later Althusser, there was enormous excitement about going beyond cold war dichotomies and 'free world' complacency to engage with racism, sexual discrimination, and poverty and to feel that new spaces were opening up and that a different future was possible. We may have started, in my case, with Kennedy's New Frontier but we ended up using the forbidden language of Marxism, forbidden, that is, by associating it only with the worst excesses of communism. We felt we were overthrowing the patriarchs as we criticised the assumptions of both 'sides'. We did not think we were embracing old dogmas, even if we may have argued dogmatically to the dismay of our elders.

As paradoxical as it may now seem, we employed the words of old-fashioned Marxism, and many of the songs and symbols of the Old Left, of our elders, to condemn what we had inherited. Depending on which political uniform we adopted, the style varied, but our arguments and practices were adorned by different combinations of Marxism–Leninism, vanguard party, barricades, spontaneity vs leadership, reformism vs revolution, utopia, freedom against authority, feeling vs rationality, youth vs age, sexual freedom vs sexual inhibition. Some of us, eventually, adopted the language of Gramsci to try to rethink left politics in terms of possibilities rather than guarantees. Indeed, this is the sense of a beautiful essay by Stuart Hall who has provided such an important role model, of integrating what is useful in Gramsci, Althusser, and more recently Foucault, to engage with what is new rather than to try to force reality into old schemas.[1]

We went on, some of us, to try to understand what challenges historical development poses to our very way of thinking. This has, of course, taken a wide variety of forms, especially under the impetus of the collapse of communism in Eastern Europe and of traditional Social Democracy. Reactions have varied from complete rejection of the past to clasping desperately to what are considered eternal verities. The biggest challenge of all, however, is to build on what is useful from the past while ridding ourselves of what is holding us back from the growth and development necessary to negotiate transitions as the construction of better futures rather than merely the destruction of the past.

We have inevitably to move on. Yet in doing so we also have to recognise that the present and future are inevitably built upon elements of the past, and that the very attempt to destroy it undermines our personal and political capacities. But if this recognition, however, is to be constructive, it must be something very different from defending the indefensible, from holding on for dear life because of the fear of loss, understandable though this may be before a better future takes concrete form. We have to acknowledge loss, to grieve for what is dead, and to face the future courageously, not as political heroines or heroes, but as naturally anxious human beings. It is this tension between what is lost, what remains, and what will or can be that delineates not only our human condition but social and historical progress, in the sense of moving forward, on a voyage of change.

LONG SHADOWS OF LOSS AND DESTRUCTION

Recently I have been reflecting on how the perception of time changes at different points in the lifecycle. In this context I have thought about the difference between growing up in the postwar period in the United States compared to in Britain, and about how little I understood at the time. The following has struck me. The experience of the war was so recent in the 1960s that both what was said and what was left unsaid or repressed in the postwar period must have cast a long shadow even over those developments which were new and different. In Britain, unlike in the US, the physical destruction and consequent rebuilding of cities and the construction of new towns, however much we might now be critical of what was built with eyes and needs formed by a later period, must have had a major impact. The demand to remake society, and support for the postwar settlement, must have related to what people saw and experienced daily. The consensus around the welfare state reflected the desire not to go back to the social and economic conditions of the 1930s. But this consensus must also have been buttressed by a sensation that society was improving. This was not false ideology or the product of social engineers or modernist writers but was rooted in the daily lives of millions of people. Not only was decent housing urgently needed, but getting rid of the rubble and filling in empty spaces would have reminded people daily that life *could* improve. This impression must have been reinforced by the experience of full male employment, along with the continuing participation of married women in the paid labour force, and reforms in health, education, and other social provision. There was 'good' and 'bad' in this, but the 'new' was literally, concretely, no pun intended (!), the stuff of everyday experience.

The lacunae wrought by war were filled, in private lives as well as the physical fabric of society. But ambivalent feelings were undoubtedly aroused. We can also understand why, in the face of postwar changes, a certain conservatism emerged as a reaction to the disruptions and terrible human and material losses of the Second World War. It is true that the return by many women to more traditional family roles and the dismantling of nurseries after the war were reinforced by the arguments of psychologists and sociologists which became embedded in the professional expertise of social workers, teachers, and others about what was 'normal' and 'good' for children and families. These arguments, which Denise Riley has analysed so well in her book *War in the Nursery*,[2] can certainly be criticised. But both their acceptance at the time and their continued persistence in British political debate, so different in most other European countries, must be explained by something more than the influence of experts.

Large-scale change never takes place unless it also corresponds to needs in the lives of millions of people who never experience such transitions merely as victims of policy or of ideology. There never was, and never can be, a complete return to the past. Women never simply go back to their pre-war lives even if they do not continue all of their wartime roles. Long shadows were undoubtedly cast by the terrible disruption of the war years. Sudden death and loss of homes and possessions, separation and physical dislocation marked the lives of millions of people of different generations in Britain, and to an even greater extent those in occupied Europe, witnessed by British troups at the end of the war and reported in the news broadcasts of the time. Moreover, it is likely that guilt caused by surviving, so well known by Holocaust survivors, was a widespread phenomenon in the population at large.

Death, destruction and loss were, of course, also accompanied by new freedoms. Untraditional paid work brought greater economic freedom, and women enjoyed wider cultural and sexual horizons, not least because of the influence of American troops. Food parcels from America, jazz and American movies and G.I. brides probably all contributed to the British love–hate relationship with the US. But millions of women also experienced heavy, multiple burdens as they laboured to look after themselves and their children, keep house, contain the fear of death, and find some laughter and enjoyment in difficult wartime circumstances. Is it really surprising then that many felt that what they wanted after the war was a husband in full-time work earning a wage to cover household needs, the so-called 'family wage' so much more common then than now, a washing machine and a hoover, a comfortable home, perhaps a house with a garden, eventually a car, and some paid work for an element of financial independence?

FREE OF FEAR, FREE TO CRITICISE

We now have the luxury, which many of us began to enjoy in the 1960s if not earlier, of being free from the fears and the deprivations of the depression, a defining moment for several generations of Americans in the same way as the war was for the British, to criticise materialism while enjoying affluence and new educational, professional, and political possibilities. We are right not to feel guilty about this. But having closed our ears to endless parental stories of earlier deprivations and why we should be grateful to previous generations, as well as having experienced the effects of so many silences about loss and fear of loss, perhaps we can now also begin to appreciate the impact of the context of our parents and grandparents on public policy and political projects.[3] We can continue to enjoy memories of the excitement of discovery while recognising that the new worlds of years gone by were neither perfect ideals nor suitable any longer for changed circumstances. We can continue to adhere to many of the aims of the past, and still admit that some were neither possible nor perhaps even desirable in the light of further understanding. We can seek better means of obtaining what is still desirable but not yet reached while also building on new insights to aim at new and better goals.

At the end of the century it is often hard to appreciate fully what the achievements of abortion and homosexual law reform and anti-discrimination legislation represent. The beginning of the end of deference in Britain including the flowering of youth culture was related to the expansion of educational opportunities and an improvement in living standards. These and other changes have represented truly major advances. They are not undone because we now can also recognise their limitations. We may now be critical of some of the effects of much urban regeneration from the 1960s. Of course 'people should have known better'. But any mature analysis would recognise that what is no longer considered acceptable, or 'progressive', could still have constituted an advance at the time. If we place Britain in a wider European context, we can acknowledge that, for example, Le Corbusier's modernist housing for workers was a good deal better than the conditions that millions of people had endured up to then. Separate kitchens – isolating as they may feel now – were an improvement on living in a one-room slum. It is important to avoid, to use an inelegant term, 'presentism', that is, condemning the past from today's standpoints. What was a reasonable decision because of contemporary understandings and widespread demands would not be reasonable today in changed circumstances and with the benefit of hindsight.

Criticism of the past should bring humility about the present and help us to avoid both old and new mistakes. But attempts to destroy the past is disabling and the mirror image, I might add, of holding on for dear life and against all odds to what we know and what is familiar however problematic it may be.[4] Our taken-for-granted 'common sense' derives in large part from previous experience. What was once exciting and new comes to be internalised and transforms what appears 'normal' and 'natural'. A deeply conservative cynicism about whether change is possible can develop, even when change is taking place all around us, because we fail to historicise and relativise past and present.

WHAT CELEBRATION OF 1968? OR
TEN YEARS IS A LONG TIME

Indeed, the past looks different at different points in time. This can be illustrated by focusing on what for many encapsulates the 1960s politically: 1968. That year represents what many people consider the political high point of the decade, the culmination of student militancy in the US and student movements in the UK and elsewhere, the May events in France, the Prague Spring and the Soviet invasion of Czechoslovakia, and so on. Yet compared to ten years ago, my impression is that very little is being said about 1968. This is probably a result of how much has changed in the last decade, not only the fall of communism, but also the undermining of a neo-liberal hegemony if not its disappearance, and the emergence of a centre-left politics which claims to be radical. Re-reading what I wrote for an Italian left journal, *Rinascita*, on the British reaction to the twentieth anniversary of May 1968, it struck me that despite many differences, some observations may still be relevant. I noted that given the political significance of 1968 in countries like France and Italy, it would have been easy to misread the media coverage which the anniversary engendered in Britain. This included television and radio programmes, several major books and therefore lengthy book reviews, newspaper articles, magazine inserts, even a festival of nostalgia and celebration. But a word of caution before we romanticise the past. What was significant about this interest was not so much the *content* which focused above all on the French May, but what these activities had to say about Britain in 1988. First, and by no means least, the men, and it was mainly men, who made the programmes, wrote the books, and organised debates were the generation who lived 1968 as a life event in its way as significant as the second world war for another generation.

There was a mixture of nostalgia, a feeling of lost youth and unfulfilled promises, the memory of sexual adventure. Questions were asked about what it had all meant. The sensation that nothing was the same afterward and that things changed and yet so much remained the same or was worse with the Right in power combined with an enormous ambivalence about lost illusions and about impossible yet marvellous utopias. Of course, all these could be dismissed as the musings of 40 somethings expressing their mid-life crisis in a public way and transferring a cycle of personal change on to a political dimension. And yet, the very fact that they were, and many still are, in positions of power as intellectuals who controlled and influenced the media or held academic positions was itself a significant outcome of 1968 and a comment on Britain both ten years ago and now.

DIALOGUE OF THE DEAF

We can understand the relative silence about 1968 today and the alienation of the 1968 generation better if we consider the following. Ten years on there has been a significant displacement with Blair in power, oppositional politics, the only kind of politics most of us know, detached from engagement with concrete programmes of reform, in a moment when it is impossible to return to pre-1979, and there are many reasons for not doing so. We confront a younger and different generation in the corridors of power who find it difficult if not impossible to articulate anything good about the left politics of a previous generation. A dialogue of the deaf ensues. The oldies have their political antennae tuned to another station whose music they recognise. They shut their ears to new accounts of a world that has changed so much compared to their youth. They do not even hear the argument that achieving social justice requires a different story line if there is to be a happy ending. And just as new worlds are opening up in Britain, the desire for the solutions of times past, so long repressed under the impact of 18 years of Conservative governments, explodes but remains unanswered by those in power.

And yet, rather like in the post-war period, but for different reasons, there are huge silences almost as if fantasy fears reality. In the leftist opposition to the government, who speaks, as we used to do, of poverty traps caused by the workings of the benefit and tax systems? Where are the demands for full employment? Why, we used to ask, was money spent on unemployment benefits when people – usually meaning men – could be working, spending money, and paying taxes? Demands were made for new opportunities for women to be in formal paid work, and for the provision of good child-care as a precondition for making women's rights a reality. After all, it was said, women were not only mothers. No one, we used to say, should be stuck on benefits. Of course, much of this was itself oversimplified. It took time to incorporate a richer understanding of the pleasures as well as the responsibilities of parenting, to put men into the equation, and to make some progress in incorporating the needs of the disabled and of the elderly. Yet what is striking is how much is being repressed. This is caused, I think, by widespread ambivalence about change and personal growth, which after all always implies loss as earlier states of being disappear.

This is certainly true of a generation of intellectuals whose world view changed forever after 1968 and who occupy important spaces, however constrained, which have formed significant threads of the fabric of Britain under Thatcherism. It was easy in 1988 to see only those aspects of a complex present which seemed to negate the hopes of 1968: the BBC was under increasing government pressure; the universities had to defend themselves by showing how they could succeed according to the logic of the market; the moral panic associated with AIDS led to a new attack on homosexuality, and the possibility of restrictions imposed on abortion. Ten years ago there was a tone of self-criticism, of 'how could we be so young and naive', a painful cry of personal and political crisis, a feeling of impotence and dismay or adolescent defiance. In 1998 now that we once more have a Labour government, howls of betrayal drown out any soul-searching as 18 years of opposition to the Conservatives appear unrecognised by those in power. Yet if we listen carefully to the ways in which that crisis was expressed in 1988 and think about it with a sensitivity formed by the needs of the present as much as the experience of the past, there is much we can learn from this ten years old 'celebration–mourning' of 1968.

PASSING THE TORCH TO WOMEN

It is not a reductive or simplistic feminism in 1988 to note that the voices we heard and therefore the message we received were masculine. This was not surprising. After all the best known protagonists of 1968 were almost all male. Women were present and were active, but it was not women's historical moment, even if, according to these 1988 commentators, it made our moment possible. And in 1988 this was a theme voiced by men on the left who, in what was in large part a romanticised and idealised view, made a ritual bow in the direction of feminism which, it was said, had continued to pursue the promises and aspirations of 1968. Feminism was granted (rather than having seized) responsibility for putting the personal on the political agenda. It was women above all who demanded an authentic politics rooted in subjectivity and reflecting the need for autonomy and self-fulfillment, and carried on questioning old roles and old authorities, above all traditional definitions of gender and sexuality. Most importantly, it was said, feminism had undertaken that historical task contained in the promise of 1968 to break with the old, to re-think society from a new perspective, to ask unasked questions, to speak the unspeakable.

Yet women of the 1968 generation know something which goes beyond a ritual gesture to what is presented as a last hope delegated to 'the others', that is, which is voiced as a delegation rather than as part of an assumption of shared responsibility. We know the pain, the effort, the exhaustion, the wounds, the disorientations, the resistances, the repetitions and the search for reassuring structures which have been part of this break with the old. We also know the excitement accompanying this growth, this experiencing life as process rather than structure, this leap into the future – without any guarantees of an endpoint, for there is none. Having experienced the fear of the unknown, we can understand if men hesitate before a similar process yet we can still be angry confronted by this abdication and delegation. We also recognise the exhaustion of juggling roles and trying to perform, made to measure, for what structurally and to a considerable extent also culturally is still, in the main, a man's world.

ASSUMING RESPONSIBILITY FOR A CHANGE

It should also, once more, be pointed out that perhaps the politically most significant immediate effect of the anti-authoritarianism, anti-statism, and the general critique of the corporatist consensus of post-war politics was the victory of the new right which was determined and able to make that break which neither the new nor the old left managed and yet prepared the way for. We cannot ignore the fact that Blair and New Labour and the support for New Labour in the last election and afterward are related to that failure. Why has the right always tended to be so much better at understanding an epoch than the left? Perhaps because the new right, itself one of the products of what Gramsci might have described as a long-term organic crisis, of which 1968 was another manifestation, learnt the lesson taught by one of the theoretical fathers of conservatism, Edmund Burke, that history is process and that institutions have no choice but to change to ensure social continuity. But the lesson is not just one of conservation. If the aim is radical change and renewal, and the establishment of legitimacy for a new political project, one which cannot simply be overturned by the next government, change not must not only be shaped in a progressive direction through public policy promoted from on high but must be based on widespread consent and reflect needs articulated from below.

The right learned to articulate and to respond sufficiently to demands to organise and maintain a social basis of consent in order to shape and manage its version of a modernising project. Many on the left, meantime, dazzled by the rapidity and apparent fragmentation of change, continued, and continue, to clasp the life-raft of the old. In fact, the past never disappears completely but has to be integrated because it serves inevitably as the basis of the new, however radical or, as we once said, revolutionary. Yet so often what is truly novel is obscured by the energy expended holding on to the old or, on the contrary, seeking a clear break, abandoning the project altogether. Will the left be able to learn to look at the new and to analyse the past without simplistic schemas? Will renewed interest in the 1960s provide the occasion for doing so which the celebration of 1968 ten years ago failed to do?

But New Labour also bears some responsibility. A hand might be held out to those of good will who could, if encouraged, make a journey of discovery and contribute to renewing the country. Social creativity and social entrepreneurship, so praised by the gurus of New Labour, often imply untidy, messy and unintended outcomes which are stepping stones to new problems as well as new solutions. A celebration of diversity as a distinguishing mark of new brand Britain, and a recognition of the social worth of providing care, both of which have roots in 1960s politics, could create connections outwards and across political generations to the benefit of the government and the society. Social consensus and social creativity could both be enhanced. If the older political generation of 1960s leftists does not respond because of problems of identity and recognition, perhaps a younger, more open and more energetic generation will.

NOTES

1.   Stuart Hall, 'The problem of ideology: marxism without guarantees', in *Stuart Hall. Critical Dialogues in Cultural Studies*, (eds D. Morley and K.-Hs. Che), Lawrence and Wishart, 1996.
2.   Denise Riley, *War in the Nursury. Theories of the Child and the Mother*, Virago, 1983.
3.   Recent reflection on how relieved refugees from continental Europe must have been to arrive in Britain before and after the war, and British intellectuals to have avoided Nazi occupation has made me understand much better than earlier a generation of intellectuals whose

view of Britain was above all of tolerance and pluralism. Of course, this reinforced a certain British complacency and self-satisfaction about the British political system in the 1960s which we criticised so vehemently. As 1960s leftists were not shy of pointing out, both the literature on British politics, forever stressing British continuity and supposed lack of profound social cleavages, in implicit contrast to France, and mainstream political debate in the 1960s appeared blind to the history of class conflict, imperialist domination, and racism.

4. This is exemplified in the exchange between Christopher and Peter Hitchens, 'Oh brother, what a time', The *Sunday Times*, 1 March 1998.

12 Crafting a New Social Settlement*
Paul Hirst

Modern industrial societies have little to hope for in common. At the top of the pile individuals may expect a big bonus or at the bottom they may dream of winning the lottery. But we no longer have collective imagined futures that are capable of mobilising and inspiring masses of people. The reason for that is that we appear to have no viable methods of how we might govern our affairs to improve them. The models that we have relied on for the better part of the century have worn out. Those of the centre left faded with the discovery that it was far from easy in the long run to manage the economy to provide full employment and steady growth. Those of the right are dying as people recoil from the true consequences of unregulated markets and overwhelming corporate power.

State *dirigisme* and *laissez faire* are both discredited. The other form of governance, that made state action effective, and the current desperate return to *laissez faire* unnecessary, was corporatism. Yet after a heroic period in which in many countries it helped to stabilise economies after the oil-price inflation of 1973, it too has become less effective. We shall return to the reasons for the failure of corporatism below.

The point is that the social changes that undermined corporatist governance as a 'third way' between state intervention and the market have created the conditions for the appearance of a new model, associative democracy. Associative democracy aims to devolve as many tasks of governance as possible – in economics, politics and welfare – to self-governing voluntary associations. The claim is that by deepening and extending democratic control, more effective because more local and, therefore, better informed decisions will be made, thus improving economic and social governance. This model is both radical and practical. It is also capable of attracting support from across the political spectrum from those who reject the decayed orthodoxies of the right and the left. It is the best option for continuing the negotiated co-ordination of market economies of corporatism and the social solidarity made possible by welfare states.

* This essay first appeared in *New Times*; the editors wish to thank the journal for permission to publish it here.

The classic form of governance through negotiation and bargaining is corporatism – the regulation of capitalism through co-ordination by organised interests at national and at plant level. Industry, organised labour and the state co-operated in order to secure sustainable commitments by each of the parties. Corporatism has been one of the most effective institutional supports of the large-firm economy in the post-1945 advanced world. But it has been threatened by economic and industrial changes that have made it more difficult to bargain through centralised organised interests.

Divisions of labour and forms of manufacturing organisation have changed radically since the early 1970s. The workforce has differentiated as a consequence of the decline of standardised mass production. Such changes have led to a blurring of the blue/white collar boundary in changing structures of skill. Unions are now less representative of labour as a whole and less able to centralise bargaining around the common interests of the labour force. At the same time, the structures of 'the firm' have been changing rapidly. Increasingly, highly-centralised top-down control has been abandoned in favour of more responsive forms of organisation able to cope with changing demand, rapid innovation, and the flexible production of a wide range of goods. Decentralisation, de-merger, the growth of inter-firm partnerships, and relational sub-contracting, weaken the classical managerial line of command and also mean that the interests of industry are more and more difficult to represent through national business federations.

The new forms of negotiated governance – networks, partnerships, trust-relationships that are emerging after the decline of national corporatism – are more specific and more evanescent, less capable of being synthesised into a 'model' on a national scale. The state too is less of an effective corporatist partner than it was in the era of the post-1945 great boom. States have fewer capacities to determine macro-economic conditions and thus have less to offer labour and business in exchange for their compliance.

The decline of corporatism and the weakening of Keynesian demand management strategies have limited the scope for distinct national responses to changing economic circumstances. Not only have general models of governance ceased to be effective guides to political actors but their embodiment in distinctive 'national' models is now increasingly under threat. Until recently, specific national capitalisms could be held up as models to the laggards in industrial performance and economic governance – West Germany, Japan and Sweden being the most often cited examples. The Swedish combination of comprehensive welfare, active full-employment policies, centralised corporatist bargaining, and highly concentrated internationally competitive industrial companies has clearly 'unravelled', even though popular support for welfare institutions remains strong. Germany and Japan are both increasingly seen as problematic models suffering from weaknesses and constraints that are systemic rather than conjunctural.

The problem now is that models at every level seem less applicable. This is not to say that there are no new forms of governance and no specific experiences from which others can learn. There are a great many examples of institutional and organisational innovation. Firms are engaged in many evolving experiences of partnership, of building networks, of creating new working practices, and of seeking new relationships with customers, suppliers and employees. Governance through negotiation continues to develop in many forms at local level: new relationships between companies, local authorities and public agencies, worker groups, and local associations and activists.

Thus the problem is not that nothing is happening in the creation of new forms of governance. It is that such changes are specific to definite localities, evanescent, and subject to constant revision. They are thus difficult to generalise or to learn from – in part because they are processes rather than a settled architecture of institutions. Models of the old kind offered firms, societies and states that were seeking to catch up, the chance to do things by numbers, to copy institutional designs and practices. Keynesian demand management was available to any medium-sized state with a large enough public-sector and a competent civil service. 'Fordism' was an ideal–typical model of industrial efficiency that could be copied and adapted to local circumstances by mediocre firms.

Models also meant that much of society was following the same script; that fact ensured a degree of uniformity and an ability to grasp the prevailing institutional architecture. Such simplicity had significant advantages – societies where institutions are localised and rapidly changing, are hard places for all but the most talented and adaptable to live in, and difficult for outsiders to break into. They make accountability above the level of the local difficult and common standards all but impossible.

Those who hanker after the uniform governance of the nation state, for social democratic fairness and common standards of life, and for settled industrial routines, will find this new and evanescent world threatening. We cannot go back to such uniformity in governance, but we need to go beyond a situation where the only certainties are perpetual learning and institutions that exist only in evolution. A world of examples cannot create an economic and political system. A patchwork world of this kind is also unlikely to be a successful or sustainable one. Modern societies need to sustain broad-based prosperity. If this cannot be had by the old social-democratic national state-based strategies then we must find new ones, adapted to less stable and standardised production regimes but which will have similar effects.

In the absence of new models, the old ones persist – increasingly inaccurate and pernicious in their effects. A good example is our unthinking use of liberal notions of a democratic state in a market society, with a clear division of public and private spheres, and of 'civil society' as a realm of voluntary action and private freedom. Yet this liberal architecture is a gross misdescription of the structure of modern societies.

There is now no clear divide between the public and the private spheres, between democracy and markets, public and private choice. In fact modern societies are dominated by very similar large organisations on both sides of the formal public–private divide: business corporations, big public bureaucracies, quangos, and many intermediate kinds of organisations. These are in the main weakly accountable to those to whom they provide services.

The space between the public and private spheres is crossed by a wide variety of large governments, which are neither answerable through democratic elections nor through the market choices of consumers. Much of private life is dominated by large corporate businesses. We thus are faced with a post-liberal organisational society in which the fundamental relationship on either side of the public–private divide is that between a service provider and its clients, and in which the old liberal relationships of citizens and representative government, sovereign consumer and neutral market mean less and less.

For most purposes people are confronted by organisations, and even though those organisations directly affect their interests they have very little to say in how they are run. The institutional architecture of a post-liberal society is so different that conventional economic liberal measures to boost accountability are no longer effective: downsizing government simply shifts the government functions of large organisations from one formal constitutional site to another, from public to private, or public to quasi-public; and attempting to restore the role of 'markets' is not to remove individuals from the scope of governance, but to shift the agencies that perform the functions from state to corporate bureaucracies.

Responding to the institutional architecture of a post-liberal society requires that schemes for democratisation and reform cross the boundary between civil society and the state, that they explicitly tackle the broader issues of the governance powers of all organisations and not confine their remedies to government and to the state. Civil society needs to be made 'public', its organisations being accepted as governing powers over which citizens with significant affected interests should have a say proportionate to their involvement and the risk to their interests. Thus organisations – state and non-state – need to be treated as political, not merely administrative or private, and the relevant publics given a greater direct role as organisational 'citizens'. If supposedly private organisations are governmental, then many public bodies and government agencies are now structured as if they were private corporations.

Traditionalists respond to this by seeking to reassert the power of the nation state. They claim that such a state, democratically accountable and imposing common standards, can check the slide away from national uniformity and common citizenship. They fail to realise that the state is weaker in certain dimensions than it was, but is ever more over-extended in providing a diverse range of services and seeking to regulate an ever-widening range of contingencies. As such it is too overloaded to act as an effective democratic overseer and too enmeshed in trying to rationalise its own activities to offer a check to the growth of private and quasi-public managerial power. Indeed, elected politicians and career officials are eager to assert corporate models of management in the public service; the paradox is that they are often the ones that business has been abandoning in practice as it tries to become flexible and responsive.

Unaccountable private government is currently able to grow unchecked – in the major financial markets, in media empires, in major corporations – because its actions are presented as non-governmental, as the private actions of free citizens in civil society. Privatisation and marketisation are failing to confront the problems of modern public management, while reducing equality and fairness in the provision of public services. Yet social democracy has not enjoyed a real renaissance in response. It depended on an economic-governmental conjuncture that cannot readily be put back together again. The range of modern public services is too wide and too diverse to be delivered to everybody in the same way. Social democratic and Christian democratic welfare measures and social provision reinforced national political identity, civic consciousness and a spirit of public service – they thus provided some of the social foundations for an effective mass democracy. A measure of cultural and social homogeneity is essential to democracy. One has to be sufficiently like one's fellow citizens to trust them with legislative power over one.

The capacity to reform and to renew the welfare system is central to our ability to find a new substitute for social democracy. Currently the centre-left has little to offer in this direction; it is in thrall to the right. The welfare state and democracy are intimately linked. One cannot build new forms of democracy without ensuring a measure of social security. Thus the decentralisation of sovereign power has to be coupled with a welfare system and set of public services that is itself decentralised, but which ensures common minimum standards of provision. This can only be achieved by maintaining public funding and common minimum entitlements. An associationalist welfare system would combine public funding related to individual membership of voluntary bodies providing services with citizen choice over providers. Public funding and common basic minima are essential in order to sustain an adequate level of welfare and a suitable range of services for all. Public entitlements and choice need to be combined, not driven apart as economic liberals who seek to privatise welfare provision wish to do. The provision of services through publicly funded voluntary associations in which individuals can choose and can craft the specific services they want is compatible with the common basic entitlements that were central to classical social democracy.

Indeed, it is probably the only way social democratic aims can survive. Unless individuals in a more differentiated society have choice and will consume the public services they pay for in the way that they want to, then public welfare will degenerate into poor relief. This advocacy of 'targeting' welfare services, concentrating them on the poor, has begun to capture socialist parties. It is a political disaster, that will promote the worst kind of social differentiation – creating services that only the desperate will consume through want of other choices but which all have to pay for.

A decentralised society can be a diverse one, but it cannot be a polarised one. A new democratic welfare system based on provision through self-governing associations requires an adequate minimum of common security. A society divided between the poor and the excluded and the rest will promote centralisation and repression, not localism and choice. Thus diversity in provision, where all can choose the services they want and the well-to-do can top up a common sufficient minimum, may actually be the only route left to a relatively fair and not grossly unequal society. Taxpayers thus will get the services they want, and will be more likely to be willing to contribute to services they consume. Associationalism is a way to crack tax aversion on the part of middle-income people.

Associative democracy provides new and clear models of governance that are applicable in the political system, in economic life and in welfare services. Associationalism does not do this by proposing the replacement of the existing social order with an entirely new alternative. Rather it is a supplement to existing institutions that has the capacity to transform their workings rather than to supplant them. Associationalist governmental means can be added piecemeal and iteratively to existing institutions in an ongoing reform process. Thus it has the gradualist and reformist potential of social democracy, but adapted to new conditions.

Associative democracy aims neither to abolish representative government nor to replace market exchange with some other allocative mechanism, rather to free the former from the encumbrance of an over-extended and centralised public-service state and to anchor the latter in a complex of social institutions that enables it to attain socially desirable outcomes.

Associationalism responds directly to the problems of how to democratise a post-liberal organisational society, since it aims to promote governance through democratically legitimated voluntary associations. The conversion of public and private corporate hierarchies into self-governing bodies answerable to those whom they serve and who participate in them, would thus answer to the greatest democratic deficits of our time – organisational government without consent and corporate control without representation.

The great advantage of associative democracy is that it offers a coherent model to guide reform initiatives across specific organisations and localities. It provides a means to link-up and to systematise local experiments. Suitably applied, associative democratic concepts provide a coherent and sufficiently loose-textured model that can help to convert many local experiments in decentralisation, democratisation, and negotiated governance from one-offs into contributions to a move towards a new style of social governance.

Index

Index

THE RINGS
OF DESTINY

THE RINGS OF DESTINY

Inside Soviet Russia From Lenin to Brezhnev

by AINO KUUSINEN

Foreword by *Wolfgang Leonhard*

Preface by *John H. Hodgson*

Translated from the German by Paul Stevenson

WILLIAM MORROW AND COMPANY, INC.

NEW YORK 1974

PRINTED IN THE UNITED STATES OF AMERICA.

LIBRARY OF CONGRESS CATALOG CARD NUMBER 74-9135

ISBN 0-688-00306-0

1 2 3 4 5 78 77 76 75 74

Contents

Preface

In the winter of 1964–65 Aino Kuusinen received permission from Soviet authorities to visit her native Finland after experiencing more than four decades of life as a functionary in the Communist International, as an agent for Soviet military intelligence, and as a victim of Stalin's terror machine. Aino Kuusinen's return to Finland was expedited by the intervention of her stepdaughter, Hertta Kuusinen, daughter of the late Soviet leader Otto W. Kuusinen and a mainstay of the Finnish Communist Party from 1944 until her death in 1974, although the relationship between these two women soon took a turn for the worse with Aino Kuusinen's unexpected defection to the West.

In the wee hours of a June morning in 1965 Aino Kuusinen left her Helsinki apartment—suitcase in hand, fur coat draped over one arm—for an alleged rest at the summer home of an acquaintance. Instead of a trip to the Finnish countryside, however, Aino Kuusinen's taxi driver started her on the last leg of the journey from the Soviet Union to Finland and finally to continental Europe, where she became a cause célèbre, first with her interviews of 1966 and then with the posthumous publication of her memoirs in Germany, Finland, Sweden, Japan, Italy, France, Great Britain, and now the United States.

Aino Kuusinen had a phenomenal ability to recall in great detail events of the past, even of the distant past, although she allowed errors of two sorts to creep into her remarkable book. With the vivid imagination of a self-centered adventuress, for example, she claims in the face of contradictory

6

evidence that she sought assistance from the U.S. Embassy in Moscow on two occasions, 1947 and 1948, after her release from the Vorkuta labor camp. The pride of a woman scorned by a man whose philosophy, as stated by Otto Kuusinen himself, was that he was too developed both intellectually and physically to find satisfaction in a single woman, no doubt figured prominently in Aino Kuusinen's conscious effort to convey the impression that it was she who severed relations with Kuusinen and that her former husband, in contrast to herself, was an embittered emigrant whose loathing for Finland and the Finnish language was epitomized in an alleged desire to march back to Helsinki at the head of the Soviet Army.

There is little reason to take issue with Hertta Kuusinen's advice that her stepmother's memoirs should be approached with great care, but objective observers will reject the claim that Aino Kuusinen was "used" for propagandistic purposes by the yellow press. The true merit of her recollections is indicated by the fact that Roy Medvedev—prominent historian and dissident in the Soviet Union—considered Aino Kuusinen worthy of mention in his well-known book *Let History Judge*. The foreword to Aino Kuusinen's memoirs by Professor Wolfgang Leonhard will convince readers that her book is an important personal account of events and experiences bringing life to the years 1918–1965 and providing a new as well as unusual perspective on Soviet politics and international Communism in the period from Lenin to Brezhnev.

Syracuse, New York, Spring 1974

JOHN H. HODGSON

Foreword

At the beginning of 1966 a number of European newspapers announced the arrival in the West of Aino Kuusinen,* the widow of the high-ranking Soviet official Otto Kuusinen, who had for many years been the secretary of the Communist International. It was reported that Aino Kuusinen had received permission from the Soviet government for a short visit to her native Finland, and had decided never to return to the Soviet Union.

At first, rather naturally, the main subject of interest was not so much Aino Kuusinen herself as the fact that she was the widow of Otto Kuusinen. Kuusinen was one of the few high functionaries who had survived all Stalin's purges.

He was a friend of Lenin's, adviser to Stalin and close colleague of Khrushchev; for more than twenty years he played an important part both in the Communist International and in the Party and State leadership of the Soviet Union. As a result his name was widely known beyond the confines of the Communist world. Kuusinen was one of the founders of the Finnish Communist Party in 1918, and from 1921 to 1939 he was the secretary of the Executive Committee of the Communist International (Comintern) in Moscow. Thus he had a place in the leading circles of the Communist world organization from its inception almost to its end. Although a Finn by birth, Kuusinen was also active in the highest Party and government circles of the Soviet Union itself. From 1940 to 1957 he was deputy chairman of the Presidium of the Supreme Soviet of the USSR; in addition he was a member of the Central Committee of the Soviet Com-

* Aino Kuusinen reached Finland on 28 February 1965 but did not announce her arrival to the press until the following year.

8

munist Party from 1941 until his death, and in the final years of his life, from 1957 to 1964, he was even a member of the Party Presidium (Politburo), the highest centre of power in the USSR. Otto Kuusinen died on 17 May 1964 and was given one of the biggest State funerals that the Soviet Union had ever known.

A few months later, Aino Kuusinen was given permission to undertake the journey which enabled her to leave the Soviet Union for ever. This was the first time that the wife of such a high-ranking Soviet politician had come over to the West— Stalin's daughter, Svetlana Alliluyeva, did not do so until a year later—and this in itself was unusual enough to arouse interest in Aino Kuusinen.

After the first interviews which she gave in the West, however —amongst others for *Expressen* in Stockholm, and an extensive one for the Italian *L'Europeo*—it became apparent that she could not be regarded solely as an appendage of Otto Kuusinen. She emerged clearly from the interviews as a strong personality with a dramatic life story, and with her own aims and opinions.

For me, the first reports about Aino Kuusinen, and above all her detailed interviews, aroused a burning interest and a desire to know her personally. My wish was granted sooner than I had hoped, for at the beginning of June 1966, only a few months after the first reports, I received a letter in which she told me that she was intending to write her memoirs and asked me to assist her in the task.

It turned out subsequently that she had read my book *Die Revolution entlässt ihre Kinder* (English translation: *Child of the Revolution*) in Finland and had seen from it that I had lived in the Soviet Union from 1935 to 1945, at the time she was there. She had also learnt in Finland that I was engaged in the study of Soviet affairs and the problems of international Communism, and had rightly assumed that I was a person who would understand her and her fate from his own experience, and would be able to help her in her undertaking.

After a brief correspondence we arranged our first meeting. My first impression of Aino Kuusinen was of an old lady with a winning personality, astonishing intelligence and quick powers of comprehension. She spoke a number of languages, including good German. I was particularly struck by her remarkable

9

memory for names and events, her gift for describing personal experiences vividly and graphically, and her sense of humour often expressed in biting irony. She was over seventy when I met her, and yet she was full of sparkle and vivacity—even with a touch of coquetry—intensely active, and possessed by the desire to write her memoirs. She had remarkable will-power for a woman of her age. She was exuberance itself as she recounted episodes from her activities in the Communist International at the beginning of the twenties, her special mission to America, her activities in the Soviet espionage service in Japan, her arrest and life in Soviet prison camps, and the last few years which she had spent in Moscow after her release in 1955.

At our first meeting I encouraged her intention to record her interesting and dramatic life-story, and also made a number of suggestions, which she readily accepted. We agreed that I would go through the portions of the manuscript as they were finished and arrange for the publication of her memoirs in Germany and other Western countries. Almost a year passed before I met Aino Kuusinen again, and in the meantime I had received the larger part of the manuscript, which I found a deeply impressive and absorbing document.

I felt that the memoirs should be published as soon as possible. Admittedly scores of memoirs have now been published by people who were active in the Communist movement and in the Soviet Union but were subsequently disillusioned by Stalinism. In my view, however, Aino Kuusinen's differ from the books published hitherto in a number of respects. Most memoirs of this kind only cover limited periods in the development of the Soviet Union or of Communism. Few of them give a picture stretching over many years or decades; but Aino Kuusinen's account covers a time-span from 1918 to 1965, from Lenin's time to the fall of Khrushchev. Moreover, during those four decades, she experienced life in the Soviet Union and international Communism at widely differing levels. The vagaries of fate carried her from dizzy heights to the utmost depths, from the life of the ruling élite to that of a prison camp inmate.

Her perspective of these events is also new, unusual and different. Her point of view is neither that of the Soviet functionary who has grown up as a Soviet citizen within the USSR, nor that of a West European intellectual who joined the Communist movement out of indignation at social injustice and political oppression, or under the influence of the Marxist view of life. Aino Kuusinen did not rise step by step through the bureaucratic system—and she was quite the reverse of an 'official' type in her feelings and attitudes—nor did social, political or ideological questions form a really essential part of her life. Her memoirs are rather those of a beautiful, intelligent, educated and self-possessed woman who joined the Communist International and later the Soviet intelligence service through a series of highly unusual circumstances—one might even say accidents. In her vivid descriptions of her life and activities, which included certain highly unusual missions, we can see clearly how little she was motivated by political or ideological considerations. One often gains the impression from reading her memoirs—beginning with the time when she left her home in Finland out of love for Otto Kuusinen in 1921—that a desire for danger, adventure and risk was perhaps the main motive in her life.

One thing emerges clearly from Aino Kuusinen's account, and that is that despite many years of activity in the Communist International, she always reacted to any situation firstly as a Finn. The official Soviet claim to have 'solved' the national question has seldom been so unequivocally disproved—although Aino Kuusinen does not take up a political attitude over this. While in no way appearing as a theoretical Marxist, she indirectly, but none the less clearly, shows up the contradiction between international Marxism and Soviet practice in this important question.

Aino Kuusinen's memoirs are a highly personal account—especially in that part which deals with her life in Soviet prisons and prison camps. In contrast to some other convicts, she escaped the danger of regarding the Soviet authorities as being in any way in the right, of looking upon them as 'comrades' who merely acted incomprehensibly. This, I believe, is due not to a basic hostility on her part, but rather to the natural authority and self-confidence of a well-born woman who has held her own in society in many different countries, Communist and bourgeois. Her courage has both a personal and a social origin. She is the opposite of an Evgenia Ginzburg or a Nadezhda Mandelstam: the former is a better Communist than her tormentors, the latter expects nothing from the Stalin regime but misery and death. Aino Kuusinen faced the atrocious reality of her situation without great soul-searching, without tragic disappointment, without allowing her whole inner world to collapse. She was determined to survive, of her own free will and because she did not want to give the Soviet authorities the victory of breaking her down and finishing her off.

The personal and often emotive nature of her memoirs leads to exaggeration here and there, as is particularly evident in her attitude towards her husband, Otto Kuusinen. In fact she secretly admired him and never identified him with the regime, and her frequent criticisms of him are more often the result of her own painful experience than an objective judgement of the facts. Otto Kuusinen is the man who has wronged her, whom she no longer loves and no longer wishes to see, and she projects this personal conflict on to the figure of Kuusinen the politician and official. Though Kuusinen undoubtedly played an important rôle both in the Comintern and in the Soviet Party and State administration, Aino Kuusinen's personal viewpoint often seems to lead her to portray him as more important than he actually was.

The life story of Aino Kuusinen makes no claim to be a work of historical analysis. It is above all and emphatically a personal account of the alert mind and passionate heart of a strong-willed woman of our times, who portrays important events and personalities in the Soviet Union and international Communism as she experienced them. As I can testify from the conversations we had together, the author was concerned to make her account as objective and truthful as possible, but clearly it is coloured by the emotional effect of her experiences, particularly in the labour camps. In addition, Aino Kuusinen was already in her seventies when she began to write her memoirs. In spite of her astounding vitality and her good memory, it cannot have been always easy for her to recall events which often lay decades in the past.

I had the impression that the writing of her memoirs was the final objective of her life. The nearer she came to the end of the task, the more she seemed to feel that her own end was approaching. Her initial optimism began to fade. Whereas in 1966 she had been full of life and had given interviews readily, she now became less and less approachable to the outside world. She complained increasingly of her state of health, and her all-embracing optimism gave way to pessimism and despair. When her memoirs were finished she urged me to delay their publication until after her death. As she wrote to me in the autumn of 1967, she had brought her life's work to an end, but now, in view of her old age and poor health, she wished to be spared all the excitement and talks to the press that would be involved in the publication of a book. She was therefore entrusting the manuscript to me to be published after her death, in the hope that I would treat it with objectivity, sincerity and understanding.

In obedience to her appeal, the memoirs remained locked in my desk for nearly three years. Though I naturally understood her wish, I also regretted having to withhold the memoirs from the public.

Aino Kuusinen died on 1 September 1970. The time had come to fulfil the agreement made between her and myself in 1966, and to accomplish her last wish. As the editor of the memoirs, my main task was to check historical facts and names and to add explanatory notes where necessary. Apart from minor stylistic changes and unimportant deletions, the book remains exactly as Aino Kuusinen wrote it. As the editor I do not necessarily accept every detail of her representation of events and persons as ultimate historical truth, nor do I identify myself with all her political views and judgements.

Aino Kuusinen's memoirs seemed to me so important that I consulted a number of experts amongst friends and acquaintances, and I would like particularly to thank those who have not only read the manuscript carefully during the past few months, but also helped me in the task of editing. The well-known expert on Soviet affairs, Borys Lewytzkyj, who now lives in Munich, concentrated on the part covering the Soviet period of Aino Kuusinen's life, checked a large number of historical data and helped me in compiling the biographical notes. Professor John Hodgson of Syracuse University—acknowledged as a leading expert on Finnish Communism, and the author of several works on the subject, including his book *Communism in Finland*— provided much valuable information about Otto Kuusinen (of whom he is at present writing a biography) and other Finnish Communists mentioned in the book. Ruth von Mayenburg (whose autobiography *Blaues Blut und Rote Fahnen* was published in Vienna in 1969) and Babette Gross (biographer and lifelong companion of Willi Münzenberg) were both connected with the Comintern in Moscow at different times and helped in checking relevant passages, as well as making corrections, some of which figure in the notes.

I have edited these memoirs not only out of personal friendship for Aino Kuusinen and in fulfilment of her last wish, but also because I consider her account to be a dramatic document of our time which goes beyond the personal framework to provide new insight to and knowledge of the development of International Communism and the Soviet Union. Historians will no doubt have objections to make here and there, but I hope at least that they will agree with me in regarding Aino Kuusinen's life story, despite any weaknesses of detail, as an important document of contemporary history in so far as it brings into the light of day people, situations and events which in some cases are still imperfectly known.

For the general public in any case, and for the many who would sooner read about contemporary events as mirrored in the experience and suffering of a remarkable human being rather than as a dry historical chronicle, Aino Kuusinen's memoirs have the inestimable value of an eye-witness account.

Manderscheid/Eifel, Autumn 1971   WOLFGANG LEONHARD

I

The Rings of Destiny

My late husband, Otto W. Kuusinen, was one of the most puzzling figures among Communists of international repute, and I hope that the record of my direct personal experience may throw some light on the mystery which surrounded him.

Otto Kuusinen once published in the Soviet Union an essay on his philosophy of life, entitled 'Choosing the Right Ring'.[1] Mindful of the Bolsheviks' enthusiasm for large machines, he asked his readers to imagine an apparatus consisting of a moving belt, from which hung rings which could be grasped by the people waiting underneath. In this life, he said, every human being has the chance to grasp such a ring and hang on to it, without knowing where the moving belt will take him. A happy life depends on grasping the right ring, which will carry one over the abysses of life, so that when one lets go of it one will be sure of landing in a safe place. But it is the lot of many men to take hold of the wrong ring, and to land in a dangerous place far removed from where they had hoped to be. Others manage to seize the right ring but let go of it too soon or in the wrong place. This parable of Kuusinen's is not a bad illustration of the human condition. In my own life, I began in the early 1920s by grasping a ring which took me out of Finland, first to Moscow and then to many parts of the earth which I had never expected to see. After seven years in Moscow, the headquarters of the World Revolution, my husband Otto Kuusinen and I chose different rings, and I left Russia to spend two years on a secret mission to the United States.

After having lived so long in New York, the drab routine of life in the Soviet capital was difficult to bear when I returned, and so I switched to another ring which took me to pre-war Japan. With the help of the Soviet military secret service I spent there the happiest and most carefree years of my life. My work brought me into contact with a man who, long after his death, was celebrated as the best spy the Soviet Union had ever had— Dr Richard Sorge. Yet when I first met him in the mid-thirties, he was certainly not held in particularly high esteem in Moscow.

Towards the end of 1937 I was ordered to return to Moscow. I obeyed, thinking that I could come to no harm, but this time I had chosen the wrong ring. Like so many others, I was to make close acquaintance with the horrors of Stalin's purges. I spent more than a year under interrogation in the prisons of Moscow, and then there followed eight long years in the notorious Vorkuta labour camp on the Arctic Circle. Needless to say, these were the grimmest years of my life. However, thanks to my robust health, and perhaps also to unseen protectors, as well as ingenuity and what Finns call *sisu* (pluck and perseverance), I survived the ordeal.

After the war I was released from Vorkut and found myself confronted with the difficulties which face all former political prisoners in the Soviet Union. I was not allowed to live in Moscow, and sought a sunny place in the Caucasus where I could live in peace with friends. But peace and quiet were not to be mine. Once again I was arrested and thrown into the same Moscow prisons which I already knew so well. Although my health was now deteriorating, I was eventually sent to the Potma labour camp, where I spent five and a half years. I was finally released in 1955, two years after Stalin's death.

I had spent more than fifteen years of my life as a political prisoner of the Soviets. During those hard years I formed the resolution to write and publish my memoirs, as this seemed the only means of avenging myself on those who had robbed me of my freedom. But if I was to achieve this goal, my main task during those fifteen years was to stay alive and make sure that I emerged from the camps with my mind and morale unbroken. It might perhaps be asked why it is so important that such a memoir should be written. Many valuable biographies have already been published containing detailed accounts of the horrors of life in Stalin's prison camps. I am, however, convinced that every account of this kind helps in its own way to enlighten the world about the regime that prevailed in the Soviet Union.

The day I regained my freedom in 1955, I swore to myself that I would stake everything on getting out of the 'workers' paradise' which had trampled upon my rights as a human being; but ten more years were to pass before I achieved this aim. Finally in 1965, almost a year after Otto Kuusinen's death, I was granted permission to visit my native Finland.

I have been through many adventures, and have suffered fate's ironies perhaps more frequently than most of my contemporaries, but none of my unhappy experiences have broken me, and I have not lost my taste for living. There is one thing at least which I have learnt in my overfull life—every man, whether consciously or unconsciously, fashions his own fate; it is ourselves and not others whom we have to thank for our bad experiences, and equally—should we choose the right 'ring'—for our happiness.

I was born towards the end of the last century as the third child of my parents and spent most of my childhood in central Finland, where I was brought up in every respect like my three brothers.[2] Our parents taught us at an early age the importance of maintaining a fearless and stoical outlook on life, and although I do not remember having ever been punished, I know that we were certainly not pampered. I learned the qualities of tenacity and daring at an early age, and could hold my own with any of the boys in skiing and swimming.

When I was not yet ten years old I conceived the idea of going to Africa as a Christian missionary. This ambition had been aroused by a travelling missionary who came to our district and to whom I gave all my savings so that he could buy clothes for the poor African children. When my father heard of this he advised me not to waste my money, since it was so hot in Africa that small children did not wear clothes or trousers. Today I often wish that all my sudden resolutions had had such harmless consequences. But this was not to be the case.

I owe much of my knowledge of historical events, foreign countries and politics to my father, for he had a fascinating way of telling us about these subjects, right from our earliest childhood. When I was young Finland still belonged to Tsarist Russia, which was then attempting a massive programme of Russianization. Our father strove to make us understand the dangers which threatened the grand duchy of Finland and how the constitutional rights which Tsar Alexander I had granted it were being infringed. Our father shared many other interests with us besides his burning patriotism, and he had a well-stocked library through which we became familiar with a wide variety of books. I probably inherited my love of the theatre from him. One of his chief concerns was the temperance movement. He had founded a temperance society in our community, of which he was the chairman, and gave impassioned addresses at the meetings. He impressed upon us children again and again the importance of abstaining from alcoholic drink.

I made good progress at school and distinguished myself in foreign languages and essay-writing. My essays were often read out by the teacher as examples of good literary style. After finishing secondary school I took a four-year nursing course at the Surgical Hospital in Helsinki. I have always remembered the doctors there with great gratitude and respect, and also the exceptionally capable matron, Sophia Mannersheim, who was loved for her attractive personality.

Very soon after qualifying as a nurse I married Leo Sarola,[3] a good and wise man, somewhat older than myself, who worked as an engineer in the railway management. It was not long before we realized that our marriage was built on sand, however: I was too active a person and could not reconcile myself to the narrow circle in which we lived. For some years we saw no way out, until one day fate changed our lives. In 1919 we were living in a small house near Helsinki, in what is now the suburb of Tapa-nila. One cold and gloomy autumn evening we heard a knock at the door and a woman friend of ours came in. She apologized for disturbing us so late, then continued: 'I haven't come for a social visit, but to ask your help for someone. There's a Member of Parliament[4] waiting outside. His life is in danger, and he is somebody worth saving. The police are after him and if they find him he is bound to be condemned to death. He has nowhere to sleep tonight. Could you take him in?' She went out and came back after a moment with a man whom we did not know. He looked intelligent and was neatly dressed. We greeted the stranger, invited him to take a seat and offered him something to eat, which he refused. He suddenly stood up and said very seriously: 'I can't accept your hospitality without your knowing who I am. It's quite possible that you will not want to have me under your roof once I have told you. My name is Kuusinen.' 'That doesn't matter,' my husband said calmly, 'you can spend the night with us, and as long as you are here you are in no danger.'

We had naturally heard of Kuusinen as one of the leaders of the Communist uprising in 1918, and knew that he had been Minister of Education in the short-lived Communist government. We also knew that, like the other ministers, he had fled from Viborg to Petrograd. We had read in the papers that there was a price on his head and that he was likely to be shot if he was discovered.

The maid brought our guest something to eat and made up a bed for him, and the next morning he left before daybreak without saying where he was going.

We later heard that Kuusinen had come to Finland shortly before because Lenin had asked him to investigate the situation and rescue the Left from its current state of disorder.[5] Little did I know that the arrival of this stranger in our house was the first link in a chain of events which was to alter the whole course of my life.

Three months later I met Kuusinen for the second time. It was during the bitterly cold winter of 1920, when I met the lawyer Eino Pekkala one day on the Iso-Robertinkatu in Helsinki. I had got to know Pekkala through my brother Toive Turtiainen; they were both Social Democratic Members of Parliament, but whereas my brother sided with Väino Tanner, Eino Pekkala belonged to the left wing of the Party and later joined the Communists. As we were near where Pekkala's parents-in-law, the Murriks, lived, Eino suggested that we went in for a cup of coffee. There, in addition to the Murriks, I met their daughter,

Salme Pekkala, and Hella Wuolijoki. To my surprise Kuusinen was present as well, and I later heard that he was staying secretly at the Murriks's home.

During the conversation I learned that Salme Pekkala was shortly going to London on a secret mission for the Communist Party. Suddenly Kuusinen produced four large diamonds from his waistcoat pocket and showed them to us all, saying: 'Each of these is worth forty thousand.' I can no longer remember which currency this referred to. Then he handed the diamonds to Pekkala's wife and said with a smile: 'Here's some money for the journey.'

Not long after this, Kuusinen left Finland and lived in Stockholm, whence he began to send me poems and letters. Instead of being posted, these were brought by a young man whom I did not know. Once I received two letters simultaneously, one addressed to me and the other to Professor Rafael Erich, the Prime Minister at that time. In his letter to me, Kuusinen asked me to forward the letter to Erich through a trustworthy person. If I thought that was too dangerous, I was to give the letter back to the person who had brought it. Kuusinen and Erich had been friends at school and university and had later been Members of Parliament at the same time, and in his letter Kuusinen begged the Prime Minister to put an end to the persecution of the Communists.[6]

I lost no time in carrying out Kuusinen's request. A nurse whom I knew well from our schooldays agreed to take the letter to Erich's house and wait there for an answer. Erich lived near the station and so I waited for my friend in the station restaurant; I was bursting with pride at the idea of being involved in such an exciting and important business. Soon my messenger came back and told me how the Prime Minister had received her in his study and, without asking her name, had merely enquired whether she knew who the author of the letter was, to which she had truthfully replied 'no'. Erich had read the letter slowly and carefully and had then turned to her and said: 'Tell the sender that I shall not reply.'

In any other country, the Prime Minister would probably have informed the police and instituted an enquiry. I sent Kuusinen my report on the affair via the same young man who had brought the letters.

I felt the need to make something more out of my life than merely being a housewife, and therefore decided to open a private clinic in Helsinki, with the help of a bank loan. At the beginning of 1922 I went to Stockholm to learn something about the running of such an establishment. In Stockholm I was advised to go to Berlin in order to widen my experience, and I followed this advice without having any idea of the current situation in Germany. As a result of inflation the economy was in a chaotic state, prices were shooting up from day to day and there was a dire shortage of food. Strikes and demonstrations were everyday occurrences. My hotel had no heating, and I would have liked to return to Sweden immediately, but the railway workers were on strike and there were no trains. I could do nothing but sit and wait for the end of the strike, and during this time something happened which gave an unexpected turn to my life.

One day I went to the police station on the Alexanderplatz, as I needed a stamp for my passport, and met a Finn whom I knew slightly, who was there for the same reason as myself. This was the newspaper editor and Member of Parliament Yrjö Sirola, a close friend of Kuusinen, who had been Foreign Minister in the revolutionary government of Finland in 1918.[7] We arranged to meet the following day, and at this second meeting he told me openly that he was working for the Comintern in Moscow. He was in Berlin on the orders of Lenin and Kuusinen —and I now realized for the first time how influential Otto Kuusinen was in Moscow. Sirola's mission in Berlin was to gather information about the finances of the German Communist Party, which had asked the Comintern for large sums of money. At the same time he was looking for people who knew German well as employees for the Comintern office in Moscow. Half-jokingly, he suggested that I should pass through Moscow on my way back to Finland—his wife had made the same journey shortly beforehand.

The railway strike showed no signs of coming to an end, and I saw Sirola from time to time, since I hardly knew anyone else in Berlin. He lived with a Finnish goldsmith from Petrograd named Koso, and one day Koso's wife invited me through Sirola to afternoon coffee. After the meal, Sirola said he had something interesting to show me. Under his bed and in the cupboards in his room were a whole lot of sacks filled with Tsarist banknotes, which according to him were 'worth millions'. Kuusinen had sent his brother-in-law, the lawyer Einari Laaksovirta, to Germany to convert the roubles into Western currency to finance Communist operations in Europe.

When the Bank of Finland was taken over by the Bolsheviks during the Communist uprising of 1918, Laaksovirta had been its deputy manager and had acquired some knowledge of banking affairs. I later met him in Moscow, where he had gone at Kuusinen's request. I could not imagine how Tsarist paper money could possibly have any value at all; when I expressed my doubts to Sirola, he admitted that the notes were losing value daily, but assured me that their exchange rate was bound to rise again.

Sirola was travelling on a forged Norwegian passport, and was constantly afraid of being found out by the police. The second time he needed an extension of his German visa he could not bring himself to go to the Passport Office. The German Communists assured him that it was quite simple: he only had to insert a sum of money in his passport and hand it to a particular official at the Alexanderplatz office, whose name he was given; the official would extend the visa without asking any questions. Sirola thought the whole thing very risky. What would happen if he was arrested for trying to bribe an official? I tried to bolster up his courage, and even offered to accompany him to the Passport Office. I had to work on him for a whole day, and thoroughly make fun of his anxiety, before he could bring himself to go to the police station, and even then I had to promise to wait for him in the café opposite. However, everything went off smoothly, and Sirola was happy and content.

When the railway strike was over, Sirola again suggested that I should return to Helsinki via Moscow, and in a somewhat frivolous frame of mind I gave way to the temptation. But it was not so easy to get to Moscow, since one had to travel through Polish territory, and at that time the Polish government were forbidding any through traffic. More weeks passed, until we finally hit on the plan of taking a boat to Königsberg from a

German port on the Baltic, and continuing by rail to Moscow. We had no difficulty in getting cabins on a small coastal steamer which would take us to Pillau, the port of Königsberg.

The ship put in at several places, and at each we stayed prudently in our cabins. At one of these ports of call we heard a band playing the march of the Finnish cavalry from the Thirty Years' War. Sirola, who was always nervous when travelling abroad, was now seized with the greatest anxiety, since he assumed that he had been recognized. This seemed to me so absurd that I decided to play a joke on him. I went on deck to find out what was happening, and saw only the quayside on which a military band was playing. I told Sirola, however, that it had been discovered that a Finnish Member of Parliament was on board, i.e. himself, and that the band was playing in his honour. Sirola turned as white as a sheet. Shortly before dinnertime the stewardess came with an invitation for us to eat at the captain's table; someone would show us the way there. I changed quickly and told Sirola that the invitation was because of his having been recognized. He had still not realized that I was playing a joke on him and he was becoming increasingly nervous. When we got to the dining room we saw that the table was laid for six. The stewardess showed us to our places, and we sat in silence awaiting developments. After a while the door opened and four officers came in. I recognized the captain by his uniform, but who could the tall officer be who sat down opposite me, while the others took their places to right and left of him? I glanced repeatedly at the old gentleman, whom I knew I had often seen in pictures, and suddenly I realized that it was Field Marshal von Hindenburg, the war hero and later President of the German Reich. It was of course in his honour that the band had been playing. The officer on his left was his adjutant, and the one on his right his doctor. Hindenburg was a gentleman of the old school, and we talked together all the way to Pillau.

After a long and uncomfortable railway journey from Königsberg, I arrived in Moscow on a hot day in the early summer of 1922. Sirola had cabled ahead to say that I would be coming with him, and I was lodged in a large yellow-painted *dacha* in the beautiful Neskuchny Park near the Moskva River. The house had belonged to a well-to-do Russian before the Revolu-

23

tion and was now inhabited by Trotsky's parents, who took me in as their guest. We conversed in German. Trotsky himself did not live in the house, and I don't believe he visited his parents during my stay. The father was a tall, slim, well-dressed old gentleman, who had been a lawyer in Kiev, and the mother was a distinguished old lady. They told me that they had spent several summers in Finland, and how unforgettably beautiful it was. They had a number of servants, including an excellent cook, and the house provided all the comfort one could wish for. Foreign Communists visited them almost every day, and there was always an ample supply of coffee, tea and cakes. The main theme of conversation was politics, but to my surprise Russian Communists came very seldom.

Kuusinen was in Petrograd at this time at a meeting of Finnish Communist leaders at which, Sirola told me, an attempt was to be made to bring together the various disunited groups.[8] Sirola soon left to take part in the meeting, but beforehand took me around Moscow a bit, and I must say that I did not get a very favourable impression: the city was extraordinarily dirty, and everything seemed disorganized. We visited the Comintern building on Denezhny Pereulok, a former palace which had housed the German Embassy in 1918 and seen the murder of the Ambassador, Count Mirbach. The place was like a noisy, bustling railway station: people ran continually from one room to another, carrying all kinds of papers and talking at least twelve different languages. People consumed sandwiches and tea to the accompaniment of clattering typewriters. Never had I seen such a strange assortment of people in the same place at the same time. When I remarked to Sirola that I could not imagine how anyone could work in such a place, he merely smiled, but I thought to myself: 'So this is the headquarters of the World Revolution.'

This was the time of Lenin's New Economic Policy, or NEP, as it was called[9], and for the average citizen of the Soviet Union there were many more important things than world revolution. Under the new principles private enterprise was once more allowed; the peasants began to sell their harvests to hungry city dwellers, and long-needed commodities began to appear intermittently on the open market. So the situation was generally somewhat better, though the frightful misery wrought by revolution and civil war could not be cured in a short time.

The time had come to think of returning to Finland; but I discovered that it was as good as impossible to leave the Soviet Union in a legal fashion. Bureaucracy blocked the way at every step, and as I had no influential friends I could see no chance of obtaining an exit permit. Then in late summer, after the Petrograd conference was over, Kuusinen returned to Moscow. He came to me immediately, and I forgot all about returning home—I knew now that it was because of him that I had come to Moscow.

We were married in the registry office as prescribed by Soviet law, and at first lived for a number of years in the Lux Hotel on Tverskaya Street (now Gorky Street). This hotel, called the Hotel Filippov before the Revolution, was reserved for high Comintern officials up to the end of the Second World War. Although it was a first-class hotel by the standards of the day, the traffic noise from the street robbed it of any real feeling of comfort.

Later we were assigned an apartment in the Kremlin enclosure which had been used by court officials in Tsarist times. The building was over two hundred years old, and although attempts had been made to modernize it, it was very damp. A further disadvantage was that anyone coming to see us had to identify themselves at the Kremlin entrance, which was highly tedious both for our guests and ourselves. So we were very pleased when we finally moved into the Dom Pravitelstva, the residence for high government officials, where we were given an apartment on the tenth floor. This building was close to the Moskva River, almost opposite the Kremlin near the Kamenny Bridge, and had only just been completed after numerous delays. The layout was not very practical, but by Soviet standards it was the best type of apartment one could get, with large rooms and two balconies. Even the lifts worked most of the time, which in Moscow was a rarity. Our nearest neighbours were Rykov, the then Prime Minister, and his family, and on the seventh floor lived the daughter of a St Petersburg aristocrat, Elena Stasova, who was a friend of Lenin's and whom I shall mention in a later chapter. Bukharin and Radek also lived in the building for a while.

Besides this apartment we had a *dacha* for the summer at

Serebrianny Bor (Silver Wood), west of Moscow. It was surrounded by fir-woods and was an ideal place to recover from the city noise. Otto, who preferred never to leave his office, only stayed reluctantly in this villa, but to me it meant a great deal.

I had not been in Moscow long before I began to realize how hard and joyless life had become for the majority of the population since the Bolshevik Revolution. I particularly doubted the concept of a 'classless society' since I could see that there was a large difference between the life led by the workers and that of the 'Soviet aristocrats', as they were popularly called. Our own example was as good as any. Each year we received a new car, which we did not pay for, and thanks to the generosity of the 'classless society' we had the free use of our apartment, our *dacha*, a chauffeur and a housekeeper. Our housekeeper, Alexandra Prokhorovna Seldyankova, who could neither read nor write, had worked as a cook for wealthy Russian families before the Revolution. When she went shopping for us she did not need any money, only three small books which she presented in the different shops. One was for the State dairy, where she got milk, butter, eggs and cheese, another for the State butcher's, where she obtained meat and poultry, and the third for the State fish shop, where she 'bought' fish and caviar.

The average housewife could not buy as much as she liked by any means. All food was rationed, and only small quantities were available. For instance, a housewife could not generally buy more than a hundred grammes of butter—she might sometimes get 200 grammes if she queued for long enough. But the high-ranking officials, who had an unlimited number of ration books, could order as much of the available foodstuffs as they wished. Queues formed from early in the morning, and a policeman was on hand to keep order. As each customer came out of the shop with a couple of small packets, another was allowed in. Our cook didn't have to queue, however. As soon as she showed the policeman the book, he called out: 'Make way, make way!' As she came out of the shop laden with parcels, the women outside would shout at her angrily, not only because she had been let into the shop before them, but also because she had been allowed to buy so much. Alexandra herself had not fully grasped the magical power of our ration books: she thought we paid for the goods, since the books were always stamped 'paid' at the end of the month, but in fact we never paid a kopeck. Many lower-ranking Comintern officials also had ration books which allowed them unlimited purchase in the State shops, but they had to pay cash for their purchases; only we, the 'aristocrats', were paid for by the 'classless society'.

All that glitters is not gold, however, and we had to put up with a number of inconveniences. One of these was a chauffeur named Razevsky, who was assigned to us by a particular government office. He always chattered endlessly while he was driving us and there was no way of reducing him to silence. Not only was he constantly turning round and ignoring the traffic, but he also drove at breakneck speed, which Otto found a nerve-racking experience. More than once my husband said to me: 'He'll be the death of both of us.' But he didn't dare complain to the office which had assigned Razevsky to us.

One day when I was alone in the car, the chauffeur asked me very earnestly whether I could do him a favour. 'You see, Comrade Kuusinen, I've written a play. Would you be so good as to read it and tell me your opinion of it? And I would also like to ask you to recommend it to the Drama Commission.'

'Certainly,' I replied, 'I'll do so with pleasure.'

'It so happens I have it with me,' he said and, fishing the manuscript out from under his seat, he handed it to me over his shoulder. It consisted of some two hundred dog-eared sheets scrawled in pencil.

I began to read it the moment I got home, and had not got very far when Otto came in. I had just laughed aloud over a particularly gross eulogy of Stalin, and Otto asked what I was reading. I replied: 'You'll never believe it, but it's a play our chauffeur has written. He asked me to read it and put in a good word for him with the Drama Commission.'

'I imagine it's hard going?'

'More than that. It's such frightful rubbish that one can't stop laughing.'

'What will you do with it?'

'I shall write to the Commission and tell them not to bother to read it.'

'But no, don't you see, this is the chance we've been waiting for. You must write and tell them this is the most important play you have ever read. Suggest they print ten thousand copies; then they'll at least bring out a small edition, and one bad book more or less in the country really won't make any difference. The most important thing for us is for Razevsky to be removed from the chauffeur class and become a dramatist—that way we'll be shot of him.'

I could not bring myself to recommend Razevsky's play, but I sent it in to the Commission, and Otto's prediction was fulfilled. We lost a bad chauffeur and the Soviet Union gained a new dramatist.

In the early days of his regime Stalin was often to be seen in public; as yet he was not afraid to appear freely amongst the people. When I began to work for the Comintern in 1924, he often came to the sessions of the Political Secretariat in the Red Hall of the Comintern building, and was almost always present at the plenary sessions of the Executive Committee in the Kremlin auditorium. He listened attentively to the Russian translations of the speeches of foreign Communists, and his summing-up of their activities was terse and penetrating, never loud and provocative like Khrushchev's utterances in later years.

When I was called to meet Stalin for the first time I was sitting high up in the branches of a tree. For many years Otto and I spent our holidays in the Caucasus, and this was in the autumn of 1926, at Sochi on the Black Sea. We stayed in the Kusliankam, a two-storey *dacha* isolated from the outside world in a beautiful, cool park. The *dacha* and the surrounding woods were used exclusively by high government officials and party functionaries, and were closely and constantly guarded. A convalescent home called the Riviera lay near by, and its employees served us also. We occupied the ground floor of the *dacha* every autumn, while Sergey Kirov, the Party Secretary of the Leningrad district, lived above us. In later years Kirov was considered to be the likely successor of Stalin, but in December 1934 he was murdered, probably on Stalin's orders. When we took our holidays together in 1926, Kirov, a carefree bachelor, was always ready to do anything for Otto and me.

Stalin was holidaying at the same time and was staying quite near us in a very elegant *dacha* on the road to Machesta, right on the sea-shore. One day I had climbed up a tree from which one could enjoy a view of the Black Sea, when I saw a car, with a uniformed chauffeur and a single passenger, stop at our garden gate. From my airy seat I watched the soldier jump out and run into the *dacha*; seconds later Otto came out and called to me. At first I did not feel in the least inclined to answer—but when I heard him order the soldier to look for me in the park, I realized it must be something important and scrambled down.

Otto was very nervous and said to me quietly, but in a significant tone: 'It's Stalin.' The visitor was indeed Stalin; he did not get out, but Otto and I got into the car with him, and before I knew what had happened I was sitting between the two men and we drove off. Stalin's manner was polite though rather stiff. He said he would like to show us his native Georgia, to which I unthinkingly answered that I had spent my previous leave in the Caucasus and knew the region a little. Otto made a frightened face and looked at me penetratingly, but Stalin did not take my remark amiss. He said he knew that I had been there, but could not imagine that I had really taken in the beauty of the mountains. Otto was obviously nervous during this conversation, and I myself could not restrain a certain uneasiness: why was Stalin being so amiable?

I asked after his wife Alliluyeva, and Stalin said she had left to spend some time with relatives. Then suddenly he addressed me in Finnish. I was taken aback, not only by his use of Finnish but by the meaning of his words: for the Secretary General of the Communist Party, and therefore the most powerful man in the country, had asked: 'Have you any cream for coffee?'

To my enquiry where he had learned the phrase he explained: 'Before the Revolution my wife and I had to flee from Petrograd to Finland. We lived at Hiekka, a suburb of Vyborg on the western side of the bay, where almost every family kept a cow, and my wife used to send me to the neighbours to buy cream for our coffee. So I had to learn how to ask for it in Finnish.'

'And what did the housewives answer?'

'When they had cream they said "*On, on*", and when they had none they said "*Ei ole*".'

I laughed long and loud, and Stalin seemed delighted that he had broken the ice between us. As he became more relaxed he slapped his boot with the palm of his hand—I never saw him wear anything on his feet but riding boots—and cried: 'I'm the only real proletariat here, for my name ends in "shvili". All the other Georgian comrades, with names in "idze" or "adze", are either aristocrats or bourgeois.' So saying, he named three of his best friends—Yenukidze, Lominadze and Ordzhonikidze—who all had high positions in the government. A few years later, however, the first two were liquidated by their good friend Stalin, and Ordzhonikidze committed suicide.

Shortly afterwards we met Stalin again, and this time I received a very different impression of him. He sent his car to fetch us and we learned that a trip on the Black Sea was planned. At the landing-stage we found Stalin's small, brown-painted, insignificant-looking motor-boat. He received us cordially in a cabin and said to a sailor: 'I shall serve these guests myself.' There was fruit on the table and a lot of wine and champagne bottles. Stalin filled our glasses and put a record on the gramophone: it was the delightful Georgian folk-song 'Suliko', but it rather lost its charm as he played it over and over again. He also drank glass after glass of wine, and after a while he began to dance. It was a gruesome sight, and the more he drank the more fearful he looked. The whole performance seemed like a bad dream. He bellowed with laughter, staggering and stamping round the cabin completely out of time with the lovely music. The general impression was not only coarse and vulgar, but so bizarre that it seemed like a kind of sinister threat. The most frightening thing of all was that, despite his drunkenness, he still seemed sober enough to observe my reaction to his conduct. We spent the whole day on the Black Sea with the drunken dictator, who seemed to me more and more like some dreadful monster. The sun shone and the water glittered, but the frightful spectacle of Stalin's wild dance spoiled any pleasure one might have had. When we returned to our *dacha*, I told Otto firmly that I would never again go on one of Stalin's excursions.

That unpleasant day on the Black Sea showed me Stalin as he really was. Later Otto revealed to me another of the dictator's peculiarities—the more ruthless and cold-blooded he became, the more he lived in an almost insane fear for his life. When he went on a rail journey, even in his Georgian homeland, the particular train and the carriage in which he sat were kept a secret from the public. Once, on a drive from Sochi to Machesta, he passed a place where the roadway had been repaired and was being sprayed with water by firemen. One of them saw the car coming up the mountain road and played the hose on it as a joke. Immediately a uniformed bodyguard jumped out and seized the offender, though none of the road workers had any idea that it was Stalin in the car.

In 1938 Stalin's mother died in Tiflis, but he was so afraid for his own life that he did not go to the funeral. When I stayed there in 1948 I was told how the local Party authorities had buried the old woman in the crypt of a church, and both they and the rest of the Georgian population had felt injured in their pride because Stalin had not come to his mother's funeral.

I have very few personal memories of Lenin, since I only met him a few times at the Comintern, in the autumn of 1922. At that time he had so far recovered from his first heart attack that he was able to work for a period of some three months. I often spoke with him on the telephone, as he used to ring up in the evenings on our private line, and when Otto was not there I had to answer. Lenin was always very pleasant; he would ask me in German how I was, and leave a message for Otto to ring him back as soon as possible.

Lenin was noted for his wit, and I once heard an example of this. It was in the Red Hall of the Comintern building: Clara Zetkin was visiting Moscow and told Lenin that she knew a very good heart specialist in Berlin. 'I would like to have him come and examine you.'

Lenin replied: 'I have already been examined by countless specialists, but I'm afraid it's all in vain. Thank you, nevertheless, for your offer.'

'But I can assure you, this doctor is the best in the world, and what's more he's a very good Communist and belongs to our Party.'

'Then I shan't let him examine me, for who ever heard of a good Communist being a good doctor?'

My personal acquaintance with Lenin consists solely of such insignificant events. Anything else I know about him I heard from Otto and others. I knew his sister and his widow rather better, on the other hand. A few Bolshevik leaders knew at that time how ill he was, and were not surprised by his death in January 1924. Everyone knew he had had heart attacks, and many believed that he had a weak heart.

In the autumn of 1925 I had an unexpected telephone call from Leningrad. To my astonishment I heard that my brother Väinö was there and would be coming to Moscow by the night train. Väinö had spent seven years at grammar school and had gone into the army as a sergeant. What was he now doing on Russian soil? When I met him at the station, my first question was: 'Why have you come?' To which he replied: 'I didn't come, I was brought.' And he went on to tell me his incredible story. He had been commanding a group of soldiers guarding part of the Suomenlinna fortress on the coast near Helsinki. One dark autumn night, Väinö had been inspecting the sentries. A violent storm sent great waves crashing against the cliffs. Suddenly he saw a large motor-boat approaching the shore. Struggling against the howling wind, he shouted: 'Who goes there?' There was no reply, but five men jumped ashore, grabbed hold of him and dragged him on to the boat, which made off to the open sea. Before he knew what had happened he found himself in Krety prison in Leningrad. When he declared that he was my brother he was taken to Yrjö Sirola's office at the 'Communist University for the National Minorities of the West' in Leningrad.[10] Sirola had received him kindly but told him that he could not return to Finland, since he would be punished as a deserter; and so now he was my guest in Moscow.

We had a long discussion as to what Väinö should do. Since he was afraid to return to Finland, there was only one solution: he must go back to Leningrad. So he went there, was given the new surname of Kanga, and the university found some work for him. He was supposed to check the Finnish translation of *Das Kapital*, since the professor at Helsinki who had translated the book had apparently distorted many of Marx's ideas, but although Väinö had a good grasp of German he was not up to this task. So he was given free board and lodging in the student hostel and it was suggested that he should study Russian. A brilliant future was promised him, and he did as he was told.

After a few years he was appointed director of the agricultural college at Petrozavodsk, the capital of Soviet Karelia, where he married a Finnish girl. Väinö had absolutely no qualifications for this post, since he had grown up in a town and had never had anything to do with agriculture. I mention this chiefly to show how indiscriminately positions were filled at that time in the USSR.

II

The Comintern

From 1924 to 1933 it fell to my lot to work for the Communist International or 'Comintern'. Before coming to Moscow I knew next to nothing about this organization, but before long I was to become closely acquainted with the 'Headquarters of the World Revolution'. In 1921 my husband had been appointed secretary of the Executive Committee of the Comintern (ECCI), which included the duty of laying down the organization's guiding principles, and in the autumn of 1922 he began to invite me to take part in evening discussions on Comintern affairs in our apartment at the Lux Hotel. Our visitors included Comintern officials, such as Pyatnitsky and Rakosi of Hungary: the discussions continued late into the night, as was the custom in Moscow then and later. I thus became a certain extent acquainted with the personnel, problems and activities of the Comintern before I began to work for it myself. Otto even enlisted my help on occasion with delicate affairs which he wanted to keep secret from his office colleagues. Although I was only a two-finger typist, my first task was to copy out a document which Otto had drawn up in German for the International Control Commission. This began with a series of charges against Alexandra Kollontay, who had allegedly conspired with Shlyapnikov against certain aspects of Comintern policy. After the accusations came Alexandra's confession and an oath that in future she would not oppose the policies of the Comintern. All this was carefully drafted and only needed to be signed by her. Otto impressed upon me that this was a delicate matter which must not become known in the office and which I must not talk about. When in my ignorance I asked who Alexandra Kollontay was, he explained that she was a very intelligent and gifted woman, who was apparently fated to fall into difficult situations because she was always being carried away by enthusiasm for hopeless causes.

In addition to copying work, Otto began to canvass my opinion of certain Comintern personalities. He admitted that he had learned from bitter experience not to rely solely on his own judgement in assessing the character and capabilities of others. The way in which he sounded out me and others before forming his own opinion showed how carefully he always planned his course of action, and how anxious he was to avoid mistakes.

I learned from Otto and his colleagues that long before the Revolution of 1917, Lenin had dreamt of founding an international body which would organize and carry out revolutions so as to overthrow the capitalist system throughout the world and replace it with Communist governments under the new Bolshevik order. In December 1918 or January 1919 Lenin had invited a few of his friends and advisers to a meeting in Moscow, including several leaders of the ill-fated Communist uprising in Finland in 1918. The aim of this meeting was to discuss the founding of a centrally controlled international organization, which would have its headquarters in Moscow and would replace the Second International. I possessed in Moscow a photograph of this gathering, which included Lenin, Zinoviev, Trotsky and probably also Kameniev, as well as Otto Kuusinen and three other Finns—Kullervo Manner, Yrjö Sirola and Eino Rahja.

The result of this preparatory meeting was that at the beginning of 1919 Lenin called a larger meeting in Moscow to discuss the founding of a 'Third International'. Apart from Hugo Eberlein from Germany, an Austrian and a couple of Russians, all the participants were political refugees or exiles who were living in Soviet Russia or were on their way through. Hugo Eberlein was the only authorized representative of a Communist organization outside Russia, and apart from him none of the foreigners had the right or the authority to speak for anyone but themselves. Kuusinen once pointed out to me the comic fact that some of these so-called delegates had never seen the country they were supposed to be representing.

Although Lenin had chosen the participants in this hurriedly called conference fairly indiscriminately, Moscow propaganda later inflated its importance by referring to it as the 'Founding Congress of the Communist International'. Most of the participants were intellectual theoreticians, like Lenin himself. The founding of the Comintern had proceeded in a fairly haphazard fashion and without great proclamations: no definite programme was drawn up, there was no organized leadership or assignment of areas of responsibility, and apart from a couple of editors of propaganda leaflets there was no permanent staff. Thus the Comintern was not in a position to do anything much beyond printing a self-glorifying leaflet and urging workers abroad to support 'the cause'. The 'little fish' was trying to convince the world that it was a 'big fish'. No one will deny the meetings of 1919 and 1920 a certain historical significance, but, to impress both friend and foe, the importance of those who were present was greatly exaggerated in later years. According to Otto, in those early years there was no real Comintern organization.

Some time after the conference in March 1919, the palace on Denezhny Pereulok was set up as the central office for the world revolution. Yet on my first visit in 1922 I could not, with the best will in the world, see in it more than a motley collection of garrulous Russians and foreign intellectuals. As I mentioned, the German Embassy was housed in this building for a short time in 1918, and it was here that the Ambassador Count Mirbach was murdered—according to the official announcement, by the Social Revolutionaries' Party (SR) as a protest against the Brest-Litovsk peace treaty. Readers may remember that a large number of Social Revolutionaries were shot after Lenin had declared that the Ambassador's murder was meant as the prelude to an uprising against the Bolshevik regime. However, I soon learnt that the SR's had not in fact been the culprits. When I came home one day, Otto was in his study with a tall, bearded young man, who was introduced to me as Comrade Safir. After he had left, Otto informed me with a smile that I had just met Count Mirbach's murderer, whose real name was Blumkin.[11] He was an official of the Cheka (the political police) and was about to go abroad on an important mission for the Comintern. When I remarked that Mirbach had been murdered by the Social Revolutionaries, Otto broke into loud laughter. Apparently the assassination was merely an excuse to get the Social Revolutionaries out of the way, since they were Lenin's strongest opponents.

At the beginning of 1921 Lenin called Otto back from Stockholm and gave him the task of planning the 'organizational principles' which were approved by the third Comintern Congress in July 1921.[12] All Communist parties in the world were reorganized in conformity with these principles, and Otto was highly praised for the way in which they embodied Lenin's teaching. I remember well the letter, now in the Lenin Museum in Moscow, in which Lenin stated that no one but Kuusinen could have formulated the principles so well. Otto wrote them in German and Wilhelm Koenen, a German Communist, had the task of correcting his style.

At the third congress Grigori Zinoviev was elected chairman of the Executive Committee of the Comintern. Some thirty-nine more or less authentic Communist Parties became members of the Comintern at this congress. As a result they gradually moved further and further away from the real interests of the workers' movement in their own countries, and during the next decade tended more and more to serve the interests of the leaders of the Third International who were resident in Moscow. I use the term 'more or less authentic' Parties advisedly, for at the time some of them consisted of only a few people or only existed on paper. They too were 'little fish' pretending to be 'big fish'.

I should at this point say something about the way in which the Comintern was organized. Theoretically and on paper, the congresses in Moscow to which each member Party sent its authorized representative embodied the highest authority of the Communist International. Yet during the twenty-four years of the Comintern's existence only seven congresses were held. In between times the leadership was exercised by the Executive Committee (ECCI), but this again only held seven plenary sessions. The Executive Committee consisted of some thirty people elected by the congresses from the delegates of all the member Parties. A few of the larger Parties, such as the German and the Russian, had more than one representative on the Executive Committee. Almost all the representatives lived in Moscow.

The day-to-day activities of the Comintern were handled by the Political Secretariat of the ECCI, whose members were likewise elected during the congresses. It consisted of some eight to ten members who always had to be available in Moscow. Within the Political Secretariat was a smaller secretariat consisting of three Comintern executives, known as the 'Inner Commission'.[13] During the nine years in which I was employed at Comintern headquarters there were only three men whose orders were obeyed to the letter, and these were the members of this closed circle: Otto Kuusinen, Osip Pyatnitsky and Dmitri Manuilsky. Kuusinen was responsible for the guilding principles of the organization and for watching political and economic developments in the capitalist countries. Pyatnitsky controlled secret activities and financial affairs, as well as questions of personnel and management. Manuilsky usually had the least to say in major decisions; he functioned to a certain extent as a liaison man and observer for the Central Committee of the Russian Party, and also looked after Comintern activities in France and Belgium, as he knew both countries from his student days. Otto's protégé, Mauno Heimo, kept the minutes of the Inner Commission.

Each member Party had the right to bring its own problems before the Comintern's Executive Committee in Moscow through its authorized representative; the Committee could also take the initiative in solving serious arguments and conflicts within a foreign Party. In the latter case, representatives of the Party in question were summoned to Moscow, and the Political Secretariat appointed Comintern officials to hold discussions with them, which sometimes lasted for months on end. Finally a resolution was voted on. Such resolutions were generally drafted by the Comintern long before the foreign delegation arrived in Moscow, but they frequently had to be altered during the discussions. After the voting, the delegation returned to their country to control their Party's activities in accordance with the resolution. Yet the decisions laid down in these resolutions were often unsuited to the particular case or unworkable, and in many instances they proved contrary to the interests of the Comintern members.

Apart from the conflict between Stalin and Trotsky, the affairs of the Russian Party were never discussed in Comintern assemblies; however, this did not prevent rumours from circulating about the power struggles in the higher echelons of the Soviet government and Party, for these conflicts often produced frightening upheavals whose effects naturally extended to the Comintern. It was strictly forbidden to mention Soviet Party affairs in the Comintern assemblies when there were foreign Communists present. They were regarded as so secret that they were above all discussion or debate. But Parties outside the Soviet Union were obliged to inform the Comintern of all their activities, and the Cheka planted agents in these Parties or recruited them from the latter's ranks, so as to keep a close check on everything they did. Foreign delegates who dared to ask—through ignorance or naïvety—why the Soviet Union's internal problems were never discussed, were fobbed off with a sarcastic or evasive reply.

Next to the Executive Committee there was the International Control Commission (ICC), which served as a sort of court of appeal for all Communist Parties and watched over the orthodoxy and morale of each one. The nineteen or so members of this commission were elected at the Comintern congresses; theoretically the ICC stood above the Control Commission of the Soviet Party as well as the others. Its director was a Lithuanian lawyer by the name of Angeretis, and he was probably the only person who was continually present in the ICC office. The Control Commission could summon before it any Cominterm employee, regardless of whether he belonged to the Soviet or another Party, and pass judgement on him for his real or alleged misdemeanours. If the person concerned was a high official he was usually severely reprimanded before a specially called assembly, and then dismissed. The sessions and decisions were generally kept secret, and no minutes were taken. Only if a record was absolutely essential were minutes taken, by the German Alice Abramowitsch. (I know that Otto once instructed her to take down every word when he made a speech indicting his long-standing Finnish rival Kullervo Manner before the ICC in 1933. Manner was arrested after this speech.) Usually only the accuser and accused appeared before the ICC judges, and no important decisions were ever taken without first obtaining Kuusinen's opinion.

Amongst the committees which decided the Comintern's policies, and of which the Inner Commission was the most powerful and most secret, there were many permanent departments of varying sizes, and as they all contributed to the work of the Comintern, they were all of some importance. The department whose secret activities overshadowed all the others, however, was the OMS, which was as it were the brain and the inner sanctum of the Comintern. The initials OMS stand for *Otdel Mezhdunarodnykh Svyazey*, or International Relations Section. From here a network of permanent agents spread throughout the whole world, receiving instructions and conveying orders and directives to the local Party leaders. One of the most delicate tasks of these agents was the distribution of Comintern funds for Party activities and propaganda. (Various organizations such as the 'Friends of the Soviet Union' or the 'League for Peace and Democracy' were created to camouflage this activity.) In the twenties these funds were sent to the OMS 'resident' by diplomatic courier: the 'resident' was generally a member of the Soviet Embassy, who could claim diplomatic immunity. In many countries there were trade organizations which saw to the distribution of the funds, such as Amtorg in New York and Arcos in London. The OMS's activities extended into many other areas: it controlled all secret undertakings and missions, the secret intelligence service, the encoding and decoding of messages, and a large part of the propaganda system.

The OMS was also the link between the Comintern and Soviet military intelligence, and also the secret police, the name of which changed constantly over the years; after 'Cheka' it was called the 'GPU', 'NKVD' and 'MVD'; at present it is known as the 'KGB'.[14] This collaboration was not always harmonious, however, and relations between the OMS and the secret police were particularly bad. This was possibly one reason why so many Comintern officials perished in the great purges of the thirties. My husband harboured a decided aversion towards the military intelligence service.

The chief of the OMS from the foundation of the Comintern was Mirov-Abramov,[15] but the veteran Bolshevik Osip Pyatnitsky, a member of the triumvirate of the Inner Commission and the right man for his job, had at least as much say in its running. Pyatnitsky was a Lithuanian and had started life as a tailor's apprentice. He had been active in revolutionary movements from his earliest youth, around 1900, and made up for a lack of formal education by his extensive experience in the field of illegal activities. Having a close knowledge of the Russian-German frontier district, he used to smuggle anti-Tsarist pamphlets and newspapers into Russia and help agents across the frontier. Later he worked for Lenin for several years in Germany, England, France and Switzerland. He was arrested during a mission in Russia and sent to Siberia for two years; he regained his freedom in 1917. Pyatnitsky was undoubtedly one of the mainstays of the Comintern, yet he received little thanks for it; he was accused of Trotskyism and perished in the purges at the end of the thirties. Mirov-Abramov met the same fate. One of the sections of the OMS was the documents office; its leader, Milter, produced excellent forgeries of visas, stamps and other documents. Passports were seldom forged, on the other hand, as it was easier to obtain used (or even better 'clean', i.e. unused) passports through the Communist Parties in the different countries, and merely change the photographs and enter the necessary visas and stamps. There was a particular demand for US passports, and a reserve of these was always kept available. When foreign delegates entered the country to take part in meetings and congresses, they had to give up their passports and only received them back on leaving. They doubtless had no idea that interesting details were copied from them. About ten people worked under Milter, who also fell victim to the purge in 1937.

One of the largest departments of the Comintern was the Press Department. It's name was misleading: instead of producing newspapers and other publications, it was the place which provided translators and stenographers in all the necessary languages—Russian, German, Spanish, French and English. Since most of the employees below the rank of departmental head had no permanent secretaries, they had to enlist the aid of the Press Department, which provided a duplicating and copying service and which high-ranking officials could also call upon for secretarial help. One of its members was a Hungarian émigré named Levin; an exceptionally gifted man, he was perhaps the best simultaneous interpreter of his time and there seemed to be no language which he had not mastered. One day I asked him how he could translate so smoothly from German. 'Surely you have to wait for the end of the sentence to know what verb the speaker is going to use? I can't understand how you manage it.'

'No,' said Levin, 'as soon as they begin a sentence I know at once what verb they are going to use, and I'm seldom wrong.'

Another large department was the Organization Department; when I arrived it was led by an Old Bolshevik, Boris Vasiliev. He later took up a post under the Central Committee of the Soviet Communist Party, and his successor was an Estonian named Mehring, who perished in the purge of 1937. The most important task of this department was the constant observation of foreign Parties, to ensure that the Comintern's directives were obeyed and also to uncover any deviations or internal disputes.

The economic and political reports which appeared in the weekly Comintern bulletin helped to reveal whether a particular Party had acted unwisely at a particular moment, or had failed to react to an important event. When the Organization Department discovered an apparent misdemeanour on the part of a foreign Communist Party, its director or his deputy went to see this Party's representative on the Executive Committee and discussed with him what directives or reprimands should be sent to the delinquents. In particularly serious cases, the director would recommend that a special instructor be sent from the Organization Department to clear up the problem in the country concerned.

Whenever people from Comintern headquarters went abroad they had to hand in their Party card or booklet, and in the case of an illegal journey all their other identity papers, to the Organization Department, which kept them until the person in question returned.

Another large and important department was the Agitprop Department, which provided the foreign Parties with propaganda material and directed activities in collaboration with the OMS. The Moscow Radio, named after the Comintern although not directly controlled by it, used material from the Agitprop Department.

I myself began working for the Comintern in 1924, in the Information Department; its head at the time was Gusev, an Old Bolshevik, but he was soon replaced by another Russian, Boris Shubin. This large department employed specialists who had to keep themselves informed of events in all the major countries of the world. Newspapers and periodicals of all political persuasions were read there; abstracts were made of any important items and published in the weekly bulletin. The Information Department had national and regional secretariats, but neighbouring countries with similar problems were often included in one and the same secretariat.

The Administration Department should also be mentioned; its director was the able Petersburg lawyer Kivilovich, supported by his not overly intelligent assistant, Kozlov. Kivilovich's department was responsible for all domestic matters in the Comintern building and in the Moscow hotels Lux and Maly Parizh. It also reserved hotel rooms, bought theatre tickets and dealt with the reception of foreign delegates in Moscow. It controlled the Financial Office under the Paymaster-General Orest, which was responsible for paying salaries and distributing funds.

Naturally there was also a Personnel Office, which controlled all the employees and above all checked on their political reliability. This office was staffed by members of the GPU, who often had little respect for the views of the Comintern leaders, and additional quarrels between the two organizations arose as a result.

There was also a Women's Secretariat in the Comintern, headed by the German Clara Zetkin. Officially she was the only female member of the Executive Committee, but as she was old and almost blind by that time, her protégée Herta Sturm, likewise a German, was the actual driving force. The Secretariat had the task of keeping informed about the activities of various left wing women's organizations throughout the world. It also had to receive the Communist women leaders who visited Moscow and make sure they did not receive a false impression of social life in the capital.

Finally three other organizations should be mentioned which maintained a close working relationship with the Comintern and received their instructions and financial support from it.

These were the Communist Youth International[16], the Krestintern (Communist-led peasant International)[17] and the Profintern[18] (International Trade Union Federation). The Youth International had its offices in the Comintern building; as the name implies, it supervised all organized youth activities and also sent agents abroad. The Krestintern, under the Georgian Lominadze, was founded to bring foreign farm-workers' and peasant movements under the influence of the Comintern, though this proved more or less fruitless. The Profintern was the only one of these three organizations that had any importance.

I should say something here about Mauno Heimo, who could be called the effective day-to-day manager of the Comintern. He was a Finnish law student who took part in the uprising in 1918 and escaped to Sweden. It was he who helped Otto to move secretly from Sweden to the Soviet Union at that time. Otto knew him well, and it was at his request that Heimo came to Moscow at the beginning of 1924. I happened to be present when Heimo arrived at our apartment in the Lux Hotel. Otto offered him a seat and began to talk about his most pressing problems: 'I have been waiting for you for a long time. There is no proper organization in the Comintern and you and I must create one. There is no proper staff and no proper delineation of responsibilities. Fifteen hundred people are being paid for their work, but no one knows who his superior is or what authority he has or even what he is actually supposed to be doing. It's a real bureaucratic muddle. We must reorganize the whole staff from the ground up.' To which Heimo replied: 'Just give me time to look around a little; first of all I would like a list of the employees, so that I can get some idea of who these fifteen hundred people are.'

Barely a week after this conversation, Heimo came to our apartment one evening and gave Otto the following report: 'I have studied the list closely and got to know most of the senior people; I have also found out what they are doing. I have made a list of superfluous personnel, of which there are about a thousand. But I need a little more time to think how best to divide up the work. One thing is certain—we need a building more suited to our work than the present one. If it's all right with you I should like to ask the Soviet CP to give us a suitable building.'

A day or so later Heimo had thoroughly inspected a building at No. 6 Mokhovaya Street, near the Kremlin, and the same evening he brought Otto a plan on which he had shown how the floors and apartments could be rearranged into offices. He was a remarkably able fellow, with a fantastic gift for organization and personnel matters. When he showed Otto the layout he also presented him with written proposals as to how the functions of the Comintern could be divided up so as to achieve higher efficiency and secrecy. Otto, who had no gift for management, was greatly impressed by this attribute of Heimo's. In addition Heimo was good at dealing with people, and well liked generally. He had organized all the work in such a way that he himself, together with Otto, Pyatnitsky, and in less important matters Manuilsky, held the reins of the organization and concentrated all the power in their hands. Thus Heimo was in a sense the executive director of the Comintern and had extensive powers to make decisions about its day-to-day running without having to consult his superiors. It is very probable that on any particular day Heimo knew better than anyone else what was going on in the offices of the Comintern. His title of 'Secretary for the Secretariats', which was created specially for him, opened all doors. Yet, like Otto, he preferred not to advertise his enormous powers, and to make it appear to outsiders that he was only an insignificant lackey.

Soon after his arrival in Moscow, Heimo married an American woman, a Latvian by birth, who had come over as an interpreter with the American Relief Commission. They had a son, but I do not know what happened to him or his mother. Heimo himself perished during Stalin's reign of terror. His rôle in the reorganization and daily running of the Comintern was far greater than is generally realized. One proof of this is the fact that he was commissioned, together with Zinoviev's secretary Tivle, to write an official history of the first ten years of the Comintern.[19]

On entering the Comintern building by the main entrance, one found oneself opposite the orderly room for the men who guarded the building and kept away unwelcome visitors. The guards, who wore plain clothes, were not employed by the Comintern itself but by the GPU, and their orders and regulations had to be strictly observed. There was always a guard on duty at the entrance door, and also on the fifth floor at the entrance to the OMS, the inner sanctum of the Comintern. All visitors were first asked the object of their visit, and most of them had made an appointment with one or another official. The visitor was then led into the waiting room, while the orderly informed Heimo's office by telephone. Heimo checked the appointment and then instructed the orderly to make out a pass for the visitor. After the pass had been made out it was checked in the adjoining room, and the visitor's identity papers were also checked. Only then was he taken to the office he had come to visit.

Employees had to clock in and out at the orderly room when they entered and left the building. This did not apply, however, to members of the Executive Committee and the highest-ranking Comintern officials.

The Comintern library and archives were kept in the basement. The librarian was the exceptionally gifted Allan Wallenius, a former Finnish student and protégé of Otto's, who had taken a librarian's course at the New York Public Library and was fluent in several languages. He perished in the purge of 1938.

The highly competent archivist was Boris Reinstein, who had studied chemistry in his youth in Paris, and had been arrested there for revolutionary activities. Later he had emigrated to the United States, but returned to Russia after the Revolution. He was a cultivated and sociable old man. I think it was one day in 1928 that I came into the archive room and found him sitting pensively with his chin propped on his hand. I asked him why he looked so mournful and he answered: 'I've been thinking that there are three kinds of people in this world—the first die too early, the second die too late, and the third manage to die just at the right time. I'm trying to put our leaders into these three categories. Obviously, Lenin died too early, and it would have been a good thing for our country if he had lived longer, whereas Trotsky outlived his usefulness; he should have died at a particular time, but he went on living. Look at this paper— I've put the names of a few leaders in the category I think they belong to.' I was dumbfounded to see that Reinstein had dared to put Stalin's name in the second column. 'But,' he went on, 'I don't know what I ought to put for myself. I often think I have

46

already lived too long and am no longer any use. I really don't know.' Reinstein was in fact one of the few Comintern officials who had the good fortune to die a natural death.

Hertta Kuusinen, Otto's daughter by his first marriage, came to Moscow in 1929 after finishing school in Finland. Under Soviet law everyone had to take employment on reaching the age of eighteen, and this applied to Hertta as well. I suggested that she should continue her education, but Otto would not hear of it, since he did not think much of Russian schools and Hertta did not speak Russian. I then suggested that she might work in the Comintern library, and asked Allan Wallenius to take her on and train her as a librarian. So Hertta got her first job in the library, and apart from a Comintern course in cryptography she did not go to any school in the USSR. Shortly after starting in the library she married the Finn Tuure Lehen, who was studying at the Soviet Military Academy. After she had learned the principles of librarianship Hertta was placed at the disposal of the Finnish Party, and was later sent on a special mission to Finland. The plan miscarried, she was arrested and spent several years in prison.[20] After her release in 1944 she was given a leading position in the Finnish Communist Party, which she occupied until her father's death in 1965. Hertta was the only one of Otto's relatives who came to live in the Soviet Union and stayed there unmolested. She never in fact saw the true face of Russian Communism, since she did no more than travel to and fro between the Lux Hotel and the Comintern building.

I myself began to work in the Comintern in April 1924. Heimo took down my particulars and I had to sign a number of papers and documents, including one which asked whether I was acquainted with Marxism. I was told that Lenin had answered this question with the words 'I'm doing my best to learn it.' Heimo then took me to a vacant desk in an office where Emelyan Yaroslavsky worked. Yaroslavsky was at that time at the head of the Control Commission of the Soviet Party, which was an extremely responsible position. I was told that he was working in the Comintern building in order to study some highly confidential documents in the archives. However that may be, he and I said little to one another. First of all I was given a pile of material in German to read, which explained how the

Comintern functioned and gave a résumé of its history and the resolutions and decisions it had made. It was the first task of every new employee to make himself familiar with this material.

As already mentioned, I was first given a job in the Information Department. Because of my Scandinavian origin I had to follow political and economic events in Sweden, Norway and Denmark, and was given the title of 'Adviser on Scandinavia'. I had to read carefully all the most important newspapers and magazines, as well as TASS news and the Soviet diplomatic reports dealing with these areas. My assistant was Willi Mielenz, a young man from Berlin, and I was able to make use of the shorthand typists from the Press Department. Our job was to prepare two reports a week, in German, on each of the three countries; one of these dealt with politics and the other with economic developments. The reports had to be delivered to Heimo's desk every Friday at four p.m. Heimo or his assistant read through the reports, crossed out anything which seemed unimportant, and then decided which parts should be translated into Russian for the officials who did not read German; I remember that the translations were sent to Stalin's secretariat among other places.

We received two kinds of TASS telegrams: the first, on grey paper, carried news which could be published in the press, while the second, on pink paper, were only to be read by a limited number of Comintern officials and members of the Central Committee of the Soviet CP. The foreign news editors of *Pravda* and *Izvestia*, as well as the midday paper *Vechernyaya Moskva*, often dropped in to see whether the telegrams contained any news they could make use of. I could sometimes give them information from the pink telegrams about strikes and such-like events, but was not allowed to show them the telegram itself.

Mielenz had worked in a Swedish factory during the first world war and had learnt very good Swedish. He was a pleasant person and a good assistant, but he had one failing which eventually put an end to his career. Not only did he criticize the way in which the Soviet government handled certain problems, but he was also so naïve that he wrote letters to the Moscow authorities in which, with a certain Germanic arrogance, he made specific proposals as to how working and other conditions

48

in Moscow could be improved. In fact I quite frequently agreed with his criticisms, but I kept my views private and only shared them with my husband. I warned Willi that it was not only useless but even dangerous to give such advice, but he was not to be dissuaded. When I returned from America in 1933 I found my former office empty, and no one seemed able to answer my question as to where Willi was.

Fortunately there were no earth-shaking events in Scandinavia during the twenties, otherwise the weekly reports would have been a much more burdensome task than they were. I only remember certain difficulties with the Norwegian trade unions; everything else in these reports has more or less vanished from my memory.

In 1925 there was a plenary session of ECCI to discuss the failure of the Swedish Communist Party to carry out certain Comintern instructions, and especially to arrange mass demonstrations of workers on May Day as had been done in Oslo and Copenhagen. Kilbom, who headed the delegation (its other members were Samuelson and Ström), answered the charge in a long and polished speech. His words and demeanour gave the impression of a man obsessed with his own importance. In fact the whole Swedish delegation had a very high opinion of itself—a view which was not, however, shared by the Comintern. Sweden was a predominantly bourgeois country with a very small Communist Party, and even a man of boundless optimism could hardly believe that it could bring about a revolution, or even a successful revolt. Kilbom admitted that the Party had been instructed to arrange demonstrations, and said that extensive preparations had in fact been made; but unfortunately it had rained on the first day of May, and the leaders had called off the demonstration because they knew that only a few workers would take part in such bad weather, and they judged that the cancellation would harm the Party's image less than an under-attended demonstration. After this effort to justify the actions of his Party, Kilbom sat down, and Pyatnitsky and other Comintern leaders weighed in with sarcastic comments. Really? So it rained, did it? And what would you have done if you had been having a revolution? Would you have called that off too? What would have happened to the October revolution if we had worried

49

about rain or snow or slush, when we were standing in it up to our waists?

At this, Kilbom got up again and answered with as much patience and dignity as he could muster: 'It may well be that we make little mistakes in Sweden now and then—a step to the right or a step to the left, perhaps—but please do not forget that we are still on the way to revolution.' Hardly had these words been translated when, to everyone's surprise, Stalin broke in with grim seriousness: 'Not a step to the right and not a step to the left—you must go forwards the whole time.' All those present were convinced that this pronouncement meant the end of Kilbom's career—such was generally the result of a strong public censure on Stalin's part, and in the case of Soviet citizens even worse was to be feared. Kilbom knew very well how these things were treated in Moscow, and I was not surprised when Otto told me later that Kilbom had come to his office in tears and had begged him to have the words about the 'step to the right and the step to the left' stricken from the minutes, together with Stalin's reply. Poor Kilbom was half dead with fear and couldn't say enough in praise of Stalin and Otto. If only they would forgive him his lapse, the whole affair could be forgotten. Otto interceded with Stalin, who smilingly agreed to put Kilbom out of his misery, with the result that a few days later Kilbom was as full of his own importance as ever.

I should say something here about the 'Zinoviev letter' affair. In the autumn of 1924 considerable alarm was caused in Moscow when the British press published a letter, containing instructions from the Comintern to the British Communist Party, which was allegedly signed by Zinoviev, the President of the Executive Committee of the Comintern, and by Otto Kuusinen. This letter caused a political stir in Britain. The facts behind it were as follows:

After its fifth congress in the summer of 1924, the Comintern had sent instructions to the British Party relating mainly to activities in India, where the ground was thought to be fertile for revolution. The British Party had also been instructed to form cells in the Army and to engineer difficulties in the colonies. The British Party had handled the message carelessly, and parts of it had leaked to certain journalists. The latter had thereupon concocted a new letter, which was read out in Parliament as the original and authentic one. It was clear to Otto from the outset that this letter was a forgery, even though it contained a few of the actual instructions. He recognized the forgery by the fact that the second initial was missing from his signature—he always signed himself 'O. W. Kuusinen' and not 'O. Kuusinen'.

Moscow was horrified that the British Communists had handled such a highly confidential document so carelessly, and sent them a sharp rebuke. But when the British Parliament began to make a big affair out of the letter and demanded explanations from the Prime Minister and the Soviet government, there was increasing nervousness not only in the Comintern but also in the People's Commissariat for Foreign Affairs. Chicherin himself paid a visit to the Comintern headquarters and held a long consultation with my husband and Pyatnitsky behind closed doors. Otto told me that Chicherin had raged against the Comintern for getting itself involved in secret activities which would greatly damage the Soviet Union's diplomatic relations. He had demanded that the Comintern should cease to involve itself in illegal work, and should leave this type of activity to the appropriate organizations. As a result of this incident certain types of secret work were in fact transferred from the Comintern to the Fourth Bureau of the Red Army (of which more later) and the GPU. But for the benefit of the British, Chicherin was instructed to declare that the Comintern never indulged in secret or illegal activities and that the 'Zinoviev letter' was a blatant forgery.

The British were not so easily put off, however, and the Trades Union Congress demanded permission to examine the Comintern's files in Moscow. At first this seemed absurd, but Otto and Pyatnitsky decided to remove all suspect material so that the delegation could examine the 'entire' correspondence relating to British affairs as much as they wished. There followed three days and nights of feverish activity, supervised by Mauno Heimo and the head archivist Boris Reinstein, during which compromising documents, and particularly those relating to the 'Zinoviev letter' and the secret instructions to the British Party, were removed from all the files which the British delegation were likely to take an interest in. Even the daily entries of incoming and outgoing correspondence were rewritten, so that the Comintern should appear in a completely innocuous light. The abstracted material was removed to another part of the town, and there was even a rehearsal for the British visit. The TUC sent three delegates, who could all read either Russian or German and inspected a number of rooms and files at Comintern headquarters. The result was that the trio were completely misled and the Comintern was absolved of any subversive and secret activities in England. After the delegation had left, there was general relief and everyone had a good laugh over the fact that they had been able to pull the wool so easily over the Englishmen's eyes.

Lenin had been firmly convinced that in countries where conditions were favourable for a revolution, competent and zealous leaders would arise spontaneously from amongst the population. By the end of 1924, however, Kuusinen had come to the conclusion that this was too optimistic and that it would be necessary to bring promising young Communists from abroad to the USSR, train them as leaders and then send them back to their own or to another country. This was the most important lesson which Kuusinen had learned from the ill-starred revolutions in Finland, Hungary, Germany, Poland and Bulgaria. Good leaders could not be conjured up out of nothing, and must be created within the USSR from the best foreign material. I don't suppose that Kuusinen was alone in this opinion—which was almost self-evident in any case—but he tried sedulously behind the scenes to convert the Soviet leaders to his way of thinking. It was due to his influence that the Lenin School, where young Communists from Western countries were carefully trained in revolutionary methods, was founded in 1925. This was a boarding establishment, kept secret from all outsiders, and was first housed in a small mansion in Kropotkin Street, dating from the time of Catherine the Great. Later, when the number of students grew, the school was moved to a larger building. Until 1939 its principal was Kirsanova, the wife of the chairman of the Party Control Commission, Yaroslavsky. At first the school had only two departments, but in the course of time departments for other nationalities were added until there were finally about ten of them. The courses lasted from two to four years and the curriculum included historical materialism, the history of the different Communist Parties, legal and illegal Party activities, revolutionary methods, the use of codes and other skills. I do not know how many students passed through the school, but it must certainly have been several hundred. A few of them afterwards reached high office in their own countries, such as Enver Hoxha in Albania. An ex-pupil of the Lenin School, Aksel Larsen, is now an important figure in Denmark. Today the school no longer trains leaders for foreign countries and its secret teaching programme has been transferred to another institute.

In 1964 I met a young foreigner in the house of some friends and learned that he was studying at a secret school in Moscow. It was a political and military academy which held five-year courses exclusively for foreigners. The students lived on the premises and both men and women were admitted. The teaching was in Russian and English. A friend disclosed the address to me, and I satisfied myself that the school did really exist there.

The 'Communist University for Eastern Workers,' also known as the Sun Yat-sen University, was controlled by the Comintern and was an indication of the importance with which Asia was regarded in Moscow. Here Chinese and other Asians were trained in revolutionary methods. The principal was Dr Maria Frumkina, whom I became friendly with many years later in the Lefortovo Prison in Moscow.

The Comintern published two journals, the *Communist International* and the *Inprecorr* (International Press Correspondence). The former was the more important, though it did not appear regularly; it contained articles on political theory which were often written by the Comintern leaders. Men like Zinoviev, Varga, Bukharin, Radek and Kuusinen belonged to the staff at different times. The editorial office was in Moscow, but the paper was printed in Hamburg, in German and sometimes in other languages. Hamburg was probably chosen because it was convenient for communication with the rest of the world.

Inprecorr was published in Hamburg at irregular intervals during the twenties. Its editor in chief was Julius Alpari, a multilingual and highly-educated Hungarian Communist who often came to Moscow for advice and material. The *Inprecorr* was the channel through which reports on the different Comintern agencies, as well as manifestos, reports on plenary sessions, conferences, theses, decisions, etc., were communicated to the Parties in different countries. It was printed in German, English, Spanish and French and was controlled by the political secretariat of the Comintern. Later on the place of publication was moved to Moscow. Its main significance was as a link between the national Parties, whom it kept informed of each other's activities. It is therefore of value for historical research, but it should be borne in mind that it often contained information designed to mislead for reasons of secrecy or propaganda.

Another journal financed by the Comintern was *World News and Views*, the organ of the World Economic Institute under Professor Eugen Varga; apart from articles on economic subjects, it also contained political propaganda.

All these publications consumed a great deal of money, and in addition the greater part of the Communist world press was dependent to a considerable degree on Comintern funds. Only a few leaders knew the exact sums involved, but they must have been considerable.

As already mentioned, at its congress in 1921 the Comintern adopted the organizational principles worked out by Kuusinen and approved by Lenin before the conference took place. These have since provided the basic constitution and operational directive for all Communist Parties in the world. One of the chief rules is that the basis of any Party organization is the Party cell, which must be set up in each work-place, be it a factory, a farm or an office. The cell may consist of only three Party members, if the number of Communists is as small as this, but in factories and similar establishments it will consist of hundreds or thousands of members. The cell elects a secretary and maintains a Party office, and these form the basis of the Party organization. The next step is the district committee, then the regional committee, and so on up to the Central Committee of the Party and the Politburo, above which there is only the Party Congress. Each of these bodies has its own secretary and executive organs. The cell secretary is responsible for the activity of the cell and for liaison with the district committee. He makes sure that the members attend Party meetings regularly and pay their dues. Anyone who does not fulfil these duties may be expelled from the Party, which can also result in his losing his job. These rules were not applied identically in all organizations, but the Comintern was generally very strict in this respect. Contributions were low, amounting to half of one per cent of each person's wages. Foreign officials working in the Comintern paid contributions to their own Parties unless they became members of the Soviet CP.

I have mentioned these details so as to make my description of a Comintern cell meeting comprehensible. These meetings were held at irregular intervals, as and when the cell secretary and the different committees thought them necessary. There were times at which they were called frequently—perhaps even once a week—such as during Trotsky's fight against Stalin, for example. The secretary acted as chairman and read out a report which was placed in his hands by higher authority. Those present were allowed to ask questions and make comments, and the secretary then read out a resolution which he had drafted himself on the instructions of the district committee. Needless to say, the resolution was passed unanimously.

The meetings were held in the club room in the basement of the Comintern building. It was no joke sitting on narrow benches for hours on end, especially after an eight-hour working day when everyone was tired and only wanted to go home. Foreigners who did not understand Russian suffered particularly and had difficulty in hiding their yawns. But no one dared to protest, or even to mention the fact that members of the Executive Committee were never to be seen at them—such important people had better things to do. In short, the meetings were the most monotonous, dull and boring that could be imagined, especially considering that the Comintern officials were intelligent enough to conduct a more intelligent discussion. The bombastic reports and resolutions were even more boring and confusing for simple workers, who had little comprehension of the political themes involved. Naturally the speakers painted an adverse picture of the living conditions of workers in other countries. A 'spokesman' commissioned by the Central Committee to visit factories in order to explain and defend the decisions made by the Party leaders once complained to me about the difficulties of his office. 'It's easy enough,' he said, 'to tell them what one has been instructed to say. But the difficulties begin when they ask questions and I can't answer them as I would like to. They simply don't believe me. A simple worker is not interested in politics; the only things that matter to him are food, clothing and housing, schooling for his children and the inadequacy of wages.'

As if cell meetings and 'purging' sessions were not taxing enough, the Comintern employees also had to attend trade union meetings, which represented an additional burden, even though they were less frequent than the cell meetings. At the union meetings the discussion was again led by the cell secretary. All Comintern employees belonged to the Union of Cultural Workers, which was later called by another name.

The word 'purge' is associated with the liquidations carried out by Stalin, in which thousands upon thousands of people perished; less well known are the comparatively bloodless Party purges (the Russian word is *chistka*), which were carried out now and then to eliminate unreliable elements from the Party. These took place within the individual Party organizations, but the purge committee was appointed by the Party Control Commission and not by the organization in question. With the exception of the Political Secretariat and members of the ECCI, all Comintern employees had to take part in the *chistka* sessions, which generally lasted from six in the evening until midnight. After an eight-hour day these sessions were a burden for everybody, but they were even worse for those who had to appear at their own 'trial', and who spent the whole day waiting in fear and trembling for the ordeal.

The sessions generally proceeded as follows: the person who had to justify himself was summoned to the platform, and the purge committee and the rest of those present began to ask questions. Some came off easily and quickly, while others were grilled at length. If the victim had personal enemies, this could have a decidedly unfavourable effect on the proceedings. The loss of Party membership, however, was generally not so quickly decided, since in this the Control Commission had the last word. If it turned out that the accused had not done anything that rendered him unworthy of Party membership, then the inquiry was terminated without a vote. If the outcome was adverse, however, no one had a good word to say for him. The chairman would ask, 'Does anyone object?', and since no one ventured to do so the matter was settled 'unanimously'. I may mention two cases which illustrate how people were subjected to these 'purges'.

An Austrian named Stange was employed in the Comintern's newspaper archives. In the First World War he had been taken prisoner and sent to Siberia. When the war came to an end he stayed there, married and later came by a roundabout route to Moscow. He got a job in the Comintern because of his knowledge of German. He found a house for his family somewhere outside Moscow, and a small piece of land on which he grew strawberries and kept a cow. From time to time he sold milk and strawberries to Comintern people, and this proved his undoing: he was accused of being a 'speculator'. When I came home after the session at which Stange had been found guilty and told Otto about the case, my husband was surprised and asked whether I had voted for Stange's expulsion from the Party. 'Naturally,' I replied, 'otherwise I might have been expelled myself.' 'You're all crazy,' said Otto, 'how can Stange possibly be a speculator?' The next morning Otto cleared up the matter with the Control Commission and Stange's expulsion was annulled. This was the only occasion on which Otto dared to intercede on behalf of one of his subordinates. Stange was too unimportant for the affair to be compromising, and anyway Otto liked strawberries.

The other case occurred in 1928 and concerned a far more important personality, namely Petrovsky, the editor of *Communist International*. A skilled journalist and a gifted linguist, Petrovsky had just returned from a mission in Great Britain. When called to defend himself, he gave a calm and dignified account of his life and there seemed to be no doubt that he would be 'acquitted'. But when the chairman asked whether anyone had anything else to say, an unknown woman stood up and asked: 'Comrade Petrovsky, were you in Berdichev when the town was occupied by the Germans?' (i.e. during the First World War). Petrovsky said that he had been, and the woman continued: 'What were you doing there?'

'I was the mayor of the town.'

'What did you call yourself then?'

'Lipets.'

'Had the Germans appointed you mayor?'

'Yes, but the Party approved my appointment.'

'Do you know who used to sign the death sentences which the Germans passed upon Jews in Berdichev?'

'It was I, Lipets.'

Several Jewish witnesses from Berdichev were present, and Petrovsky-Lipets, himself a Jew, was violently attacked and abused. A unanimous vote was passed that he was unworthy of remaining in the Party, and his case was referred to the Control Commission; at this stage further crimes were discovered, and Petrovsky was condemned to death and shot. Among other things it came out that at the time when Trotsky was Commander in Chief of the Red Army, Petrovsky had been an Inspector of military schools and had functioned, so to speak, as his right hand. This in itself was enough to ensure the death penalty. It was further discovered that around 1927 Petrovsky had been the editor of a secret Trotskyist newspaper which was printed in the basement of a building in Mokhovaya Street. Petrovsky's sister, a distinguished lawyer who called herself Nurina (a modified version of the original family name Nürnberg), was also shot as a Trotskyist.

Foreign employees of the Comintern who were members of the Soviet Party all had to undergo the ordeal of the *chistka*, and since many of them spoke little Russian their statements had to be translated by interpreters. All of them were terrified at the prospect of facing the committee.

A West European girl once came into my office in tears to ask my advice as to what she should say at her 'trial'. She was the daughter of a government minister in her own country, and feared that she would certainly be expelled from the Party. I advised her to say that her father had been born somewhat earlier than she and that she therefore did not know in what circumstances he had come to be a minister. The girl actually gave this explanation at the 'trial', and was acquitted amid general laughter. She was employed in the Press Department, and I do not know when it was that she later purged herself from the Comintern.

A small number of personnel at Comintern headquarters were regarded as specially suited to undertake missions abroad. They were known collectively as 'international cadres', but did not form a separate department, as people might be sent abroad from any section or grade in the hierarchy including the Executive Committee itself. However, the chosen band all had certain aptitudes for secret work; they were political rather than technical operators, knew foreign languages and had lived and worked outside the Soviet Union.

They might be sent abroad on a variety of tasks, but their usual rôle was to observe and mediate in the internal quarrels of national Communist Parties. They were seldom sent to the countries in which they themselves were born and brought up. I do not remember them all, but they numbered about forty, and I think Elena Stasova and I were the only women among them. The assignments on which they were sent had to be approved by the Inner Commission; they were not separately announced, and were generally kept secret. The person in question would simply disappear for a time, and his colleagues would assume that he had been sent abroad. Among the members of the ECCI who were sent on missions of this kind was my old friend Yrjö Sirola and also Kullervo Manner, Arthur Ewert, Jules Humbert-Droz, Elena Stasova and Chemodanov. 'International cadres' not on the Executive Committee were Mauno Heimo, Niilo Virtanen, Mehring, the twin brothers Glaubauf, Joseph Pogany (who used the name John Pepper in the USA), Feinberg, Petrovsky (known in Britain as Bennet), and Pyatnitsky's assistants Grollman and Idelson.

Comintern officials were often sent abroad for a few weeks to conduct special training courses. Thus Niilo Virtanen went several times to Norway to give instruction in Party and trade union work. Sirola, Manner and Hanna Malm taught Comintern work in Sweden, and Jussi Lumivuokko was active in trade unions there. The Danish Communist Party was regarded as of little account, and I do not remember who went to Denmark; but Thoger Thogersen was invited to Moscow to study, at the Profintern, ways of organizing Communist workers in trade unions.

Of course, every agent who was sent abroad used a cover name and a forged passport: this was taken care of by Milter, the Comintern passport expert.

To understand the workings of the Comintern one must realize two things. Firstly, it was always being reorganized, and secondly, a great deal of its activity was fictitious, especially as regards the supposed influence of national Parties on Comintern policy. Foreign Party representatives were given imposing titles and elected to the leadership; they took the chair at plenary sessions and were given the principal posts on committees that sounded important, but these jobs were honorary and did not amount to much in reality. At congresses and sessions of the Executive Committee the chairmanship was held by no one for more than a day; when I once naïvely asked Kuusinen why this was, he smiled (a thing he rarely did) and said: 'It's so that the foreign comrades have a chance to sit up there and imagine that they're running the show.' All political questions were in fact thrashed out and decided as far as possible before the sessions, so that it did not matter much who was in the chair or what speeches the foreign delegates made. It often happened that draft resolutions which were moved at the end of a congress or a session of ECCI had been minutely prepared and drafted weeks before.

The Comintern leaders had various ways of controlling member Parties. If, for instance, an issue affecting the German Party was to be discussed in Moscow, the Germans were asked to send delegates, but to be on the safe side instructions were sent at the same time indicating which delegates were required and what their mandate should be. In this way the Comintern leaders had a strong hold over the national Parties, but despite all their precautions and exertions they were seldom able to bring about a state of harmony among them, and much time and energy was expended in attempts to resolve their internal disputes. Again and again the Comintern made elaborate efforts to instil reality into Marx's slogan 'Workers of the world, unite!', but it must be admitted that these met with very little success.

The first major activity by the Comintern reached its climax in the plan for a revolution in Germany in October 1923. In Lenin's opinion, three conditions were required for a successful revolution in a capitalist country:

Firstly, it must be ripe for revolution, i.e. the government must be weakened politically and economically by such calamities as war, widespread unemployment and grave social upheavals.

Secondly, there must be a well prepared Communist Party in

the country which is ready to exploit the hardship and discontent of the masses and is capable of uniting them round its banner and organizing and directing them in the ensuing battle.

Thirdly, there must be a sufficient supply of arms and people who know how to use them at the right time.

At the beginning of 1923 Lenin and his closest advisers had spent a considerable time analysing the political and economic situation in Europe, and he and the Comintern had come to the conclusion that the preconditions for revolution in Germany were present in full measure. The moment had thus come to wipe out the humiliating fiasco of the first German Communist uprising, that of March 1921 which had been directed by Bela Kun. One of the principal 'experts' who encouraged Lenin in this belief was Otto Kuusinen : he told me so himself, and boastfulness was not one of his failings.

Germany, the centre of Europe and a leading industrial power, had long been regarded as the key to world revolution, and it was only fitting that this should break out in the homeland of Marx and Engels. But apart from such theoretical and sentimental arguments, there were more important reasons for choosing Germany as the proving-ground for Lenin's theories. Since the end of the world war there had been well-organized groups of the extreme left which were now coming more and more into the foreground and were exacerbating the national crisis by provoking internecine disputes, as I had seen for myself before leaving Berlin for Moscow. After 1919 Lenin, who was convinced of Germany's key importance, had sent some of his most trusted advisers to Berlin to observe the situation and recommend action. Karl Radek and Elena Stasova were among the chief of these, and despite the misadventure of 1921 Bela Kun continued to be regarded as an expert on Germany. There were indeed plenty of such experts in Moscow in 1923, as a number of German Communists lived there and were a fertile source of ideas and advice; they too were prone to believe that the German working class was ready to overthrow the government and grasp the reins of power. Then, in March 1923, Lenin suffered a third stroke, which brought him to death's door. The effect of this on the Comintern leaders was to make them determined to engineer at least one successful revolution in a foreign country before the father of Soviet power departed this life.

Otto told me, with reference to this time, that he had never expected any lasting good to come of the chaotic and ill-organized attempts at revolution in such small areas as Hungary, Bulgaria and Bavaria, but that he shared the optimism and enthusiasm about a revolution throughout Germany, for which the time indeed seemed to be ripe. Once Germany was Communist, he was convinced that the neighbouring countries would present no difficulty. This conviction, and the belief in the imminent Communization of Europe, became an article of faith in Moscow and was not seriously doubted by anyone.

The exact date of the intended *coup d'état* in Germany was decided months beforehand: it was to be midnight on 22/23 October 1923. Berlin, Hamburg and other large cities were to be in Communist hands by dawn on the 23rd. Shock troops in Berlin had been trained and armed for the purpose of carrying out surprise attacks on the town hall, several ministries, the State Bank, police headquarters, the main stations and so on. Members of the national government were to be arrested and shot. Berlin was chosen as the main target in the belief that once it was captured it would be an easy matter to take over the other cities. Detailed plans had been worked out for the consolidation of Communist rule, and a government programme together with proclamations had been drafted months before the appointed date.

Arms were transported in a cargo steamer which plied regularly between Petrograd and Hamburg; there they were unloaded by Communist dockers and stored on wharves under Communist control. A small, slim, unimportant-looking man named Kleine (actually Guralsky) paid several flying visits to Moscow to arrange for the shipments, which included thousands of rifles.

All these preparations were carried out in such secrecy that even at Comintern headquarters only a few people knew what was afoot. The plans were discussed at nocturnal meetings with German leaders, the utmost importance being attached to concealment and surprise.

A high-level meeting discussed the appointment of a delegate to be sent to Berlin, with the necessary authority to direct the revolution on the spot. Lenin hinted that his own choice would be Kuusinen, but Otto, who was afraid of burning his fingers, at first raised minor objections without actually turning down the job. Finally he told Lenin that, while he felt highly honoured by having been selected for such a responsible task, he had decided after much thought that he was not the right man, on account of his part in the unsuccessful Finnish revolution of 1918, and that it would be better to send someone who had distinguished himself in the October revolution. He suggested Karl Radek, who had carried out several missions in Germany and knew it well. In this way it came about that Radek was sent to Germany to start and supervise the uprising.

I well remember the evening of 22 October in our apartment in the Lux Hotel, where Otto, Pyatnitsky and Manuilsky sat waiting for the telegram from Berlin which was to inform them that the revolution had broken out. They remained for hours in Otto's study, smoking and drinking coffee. There was a direct telephone line to Lenin's sick-bed at Gorky, and this was kept open all night: Lenin could not speak except to mumble a few syllables, but his mind was fully alert and he was intensely interested in the experiment which was to put his theories to the test in the most important country in Europe. Doubtless other high-up leaders were with him, waiting for the decisive news.

Midnight came and went, but no telegram. One o'clock, two o'clock—still nothing, and so it went on until Pyatnitsky and Manuilsky went home at dawn, having first sent a terse telegram to Radek asking what had happened. A few hours later came his reply: 'Nothing.'

During the day we heard that there had been a regular battle during the small hours in Hamburg, where workers led by Ernst Thälmann had attempted to begin the uprising and had suffered heavy losses. But that was all. After the long and toilsome preparations, nothing had happened—the German revolution was still-born. The Comintern leaders were beside themselves with fury and disappointment, and could not wait to discover what had gone wrong and, no less important, whose fault it was. An angry telegram was sent to Germany ordering the principal agents from all parts of the country, such as Radek,

Thälmann, Bela Kun and many others, to report to Moscow and explain 'who had betrayed the German proletariat'.

A few days later there was a knock at our door; I opened it and was greeted by a tall man speaking German. He said he was Thälmann from Hamburg, and asked if Comrade Kuusinen was at home. I said Otto was not yet back from the office; he replied that he had been told to come to our apartment at that particular time, and asked if he could come in and wait. I had hardly closed the door when there was another knock: this time it was Karl Radek, whom I knew, accompanied by a very good-looking woman. He introduced her; the name meant nothing to me, but he did not explain what she was there for.

A third knock, and Bela Kun appeared. He had scarcely crossed the threshold when a furious argument began between him and Thälmann, each accusing the other of disobeying instructions and betraying the German revolution. I sat on the sofa with Radek's friend, while the two men remained standing and continued to argue fiercely. I was amazed that they did so in the presence of an outsider, for the young woman did not belong to the Comintern and I had no notion why she was there. Radek was calm at first, but suddenly he joined in the quarrel and all three men shouted at once. I longed for Otto to appear, as the situation was getting worse and worse and I had no idea how to control it. Suddenly, to my astonishment, the woman jumped up and stood between Radek and Thälmann, shaking her fist at the latter and calling him a brainless prize-fighter and other uncomplimentary things. The quartet had reached the acme of frenzy when Otto appeared in the doorway, looking calm but somewhat startled and carrying a huge brief-case. The others took no notice of him, but went on shouting and hurling abuse. Otto moved cautiously round to the dining-table where he usually sat, clutching the brief-case to his chest as if he feared someone might try to snatch it. Suddenly the woman flew at Thälmann, tugging at his coat and hammering with her fists. A regular fight began, with Radek and the woman on one side and Thälmann and Kun on the other. But Radek was a puny fellow compared with Thälmann, who did not move an inch but stood there with his legs apart and his hands in his trouser pockets, the image of a brawny docker. Then, just as Kun was about to spring at Radek, Thälmann stepped back, grasped Radek by the lapels and said: 'Look here, Radek, since when has a Galician Jew been able to thrash a Hungarian one?' This disconcerted the others; there was a moment or two of rather forced laughter, and the fight was at an end.

Otto, who was now able to get in a word, said to Thälmann: 'Look, why don't you go home for the present? Then we can meet after dinner and discuss it all calmly.' Thälmann went off to his hotel, and Otto advised the others to do the same, as obviously none of them were in the right frame of mind for an objective argument. The representatives of the proletariat thus took their leave.

To Otto, when they had left our apartment, I said: 'Isn't it disgraceful of the men to go on like that in front of an outsider?'

He replied: 'She's not an outsider—she's Radek's friend, Larisa Reissner, the daughter of a Polish professor, and she was sent to Germany as Radek's assistant there.'

Pondering the encounter later that evening, I wondered if it was the sort of thing Marx had in mind when he said: 'Workers of the world, unite!'

The post-mortem duly took place, and it came to light that Radek and Larisa, without consulting Moscow, had decided at the last moment to alter the plans and postpone the revolution for three months. The reason was that they agreed with the German Communist leaders, and particularly Brandler, the Party chairman, that the situation was not yet ripe and that there was insufficient preparation for a full-scale revolution in so many different parts of the country. Through some blunder they had failed to inform Thälmann of the change of plan, and he and his men had attacked the Hamburg police headquarters and other centres in the belief that similar attacks were taking place in Berlin and elsewhere.

The chief blame for the fiasco was finally attached to Radek and his companion. Otto Kuusinen, who had had so much to do with the plans, escaped scot-free as usual: he was much too clever to compromise himself in such a risky enterprise. He generally preferred to let praise or blame be reaped by others, but this was not because he was modest or unselfish. Many of the directives for the German revolution were his work, but he

65

was careful to have them signed by Zinoviev, the chairman of the Executive Committee.

Years after the collapse of the German rising, Otto continued to wonder what the mistake had been. Had not the time been ripe in accordance with Lenin's theories, and had it not seemed as though all the conditions for a successful revolution were fulfilled? It was not till much later that he thought he had found the answer: it was the leadership that had failed, and he decided that Lenin had not sufficiently analysed the rôle of leaders and their subordinates in preparing and carrying out successful revolutions.

The German fiasco of October 1923 was a turning-point in the history of the Comintern, causing it to rethink all its strategy.

As Germany had proved too hard a nut to crack, the leaders decided to have a try at something smaller, and the choice fell on Estonia. This newly independent republic certainly did not fulfil Lenin's conditions for revolution: it was politically and economically on the up grade, and there was no question of an internal crisis. However, the Estonian Communists in Moscow and Leningrad were convinced that a band of shock troops would suffice to overthrow the detested capitalist regime. The Comintern leaders believed them, and on 1 December 1924 a scratch unit of a few hundred men attacked strategic points in Tallinn, the capital. But the workers paid no attention; the assailants were repulsed everywhere, and only a few of them made good their escape to the Soviet Union. This was a comparatively small venture, but I remember how disappointed Otto was at the result: he had hoped to see the southern shore of the Gulf of Finland in Communist hands, which would have undermined the strategic position of Finland itself. Naturally little was said in Moscow about the Estonian affair, and few were informed of it; apart from Otto, I knew of it from Heimo and Yrjö Sirola, who had had the curious idea of going to Tallinn as an observer.

The Comintern's attention in the twenties was mostly focussed on the Balkans, but there was little success to record except in Bulgaria, and this was mainly due to the tradition of Russo-Bulgarian friendship. Stamboliiski, the leader of the left-wing Agrarian Party, was ousted from the Premiership in June 1923 by a military coup which installed Professor Tsankov as the new Premier. The Comintern ordered the Bulgarian Communists to stay quiet until a counter-stroke could be prepared. This came in April 1925, when the order was given to assassinate the government and the royal family. A bomb was set off during a service in Sofia cathedral; over a hundred were killed, but the King and his ministers escaped. It was said later that George Dimitrov was responsible for the *attentat*, but I could never find out if this was so.

Apart from European affairs, the Comintern kept a watch on developments in China and India, and in 1926 Kuusinen himself took over the chairmanship of the Far Eastern Study Group. China was envisaged as the scene of the next major Comintern coup, and so chaotic were conditions there that there seemed to be a good chance of establishing a Chinese Soviet republic.

Among the many Chinese students at the Sun Yat-sen University in Moscow was the son of Chiang Kai-shek, leader of the nationalist Kuomintang party. Moscow was at pains to strengthen its relations with the Kuomintang, and, while Chiang Kai-shek received financial and other help, Communists were infiltrated into the upper ranks of his party and its fighting forces. I well remember a day in 1926 when the Chinese students paraded in front of the Comintern building, singing songs and waving flags to express their gratitude. At about this time the Russians lent Chiang Kai-shek a military adviser in the shape of General Blücher (Blyukher), who was liquidated by Stalin in 1938. But the friendship did not last long, for relations between the Kuomintang and the Chinese Communists began to cool in 1926; in the spring of 1927 there was a complete breach, and Chiang Kai-shek turned against the Communists. In December of that year the Comintern staged a rebellion in Canton, but Chiang put it down without difficulty.

Thus the Comintern's plans had again miscarried; who was to blame this time? Among the advisers whom Otto trusted was Feinberg, who came from London, and Niilo Virtanen, Otto's secretary; he now sent the latter to China to investigate. When Niilo returned Otto questioned him in great detail, and a few days later Niilo said to me laughingly: 'Otto doesn't know the first thing about China. I could hardly help noticing it, he asked me such silly questions about the trip.'

The failure at Canton convinced Otto not only that the Comintern could expect nothing of importance to come out of China, but also that there was no one in Moscow who really understood that country. He was as right on the second point as he was wrong on the first.

It may be wondered why, for the purposes of the Information Department of the Comintern, Finland was combined with Poland, Lithuania, Latvia and Estonia and not with the other Scandinavian countries. The reason was that in all the countries of the former group the Communist Party was forbidden by law, so that clandestine activity presented similar problems in each. The top Communist leaders of all five countries lived in Moscow, and Party members who remained in their native countries concealed their identity as such. All Party activities were directly controlled by the Comintern, which used couriers and clandestine news services to maintain contact with Party cells in the five countries and convey instructions to them. It happened often enough, however, that couriers were arrested and the secret channels of information brought to light.

Everything to do with illegal Communist Parties in these countries was wrapped in mystery at Comintern headquarters. The door of the Polish section, for instance, was kept locked, and apart from the few people who worked there only high officials were allowed to enter. The Finnish section had a small office on the fourth floor, where Kullervo Manner and Hanna Malm worked, and the three Baltic States sections had similar premises. No one talked in the corridors about the affairs of the five parties, and they were never discussed at plenary sessions of ECCI or in the Political Secretariat. Decisions concerning them were taken by Kuusinen or Pyatnitsky according to the subject. Many members of the Executive Committee were foreigners, and it was undesirable for them to learn the secrets of the clandestine Parties. There were no officials with the duty of circulating reports on these countries, and the Comintern Bulletin made no mention of their affairs.

After I had been living in Moscow for a few months, I began to wonder where the Comintern got all its money from. One day I heard a conversation between my husband and Pyatnitsky in our hotel apartment, from which I learnt with astonishment that every Communist Party and newspaper in the world had to be subsidized by the Comintern. To keep up appearances, the public was led to suppose that the workers in all countries who joined the Communist Party to further the cause of world revolution also contributed to the Comintern's expenses, and, to make the illusion more complete, a sum was fixed every year representing the supposed contribution of each national Party. The annual published budget of the Comintern, drawn up by Otto and Pyatnitsky, contained a section entitled 'Contributions from brother Parties', and they had great fun inventing the amounts. Otto often told me that in actual fact the Comintern never received a penny from any foreign Party. All the time I worked there, on the other hand, there was an endless stream of visiting foreign Communists who wanted money to help their Parties out of one difficulty or another. They were usually referred to Pyatnitsky, and if he approved the request it was taken up at the next session of the Inner Commission. Pyatnitsky alone knew the exact amounts paid to each Party; he seldom mentioned the figures to his two fellow-members of the Inner Commission, and not even the People's Commissariat for Finance knew how much money was received and paid out by the Comintern.

The Comintern's funds, however, all came from the Soviet government in one way or another. In the early years a small proportion came from the sale in foreign countries of jewels, works of art and other valuable relics of Tsarist times which had been confiscated from their owners. For the most part, however, the money came from ordinary public funds, though not directly from the Finance Commissariat but, for concealment's sake, from one or other of the offices dependent on the Central Committee of the Soviet Communist Party.

Considering how much was known to Pyatnitsky and his two immediate assistants, Grollman and Idelson, it is not surprising that they were tried and shot at the end of the thirties. The main charge against them, it is interesting to note, was that they had secretly sent financial aid to Trotsky in exile.

In connection with the subsidizing of foreign Parties I remember an amusing anecdote about Kalinin, who was for many years the titular head of the Soviet State. I heard it from Tovstukha, a high official responsible to the Central Committee, who was present when the Latvian Minister called on Kalinin to present his credentials. The old man imagined that his visitor was a prominent Latvian Communist, and greeted him cheerily with the words: 'Well, Comrade, what's the news? Any complaints? Not getting enough money for your Party? I'm not the man for that, you know, you must go over to the Comintern and see Pyatnitsky—he's the one with the money-bags.'

Kalinin was one of the few really likeable men among the Soviet leaders whom I met. He had a fondness for playing tricks on people. In 1929, I think it was, Otto and I spent our holidays at the beautiful Black Sea resort of Gagry, where we shared a *dacha* near the beach with Kalinin and his assistant Valerian Zorin (who was drunk most of the time). The villa was surrounded by flower-beds and by a delightful park, the only entrance to which was guarded by GPU men. The inmates of the villa were supposed on medical advice to rest for two hours after lunch; some did so, but others paid no attention to the rule. One afternoon, at about four o'clock, Kalinin's room was found to be empty; he was sought in vain, and the resulting excitement can be imagined. Behind the villa was a gloomy mountain-side, and the GPU feared that he might have been kidnapped by a hostile native tribe. Cars with screaming sirens raced along the beach to Sukhumi and Tuapse and back, but no trace of Kalinin. I heard the men telephoning to Moscow in desperate tones, and summoning troops from the nearby garrison to search the area with police dogs. Then—it was nearly six o'clock—a bather who had been lying face downwards in the sand, his head covered by a towel, got up and started walking towards the villa. It was Kalinin, dressed in a bathing-suit, with the towel round his neck and a broad grin on his face. He told us cheerfully how he had enjoyed giving his 'guardian angels' the slip for a while, and what fun it had been to watch the general uproar: he had lain there peeping out from under his towel, and the searchers had not dreamt of looking for him among the crowd of bathers. Who but President Kalinin would ever have dared to play such a joke on the GPU?

Kalinin may have lacked the correct background for a head of State, but he made up for this by his sense of humour. He was also kind-hearted and genuinely did his best to help people in difficulties. When I was in the Butyrka prison in 1938, a cell-mate told me the following story about her son. When the boy reached school age, the head of the elementary school in the village where they lived near Moscow refused to take him because his father had been shot as a *kulak*.[21] The family farm had been incorporated into the collective where his mother worked. The boy was lively and intelligent, and one day he announced that he was going to Moscow to ask Comrade Kalinin to help so that he could go to school. His mother tried to dissuade him from this 'hopeless' idea, but he insisted, so she took him to the station and sent him off with food for the journey. With the help of the police he found the house in Moscow where Kalinin received visitors; he had to await his turn for two days, spending the night at a nearby hostel for peasants. On the third day he was finally admitted, and left Kalinin's office with a paper in his pocket instructing the headmaster to enrol him as a pupil. According to his mother, he proved a good scholar. She herself was in prison for having dared to criticize the work of the agronomist assigned to the collective farm. I do not know what became of her, or what effect her arrest had on her son's education, but perhaps he was allowed to continue his schooling on the strength of Kalinin's letter.

Members of the Comintern naturally suspected that not all the funds earmarked for foreign countries reached their proper destinations, and I know many instances which prove that these suspicions were justified.

During the British General Strike in 1926 the Comintern, using the Profintern as a cover, decided to send about £30,000 to the Communist leaders of the London dockers. The task of handing it over was entrusted to Allan Wallenius, the Comintern librarian, who spoke English well. He set out with a forged Swedish passport for Stockholm, where he was to board a British ship for England. When he got back, Otto asked him how the journey had gone. Allan replied that he had travelled on the British ship as a stowaway, fearing that the police might catch him; a friendly stoker had hidden him in a bunker till they put to sea, and Allan had come on deck covered in coal-dust. In the course of the voyage it turned out that the stoker was a good Communist and actually knew the man to whom Allan was to give the money. Allan gave a long and entertaining account of the trip, until Otto grew impatient and said: 'Well, come on, did you meet the man in London and hand the money over?'

'No,' said Allan, 'I didn't have to. I thought it was too risky to let the British see my forged passport, so I gave the money to my friend the stoker, who promised to deliver it to the right quarter.'

'What was the stoker's name?' asked Otto drily.

'He told me his name, but I've forgotten it.'

Speechless with fury, Otto pointed to the door. Needless to say, the money never got to its destination.

Another misfortune befell the Finnish Communist Party. Instructions were sent to Helsinki to send a reliable man with some knowledge of precious stones to open a jeweller's shop in Stockholm, where valuables confiscated by the Bolsheviks could be sold for Swedish currency. The Finns chose a man (I forget his name) who duly opened a shop, which I once visited on a trip to Sweden: the window was full of all kinds of elaborate ornaments, silver jewel-cases and small works of art. But the manager had other talents besides window-dressing, and a few months later he and his valuable stock disappeared. The Comintern never saw a penny of the proceeds, and there was nothing they could do about it.

This story is reminiscent of the Scheinmann scandal, which had nothing to do with the Comintern but which was typical of the times.[22]

One of the Soviet financial experts in the middle twenties was Comrade Scheinmann, who, Otto told me, had been a Bolshevik adviser and liaison man with the Finnish Communists in the 1918 rising. Otto regarded him as a financial wizard, and it was no surprise when he became head of the State Bank in Moscow. His main task was to stabilize the rouble and bridge the foreign currency gap, and for this purpose to negotiate with foreign banks and governments about various problems including the redemption of Tsarist bonds.

Lenin himself attached the utmost importance to stabilizing the rouble, and once said that if this were not done, the revolution was doomed to failure and collapse. Scheinmann's negotiations frequently took him abroad, and in 1927 or so he asked if he might take his wife and children on his next trip, as his Western friends were teasing him because he never brought them. Permission was granted, and the whole family went abroad. Then came a letter from Scheinmann, posted in Prague, to the effect that he must honestly state, with profound regret, that he would never be able to stabilize the Soviet currency; he had therefore decided that he must give up his post as director of the Bank, and would not be returning to the Soviet Union. He did not indicate what his plans were; but it occurred to someone to open the safe and strong-boxes to which the director had had access, and naturally they were empty. Scheinmann had taken all the negotiable foreign assets that he could lay his hands on, and Otto told me in strict confidence that he had made off with a substantial part of the Bank's funds. Ironically, the Russians could do nothing about this either, and very few people in Moscow were told about the robbery. Scheinmann had shrewdly calculated that the viability of the Bolshevik regime was not rated very high in Western financial circles, and that Soviet foreign trade would suffer a rude blow if the extent of his depredations were to leak out. Consequently there was no hope of either laying him by the heels or recovering the stolen money.

After Scheinmann's disappearance exhaustive attempts were made to find out who had known him before the Revolution. It proved that he had been an expert name-dropper and had given many of the Old Bolsheviks the impression that he was a protégé of some eminent figure, but no one could discover who had actually recruited him. Perhaps he had simply appeared on the scene one day and invoked some magic name. At all events, he had been cunning enough to worm his way into the innermost Party circles and to rob the State Bank.

In all probability there were many other losses and thefts of a similar kind, though I did not happen to hear of them.

Despite the Comintern's extreme precautions, many of its secrets were penetrated by agents of foreign governments. The delegate of the Japanese Communist Party was Sen Katayama, who Otto said was a nice old man, but he had no talent for secret work and could not keep his mouth shut about delicate matters. He was sent on a few foreign missions, but was so inefficient that eventually he was kept in Moscow. One day Heimo discovered that a Japanese girl had been living in Katayama's apartment for some months, where she did the honours to visiting Comintern officials; it was explained that she was his daughter, on a visit from Japan. However, someone looked up his personal file and found no mention of his being married. When Heimo asked him about it in a friendly way, Katayama said he had not thought it necessary to mention his wife because the marriage had been arranged by his parents in the Japanese style and he had only lived with her for a short time before leaving Japan for good. The daughter had been born after his departure, and the Japanese Party had now been good enough to pay her fare to Moscow so that she could visit him.

The Comintern made enquiries in Japan, and discovered with alarm that the local Communists knew nothing of the girl and had certainly not sent her to Moscow. It also came to light that Katayama's wife, who had married him at a very early age, had never had a daughter.

This was an awkward situation. The Comintern were convinced that the girl was an agent of the Japanese secret police, but if the GPU were allowed to arrest her, it would be said that the Comintern had shown negligence in allowing itself to be penetrated and must in future be more closely supervised by the GPU. In this dilemma it was decided that the most prudent course was to send the girl back to Tokyo as unobtrusively as possible and without telling her or Katayama the reason. No doubt she reported fully to the Japanese authorities on all she had seen and heard in Moscow.

I heard about another Japanese spy from Otto Hall, a Negro whom I met in New York in 1932 and who had studied at the Lenin School in Moscow; he arrived there in 1928 and was first sent by mistake to the Sun Yat-sen University, where he slept in the dormitory. During this time he and another student formed the impression that one of the Japanese 'comrades' was a spy: they discovered that he was attending suspicious meetings, and resolved to take the law into their own hands. As he was returning one night they hit him with a crowbar and he fell downstairs with a cracked skull. The doctor found that his death could not be due to the fall alone, whereupon the GPU stepped in and discovered who his assailants were. As the GPU themselves had been on his track, they let Hall and his friend off with a warning.

I remember another attempt to penetrate the Comintern in about 1927, when Otto introduced me to a Hungarian Communist named Thomsen: he made a good impression, spoke fluent German, and seemed a highly promising addition to Otto's staff. But, less than a week later, he was arrested, as his photograph and details were found recorded in a list of anti-Communist agents drawn up by the German Party. Naturally he was executed.

The Comintern leaders did their best to see that the foreign colleagues in Moscow lived as well as possible, and they certainly had a far better time of it than the ordinary Soviet citizen. But conditions were so chaotic and unreliable that they nearly all felt ill at ease, if only because of the many thefts to which they were exposed. The following example is not without its humorous side.

Some time in the middle twenties Otto was invited to represent the Comintern at a military celebration at Minsk; the invitation stated that the festivities would last a whole day and that he would be the guest of honour. Otto detested nothing more than such occasions, where he had to make speeches in Russian, and he told me frankly that he had no intention of wasting time in this way; it was an overnight journey to Minsk by train, so that he would have to be away from Moscow for thirty-six hours. I replied: 'If you don't want to go yourself, you must send a substitute. What about Vasili Kolarov [the Bulgarian Party representative on the Executive Committee]? He likes the sound of his own voice—you often send him to factory celebrations, and he loves to parade about and show off his handsome appearance.'

Otto thought this an excellent idea, and we agreed that I would tell Kolarov that the Comintern had been invited to send a representative and that he, Kolarov, would be the ideal man for this important mission. Kolarov, as I foresaw, was delighted. He set off by train, and reappeared a few days later to tell us of his adventures. Expecting to be away only a day and a half, he had taken nothing but a brief-case with some clean collars and handkerchiefs. He had a first-class compartment to himself, as befitted his position, and soon after the train started he undressed and went to bed so as to be properly rested next day. Remembering that there had been cases of extremely daring robbery in trains in the past few months, he locked his compartment with great care. He had had a few glasses of vodka before the journey, and slept soundly in spite of the poor condition of the permanent way. He was awakened by the conductor knocking on the door and calling out that they were just arriving at Minsk. Jumping out of bed, he saw that the train was pulling into a siding; but, when he looked for his clothes, he saw with horror that everything was gone, including his shoes and the brief-case. A thief had got in during the night and stolen everything that was not red-hot or nailed down. Thus poor Kolarov, representing the Comintern, had arrived in Minsk in nothing but his underclothes and socks. He collapsed on to his sleeping-berth as the train stopped with a jerk and the waiting band struck up a military march. Peeping out of the window he saw a group of officers standing to attention, while someone could be heard asking the conductor in which compartment he was. The band played one march after another, while the honoured guest sat on his bunk in a state of consternation. The suspense increased as the guard and its officers stood stiffly to attention, wondering what had become of the distinguished delegate. The train, of course, remained stationary; the departure signal could not be given, and passengers were poking their heads out of the window to discover the reason for the delay.

At last the welcoming committee found out what had happened; someone came to the rescue with an overcoat and boots, and the trouserless but distinguished visitor was smuggled off the train on the far side and driven away without exciting undue attention.

Only a few people in Moscow heard of this episode; generally no one took notice of such 'petty' robberies, except as material for jokes and anecdotes. I would quite probably have forgotten it myself, if it were not for the fury with which Kolarov told us what had befallen him.

One day in the summer of 1926 or 1927 I met in a corridor of the Comintern building the Italian representative on the Executive Committee, well known since then as Palmiro Togliatti but in those days using the cover-name Ercoli. He asked me if I knew where he could stay for a while with his wife and small son: they were arriving that evening from Italy and he thought the air of a Moscow hotel room would be bad for the child. I invited him to bring them to our *dacha* at Serebrianny Bor, the third floor of which was occupied by the chauffeur and his wife. Togliatti accepted gratefully, and a bedroom was prepared for the family on the second floor; it had a large window and a balcony with flower-boxes. The Togliattis went to bed early; I had told the chauffeur's wife to get them breakfast next morning, but when I awoke there was no sound. Later I asked the woman if she had taken our guests their coffee; she said she had waited in but had heard no sound from their room, and had not knocked in case they were tired after the journey.

Finally, at about noon, I decided to see what had happened to them. I knocked at the door; Togliatti answered, but said he could not open it as he had nothing on. All their things had been stolen during the night. When I entered the room I found all three of them lying in bed with sheets drawn up to their chins. Not only their clothes and luggage had been taken, but their watches and money as well. Evidently the thieves had climbed in by way of the balcony and the open window as the occupants of the room lay fast asleep. Fortunately Togliatti had some clothes at the Lux Hotel, and we could send the chauffeur for them; but it was less easy to find something suitable for his wife, and it must have been a long time before she forgot this introduction to the Soviet way of life.

While the true importance of some of the Comintern leaders, like Otto Kuusinen and his protégé Mauno Heimo, was often underrated because they did not advertise it to outsiders, there were others who were overvalued for the opposite reason. Among these were Grigori Zinoviev, Karl Radek and Georgi (George) Dimitrov.

Zinoviev was re-elected chairman of the ECCI in 1921, but he was little more than a figurehead as far as the Comintern was concerned; his political ambition lay in other directions, and his job of Party secretary at Leningrad occupied nearly all his time. He made important speeches, it is true, at international meetings, and published articles from time to time; but many of these speeches and articles were written by others, including Otto. He had two nicknames in Comintern circles: 'the Tsar of Leningrad' and 'the Satrap' (this was Otto's invention). When in Moscow, he mostly worked on matters unconnected with the Comintern. His office and home were in the Kremlin, and I only saw him twice in the Comintern building during the years I worked there. As chairman he was required to sign certain documents, and I remember occasions when Otto would send Mauno Heimo to Zinoviev's office with papers for signature, and Heimo would return with the news that he was out of town. In theory Zinoviev was Otto's superior, but as far as I knew Otto always reported to Lenin, and afterwards Stalin, direct and not through Zinoviev.

Zinoviev did not inspire respect, and was heartily disliked by all who knew him well. He was selfish, sly, ambitious and boorish in manner. Most women at the Comintern hated him: he was an inveterate skirt-chaser and convinced that no female could resist his charms. My husband, who was himself far from blameless in official relationships, referred to Zinoviev in private as an unscrupulous opportunist, cringing to his superiors and pompous with his subordinates to the point of absurdity. I say 'in private', because for a short time Otto found it prudent to make a show of unconditional support for Zinoviev. The latter had enjoyed Lenin's patronage, but after Lenin died in 1924 Stalin soon outwitted him; Zinoviev's career began to crumble, and in autumn 1926 he was ousted from the party Central Committee and from the Comintern, where his departure caused no tears to flow. He was succeeded as chairman of ECCI by Nikolay Bukharin, which was a good thing for Otto as Bukharin was his closest friend among the Russian Communists.

Karl Radek represented the Soviet Union at a congress held at The Hague from 10 to 15 December 1922: this was organized by the Social Democratic trade union international and had as its object the prevention of a new world war. Many foreigners assumed from his rôle at the congress that he must be an important Bolshevik leader; this reputation, together with his Austro-Hungarian origin and his involvement in German Communist affairs, led to his becoming a member of the Comintern, where he did his best to keep in the limelight, posing as an expert on every possible question. But even in those days he never had much influence on Comintern policy, as is shown by the fact that he was never a member of the Political Secretariat. As editor of *Izvestia* he certainly ranked as the ablest journalist in the Soviet Union, but his good fortune deserted him by degrees after he was saddled with the main responsibility for the German fiasco in October 1923. He lost his position on the Executive Committee of the Comintern and the Central Committee of the Soviet Communist Party, and for many years held very subordinate appointments.

He was not prepossessing to look at, and despite his gifts of oratory and satire he did not give the impression of a great political leader. As far as I know, Larisa Reissner was the only person who ever found him lovable. Otto had little respect or confidence in him, and the feeling was mutual. Once when Otto was making a speech at an important meeting, Radek interrupted with the words: 'Comrade Kuusinen is so helpless that he would not know what to do if all his trouser buttons came off—he would just stand there holding up his pants with both hands.' This may give some idea of how friendly the two men were.

I have mentioned Georgi Dimitrov in connection with the bomb incident in Sofia cathedral in 1925. After that time he worked in various departments of the Comintern, but was always moved on after a few weeks as he could never get on with anybody. When the complaints, agitation and confusion reached a certain pitch he would be transferred without notice to another department. It got to the point when everybody at Comintern headquarters refused to work with him, and he was then foisted on to old Meshcheryakov in the Krestintern, which worked in a separate building. One day when I was in Otto's office, Meshcheryakov burst into the room and spluttered out: 'Comrade Kuusinen, I must talk to you. For goodness sake take that Dimitrov away. He doesn't understand our work and doesn't give a damn for it, and he's always losing his temper. I can't run the department with him there—you must take him away!'

Otto promised to help. When Meshcheryakov had left the office he laughed and said: 'Nobody can get on with Dimitrov. What are we to do with him? I think we had better send him back to the Balkans and get rid of him that way.' So it was decided, and Dimitrov went to carry on clandestine work in the Balkans with the aid of Tanev and Popov, two graduates of the Lenin School. Later on, about 1930, all three were sent to Berlin. After Hitler became Chancellor in 1933 they were arrested and charged with responsibility for the Reichstag fire. Otto took this opportunity to launch a world-wide anti-Fascist campaign in which the three were cast for the rôle of martyrs. Innumerable appeals and demonstrations were organized throughout the world, and were especially effective in trade union circles. The trial at Leipzig was a moral defeat for the Nazis and gave Dimitrov a platform for his famous speech. The comrades in Moscow did not, as a matter of fact, think him capable of making an effective speech in court on the right political lines, especially as his German was very bad; so Otto himself had composed an anti-Fascist harangue in the hope that its text could somehow be got to Dimitrov.[23]

The speech Dimitrov actually delivered made a great stir. He and his companions were acquitted, and when they returned to Moscow they were acclaimed as champions not only by Communists there but by many anti-Fascists throughout the world. His comrades' subsequent fate is less well known: Tanev was shot in the purges, and Popov disappeared in a forced labour camp. Dimitrov became secretary-general of the Comintern in 1935, but his authority was something of a façade, as all important decisions concerning the Parties were taken by the same people as before, namely the Soviet Communist leaders.[24]

Around 1927 the Soviet Politburo considered the possibility of transferring at least part of the Comintern to Berlin as communications with the rest of the world would be easier from there than from Moscow; moreover Germany in the middle twenties had a democratic government and a strong Communist Party. Another motive was probably the fact that the Comintern did not enjoy the best of relations with the People's Commissariat for Foreign Affairs. Chicherin, the foreign commissar, thought the Comintern's under-cover relations with Soviet embassies abroad were bad for the government's prestige. The German officials at Comintern headquarters were also keen on the change, but the idea was dropped as the situation in Germany became more confused and the Nazis started to gain ground.

In May 1943 the world was startled to learn that the Comintern was being dissolved.[25] I was not surprised at this, as I knew how its staff had been decimated: so many of the ablest had perished that the organization could scarcely function any more. One reason for the dissolution was of course that Comintern agitation in capitalist countries was a hindrance to Soviet co-operation with the Western powers; it was important to convince the latter that plans for the overthrow of capitalism and for world revolution had been given up. But the chief reason, in my opinion, why the Comintern was regarded as superfluous was that Stalin had abandoned the idea of a world revolution brought about by uprisings in individual countries. He seemed more and more to take the view, which Otto Kuusinen had expressed to me years before, that the spread of Communism would be brought about by armed force and the conquest and incorporation of new territories.

For decades past, many human lives had been sacrificed and huge sums expended by the Comintern in order to overthrow foreign governments. Even before the Soviet regime was firmly established in Russia, the Comintern had bent every nerve to export Communism to the capitalist world. But scarcely a trace has remained of all these efforts, and practically all those who took part in them are now dead.

III

My Mission to America

In the spring of 1930 I attended a meeting of the American
section of the Comintern, summoned and chaired by my husband. It was attended by Manuilsky, Pyatnitsky and Ewert, and
the US Party was represented by William Z. Foster, Jay Lovestone, Earl Browder and two prominent American Finns, Henry
Puro and Matti Tenhunen,[26] who belonged to the Finnish
workers' association of New York. Mauno Heimo was at the
meeting, and one or two others whose names I have forgotten.
Its purpose was to discuss differences that had arisen between
the American Communist Party and the Finnish association.
From the outset the American Party was sharply criticized for
its many splinter groups and for failing to recruit native-born
Americans. Otto led the attack by complaining that the American leaders spent most of their time quarrelling with one another instead of fighting capitalism.

The second speaker was Ewert, a member of ECCI and a
high official of the German Party. He had just returned from
a month in the States, where he had tried to restore harmony
among the Party leaders and find out the reasons for the drop
in recruiting. The American Party, he declared sarcastically,
was so feeble that no self-respecting worker would join it; and
he went on: 'In the course of my career I have come across all
kinds of disputes within Parties and have generally managed
to get to the bottom of them. But the internal disputes of the
American Party are a science of such complexity that I don't

believe anyone can master it. Send anyone you like to America; you won't succeed in finding out what are the rights and wrongs of the quarrel or even what it's about. I can only tell you one thing, it absorbs every moment of their time, and that goes for everybody, even the postman. I'll explain what I mean. One evening Foster posted a letter in a mailbox near his apartment, and next morning Lovestone, his rival, received a copy of it in his own mail. No one has any idea how and why the quarrel started, and no one can think of a way to end it.'

Manuilsky, the next speaker, attacked Foster violently for the failure to recruit members, and said that American workers were ready enough to join trade unions but not the Communist Party. 'You, Comrade Foster, belong to the international trade union movement, and your whole attitude is that of a union man and always will be. That's why you'll never be a good Communist; you don't begin to understand what Communism is about.' To which Foster replied with no less vehemence: 'Yes, I'm a tough trade unionist. The movement has made me hard-boiled, and you can't turn a hard-boiled egg into a soft-boiled one.' This was greeted with laughter and applause.

The US Party was chronically short of money, as it consisted for the most part of recent immigrants who could not or would not pay their dues; yet the many associations and clubs where the immigrants met to talk about the old country in their own language were prosperous organizations. All the nationalities of Europe had their associations and clubrooms in New York, and there were branches in important cities throughout the country. Many of these bodies were richer than the Communist Party, and the latter was keen to get them into its net. The American Party leaders made no secret of their intention to use the clubs and thus reduce their own financial dependence on the Comintern; they claimed to have had some success in this way with Jewish organizations.

Their present target was the Finnish workers' association—a flourishing, more or less non-political body with its headquarters in New York and branches in several other states. The New York centre was in a large building called the Haali, on 125th Street in Harlem: it had been bought with the aid of loans from members and contained public rooms, a sauna bath, a restaurant, a theatre and a big assembly hall, which was much used and brought in a good income. At a time when the Communist *Daily Worker* could only keep going with lavish subsidies from Moscow, the Finnish community possessed five financially independent newspapers.

Most of the executive committee of the Finnish association were in fact members of the Communist Party, and Puro was even a member of its Politburo, but the committee as such had many disagreements with the Party. The latter used the Haali for its meetings and refused to pay rent; it also demanded that members of the association should pay individual contributions to party funds—the association agreed to this for the time being —and should subscribe to the *Daily Worker* whether they could read English or not. The resentment this caused among the Finns was perceptible at the Moscow meeting, although Puro and Tenhunen clearly wanted to keep on the right side of the top Communist leaders and hardly uttered a word in public. Browder, the secretary of the American Party, condemned the Finnish association as lacking in discipline and working against Party interests. The Moscow leaders, however, took the Finns' side and held that they were better entitled to remain independent of the Party than were, for instance, the Jewish organizations: for the Finns, both in their own country and in the émigré community, were workers in the true sense of the word, while the Jewish Communists in New York were mostly shopkeepers and small business men who employed workers and therefore were capitalist exploiters. This was the theory, but in reality the Moscow Communists forgave the Jews for the sin of capitalism because their organizations furnished the Party with substantial contributions of both money and personnel.

After a few days filled with discussion, the American delegates were told that they had made a mistake in trying to recruit organizations instead of individuals, in violation of the principles adopted at the third Comintern Congress in 1921. It was the Party's right and duty to urge individual immigrants to join its ranks, but it had no business to seek to incorporate whole groups and then oblige the members of these groups to pay Party dues and buy newspapers they could not read.

The US Communists remained in Moscow for several months,

doing their best to make things uncomfortable for one another and to curry favour with Pyatnitsky, who held the purse-strings of the Comintern. The Moscow leaders finally grew weary of their complaints and admonished them to stop quarrelling and use their energies for the good of the Party as a whole. When they at last went home, Kuusinen addressed an 'open letter' to the Finnish workers' association stating that its independence was recognized in accordance with the decision taken at Moscow, but that an endeavour should be made to resolve its dispute with the Communist Party. This letter was published in the association's newspapers, and for the time being the Party was obliged to ride the Finnish workers with a lighter rein. The decision came as a blow to the US Communists, although the dispute was after all only a question of recruiting methods. The Comintern knew well enough that the world revolution would never break out in the USA, and they did not pay much attention to the US Party; but they did attach importance to winning over the Finnish organization, and it was only a matter of time before new tactics could be devised for the purpose.

Complaints about the American Party continued to come in, however, as the Moscow resolutions were clearly being disregarded; and the Comintern leaders decided to send someone to New York to investigate. They proposed to send Yrjö Sirola, who had been on a previous Comintern mission in America, had taught at a Finnish school there and spoke English well; but he did not want to go, and suggested me instead. I had learnt English at school and had taken lessons in Moscow from Mrs Bittelman, the wife of an American official at the Comintern. When Sirola asked if I was prepared to go, I said that I would if Otto gave his consent; I was careful not to say how pleased I was at the prospect.

For a long time I heard no more, till one day Otto came home from the office and sat down to dinner. He was unusually quiet for a time, and then said: 'Would you like to go to America and report on the trouble between the Party and the Finnish workers' association?' I said I would, to which he replied angrily: 'Aha, now I know you want to leave me.' I made no answer, and neither of us spoke another word that evening.

On the following evening Otto told me that the Inner Commission, which was responsible for missions abroad by Comintern officials, had approved my journey.

At the end of January 1931—more than six months after the plan had first been mooted—I took a train from Moscow to Berlin, on my way to America at last. I went with Kullervo Manner,[27] who was bound for Toronto as ECCI representative at a Canadian Party Congress; he knew no English and was unaccustomed to travelling alone, so I was to accompany him all the way to Toronto. I knew him well and was glad of a chance to see Canada, but I thought to myself how extraordinary it was to send someone there who could not speak English. I learnt much later that Kuusinen had sent him there to get him out of the way, so as to make it easier to bring about his downfall.

I had no regrets at leaving Moscow, and was glad of a respite from the petty bureaucracy of the Comintern and the growing atmosphere of depression generally. The forced collectivization campaign that had just begun threw a dark shadow over daily life. There were frightful tales of cruelty and starvation due to the compulsory division of peasant holdings, and we heard of the arrest and execution of farmers who refused to give up their land and livestock. The government had tried to prevent a food shortage in Moscow, but they had failed: people went hungry in the capital, and food shops were empty. So I was pleased to be going to America, though I had as yet no idea how long I was to stay there.

I travelled under the name of Fru Elisabeth Petterson, with a Swedish passport obtained by Signe Sillen, the Comintern agent in Stockholm, who also procured a forged passport for Manner. From Berlin we went by rail to Cherbourg, and after ten days of a rather boring sea voyage we arrived at Halifax. Manner was on edge throughout the journey because of his forged passport— he really did not have strong enough nerves for secret Comintern work. He was thoroughly alarmed when a Customs officer at Halifax spoke to him in Swedish, and he would not believe that it was a coincidence when another man who spoke Swedish sat near us in the train.

I do not know what his exact assignment was in Canada, apart from representing the Comintern at the congress and sorting out some difficulties between the Canadian Party and the local Finnish workers' association. In any case I left him with Canadian friends and went on to New York, having obtained a visa without trouble from the American Consulate in Toronto.

I had heard a good deal about America before my journey, but the reality was beyond all my expectations. The New York skyscrapers were an unforgettable sight, and I admired the systematic layout of the city which made it easy for a newcomer to find his way in the concrete jungle. What impressed me above all was that it was so easy for a foreign tourist to get a hotel room: one had only to fill in a registration form, and nobody asked for identification papers.

The leaders of the Finnish workers' association gave me a most friendly welcome, and actually paid all the expenses of my stay in the US. They rented a number of rooms in the large building that served as the headquarters of the Communist Party, and two of these were assigned to me and a secretary. Although I had no official standing in the association, its leaders gave me a free hand and always listened to my proposals with interest.

I regarded it as my first important task to get an idea of the five Finnish newspapers. The chief of these, *Työmies* (The Worker), was published at Superior, Wisconsin, and paid its way thanks to the many local Finnish subscribers; associated with it was an enterprise for publishing books and periodicals. A humorous weekly, *Punikki*, was also published at Superior. At Astoria, Oregon, there was a daily, *Toveri* (Comrade), and a women's weekly, *Toveritar*, which shared a single printing-press; but there were few Finns in the area, the circulation of these papers was small and they had difficulty in keeping afloat. The same applied to *Eteenpäin* (Forward), which was published at Worcester, Massachusetts.

Although New York had much the largest Finnish colony, I found to my surprise that no Finnish newspaper was published there. It seemed much more sensible that the chief paper should be published in New York, where the association had its headquarters, and so I proposed that *Eteenpäin* should be transferred there and made into the principal paper, catering especially for the eastern part of the country while *Työmies* served the west and middle west. I also suggested that *Toveri* should be wound up, and that *Toveritar* and *Punikki* should be merged into a single paper published in New York and entitled *Työläisnainen* (Working Woman). All these proposals were accepted and carried out. Until the Moscow meeting of 1930 all these papers had had to describe themselves as organs of the American Communist Party, but from now on this was not necessary.

As it would not have been worth bringing the old-fashioned printing-press from Worcester to New York, the association's committee bought new, up-to-date equipment which they installed in the cellar of the Party headquarters. They also rented some more rooms at the top of the building, little realizing how these arrangements would be exploited by the Party chiefs: the new press soon began to be used for the *Daily Worker* and other publications, without compensation for the cost of newsprint and labour. After much argument the Party agreed to pay a small contribution to the printing costs. To be sure, the Party's coffers were always empty, and apart from Moscow all its money came from the Communist members on the committee of the workers' association. The mass of the Finnish immigrants were uninterested in Party membership, and got all the political and social activity they required out of belonging to the association. At a general meeting of the latter it was thus decided that each member should choose for himself whether he wanted to join the Communist Party or not.

I was given *carte blanche* as far as reorganizing the newspapers was concerned, and this was a full-time job. New staff was required for some of the editorial posts, and I was in general charge of finance and personnel questions. I paid particular attention to the advertisement section, the head of which was a good business man, so that we secured advertisements from non-Finnish firms, doctors, lawyers, etc. The staff of *Eteenpäin* always consulted me on important questions, and I conferred with the editor almost every evening. I took care to eliminate mistakes in Finnish idiom and to improve the general level of the paper, making sure that there was plenty of news about events in the old country.

After much thought it was decided to sell the press in

Worcester; we told Moscow of this, and Sirola wrote that the Leningrad Finnish paper *Vapaus* (Freedom) would like to buy it. The committee of the Finnish association thereupon decided to make the Leningrad Finns a present of it. The press was dismantled and shipped off to Russia, but as no one there knew how to reassamble it they asked New York for help. The association sent three Finnish-American printers who finished the job in under three months; two of them, Virkkula and Jurvelin, returned to America, but the third, Hietala, offered to remain and show the staff of *Vapaus* how to work the press. His real reason was that he had fallen in love with a Finnish girl in Leningrad, whom he married. The GPU lost little time in 'discovering' that he was an American secret agent, and arresting them both. I got to know his wife in later years in the camp at Potma; she spent twenty years in prisons and camps, and discovered after her release that her husband had died in a camp in Siberia.

I had supposed that Manner was only staying in Canada for a short time, and was surprised when he turned up some time later in my New York office. He said Kuusinen would not let him return to Moscow, although his assignment in Canada was finished and there was nothing whatever for him to do there. He was furious with Otto who, he said, wanted to get him arrested in America. At his entreaty I wrote to Kuusinen asking for him to be recalled, and stating plainly what I thought of the business. The required order soon came from Moscow, and Manner was delighted and full of gratitude. Although I did what Manner asked of me, I did not really believe at the time that Kuusinen wanted to get rid of him; but when I returned to Moscow in 1933 and heard of the dispute between them over the affairs of the Finnish Party, I realized that Manner had been right and that Kuusinen would stop at nothing in his desire for revenge. In 1935 he submitted a long report to the International Control Commission of the Comintern denouncing both Manner and his wife, who were thereupon expelled from the Party and shortly afterwards arrested.

1932 was the year of the US presidential election; the Comintern decided that there should be a Communist candidate, and the choice fell on William Foster, the chairman of the American

Party, whose trade union background would, it was thought, bring in the votes of the working class. Jim Ford, a Negro, was chosen as his running mate: he was studying at the Lenin School in Moscow at the time, and was ordered to go back to the USA and take part in the election. The Comintern, who were financing the campaign, understood so little of US politics that they expected to win the election by concentrating on the Negro vote. Their endeavours were vain: they could not even collect enough signatures to enable Foster and Ford to run as candidates. Consequently the Communist vote was switched to Roosevelt, who was expected to recognize the Soviet Union and open diplomatic relations with it, as he actually did in November 1933.

After this fiasco the US Party was more discredited in Moscow than ever, especially as it could not even deliver the Negro vote. So the Comintern decided to make a play for Black Africa instead, and sent Jim Ford to Hamburg to study African languages. However, for some reason he left Hamburg suddenly, and the plan fell through.

For the most part, the American Negroes did not take the faintest interest in the Soviet Union, but I met with one touching exception. One day a good-looking coloured woman appeared in my office in New York and introduced herself as Mary Adams, a teacher in Harlem. She wanted to send her two sons, aged seven and eight, to the USSR to be brought up as good Communists, and asked my advice. I replied that education was not within my field, but that if she addressed a letter to 'The Soviet Government, Moscow' it would certainly reach the proper quarter.

In 1956—twenty-five years after this meeting, which I had long forgotten, and nearly a year after my release from Potma—I had an encounter which showed once again how small the world is. I boarded a bus in Moscow and was surprised to see that the driver was a Negro; another Negro was sitting behind him. I was near enough to hear that they were talking to each other in Russian; suddenly I remembered Mary Adams's visit, and asked the astonished young men if they were by any chance her sons. Sure enough, they were. It seemed a little sad that after their mother's ambitious plans they had not become anything more than bus-drivers, since she, after all, had been a teacher.

One morning in November 1932, I saw headlined on the front page of the *New York Times* that Stalin had murdered his wife, Nadezhda Alliluyeva. My first reaction was that this could only be a malicious invention by the sensational bourgeois press. The official version was that Stalin's wife had fallen seriously ill and had died as the result of an operation; but what could have started the rumour that she was murdered? I did not believe it, but I could not altogether repress my suspicions, as references to the story kept cropping up in the press.

I returned to Moscow at the end of the following July, and on the day after my arrival I received unexpected confirmation of the rumours from an old friend, Dr Muromtseva of the Medical Academy. She was a loyal Communist who used as a matter of course to defend all the strange goings-on in the Soviet Union, and her husband was a highly-placed Old Bolshevik. After showering me with questions about life in America, which I answered to the best of my ability, she suddenly asked: 'Did the American press say that Stalin had murdered his wife?'

'Yes, the papers were full of stories about her death, and they did say she was murdered.'

'And what did you think?'

'I didn't believe them.'

'Well, it's true.'

I stared in amazement and asked her how she knew, whereupon she told me this story.

'One morning as I was just setting out for work, the telephone rang and an unknown man's voice told me to go straight to the guardroom at the entrance to the Kremlin and show my Party membership booklet. I was paralysed with fear, as anyone in Moscow would be on receiving such an order. When I got to the Kremlin, the commandant was there with two other women doctors, and we three were led through various corridors to Nadezhda Alliluyeva's room. She was lying on the bed, quite still, and we thought at first that she was ill and unconscious, but then we saw she was dead. We were alone with the body of Stalin's wife. She had been a student at the Industrial Academy, and her books and lecture notes were still on the table.

'After a while two men brought a coffin, and we were told by an official to lay the body in it. We looked about for some appropriate clothing, and chose a black silk dress from one of the wardrobes. Suddenly Dr N. made a sign and pointed to some great black bruises on the corpse's neck. We looked closer, and then exchanged silent glances—it was clear to all of us that she had been strangled. As we gazed in horror at the body, the marks became larger and clearer, and finally we could distinguish each finger of the murderer's left hand.

'We realized that when the body lay in state, anyone who saw the marks would know what the cause of death had been, and so we put a bandage round the neck so that the many thousands who came to pay their last respects to Nadezhda Alliluyeva would suppose that she had died of a throat disease.'

My friend ended her account with the words: 'I'm sure you will understand when I say that we three doctors have had many a sleepless night since then—we know too much.'[28]

Although the doctors thought they had concealed the truth so well, I found as I went round visiting old friends in the next few days that the rumour of Stalin's guilt was widespread. Most people thought he had attacked his wife in a fit of anger because of her reproaches over the policy of forced collectivization, which had meant misery and starvation for millions of peasants. The rumour was corroborated by the fact that after Nadezhda's death her closest relations began to disappear mysteriously. It was of course extremely risky to breathe a word about the matter, and it remained taboo for at least six years afterwards. This was shown by the case of an old cleaning woman who had worked at the Mint for twenty years and, like me, was thrown into Butyrka prison in 1938: her neighbour, a Party member, had reported her to the authorities for asking what illness Stalin's wife had died of. Even such measures did not kill the rumour, and when I came back to Moscow in 1955—twenty-three years after Alliluyeva's death, and with fifteen years of prison and camps behind me—the murder was still a frequent topic of conversation.

Another friend of mine, also a Party member of long standing, repeated to me a tale she had heard from some of the Kremlin servants. Marshal Voroshilov, whose apartment was next to Stalin's, had heard through his bedroom wall Stalin's explosion of anger and Nadezhda's cries for help. He ran across in his night clothes to help her, but she was already dead. Naturally he never said anything—to do so might have cost him his life, and he was in danger for many years as the sole witness of Stalin's crime. Khrushchev, in his famous speech to the twentieth Party Congress in 1956, spoke of Stalin's vengeful designs and declared that he suspected Voroshilov of spying for the British. I heard an echo of this in 1938, when an officer in the Lubyanka began my interrogation one evening by boasting of the daily executions in the prison cellar, and showed me a list of those who were soon to be liquidated: the first name on it was Voroshilov, the second Otto Kuusinen, and the third Mikoyan.

In later years in Moscow, when the weather was fine, I often used to sit and read on a bench in the garden of the Novodevichy convent, an oasis of peace and beauty near the city centre. The fine old buildings and churches stand in the foreground, and behind a wall is a cemetery where people of importance are still buried. Walking among the graves one Sunday I came upon that of Nadezhda Alliluyeva, and was amazed at what I saw. It was ornamented by an impressive marble statue of the dead woman with a large white veil over her shoulders, and with her left hand touching her neck at the very place where, according to my doctor friend, the marks of the strangler's hand had been visible.

Nadezhda was a woman of great beauty and character; I had met her several times at the Kremlin, the last occasion being a women's congress. She told me then that she had taken up the study of weaving and textiles in order to have an independent profession of her own. I thought her intelligent but very much on edge, and irked by the attentions she received as Stalin's wife. As I stood now fascinated by the snow-white statue, my thoughts were of the past—not my own life and trials, but those of this woman who had suffered so much at the side of her tyrant husband. She had uttered no word of complaint, but had been as mute as the statue itself. But what sculptor could have dared to allude so clearly to the manner of her death? And why is it still a forbidden subject? These questions remain unanswered, and the mystery is still unsolved.

But I must return to my American story. I was of course close to the American Finns, whom I knew better than any other section of the population; they numbered about half a million and were ambitious, energetic and nearly all well off, with a solid reputation as honest, law-abiding citizens. But after 1929, when the world depression began and unemployment was rife in the United States, many Finns lost their jobs, and this state of affairs was exploited by the Soviet Union. The current five-year plan called not only for machines but for skilled workers and above all dollars; this applied to Karelia among other places, and a campaign was launched to induce Finns to settle and 'build socialism' there. At least twelve thousand had gone from Finland itself, and an appeal backed by glowing promises was now directed at the Finnish-American community. 'Karelia fever' spread like wildfire: no fewer than five thousand succumbed to it and to the blandishments of a wily agent whose true name was Gorin. He was sent out by the State security authorities and was ostensibly a member of Amtorg, the Soviet-American trade organization; many secret assistants worked for him, especially an American Finn named Oskar Korgan. The victims of this propaganda were promised work, good wages and housing and of course free passages to Leningrad and the Karelian Utopia. Destitute Finns were not accepted, but there was a welcome for those who possessed expensive tools, factories or workshops; they were persuaded to take all their movable property with them, it would be transported free of charge and they would receive compensation after their arrival in Karelia.

Mass meetings were held at which prospective emigrants were enrolled, and the exodus began: Amtorg-chartered steamers sailed one after the other from New York, taking Finns across the Atlantic to the promised land. Many arrived from remote States like Oregon and California, in cars bought with the proceeds from the sale of their houses and other property. Money was scarce, and banks acquired the houses, which were often unencumbered, for a fraction of their true value. As a rule there was no room for the cars on shipboard, so they blocked the streets leading to the piers and were sold at a considerable loss.

The rush to Utopia ended in a colossal tragedy, as it was bound to do. I had visited many of these Finnish-Americans in their flats and houses and had admired their secure, comfortable way of life. What could Karelia offer them in its place? A wretched fate awaited them, and how would their children survive the food shortage? I knew only too well that people were starving and that even in Petrozavodsk, the capital, these newcomers would not get enough to eat or find decent places to live.

Kuusinen wrote at that time and urged me to do my bit to persuade the Finns to emigrate; but I replied describing the effects of the 'Karelian fever' and refusing to take part in such a monstrous swindle. I would have liked to denounce it openly, but in the position I occupied this would have been difficult and perhaps even dangerous. I did try once or twice to warn people I knew well what a miserable place Karelia was, without adequate housing or any of the comforts they were used to; but my words fell on deaf ears. One of my friends simply replied: 'I'm sure we can adapt to conditions there as well as the Karelians. We're going to live there and build up socialism.' One woman bought a crateful of electrical appliances and said proudly: 'I'll fit up an electric kitchen there.' I thought to myself: 'You'll be lucky to have a kitchen of any kind.'

Gorin got wind of my attempts to warn people and informed Moscow, whereupon I received a letter from Edvard Gylling, the President of the Karelian Autonomous Republic, complaining of my conduct and requesting me to cease dissuading the Finns: he needed the immigrants and their property so as to carry out the plan, which he described in detail, to make Karelia a flourishing community. I wrote back that his plan was an excellent one on paper but was quite unrealizable, and that I wanted no part of the disgraceful business. I described to him how the Finns lived in America and how disgusted I was by Gorin's false promises.

The final result of this mass deception was an even more frightful chapter of human misery than I could have imagined. What happened to the immigrants' dollars, and the expensive machinery and tools they brought with them? Both were taken from them, without compensation, as soon as they arrived in Leningrad, and, more shameful still, these credulous and well-intentioned folk were persuaded to hand in their American passports, so that when they reached the Karelian forests they were completely at the mercy of Stalin's officials. Living in desperate conditions, on starvation wages, they soon realized the deception that had been practised on them and did their best to escape from the 'workers' paradise'—but this was only legally possible for the few who had had the sense to hold on to their passports. One or two others had enough *sisu* to make their way on foot through the trackless forests to Finland, whence the American Embassy could help them return to the USA; but soon this way out was closed, as the frontier was sealed off and strictly guarded. Then came Stalin's reign of terror, and the Finns who had not succumbed to the privations of Karelia were either packed off to labour camps or shot. Among those who suffered the latter fate, as several friends told me in Moscow later, were a group of skilled workers from America who built the new Finnish Legation there; the work was a great success, but once it was completed they were executed.

The few who managed to get back to America tried, on Gylling's advice, to recover compensation for their property from the American Communist Party. I do not know whether Gylling was serious, but certainly they never received a penny; it was sufficient that they had escaped with their lives. I did not hear the details of the Karelian tragedy until I returned to Moscow in summer 1933; during my fifteen years as a political prisoner I came across many of its victims.

Perhaps the best known of those who obeyed the call to Karelia was Martin Henrickson, who had lived in America from his early years and enjoyed some celebrity as a spokesman for the Finnish workers. At the time of the 'Karelian fever' he was an old man, but he wanted to see socialism with his own eyes and so he went to Karelia. Kuusinen gave him a letter describing him as 'the oldest Communist in the world', and on the strength of this he was admitted to the Russian Communist Party. But fate overtook him like the rest. I heard news of him on a visit to Petrozavodsk in 1958. He had been summoned before the Party Control Commission one day to answer for the crime of uttering a contemptuous anti-Soviet remark, to wit that the Russians were 'a lot of goats'—this in connection with the degree of sexual liberty that prevailed in the USSR. He was punished by expulsion from the Party, which was equivalent to a death sentence. Kuusinen's letter was of no avail; no one would give him any work, and since even those who did work had not enough to eat, it may be imagined how the veteran Henrickson, once a corpulent man, dwindled away to a skeleton and could scarcely walk. He kept his sense of humour, however. One day he was going along the road to Petrozavodsk with some American Finns, when they met a billy-goat. He wagged his finger at it and said: 'Pay attention, my friend, and don't tell anyone that you are a goat, or you'll be in trouble.' This was how one old man, formerly a convinced Communist, learnt the truth about life and happiness in the Soviet State.

Not only was 'Karelian fever' disastrous to individuals, but it dealt a death-blow to the Finnish-American workers' movement. Most of those who went to Karelia belonged to the association, whose funds, including the money borrowed for the purchase of premises in New York, were despatched to Russia in the guise of 'technical aid for Karelia'. The loss of cash was too much for the association, which had to wind up its activities.

Another tragic experience was that of a colony of Finnish-Americans who migrated to the Soviet Ukraine in the early twenties under the leadership of Leo Leino, a victim of Soviet propaganda, who had no political views but merely wanted to live there and cultivate his own land. He told friends of his dream and collected a group of followers, after which he came to Moscow, where I met him; he had previously seen Yrjö Sirola, who put him in touch with the authorities. The Soviet government welcomed his plan and set up a special commission to help find a suitable piece of land. He was offered, and accepted, a fertile black-earth area near Rostov-on-Don, and went back to America to push on with his preparations.

Money was collected, lists of interested persons drawn up, great modern agricultural machines were bought and a considerable number of families sailed overseas to cultivate the land which, Leino assured them, was there in abundance. They had to live out of doors until they had built their houses, but this did not deter them. Some time afterwards Leino visited Moscow and told me that they had built a large hut which served as a kitchen and canteen; the young men had sent for their fiancées and some had already been married in the new colony. Cultivation was going well, everybody was contented and cheerful, and the place was more and more like a large American farm. There were setbacks, but they were able to overcome them and go on to bigger plans. On one occasion when they had difficulties with the local authorities, the community sent Leino to appeal to no less a person than the President of the USSR. He actually saw Kalinin, explained the trouble with the aid of an interpreter and returned with a signed and sealed document authorizing the American Finns to farm as much land as they chose without interference.

The future appeared rosy, but one day an order came, like a bolt from the blue, that the whole area was to be turned into a State farm under the name of *Gigant*. The settlers' land and machinery was taken over without compensation, leaving them penniless. Some drifted back to America, but Leino remained in Russia to defend his rights. As Sirola told me, like so many other innocents he was finally shot.

I was recalled to Moscow in summer 1933; but before describing my return I will say something about the impression that the United States made on an ordinary Soviet citizen. Fed on the distortions of Moscow propaganda, one expected to see nothing but exploitation, poverty, race hatred, people out of work and so on. The reality, of course, was far different, as may be illustrated from the work of the well-known Soviet humourists Ilf and Petrov. These writers visited the USA in the early thirties to gather material for a book entitled *One-storey America*, by way of indicating that most Americans did not live in skyscrapers but led a plain, humdrum sort of life. (An English translation was published as *Little Golden America*.) They hired a car and drove all over the States, from New York to California and back via Mexico; sometimes they spent the night in city hotels and sometimes on farms. Their description is both shrewd and witty, and they rank among the great humorists of world literature.

They began paradoxically by saying that, to their surprise, they could find nothing in America that really made people happy. Once, for instance, they stopped in a suburb full of neat bungalows and two- or three-storeyed houses. The breadwinner drove to work every morning, while his wife and children stayed at home. Milk, butter, eggs and other provisions were delivered on the doorstep at dawn, and every day a white van drove round with plenty of other goods, so that the housewife did not need to go shopping to feed her family. The Americans took all this as a matter of course, and were used to being able to buy anything they wanted. Consequently they got no especial joy out of all these conveniences, and the authors drew the conclusion that America was a joyless land—quite unlike the Soviet Union, where the scarcity of goods and difficulties of everyday life meant that everyone was grateful for the smallest mercies.

In mid-July 1933 I embarked on a German steamer, one of those chartered by Amtorg to take American Finns to Leningrad. We called at Southampton, where I took a train for London, and next evening I sailed for Leningrad on the Soviet motor ship *Krasin*. It was a small, old-fashioned vessel, and both the passengers and the ship had a bad time of it during a heavy storm in the North Sea.

The journey from America gave me time to think over my personal problems, and I formed the decision to separate from my husband. During the two and a half years I had been in the United States my affection for him had vanished. Sometimes a long period of absence can help a marriage by giving each partner a chance to remember the other's good qualities; but this was not so in my case, and the nearer we got to Leningrad, the surer I became that I would not go back to Otto. I did not doubt that I would find it possible to make an independent life for myself.

I had my first rebuff from the Soviet system immediately after arriving in Leningrad. I had bought a lot of clothes and shoes in New York, knowing how hard they were to acquire in the Soviet Union, and, although this was in no way against the law, all my best things were confiscated by the Customs. I was given a receipt and told I would get them back in Moscow. but of course I did not. At the main Customs Office there I was told sneeringly: 'You can buy anything you need in the Soviet Union.'

The day before I left New York I had received a letter from Niilo Virtanen warning me against talking to anyone about my stay in America until he had a chance to tell me about the 'altered situation' in Moscow. I therefore telegraphed from Leningrad asking him to get me a hotel room, and he met me next morning at the station. We took a taxi to the Lux, and on the way he informed me that many junior Comintern officials had been arrested and that Otto's relations with the Finnish Communists were very strained. Niilo said I should not have come back from America at all, to which I could only reply that I had obeyed orders; I could have done nothing else, and I wanted to go back to my old job in the Scandinavian section of the Comintern. He looked dumbfounded at my naïvety and exclaimed: 'Whatever you do, don't do that. The Comintern is quite different from what it was when you left; the whole atmosphere is unhealthy.' He himself was still working there, but was doing his best to get a foreign assignment. He hoped either to be sent to China for military intelligence—the Fourth Bureau of the Red Army general staff—or, failing that, to Berlin, dangerous though it was since Hitler had come to power.

I knew that Niilo was a shrewd, sensible man and that I could rely on his judgement. I also knew it was risky to leave Kuusinen. I would no longer enjoy security on account of his high position, and if he did not actually take revenge he would certainly not help me if I got into trouble.

Next day I had a long talk with Otto. He reproached me for not telling him beforehand of my arrival and especially for staying at the hotel, but I made no secret of the fact that I regarded our life together as finished. I then gave him a report on my work in America, emphasizing that the conflict between the American Communist Party and the Finnish workers' association was still acute, especially as the latter had been paralysed by the effects of the 'Karelian fever'. The Party were still using the Haali for their meetings and printing the *Daily Worker* on Finnish presses, and were dilatory in paying for these services. I told Otto that I thought I had done some good by reorganizing the Finnish newspaper system. I also repeated to his face what I had written from New York, that in my opinion the deliberate deception over Karelia was a crime that would have tragic consequences. Otto, however, was unmoved by this: all he cared about was getting machinery and skilled workers to Karelia.

I told him of the American Party's financial troubles and the incompetence of its leaders. 'However,' I added, 'they have plenty of imagination'; and I told him that one of them had said to a

Finnish friend of mine: 'When the revolution comes, the Central Committee will have its office in the Empire State Building. We've already decided which floor.'

In reply to a question about the Finnish-American Communists, I told Otto of the Finnish families I had visited in Detroit. The men were mostly factory workers, well paid and satisfied with their conditions of work; nearly all of them ran a car and owned their houses. 'What about politics?' I replied that these men read the left-wing newspapers, but they would never rise in revolt at the party's behest; they had faith in the way things were. Otto interrupted and said: 'Mind you don't talk like that to Pyatnitsky: he wouldn't believe you, and would only be annoyed. In fact, if you don't want trouble I would advise you to keep all your opinions to yourself. It seems to me you've become completely Americanized—you only see what is good in the USA.' I retorted that if Otto did not believe me he could send someone else to see. 'Why should the American workers want a revolution, anyway? They have everything they need as it is.'

Unemployment in the United States was a key point at that time in the Comintern's propaganda directives to Parties all over the world. I told Otto that I thought this absurd, and that it would have no effect on workers in America, where conditions were quite different from Europe.

I mentioned that I had read with surprise a statement in the *Daily Worker* that there were twenty million unemployed in the USA, whereas the true figure was two million. I had challenged the editor, Mr Weinstone, for printing such nonsense, telling him that the left-wing European papers would copy it and make fools of themselves and the *Daily Worker* alike. To which Weinstone replied sarcastically: 'What's a zero more or less?'

'But,' said Kuusinen, 'what about the May Day demonstrations? Thousands of workers turn out every year at the Party's call.'

'Certainly they march in the procession, but that has nothing to do with Communism. The demonstrations are organized by the trade unions, and neither the capitalists nor the American government care in the slightest.'

Otto asked about the Negro problem; I agreed that it was a serious one, but the Comintern exaggerated its importance. He was astonished to hear that the blacks in Harlem had their own clubs and restaurants, owned cars and were well dressed. To his evident disappointment I added that, while I knew nothing of Negroes in the south, their living conditions in and around New York were by no means as bad as the Comintern imagined.

Finally Otto asked about the Party building where I had worked. Hearing that it had nine storeys, he asked if there was a lift.

'Certainly—three, in fact.'

'But when the lifts are out of order, it means they have a lot of stairs to climb. Why didn't they get a building with a larger area and fewer floors?'

'Why, the lifts never are out of order—I can't remember it happening all the time I was there.'

'Look, you don't think I'll fall for that propaganda, do you?'

'Well, now that we're talking about it, I do recall there was an accident once. One afternoon when the lift was full of people it dropped down to the cellar, and it was a miracle nobody was hurt. But by next morning they had it working properly again.'

'Well,' said Otto sarcastically, 'at least you've shown me that the American Party have learnt something from us Bolsheviks.' (Lifts in the Soviet Union are more often out of order than otherwise.)

Otto took it for granted that I would be returning to my work at the Comintern, and I did not undeceive him. Neither of us said a word about the arrests of Comintern officials that had taken place during my stay in America.

I also had a long talk with Pyatnitsky, who as treasurer of the Comintern was chiefly interested in the American Party's finances. He could not understand why they kept asking Moscow for subsidies and could not lay their hands on America's own wealth.

IV

Japan, the Land of Smiles

With every day that passed, it became clearer that I must act quickly to get out of the Soviet Union. I had another talk with Niilo Virtanen, who said that the Fourth Bureau of the general staff needed people with languages and foreign experience. This was the department in charge of military intelligence abroad; its chief was General Jan Berzin, whom Virtanen seemed to know well and to think highly of as an intelligence officer. He promised to get me an interview with him. Berzin was a Latvian who had joined the revolutionary movement at the age of sixteen. He was arrested in 1906 and, being under age, was not executed but sent to Siberia, whence he escaped to continue working against the Tsarist regime. After the Revolution he became an adherent of Trotsky, who was then commander-in-chief of the Red Army. According to Virtanen, I could expect him to welcome me with open arms.

A few days later I went to see him in his office. He was a personable figure in uniform and carried himself stiffly; his face was angular, and his blue, bloodshot eyes blinked continually as he spoke. He did not waste time on trivialities. Hearing that I had worked on the Scandinavian desk in the Comintern, he said he could find me a similar job in his organization, but he wondered if Kuusinen would let me go; had I not better discuss it with him first?

So I went back to Otto, who told me he had heard of Berzin's attempt at 'poaching', as he called it, but did not want me to leave the Comintern; if I did not like my present job there, he could find me another. Finally I said: 'You don't seem to understand that I don't want to have anything more to do with you. And if we are to live apart, surely it's better for me to work for Berzin.' I did not tell him I was determined to go abroad. After much argument he realized that he could not persuade me to stay with the Comintern; he absolutely refused, however, to agree to a divorce.

I returned to Berzin to tell him of Otto's consent to my change of job. He telephoned in my presence to Pyatnitsky to ask about the quality of my work, and said that Pyatnitsky had praised it highly. He asked if I had ever been in the Far East, and, when I said no, suggested a mission to Japan. I hesitated at the idea of going to a completely strange country, ignorant as I was of everything to do with military intelligence. However, Berzin continued: 'Don't worry; we shan't make you engage in espionage. If you go to Japan you can live there just as you like, get to know the country and learn the language. We will pay your expenses, and you will be responsible only to me. The only condition is that you must agree to stay there for a long time.' He hinted, however, that when I had thoroughly settled down he would have some special tasks for me.

Not wishing to be precipitate, I asked Berzin to allow me a few days to make up my mind. During that time I had several more talks with Virtanen, though I should have known in advance what the answer would be. Niilo was certain that we were both in grave danger in Moscow and should take any opportunity of leaving the Soviet Union. For this reason, he told me, he had allowed Kuusinen to persuade him to head the new Comintern office which was to be set up in Berlin, since there was no hope of getting to China instead. For my part I admitted to him that after the 'fresh air' of America I found the oppressive Moscow atmosphere unendurable. Several of my friends had disappeared, and it was easy to tell that I was mistrusted because of the long time I had spent abroad. At every turn one noticed the shortage of food in Moscow, and the poor quality of the few goods to be found in the shops. The general discontent was unmistakable, but Stalin's dictatorship rested on firm foundations. So Berzin's offer seemed the best solution, and I made up my mind to accept.

My new assignment began with four weeks' holiday at Kislovodsk in the Caucasus. On returning to Moscow I expected to be given instructions about my work in Japan, but to my relief there were none; I was strictly enjoined, however, to say nothing to anyone about my new employment.

I could now begin my preparations for the journey, the first step being to obtain a forged passport. As I was travelling under Swedish colours again, this was provided by my old friend Signe Sillen in Stockholm, who worked for the Fourth Bureau as well as the Comintern. My assumed name was Hildur Nordström; I was supposed to have arrived recently from Berlin, and the passport contained visas for the return journey via Warsaw, Vienna, Paris and Berlin to Stockholm.

I was provided with a large sum of money, and left Moscow in October 1933. I stayed a week in Vienna and a week in Paris, where I bought plenty of clothes—the Customs officer who took my American purchases away from me had not been so wrong when he said I would soon be able to replace them.

I spent one day in Berlin, and by pure chance met Virtanen in a restaurant: a dangerous thing in itself, as foreigners were strictly supervised under the Nazi regime. As Virtanen spoke Norwegian fluently he was living there under a Norwegian name, with a passport provided by the international section of the Comintern. The name, if I remember right, was Johan Luis Korsell, and the passport had belonged to an obscure Communist from Oslo who was in Moscow on a visit. Virtanen was nervous because he thought it was not forged skilfully enough, and he had asked Signe Sillen to get him a Swedish one. He was therefore delighted by our chance meeting and asked me, as soon as I got to Stockholm, to tell Signe that he would be expecting the new passport at a certain hour on a certain day at the Terminus Hotel in Copenhagen. Signe had his photographs and personal details, so he thought she should have no difficulties.

Niilo was discontented with his work, as he could achieve nothing with conditions in Germany as they were, and he hoped to be recalled from Berlin soon and sent to China. This eventually happened, but unfortunately he was then ordered to return to Moscow, where his wife and son were, and thus fell victim to the purges.

At the end of November I travelled to Stockholm without difficulty and put up at the Kronprins Hotel. Next morning I went to Signe Sillen to give her Virtanen's message. She had his passport ready, but before she could go to Copenhagen a letter in German arrived from Virtanen in Berlin, saying that he was in prison and asking her to get a Norwegian lawyer named Falk to go there and take steps to obtain his release. Falk, I knew, was a Communist who had made friends with Niilo in Moscow. We thought it surprising that the letter was addressed to Signe, which might have led to her discovery as a Soviet agent, and still more surprising that it was in an envelope franked by Berlin police headquarters; but we assumed that Niilo had got hold of a warder who was a Communist Party member, who had thought it safest to forward the letter under official cover.

Signe telegraphed to Moscow for authority to pay the cost of Falk's journey; she then went to Oslo and gave him the message. He was ready to go to Berlin, but meanwhile the police there found out that the real Johan Korsell was under arrest in Oslo for some small offence, and also that Virtanen was Finnish by birth. They kept Niilo in prison for months, but fortunately he was able to conceal his links with the Comintern, and finally he was deported to Helsinki. As he was a Soviet citizen and there was no charge against him, the Finns handed him over to the Soviet Legation.[29] He may have been right to suspect the quality of his Norwegian passport, but he told me in Moscow in December 1935 that the signature of the Governor of Oslo had been so well forged that the Governor himself authenticated it.

Before continuing my own journey I needed a new passport, as I could not go to Japan with the one bearing a Soviet visa. Signe got to work again, and in a month I had a new identity as Mrs Elisabeth Hansson, a journalist from Luleå. Apart from bearing my photograph, the passport was that of a real person, whose husband, a Communist, simply applied for it to the Swedish authorities. All Signe and I had to do was carefully to memorize Elisabeth Hansson's curriculum vitae.

I spent Christmas with Signe's family, but my New Year

present from Moscow took the form of an order to return there as Hildur Nordström. I felt sure this meant that the Japanese assignment was off, but my fears proved to be groundless. I still do not know why I was recalled, as my final instructions could equally well have been given me in Stockholm, but apparently Berzin wanted to go through everything once more in detail before I left for the Far East. He emphasized, as he had done previously, that I was to live in style and cultivate the most prominent Japanese politicians, but have nothing to do with the Germans—I learnt the reason for this afterwards. I would receive orders from Berzin alone, and was to use the name 'Ingrid' for communicating with him, the procedure for which would be explained to me after my arrival. The person responsible for liaison in Japan would be an old acquaintance of mine, whose name I was not told for the present.

Berzin catechized me on the life and circumstances of Elisabeth Hansson, and was pleased that Signe and I had foreseen every detail. He then told me my itinerary. First I was to go back to Stockholm to get money for the journey and the necessary visas on Elisabeth Hansson's passport. At 3 o'clock on 23 February I was to be sitting in the dining-room of the Grand Hotel at Stockholm, wearing a blue dress with a red rose on the left side; an agent of the Fourth Bureau would contact me there. From Stockholm I was to go to Oslo, deposit a thousand dollars in a bank there and proceed via Copenhagen to Paris, where I would book a first-class cabin on the Italian S.S. *Conte Verde*, sailing from Trieste to Shanghai at the end of July. At Shanghai I was to stay at a hotel in Bubbling Well Road, where I would be contacted and given instructions for the further journey to Japan.

In conclusion Berzin gave me a talk on politics. He expected Soviet-Japanese relations to continue deteriorating on account of the armed clash between Japan and China which had begun in 1931, leading to the occupation of Manchuria by the Japanese and the creation there of the puppet state of Manchukuo. The Japanese had also seized Shanghai, and although they had given it back again, they were threatening the borders of China proper. In May 1932 the Prime Minister, Inukai, had been murdered by fanatics who demanded a more active war policy.

His successors were subservient to the military, and a year later Japan had announced her withdrawal from the League of Nations.

I was not deterred by these rumours of war, however, and waited impatiently for orders to set out on my journey. These came in mid-February 1934, and on the 21st I booked in at the Grand Hotel in Stockholm. Two days later I was sitting in the restaurant, dressed in the prescribed manner, at exactly three o'clock. No one else was there except two old gentlemen sipping brandy. I sat anxiously until four o'clock, when two men in slovenly clothes came in; one of these gave me an unobtrusive sign, and I followed them out of the building. In a minute or two I caught up with them; they turned into a side street, and one took from a brief-case an untidy parcel wrapped in torn newspaper, telling me in Russian that it contained a lot of money. We parted after arranging to meet at Signe Sillen's home.

I was embarrassed at having to walk past the hotel porter with this clumsy package, and was surprised at the agents' slipshod methods. However, I was now in funds to the extent of several thousand dollars. When I met the two men at the Sillens' I learnt that their names were Kramov and Ilyin, and that Kramov's wife was the sister of General Uritsky. Kramov was the permanent representative or 'resident' of the Fourth Bureau in Stockholm, and Ilyin was his assistant. Like Berzin, they eventually fell victim to the purges.

Signe gave me the names and addresses of people to whom 'Ingrid' was to write from Japan, including the librarian of the city of Stockholm; I have forgotten his name and address, but he bore the title of Doctor. Also on the list was his assistant, Margaretha Sandberg, at Bodegatan 60. We agreed that Signe would use the name 'Karin' in her letters to me.

There was no particular difficulty in getting my European, Chinese and Japanese visas. It was rather a long process, but by the middle of April my papers were in order and I went on to Paris. For the next three months I had a pleasant time there, chiefly reading books about Japan and Japanese culture.

On 26 July I went to Venice and embarked on the *Conte Verde*. I always enjoy sea voyages, as I am never seasick, and this one was especially pleasant owing to the many interesting people aboard, who were most friendly and gave me useful advice about China and Japan. The ship called at Port Said and Massawa (Ethiopia), and we encountered a heavy storm in the Indian Ocean before reaching Bombay, where I got some idea of the poverty and superstition of India. I was much impressed by Ceylon, where an excursion was arranged for us, and which I felt must have been the paradise from which Adam and Eve were expelled. Then came Batavia (Jakarta) and Sumatra, which were rather dull, several Indochinese ports, Hong Kong, and finally in the middle of September we reached Shanghai. The journey had taken six weeks, and I felt regretful at leaving the *Conte Verde*, where I had had such a relaxed and pleasant time. I did not guess that I would be doing the same trip on the same steamer two years later.

Some Italians on board had advised me against staying at the hotel in Bubbling Well Road indicated by Moscow, as it had a bad reputation. (How extraordinary it was that Berzin's office knew so little about conditions and customs outside the USSR!). Instead they recommended the Palace, which proved to be excellent. I felt sure that the liaison officer would find me there, but to be on the safe side I telegraphed to the librarian in Stockholm that I could not find the book he wanted and had decided on the Palace Hotel.

A few days later, a young woman turned up who spoke German and said she had orders to take me to the 'chief'. We drove in a taxi to the Avenue Foch in the French Concession. The chief's name proved to be Dr Bosch, and the girl, his wireless operator, was called Elly. Bosch began by reproving me for choosing my own hotel. He as 'resident' was the senior officer of the secret intelligence service in Shanghai, and all Soviet agents in the Far East were subordinate to him; he admitted, however, that I was in a special position as I was to receive orders direct from Moscow. He asked what my duties were, and I replied that so far I had no specific instructions. This evidently displeased him, and he said that I must not continue my journey until he obtained confirmation from Moscow. He added that in recent weeks radio communication with 'Wiesbaden' (i.e. Vladivostok) had been difficult, and as he had no direct link with 'Munich'

(Moscow), I must have patience. It seemed to me unnecessary and imprudent for him to tell me these cover names, and another piece of carelessness was that he left the room for a moment and I was able to have a look at his passport, which lay among some papers on his desk. From a quick glance I saw that he was using the cover name of Abramov, a Latvian.

Elly also committed a breach of security by showing me where the radio transmitter was hidden behind a cupboard. She told me she was a native of Luxembourg and had arrived from Moscow a few weeks before. Years later I heard that the chief's real name was Bronin, that he had married Elly and that they were living in Moscow. They both seemed to be uncultivated people, and I had as little to do with them in Shanghai as possible. At Bronin's apartment I once met an agent of his who was introduced as Dr Voigt and claimed to be the Shanghai representative of the German firm of Siemens.

I stayed in Shanghai for nearly a month, till 'Wiesbaden' finally gave permission for me to continue my journey. Bosch gave me some cash, told me I should make for Tokyo, and asked what my address would be. My Italian friends had recommended the Imperial Hotel, and we agreed that a Dr Somebody would call on me there at a certain day and hour. I embarked on a US ship, the *President Jackson*, and after an eight days' voyage reached Kobe at the end of November; a group of my Italian friends were on the quay to greet me. After a week in Kobe I went on to Tokyo, and there began one of the happiest periods of my life; the two years I was to spend in Japan passed only too swiftly.

The Imperial Hotel, situated near the Emperor's palace, was a long low structure of red and yellow brick, designed by the American architect Frank Lloyd Wright; it was quite unlike the other modern buildings in the area, and somehow reminded me of Indian architecture in Central America. Because of the earthquake risk it had no fixed foundations but was built, extraordinary as it may seem, on marshy soil near the harbour. It had survived the great earthquake of 1923, and when Wright was told of this he wired back: 'I knew it would.' The hotel lobby and restaurant were a meeting-ground for the whole of international Tokyo, including diplomats, business men, journalists and spies. The arrival and departure of travellers, and social events in the foreign community, were reported in the English-language *Japan Times*. The Imperial was not exactly the place for a long stay, but it had a certain comfort and the public rooms were of refined elegance.

The day after I arrived, the telephone rang in my room and a man's voice asked politely if I would give an interview to the daily *Asahi*. I saw I could not refuse, and the interviewer turned up at once, accompanied by a photographer. His name was Baron Nakano; he said he worked for the newspaper, but I could not help suspecting that the police had sent him to keep tabs on me. In any case he carried out the interview, which was published next day, in a most tactful manner. Later he became a good friend, and opened many doors for me which were usually shut to foreigners. Another journalist who helped me a great deal, a highly cultivated man, was Uyehara of the *Japan Times*.

I had determined to learn Japanese, and a week after arriving I took my first lesson at the Vaccari language school. Vaccari, an Italian, taught English to Japanese, while his wife Enko taught Japanese to foreigners, including many of the diplomatic corps. She was an excellent teacher, and we became such close friends that I could ask her about Japanese topics that were never discussed publicly. I found it easy to learn spoken Japanese: it has a pleasant sound, the sentences are short and the pronunciation clear. The written language with its hieroglyphics, on the other hand, is almost impossible for foreigners. Everyday speech is full of honorific embellishments, but there are not many words to express tender feelings. With foreigners especially, the Japanese hide their inmost thoughts behind a veil of politeness. It is wrong to think they are incapable of emotion, but they do not show it: whatever sorrows they may have, they do not complain, and they may smile or laugh even while suffering deeply. They consider that one should not burden one's fellow-creatures with one's own troubles, and self-command is thus a prominent feature of the national character.

I spent Christmas with my cheerful Italian friends in Kobe. Remembering the previous Christmas in Stockholm, I thought how many new and interesting experiences had come my way in the past twelve months and what cause I had to be contented with my lot. I mused upon the future, wondering what 1935 would bring.

The Imperial Hotel was expensive, and I planned to take a flat as soon as possible in the Nonomiya Aparto building; but first I had to await the mysterious 'Doctor' who was to contact me in the first week of January. At the appointed time I was sitting in the hotel lobby and saw a man by the main door, who gave me a slight nod. This was Dr Richard Sorge, whom I had met ten years earlier when he was working in the German Secretariat of the Comintern; he and his wife had paid us a visit shortly after he arrived from Germany. So he was to be the liaison officer between General Berzin and me.

I remained sitting for a moment and then went out to the street, where Sorge was waiting in a taxi. We had a short conversation, in which I told him of my intention to move. He said he knew my cover name was Ingrid, but had not been told what my duties were; he was not authorized to give me orders or instructions, but all my communications with the Fourth Bureau were to go through him. We agreed to meet again in a week's time, and meanwhile I moved to the apartment house. The rendezvous appointed by Sorge turned out to be a low-class German bar, and I asked him reproachfully how he could expect a lady who had been living at the Imperial Hotel to meet him in such a place. But he paid no attention and merely said that he had to go to Moscow shortly, travelling via America both ways. He did not know when he would be back, so he gave me enough money to cover my expenses for a year.

I lived peacefully till November 1935, and made many acquaintances among journalists and important politicians. Then, quite unexpectedly, a fair-haired woman whom I did not know came to my apartment and told me in German that she had a message from 'our friend the Doctor': I was to leave for Moscow at once, but first he wanted a few words with me. A man would be waiting for me that evening at the flower shop in the Roppongi market; he would also speak German and would take me to where the Doctor was. My visitor emphasized once more that I should get ready to leave as soon as possible and travel by the fastest route to Moscow.

I could scarcely believe my ears. Had I not been told that I was to stay several years in Japan? Why this sudden change, when I had just learnt enough Japanese to conduct a simple conversation, and had made a number of useful acquaintances? And how was I to explain my departure to my Japanese friends?

I went to the market as instructed, bought a few flowers and met there a corpulent German who did not tell me his name, nor did I mention mine. We drove in a taxi to Sorge's modest two-room flat. Sorge confirmed the message but pretended he did not know the reason for it; I was to take the Trans-Siberian railway and put up at the Metropole in Moscow, where I would be contacted. He gave me messages for people in Moscow, asked if I had enough money for the journey and gave me the fare.

The fat German was Sorge's assistant and wireless operator; I afterwards learnt that his name was Max Klausen. He asked me to tell Moscow that if they would send twenty thousand dollars he could open a radio and electrical store in Yokohama, which would be excellent cover and also help to pay his expenses.

A few days later I read in the *Japan Times* that a spy named Abramov had been arrested in Shanghai—apparently Elly had escaped. It occurred to me at once that this was the most likely reason for my recall: I had not seen Bosch since October 1934, but something might have leaked out that was compromising to me. As he was the key man of Soviet espionage in the Far East, his arrest might well have thrown Moscow into a nervous state.

The Intertourist travel bureau told me that my best route was from Shimonoseki to Dairen, thence by train to Harbin and across Siberia. This would get me to Moscow eight days earlier than if I waited for the next boat to Vladivostok. I therefore booked for the journey via Manchuria, the USSR and Berlin to Stockholm, ostensibly my home town. I also needed a Soviet transit visa for 'Elisabeth Hansson', and this was not so easy as it sounds. I feared that the Soviet Embassy in Tokyo was under observation, and I wanted at all costs to avoid attracting notice. So I went to Kobe, where there was a Soviet Consulate, and paid the cost of a telegram seeking authority to grant the visa. This came before long, and I was duly entitled to stay three days in Moscow.

I told my friends in Tokyo that I had to return to Sweden on family business, but would be back as soon as possible. When I boarded the train for Shimonoseki I realized how many friends I had acquired in the course of a year: a score of people came to the station, including Baron Nakano and his mother. It was a wrench to leave these people and their charming country.

The journey was uneventful. The Japanese boat was clean and pleasant; the Harbin hotel, at which I stayed one night, was filthy, and Manchuria was teeming with Japanese soldiers. The monotonous trip across Siberia took nine days, and in the first week of December I was back in the familiar Metropole. The weather was grey and gloomy, and so were my feelings.

A Major Sirotkin of the Fourth Bureau came to the hotel next day. I told him how angry and disappointed I was at being recalled so soon, when I had just made a good beginning in Japan. 'But we thought you were in danger,' said Sirotkin, 'and anyway General Uritsky, the new chief, wants to see you. He thinks you should go back to Japan.' I asked with surprise what had happened to General Berzin, but the major made an evasive answer and started talking about Sorge, whose reports, he said, were vague and often inaccurate. Then he went on: 'Between ourselves, the place is in a state of confusion, and even the people at the top don't know what they want.'

Sirotkin promised to secure me an interview with Uritsky as soon as possible. I asked him what the new chief was like: it has always been my habit to learn as much as I could about people I was to meet, especially their personal qualities and level of education. The major would not say much at first—no doubt he considered such matters confidential—but he finally told me that since Uritsky took over he had shown himself to be experienced in intelligence work. He had commanded a cavalry brigade with success in the Civil War. I asked if he was related to Moisey Uritsky, the head of the Petrograd Cheka, who was murdered in August 1918 on the same day that Dora Kaplan fired at Lenin in Moscow; Sirotkin replied that Moisey was the present man's uncle. He added that I had nothing to be afraid of as the new chief was a friendly and cultivated man.

On the same day I rang up Niilo Virtanen, who came round to the hotel at once and, without preliminaries, spoke in the same way as he had done in 1933 when I came back from America. Why on earth had I returned, and did I not know of the frightful purges? Berzin had been dismissed, and so had the Finnish officials in Karelia, many of whom were in jail. He urged me to return to Japan if I possibly could, and in any case not to stay in Moscow. The Bureau were sending him to China shortly, but he feared that his wife and son would not be allowed to leave Russia. He also told me that he had run into Sorge in August, and they had had a pleasant evening at the Bolshaya Moskovskaya Hotel. Sorge, as usual, had had too much to drink and had talked frankly about his own troubles. He had had enough of spying for the Russians, but did not see how he could pull out and start a new life. He felt unsafe in the Soviet Union, and if he went to Germany he would be arrested by the Gestapo. So he had no choice but to go back to Japan, though he was afraid the game would soon be up as far as he was concerned.

Virtanen had hardly left me when the telephone rang: it was Otto, who welcomed me back and said he was sad that I had not come straight to him. He had an important matter to discuss, but could not do so on the telephone; would I go and see him that evening? After some hesitation I said yes, and at nine o'clock I went to the huge government building I knew so well.

Otto had visibly aged: his movements and speech were slower and heavier than when I had last seen him two years before. He asked me about my journey and my life in Japan, but obviously did not believe all I told him about my friends and interests there. Heaving a deep sigh, he said gravely: 'One of these days you'll be arrested for espionage and condemned to death.' I assured him that I had no dangerous mission and was left a free hand while I studied the Japanese language and customs. Then I asked why I had been recalled and what it was he wanted to see me about. But he looked at me absently and said he could not discuss the 'important matter' until next day; when I knew what it was, he was sure I would change my mind about returning to Japan. I was very cross, but promised to see him again at eight o'clock next evening.

I felt sure by now that he was responsible for my recall, and next evening I taxed him with it, making no secret of my annoyance. He was silent for a while and then answered in his dry, almost phlegmatic way. 'It wasn't I who gave the order.'

'Then who did?' I demanded angrily.

'Stalin,' said Otto calmly. 'Sit down and don't get excited. I'll tell you the whole story, and then you will see that it was Stalin ... You know how fast the world situation changes nowadays, and how hard it is to keep abreast of everything. You remember the autumn of 1923, when Germany seemed ripe for revolution. The economic situation was desperate, the currency worthless, the Communist Party and the workers were prepared, with enough arms and a detailed programme; yet on the 22nd of October, when the revolution was to break out, absolutely nothing happened. Since then I have been wondering day and night what the reason for the collapse can have been, and I have finally come to the conclusion that our old revolutionary theories are invalid. We live in a new age with new demands, and in 1923 we failed to realize that. Now I have worked out a new theory, and I have gradually convinced Stalin that it is right and that it was he who thought of it. That being so, I don't have to discuss it with anyone else in Moscow, but I am now going to explain it to you—so please do me a favour, sit still and don't interrupt.'

I said nothing, and he went on. 'The Russian Revolution was a spontaneous event, and it took the Tsarist regime by surprise. The ruling class were so short-sighted that they couldn't imagine a successful revolution, and, incredible as it may seem, the revolutionaries themselves didn't expect to succeed at that moment, Lenin least of all. But today things are different. The capitalist governments are aware of the danger of Communism and are ruthlessly determined to nip it in the bud. The Communist Parties, the trained cadres of revolution, are persecuted by governments, and all the prisons in Europe are full of Communists. Firms and factories expel Communists or treat them badly, and our press and propaganda are savagely suppressed. In this state of things, any preparation for revolution is practically impossible. The training of national cadres in the Comintern is a slow business, and those who could be effective leaders are not given the right jobs in the capitalist countries. Only yesterday Stalin admitted to me that the Comintern has some very able people among its international cadres, but that most of them are not given the right work to do.'

Having said this by way of introduction, Otto proceeded to describe the plan with which, he said, Stalin was in agreement.

'I am speaking to you now in perfect frankness. In all probability there will soon be a war. The Finns are secretly preparing to attack us, and they intend to annex Karelia and an area up to Murmansk.'

I had kept silent so far, but this was too much for me and I exclaimed: 'You can't seriously believe that the Finns would be so mad as to attack this huge country—it would be like a fly attacking an elephant! Where can you possibly get such reports from? They don't make sense.'

He made no direct reply, but continued: 'You know how pro-Finnish Gylling is, and you remember how he admired the Finnish system of dividing up their country into provinces with a separate administration for each, and said how well it would do for Karelia.'

'Yes, I remember, but we were talking about economics then, not military matters.'

'Gylling is not to be trusted ... In any case, there's going to be a war soon, and probably a big one. As you know, the Germans have always had their eye on Finland, and they're waiting for the moment when the Finns attack the Soviet Union, so that they can rush to their aid. The Germans don't mind who they help so long as it's against the USSR. The British too have designs on the Murmansk coast, and Norway would not be left out. So it is absolutely vital for us to defend the achievements of the Bolshevik Revolution. Finland is a small country, but it's of the first importance, and we must think how to defend it against threats from outside. I know exactly what material we have in the international cadres of the Comintern, and, as I said, we must get them into positions abroad where they can be most effective. This is where your talents can really be useful. Stalin has had an eye on you for a long time, he knows about your life and work, and he has in mind an important post where you could really influence the future. Of course you've been in Japan, but what could you hope to achieve there? This other job is the one for you.

'You know Alexandra Kollontay, and how unreliable she is politically—she's one of the old Mensheviks who opposed Lenin, and after the Revolution she joined Shlyapnikov's gang and was put in prison. Then she went over to Trotsky, and when she was

Minister in Norway she supported Tranmael against the Comintern. Her next post was Mexico, where Trotsky lives. Now she's in Sweden, but Stalin means to recall her and not send her abroad again. And he's picked you to represent the Soviet Union in Sweden and Norway.'

Up to this point I had listened to Otto's monologue in silence, though with some amusement and with growing surprise. I now interrupted angrily to say that I was not a diplomat and had no interest in the post offered to me.

'But Stalin is convinced you're the best person for it. The Scandinavians are used to our appointing women as ministers. You speak Swedish and know the country, and everyone here has full confidence in you. It doesn't matter that you haven't any diplomatic experience: you'll have plenty of advisers. After all, you've worked for years at the centre of a big international organization, and the work in Sweden wouldn't be so very different. You can be sure that we'll all stand by you here, and you can turn to us in any difficulty.'

My patience was exhausted. 'So now I see what it's all about. The USSR wants to go to war with Finland, and I'm to go to Stockholm as Minister and help the Red Army to plot against my own country and my own people. No, thank you, I'll have nothing to do with it. You can tell Stalin what you like.'

'Stalin will send for you and tell you himself how important the assignment is. What will you say to him?'

'I don't know what words I shall use, but one thing is certain —I don't want to be a diplomat, and I will have nothing to do with planning a war.'

So ended my conversation with Kuusinen in December 1935. I left him without a word of farewell, and I never saw him again.

I spent a sleepless night wondering how I could get out of the trap, but determined not to be a party to the intrigues of Stalin and Kuusinen. Next day Sirotkin came and gave me General Uritsky's telephone number; I called and was given an appointment at seven the following morning in his apartment in the Dom Pravitelstva. He proved to be a thin, dark man of middle height, with a small moustache. He greeted me in a friendly way; I mentioned my conversation with Otto and begged him to send me back to Japan if he possibly could. He said he would do his best, but feared it would be difficult to reverse a decision on which Stalin and Kuusinen had agreed. Our interview was short as he was in a hurry to get to his office.

For a full week I waited in my hotel, devoured by anxiety and wondering if Stalin would send for me. But at last Sirotkin came with the joyful message that I was to go back to Japan, and Uritsky wanted to see me beforehand. I went with Sirotkin to the Fourth Bureau where I found Uritsky and an unknown civilian; I did not like the look of him, and, although he said nothing, his expression suggested that the feeling was mutual. Uritsky said he was glad that the question of my return to Japan had been settled to my satisfaction. My recall, in his opinion, had been a mistake—this he said with a disapproving look at the civilian, as though to indicate where the responsibility lay. He then questioned me in detail about Japan, my experiences and contacts and what I thought of the internal situation. I emphasized the danger to the parliamentary system from ultra-patriotic terrorist organizations. He agreed with me, and thought this was also a threat to Soviet-Japanese relations.

Like Berzin, he gave me no specific instructions, but told me to go on studying and cultivating acquaintances. He advised me, however, to avoid contact with Dr Sorge, with whom he was dissatisfied. When I told him that Sorge's assistant had asked for twenty thousand dollars to open a radio shop, he exclaimed angrily: 'The rogues, they do nothing but drink and spend money. I shan't give them a single kopeck.'

In conclusion he suggested that I should write a book about Japan, describing the country and people in complimentary terms so as to improve my own status with them. I was on no account to criticize Japanese policy, but I might speak a little harshly of the USSR if I chose. What was one piece of anti-Soviet literature more or less? Expense was to be no consideration. As I already had plenty of material, including photographs, I greeted the suggestion with enthusiasm, and we agreed that I would go to Stockholm as soon as possible to write the book. That was the last time I ever saw General Uritsky.

Neither he nor I said anything about the diplomatic post in Stockholm; I never heard what came of the plan, but I felt more and more convinced that it was a brain-child of Kuusinen's and that Stalin, if he knew of it at all, had not yet endorsed it, or he would not have backed down so easily. I doubted whether the commissariat for foreign affairs would have approved the idea of appointing me, still less the Swedish government, which would probably have regarded it as a provocation to Finland. In short, I was puzzled to know how to interpret Otto's proposal, and could only think that he was determined to prevent my returning to Japan lest I be arrested as a spy, thus exposing not only the Comintern but Kuusinen himself. I had no means of confirming this, but, curiously, I gathered from a cell-mate in Lefortovo prison in 1938 that the account Kuusinen gave me was not wholly devoid of foundation.

As I was still awaiting orders to leave, I preferred to move out of the noisy hotel into an apartment, which Sirotkin found for me in a house on Frunze Embankment used by members of the Bureau. Yrjö Sirola visited me there several times and spoke of quarrels among the Finnish Communists, especially Manner and Kuusinen. Manner and his wife came one evening, shortly before they were arrested. Years later, in a labour camp, I chanced to hear of his fate, which I shall describe in another chapter.

I was much worried about my brother Väinö, of whom I had heard nothing since he was appointed head of the agricultural college at Petrozavodsk. I travelled there in secret one day and found my fears confirmed: his wife, in great distress, told me that he had recently been arrested and taken to Leningrad. Gylling, Nuorteva and Rovio had lost their jobs, like many others, and were soon to be executed in the purges. I went to the head of the NKVD in Petrozavodsk to ask him about Väinö's arrest, and he replied politely: 'There is no charge against your brother, he's an able and popular young man. He has just gone to Leningrad to clear up a certain matter, but he'll be back soon.' Väinö never came back.

In mid-January 1936 Sirotkin brought me my orders and journey money. I was told to contact Kramov in Stockholm and, when I had finished my book, to travel via Paris and embark, as before, on the *Conte Verde* for Shanghai, where I would receive instructions for the onward voyage to Japan.

Before leaving Moscow I asked my old housekeeper Alexandra to keep for me the clothes and other things I had brought from Japan and did not want to take back there. They were to be a precious source of funds a few years later.

In the second week of February I set out, as Elisabeth Hansson, for Stockholm via Warsaw, Vienna and Paris. I took a room in the Grand Hotel and began at once to write my book in Swedish, under the title *Det leende Nippon* (Smiling Japan). Its purpose was to describe the charms of that sunny land and its engaging and friendly people. I spoke of Japanese customs and interests and devoted a chapter to Buddhism and the influence of Oriental philosophy on the Japanese outlook. I was surprised at my own rate of progress: the book was completed in a few weeks, and Hugo Sillen found a publisher who promised to bring it out in June. I thought it best to leave Stockholm for a time, so as not to attract attention, and invited Signe Sillen to come on a trip to Copenhagen. I then went to Paris to book my passage on the *Conte Verde*, and returned to Stockholm just as the book was published. I was very proud of my first literary venture, and pleased with its appearance and the reproduction of the photographs. I sent copies to Uritsky and Kuusinen and to my Japanese friends, and received a message through Kramov saying that my chief was delighted with the book and congratulated me on it.

The *Conte Verde* sailed this time from Genoa; I was thrilled to be on board again, and enjoyed the journey no less than two years before. We reached Shanghai at the end of August, and I stayed at the new Park Hotel. A few days after my arrival a young Russian-speaking woman appeared and told me to go at seven o'clock that evening to the flower shop in the market, where a man I knew would be waiting. I went at the appointed hour, bought some carnations and, as I was leaving the shop, saw a man of disagreeable but somehow familiar appearance: it was the one in whose presence Uritsky had given me my instructions. We drove off in his car. All he said was: 'You can go to Japan, here's the money'; I left him with a curt 'Goodbye'. I never heard his name or saw him again, but he was evidently Bosch's successor as 'resident' in Shanghai. The sum of money he handed over bore witness to the Bureau's generosity. I booked a cabin on the *President Wilson*, the next ship sailing for Japan, and was in Yokohama by the second week of September.

I was delighted to be back in the smiling land where I had so many good friends. An English translation of my book appeared shortly afterwards—no doubt through the good offices of the ministry of foreign affairs—and I received compliments on every hand. I felt especially honoured by a letter from a Japanese professor who praised and thanked me for the way I had described the national character and view of life.

I stayed for a few weeks at the Imperial and then took a flat in the Nonomiya building as before. I resumed my lessons at the Vaccari school and was pleased and surprised to find that I had forgotten nothing, though it was nine months since I had spoken any Japanese.

I had always been interested in philosophy, and was much gratified to receive an invitation to attend lectures at the famous old Taishouni University: this was conveyed to me by three students on the Rector's behalf. I engaged in a serious study of Buddhism and Oriental philosophy; there were no other foreign students, and, although I could only follow the lectures in Japanese with difficulty, there were plenty of useful books in the huge international library to which foreigners in general had no access. My new hobby gained me considerable prestige in Japanese circles, especially after the *Japan Times* published an article of mine discussing a lecture on Buddhism that had been given by an Italian professor.

Thanks to Baron Nakano, 'Elisabeth Hansson' was invited to the highest social functions and once to an Imperial garden party; she also had the honour of being admitted to a reception given by the Emperor Hirohito for some long-distance aviators. The palace lies in the centre of a large park bounded by canals which are crossed by means of drawbridges. Japanese who walked past the palace grounds would pause and bow deeply three times in token of their respect for the Emperor. After the defeat of Japan in the Second World War, the newspapers reported that the bodies of officers who had committed harakiri were found lying near the park.

I met the Emperor's brother, Prince Chichibu, several times. He was a man of unusual character, with excellent manners, who spoke very good English and was often seen with foreigners. His democratic views were well known, and he was popular with the Tokyo intelligentsia. On one occasion there was a student demonstration in his favour near the palace, and it was rumoured that this had caused bad blood between him and his brother.

The Emperor's cousin, Kangfusu Umewaka, was a much respected Buddhist priest: I met him several times, and he once even paid me a visit. Our acquaintance began when I was invited to an ancient Buddhist ceremony which the Imperial Court arranged for the benefit of foreign diplomats on the premises of an exclusive club, and at which Umewaka was the chief celebrant. He helped me, among other things, to witness the Noh plays, which were performed at temples in conjunction with religious ceremonies and are in an archaic language unintelligible to the ordinary modern Japanese.

Of the many traditional rites, I was especially moved by the cherry blossom feast and the commemoration of the dead. Each months has its own particular flower and tree; April is the month of cherry blossom, and is celebrated with especial fervour. The thousand-year-old festivities culminate in the Miyako Odori or 'cherry dance' at Kyoto, to which people come from all over Japan. When I saw it in 1935 the scenes representing the four seasons were taken from the Noh drama, but the production was modern, with a revolving stage, and the effect was delightful. Summer and autumn gave place to winter with its dazzling snow and sparkling ice, and then came spring blossom on the shores of a crystalline lake. Magical lighting effects, glorious shades of colour, the silvery voices of a women's choir accompanied by modern music on a three-stringed *samisen*—all this produced a fairy-like atmosphere that held the audience spellbound. The orchestra and the choir were on platforms to either side of the stage: the singers on the right wore black kimonos, while those of the women on the left were resplendent with colour. Their hair was adorned with cherry blossom and glittering jewels, and with their motionless faces and whitened complexions they looked like beings from another world.

The dead are honoured in Japan perhaps more than in any other country, and the relationship between them and the living is one of great beauty and intimacy. They are commemorated annually for three days, from July 13 to 15, when it is believed that they revisit their former homes. White lanterns are lighted throughout the cemeteries so that the dead can find their way back to the house, where a special meal is prepared for them. They are brought into the conversation and told of any special family events.

Not long after my return to Japan I was reminded of Uritsky's warning: the anti-Comintern pact (November 1936) between Germany and Japan was a clear symptom of the increasing tension between these countries and the USSR, while the Chinese-Soviet non-aggression pact of August 1937 could only be directed against Japan.

For most of 1937 I was left to myself, but at the end of November I was rung up by the German-speaking woman who had conveyed the order for my return to Moscow two years earlier. She asked me to dine with her that evening at the Mitsubishi Restaurant, an invitation which I thought boded no good. When I got there she told me that, by Sorge's instructions, I was to go next evening at eight o'clock to the flower shop in the Roppongi market and meet his assistant as I had done two years before. During dinner we were joined by a presentable man whom she introduced as her husband. Sorge later told me he was a chemist by profession and was connected with the Soviet Embassy; he spoke German with an Austrian accent.

Next day I duly met the assistant, who took me to Sorge's flat. I was distressed to find Sorge lying on the sofa half-seas-over, with the remains of a bottle of whisky beside him on the table; he had evidently dispensed with a glass. He said that we had 'all of us', including himself, been ordered to Moscow, and that I was to go to Vladivostok for further directions. He did not know the reason for the order, but, although the atmosphere in Moscow was 'unhealthy', I myself had nothing to fear. For his part he would obey the order of recall if it was absolutely necessary, but I was to report to the Bureau that if he left Tokyo—which he could not do before April anyway—all his special connections there would be ruined. He then said something on which I ought to have reflected, and which I remembered many times afterwards: 'You are a very intelligent woman, the clearest-minded I have ever met; but I am cleverer than you.' It was only later—

and too late to be useful to me—that I understood what he meant: he was cleverer than I because he had sensed, before I did, the danger that awaited us both in Moscow. The reason he did not warn me more explicitly was not that he no longer wanted the task of maintaining liaison with me—this had never given him much trouble—but rather because he trusted no one and assumed, as he was bound to do, that if he spoke in plain terms I might use his words against him at some later date.

If he had obeyed the order of recall at that time he would certainly have been executed, and the Soviet Union would have lost what proved to be an invaluable source of intelligence during the Second World War. Sorge had spun a web of espionage that extended to the inmost circles of the Japanese government. Thanks to his reports the USSR was able to rely on Japan's temporary neutrality and to concentrate its forces in the west to meet the German attack in 1941. What is more, Sorge gave timely information of the date of that attack and of the Japanese onslaught at Pearl Harbor. But ingratitude is the way of the world: much of Sorge's information was not believed, and he ended on a Japanese gallows. He must have hoped that Stalin would save him from that miserable end by exchanging him for Japanese spies arrested in the Soviet Union, but if so his hopes were disappointed: he was left to his fate. Not until 1964 did the Soviet Government decide to honour his memory: he was posthumously created a Hero of the Soviet Union, a film was made in his honour, a street in Moscow was named after him and a commemorative stamp issued. But today I ask myself: which of us, after all, was really the cleverer one?

The order to return to Moscow placed me in a dilemma. I had no close connections there, but I had read in the press about the purges that were in full blast, and might well expect to be caught up in them if I returned. But if I refused, how could I escape the Soviet government's revenge? Where would I live? Should I tell the Japanese authorities who 'Elisabeth Hansson' really was? Apart from using a false name I had done nothing illegal; my whole behaviour had been pro-Japanese, and I thought I could reveal my identity to them without fear. But I rejected the idea at once, since if I did so I would be responsible for endangering Sorge and other agents who knew my secret.

Should I take refuge in the United States? My passport was ostensibly in order, and I had enough money; but what would happen if I entered America twice with a forged passport? I would have to declare myself an anti-Communist, and put people at risk who had befriended me on my previous visit.

There was no way out—I was between the devil and the deep sea. If only I could have asked somebody's advice. But I had to make up my own mind, and finally I decided to obey the order, trusting to my clear conscience and clinging to the hope that I could not be accused of any crime.

The parting from my Japanese friends was a very sad one, for this time I could not promise to return soon. As before, many came to the station to see me off. For the last time I thanked them for all their kindness; I was especially sorry to take leave of Baron Nakano, who had helped and advised me from my very first day in Japan and had carried out the role of 'observer' so tactfully. Finally the train for Shimonoseki moved out of Tokyo station; I felt that at that moment Elisabeth Hansson had left this world, and had taken part of Aino Kuusinen's heart with her.

At Vladivostok I was met on the quay by an officer of the Fourth Bureau, who had reserved a hotel room and handed me my ticket for the Trans-Siberian express; he told me that I was to stay at the Metropole in Moscow. So in the second week of December 1937 I found myself once more in those familiar surroundings with Sirotkin, who came round directly after my arrival. His news was ominous and depressing. Uritsky had been arrested and probably shot. Many officers of the Bureau had vanished, and Sirotkin was surprised that he himself was still at liberty. His fears proved to be well justified; he was a decent man, and I ran across him more than once when we were subsequently sharing the same fate.

I was given one further assignment. Just before Christmas, a woman employed by the Bureau came to the hotel and asked me to help her meet a couple who were due to arrive next morning by the Trans-Siberian, as I knew them and she did not. She did not mention any name, but when the train drew in I heard a voice exclaim with pleased surprise: 'Fru Hansson, how nice to see you!' It was the blonde woman who had acted as Sorge's messenger, and who was now returning to Moscow with her husband in obedience to orders. They were taken to a waiting car and disappeared. I too was soon to disappear—for nine years...

V

In Moscow Prisons

There was no way of escape, and all I could do was wait. After a few telephone calls and visits to old friends I realized that those who had not already vanished without trace were in a state of paralysis, awaiting events. So the Japanese newspapers had told the truth after all, and I had been credulous enough to imagine that their stories were exaggerated bourgeois propaganda. My only hope lay in my clear conscience, and I clung as best I could to that doubtful security.

One day I went to see an old Finnish friend named Alexandra, married to the Bulgarian Danko Sapunov; they lived in Kuznetsky Most near the Metropole. I had known Danko for many years since he and Kolarov were put in charge of Bulgarian affairs at the Comintern, one of his tasks being to help Communists who had left Bulgaria to find homes in the Soviet Union.

The Sapunovs asked me to spend New Year's Eve with them, and I was happy to accept as I felt lonely and depressed, especially when I thought of pleasant times in Japan. I had noticed that food was again short in Moscow, and I offered to take something along, knowing that Alexandra was an excellent cook if she could get the right ingredients. She assured me that she could manage, but I felt I ought to contribute something, and I remembered that there used to be a black market on the Arbat. I went there and soon caught sight of a peasant woman with a basket over her arm, its contents concealed under a cloth. I asked innocently if she knew where there was any meat to be had. She looked cautiously around to make sure we were not being watched, and then began talking, obviously to make sure I was trustworthy. Finally she lifted up a corner of the cloth, and there lay a beautiful frozen goose—our New Year's dinner! I haggled a bit, bought the goose and took it straight to Alexandra, who reproved me jokingly for paying too much: 'You've been abroad too long!'

New Year's Eve came round; depressed though I was, I put on my favourite dress as a good omen for 1938. Alexandra and Danko gave me a friendly welcome, and when I had admired the festive table they introduced me to the other guest, a young ballet dancer whom they knew well. She appeared shy and melancholy, but brightened up a little when it turned out that we had a mutual friend in Willi Mielenz, the German with whom I had worked at the Comintern.

In spite of the seasonal decorations, we found it impossible to be cheerful. We tried to talk of harmless and trivial subjects, but each of us knew that the others were pretending: recent events weighed too heavily on all our spirits. On this, the last evening of a year of terror, our minds kept returning to our friends and dear ones who had been arrested or had vanished. We talked with difficulty and in subdued tones, and felt impelled to mention recent arrests and fearful tragedies. An indescribable terror held us in its grip. We hardly touched the delicious goose, and tears began slowly to flow down Danko's cheeks. Suddenly the little dancer burst into wild, desperate sobs, while Alexandra and Danko stared dumbly at their plates. After a time she recovered herself, and I learnt that Mielenz, of whom she was obviously very fond, was one of those recently arrested.

Danko turned on the wireless, and just before midnight he stood up, forced himself to smile and said: 'Dear friends, let us end this year of horror in the faith and hope that the next will be a happier one, and that the dreadful events of 1937 will be lost in oblivion.' We sat in silence as he opened a bottle of champagne and filled our glasses. As the Kremlin clock struck twelve we drank to a more happy and successful year. Soon after, feeling sleepy and exhausted, I took my leave and Danko walked back with me to the Metropole.

I sat for a while in my room, trying to cheer myself with

memories of past New Year's Eves in Japan and America; then I undressed and went to bed, but could not sleep for thinking of the horrible stories I had heard that evening. I was still wide awake at five, when a knock came at the door. 'Who is it?' 'It's the chambermaid,' said a female voice, 'I have an urgent telegram for you.' I opened the door slightly; at once two men in uniform pushed into the room and locked the door. One of them said fiercely: 'Show us where your guns are hidden.' I replied that I had never had a gun in my life, whereupon one of them started to rummage in my handbag while the other told me to dress at once. They refused to leave me alone, and sat there silently while I dressed. So this was the Ogpu, and this was what an arrest was like! A few minutes later we walked downstairs, got into a rickety old Ford and drove off. It had all happened so fast that I had no time to collect myself, and it was only when the engine started that I realized with horror that the blow had fallen and that I was in the hands of Stalin's myrmidons.

After a short while the car stopped; the men jumped out and told me to accompany them. I was shoved through a door into a small unlit room, and when my eyes got used to the darkness I discovered that it was full of women squatting on the floor or sitting back to back. I had to stand against the wall, as there was no more room. Nobody said a word; we seemed almost too terrified to breathe. I had often tried to imagine what a prison cell was like, but this was worse than I had dreamed—there was no room to sit, let alone lie down or sleep. As the dawn gradually broke I found that we were in the Butyrka prison, a place of terror from Tsarist times onwards.

Having always been an incorrigible optimist, I told myself that there must have been a mistake—I had done no wrong and committed no crime, and I would certainly soon be released. I tried in vain to engage my fellow-victims in conversation; the only sound to be heard was that of sobbing. Many of them must have had small children, who were now helpless and unprotected as their fathers had already been executed or imprisoned. To distract myself I thought of the excellent dinner to which I had been unable to do justice the night before; I was hungry and thirsty now, as we were given nothing to eat or drink. Such was New Year's Day of 1938!

Evening came; we still had to squat on the floor or else lie on top of one another. Most of the women kept on weeping and bemoaning their fate, but I felt numb and paralysed.

One of my companions proved to be General Uritsky's seventeen-year-old daughter, who said her father had been arrested at the beginning of November but that she knew nothing of him; her mother, she had heard, was in the next cell to ours. Both women, I believe, were condemned to long terms of hard labour, but escaped being executed.

Late in the evening of 2 January, I was taken from the cell and driven in a police car for a long distance through the streets of Moscow. We stopped in front of a large building, and I began to hope that I would be set free with apologies; but this hope disappeared as the warder led me, without a word, through long, silent corridors, opened a door and ordered me into a large room. It was clean and well-lit and contained eight beds, seven of which were occupied. 'Can it be a hospital?' I wondered; but I was not ill, only dead-tired. I asked one of the women what the building was, and she replied: 'The Lubyanka prison, of course.' They all stared at me, until a cheerful voice called my name and one of the women actually began to laugh. 'Irma ... is it you?' I cried in amazement. Yes, it was Irma from Berlin, the charming and helpful young secretary whom I had known years before at the Comintern. I don't know what finally became of her, but I fear she was executed like so many of the Comintern staff.

A stern-faced wardress now opened the door and took me to the bathroom, where I had a welcome bath and was issued with prison clothing. (Later, at Lefortovo, I had to wear men's clothes, which were far too big; it was a men's prison, and during my two stays there I heard of only eight female prisoners in all.) I was allotted a bed and given some food, and so began my life as an inmate of the notorious Butyrka prison.

By degrees we told one another our past history, and I soon found that although I had not previously met all my cell-mates, I had heard of each one at some time or another. In the bed next to me was the wife of Yakovlev, formerly People's Commissar for heavy industry for the whole Soviet Union. She had been a senior factory engineer and was now accused of deliberately infringing regulations for purposes of sabotage. Her husband had been shot, and she was under sentence of death. So was Maya Kuibysheva, an active, intelligent woman who spoke several languages and had been known in her youth as a figure skater. Her husband, General Nikolay Kuibyshev, had already been executed; he was the brother of Valerian Kuibyshev, the celebrated Bolshevik leader, who died in 1935.

Another of our companions was the wife of Tupolev, the aircraft designer; he himself was in the Lubyanka on a charge of selling to the Germans fighter designs which had allegedly been used for the Messerschmitt 109. His wife had worked with him as a draughtswoman and was accused of failing to inform the NKVD of his 'treasonable' activity. Shortly after my arrival, she was condemned to death and disappeared. Tupolev, however, remained alive; he was allowed to go on working while under arrest, was released in due course and promoted lieutenant-general for his services to aircraft construction. When I left Moscow in 1965 he was still living there and could be seen walking proudly around, in a well-cut uniform, his chest bedecked with orders.

The saddest of our group was Chaikovskaya, whose husband, like Tupolev, was an aircraft designer and was also allowed to work in the Lubyanka, where he had been for some time. His wife was completely broken up and wept continuously. After her husband's arrest she had looked after their two small children until she too was taken away, and her last memory was of them standing helplessly on the landing while the NKVD put seals on the apartment door. We were all deeply moved by her grief and did our best to console her with assurances that the children would be brought up in a State orphanage.

All of us were frequently called for interrogation, which was always by night. On one of these occasions Chaikovskaya, to our delight, returned to the cell dry-eyed and with a calm expression, and told us that she had been promised a fifteen minutes' interview with her husband next day. In the morning she was duly summoned, and we shared her joy at the prospect of seeing her husband and knowing that he was still alive. We waited eagerly for her return from the interview, but she did not come back until afternoon, when she stumbled in and threw herself on the bed, sobbing. To our surprise her hair was carefully done, her lips made up and her nails manicured; but she lay bitterly weeping, and none of us dared say anything. At last, when she was able to speak, she told us what had happened. She had been taken into the interrogation room and told to write down the description of a dress, hat and shoes to be brought from her flat; then she was taken to a hairdresser and a manicurist and made to look like her former self. Back in the interrogation room, they made her promise not to tell her husband that she too was under arrest: she was to say that everything was fine at home, the children in good spirits and so on. If she disobeyed, the consequences would be disastrous for both of them.

Chaikovsky was then brought in, and she was appalled to see how ill and miserable he looked. They were made to sit opposite each other, with a warder close by observing every word and gesture. The conversation went as follows:

'How are you all at home?'

'Fine. How are you?'

'Are the children well?'

'Yes, quite well and happy.'

'How do you get money to live on?'

'We manage. They give us some.' This of course was a lie too.

Chaikovsky then said that he had a nice bright room in the Lubyanka where he could work at his drawings and had all the instruments and technical literature he needed; however, he had been too worried about his family to work properly. 'But now I have seen you and know everything's all right at home, and that they even give you money, my mind is at rest and I can get on with my work—I can bear anything now.'

A few days later, his wife was taken from the cell and shot. I later heard that the same had happened to him: apparently he was less successful than Tupolev at proving his value to the Soviet State.

When I was arrested I was not told what crime I was supposed to have committed, merely that I was one of those who were going to be shot. My first interrogator in the Lubyanka—a man named Zaitsev, who spoke Finnish well—began by explaining to me the theory of Soviet jurisprudence. He asked me if I knew the difference between bourgeois and Soviet justice, and when I replied 'No' he wagged his finger and said: 'In bourgeois justice the prosecutor has to prove that the accused is guilty, but under our system the accused has to prove that he is innocent.' The Soviet principle is illustrated by the joke about a rabbit which escaped from the Soviet Union into Poland, explaining that it did so because all camels in the USSR were to be shot. 'But you aren't a camel!'—'No, but how can I prove it?'

At the first few interrogations Zaitsev was all smoothness and flattery; then, as this failed, he laid several traps for me, and finally thrust an astounding document across the table—an elaborate indictment of many pages, not against me but against Otto Kuusinen, my husband and Stalin's friend. Zaitsev ordered me to sign it, as I was the person who knew most about Otto's criminal anti-Soviet intrigues. I told him without hesitation that there was not a word of truth in the charge and that I would not sign. He then switched to a persuasive tone once more, but, finding it useless, began to utter fearful threats, including that of torture. He shouted at me that they knew for certain that Kuusinen was a British spy, to which I retorted: 'If you are so sure of it, why do you need my signature?'

In this and later interrogations, Zaitsev and others kept mentioning the name of Hella Wuolijoki, and asking me about the friendship between her and Otto. I replied that it dated from the time when Otto was on the staff of *Työmies*, the social-democratic newspaper in Helsinki, for which Hella wrote articles, and that there had never been anything more between them.[30]

I asked several times why, instead of bothering me, they did not get the signatures of those who were so positive that Kuusinen was a British agent; but they replied that it was the wish of the Party leaders that I should be the one to authenticate the charges. I persisted in my refusal, and Zaitsev finally threatened me with imprisonment at Lefortovo. He gave me a frightful and detailed description of the three-hundred-year-old fortress, where the assassins of Alexander II had been confined in 1881; it was in general not a prison for women, but for the most dangerous enemies of the people. He made a last effort to change my mind: 'If you sign, you can go straight home. If you don't, it's Lefortovo, and you'll never get out alive.'

But I stood my ground, and one night in midsummer 1938 I

was taken off in the Black Maria. The bench was so narrow I could hardly sit on it, the walls seemed to close in on me and my head kept hitting the ceiling. I had no idea where we were going: it was pitch dark, and the darkness in my heart was even greater. At last the ride was over, and we were in Lefortovo. Two warders took me up a broad stairway to the fifth floor; I was locked into a solitary cell, and told to undress and go to bed.

Even today, after thirty years, I can hardly describe the horror of that first night at Lefortovo. In my cell I could hear every noise from outside. Near by, as I later discovered, was the 'interrogation department', a separate structure which was in fact a torture-chamber. All night long I heard inhuman screams and the repeated sound of the lash. A desperate and tormented animal could hardly have uttered such dreadful cries as the victims who were assaulted for hours on end with threats, blows and curses. So these were the terrors Zaitsev had spoken of! No doubt I would be tortured in the same way; even listening to it made me fear that I would lose my reason, until I said to myself: 'Keep calm, you can't do anything about it. Pull yourself together and wait till it's your turn.' So I stifled my feelings of pity for the wretched victims and forced myself to think of other things. But I still shudder when I remember that night at Lefortovo, and I shall never be able to forget it.

The torture-chamber was only a few yards away from my cell; its windows were open, and the horrors were repeated every night from nine to six. By day all was peaceful—that was when the torturers got their rest.

Eventually, also at night, I was called up for interrogation. Zaitsev sat at his desk awaiting me, with a mocking half-smile on his face. He started to tell me where I was, but I broke in: 'You surely don't think I haven't found that out by now.' He replied: 'Yes, but I don't suppose you thought we'd dare to bring you here.' To which I retorted: 'Why not? There's nothing you people wouldn't dare to do.' He then presented the document again and pressed me to sign as before, saying: 'You know where you are, and that you won't get out till you confirm the indictment against your husband. So sign now and be done with it.' 'Never!' I shouted back.

This went on month after month. One night they began thrashing a man in the next room: the partition was a thin one, and I could hear all the frightful sounds and curses. Tables and chairs were hurled at the prisoner, who protested his innocence amid cries of pain. After about two hours of this torture I heard him call out my name: 'Aino! Aino!' 'Do you know who that is?' asked Zaitsev maliciously. 'No, I don't, and I don't want to.' But Zaitsev went on: 'It's Otto Kuusinen, your husband. He wants you to sign, because he really was a British spy.' I heard the voice next door cry out again: 'Aino, Aino! Sign, sign!' I was not certain whether it was Otto's voice or not, and I said nothing. The torture went on till dawn, and suddenly all was quiet. Zaitsev got up and said: 'Let's see what has happened'; then, in a minute or two, he came back and told me that Otto had calmed down and was writing out his confession.

When I was being taken back to my cell that morning, I was led past the open door of another room in which lay a dead man, his body covered with blood. I was made to stand and look at it for about a minute, after which the warder said: 'That's what happens to the ones who don't confess.' I made no answer. On the stairway I was made to stop again and look at the mangled corpse of a man who had been thrashed to death.

Such were the methods used to intimidate prisoners and make them confess, and it was not unusual for the victims of these bestialities to lose their reason and be packed off to an asylum. I kept telling myself that I must not allow this to happen to me; and I vowed that if I escaped alive from that inferno I would proclaim to the world what tortures the Stalin regime inflicted on defenceless people. The prisoners, many of whom were Party members, had committed no crime and had nothing on their consciences, except possibly that one or another of them might have repeated an anti-Soviet joke to a circle of friends.

I remained in solitary confinement for a long time, and the document incriminating Kuusinen was thrust at me night after night. My inquisitors tried the most varied methods, and at times I felt I could hold out no longer, but I knew my only hope was to stand firm on my refusal.

One Saturday evening, late in the autumn, I was taken to the interrogation room and found Zaitsev with another man who, he said, was his superior officer. This man looked so sinister that his appearance alone might have caused an inexperienced prisoner to die of fright. He made me sit down and started on a flattering note, which I knew to be a bad sign. I was an intelligent woman, he said, and I must realize that it was to my advantage to sign the indictment without demur. He put a pen into my hand, but I replied calmly and firmly: 'As I have said before, I will never sign.' He then flew into a rage and ordered me to stand in the middle of the room, keeping my feet still. He was shouting so loudly that his voice reverberated from the walls. I prefer not to describe the rest of the interrogation in detail, but it was not until noon on Wednesday that I was released, having been overwhelmed with threats and insults and, I need hardly add, given nothing to eat and not even a drop of water to drink. None the less, I did not give in, though I was so exhausted at the end that I could hardly stand. The head inquisitor roared at me: 'I have never in my life known such an impudent, obstinate woman. I have had to do with thousands of prisoners, and not one of them refused to sign.' 'So I'm the first,' I replied indifferently. Pointing his revolver at me, he screamed in a rage: 'You will never leave this building alive!' I screamed back with equal fury, as loudly as I could manage after my ordeal, 'Alive or dead, I won't sign anyway!' He looked dumbfounded and said to Zaitsev: 'This isn't a woman, it's a she-devil!' Then he called the warders to take me back to my cell. The last thing I heard him say was: 'Don't let me ever see her again.' When the warders threw me on my bed I asked them what day and hour it was, and worked out that the interrogation had lasted eighty-nine hours.

I was still kept in Lefortovo, but the period of isolation seemed to be at an end. I was put in a cell with Maria Yakovleva Frumkina and Tamara Postysheva. Maria, whom I had known for many years, was an energetic, educated woman and had been head of the Moscow university for Oriental workers. Her father had been chief rabbi at Minsk; he was much upset that his firstborn was a girl, and, as she related graphically, she was brought up in the manner prescribed for the eldest son of a Jewish family. She was dressed as a boy, and her father took her to synagogue every morning and taught her the Hebrew prayers, which girls do not ordinarily learn. She went to school in Minsk, grew up to be a robust, boyish creature and wanted to go to St Petersburg University, but, being a Jewess, was refused permission to live in the capital. She found out, however, that Jewish girls were allowed to live there if they registered as prostitutes, so she did so and received a 'yellow permit' with which she had to report to the police once a week. She was allowed to attend the university; her father sent her money, and she rented a room to live in. Afterwards she returned to Minsk and became a teacher. She wrote novels under the pseudonym 'Esther', which are still popular with the Jews in the USSR. In Minsk she belonged to the committee of a Zionist organization and took an active part in its work. During our imprisonment she explained to me the differences between Zionists and other Jewish bodies, and told me many interesting things about religious questions and schools of thought among Jews in the Diaspora.

The charge against her was one of conspiring to found anti-Soviet Jewish organizations. She had a very bad time in Lefortovo and suffered much physical injury. Two of her Jewish friends—Rafes, who was for years on the staff of the Comintern periodical *The Communist International*, and Karl Radek—were imprisoned for the purpose of testifying against her, and she was convinced they had done so. She was constantly told she would never leave Lefortovo alive, and she was in fact executed while I was still there. Her sister-in-law Rosa Frumkina was also arrested; I heard at Vorkuta that she had been in the camp there, but her subsequent fate was unknown.

Maria was diabetic and therefore suffered more than most of us from prison conditions; she was often so weary that she could hardly keep her eyes open, but it was against prison rules to lie down in the daytime or even sleep in a sitting position. She often lamented her fate, and had a foreboding that she would be executed; but, she once said to me: '*You* won't be shot, you'll be sent to Stockholm to replace Kollontay.' I asked what gave her such an odd idea, and she said Radek had told her: he had it from Stalin himself, when he was working in Stalin's secretariat. I asked no more questions, but I remembered what my husband had told me about there being such a plan; I had not entirely believed him, but perhaps there was something in it after all. Naturally I did not delude myself that there was any hope now of such a pleasant outcome.

My cell-mates told me that the authorities had recently discovered a conspiracy of members of the Communist Youth League (Komsomol) whose fathers had been imprisoned or shot; the chief centres were Moscow and Orel, and the plotters were mostly Jews. One of the suspected organizers was Tamara Radek, the daughter of Karl Radek by his wife Olga, who was Trotsky's sister; another was Rosa Frumkina's daughter, also called Tamara.

Tamara Postysheva, my other cell-mate, was one of the most remarkable women I have ever met. She was a Ukrainian, very well educated and of extraordinary will-power. Before her arrest she had been a legal officer of the NKVD at Kiev, a post she had accepted in order to help Ukrainian victims of Stalin's purges. She was accused with some reason of being a Ukrainian nationalist: she loved her country and its people, their literature and especially music, and told me much about Ukrainian history and the persecution of her compatriots through the centuries.

Tamara was treated in a more devilish manner at Lefortovo than I had ever thought possible in the case of a woman prisoner. She was interrogated almost every night, and beaten so badly that she had to be carried back to her cell. On the first night after I arrived in the cell, the warders brought her back at dawn and threw her on her bed; when they had gone I asked her if I could do anything, and she was just able to say: 'Please have a look at my back.' It was covered with bleeding wounds. I dipped a towel in cold water and spread it over her back; this seemed to help a little, and I continued the process through the next few hours. On the following night, and on many others, I remained awake in order to apply damp compresses to her bleeding, burning wounds.

During the day she spoke not only of the frightful interrogations but of her fears for her husband, who was also in Lefortovo, having been dismissed from an important Party post at Khabarovsk. He had been a confidant of Lenin's and had held several important offices; he was popular with the ordinary people, not least because of an article which had led to the reintroduction of Christmas trees. But, said Tamara, he had no powers of physical resistance and under torture would confess anything he was told to.

Once, unexpectedly, Tamara was called up in daytime and came back a few hours later; this time she was able to walk. She sat down on her bed and was silent for a while; then she said stonily: 'It has happened as I feared. They showed me a confession signed by my husband. He simply couldn't endure what they did to him.' I asked if it might not be a forgery, but she insisted that Postyshev had made and signed the confession himself. It said that he had disagreed with Stalin on three points: rural collectivization, the school system and the stabilization of the rouble on a gold basis. Not long afterwards Postyshev was put to death, and so was his brave wife Tamara, who had confessed nothing.

I could give many more details of brutal methods and the slaughter of innocent people. Once at the Lubyanka the man who was questioning me pointed to the smooth panelled wall and said: 'Do you know what that is?'

'A wall,' I answered.

'Yes, but not an ordinary one.' And he showed me proudly that what appeared to be a wall was in fact a cupboard filled with files, reaching from floor to ceiling. He pulled out one of the drawers, set it before me and made me look at the contents. Each card bore the photograph and personal details of an officer. 'Do you know any of these?'

'No, and I don't want to.' He then told me that the officers, whose numbers ran into thousands, had all been executed. He watched me as he spoke, to see if I would burst out crying or faint as many women might have done; but I had made it a rule, on the way to every interrogation, to take a special grip on myself so that my tormentors should not have the satisfaction of destroying my composure, whatever cruel things they might say. As he went on waiting to see the effect of his card-index, I forced myself with a great effort to ask in a calm voice: 'If you execute so many people, how do you manage to bury them without its being noticed?'

'Who says they are buried?' he replied scornfully. 'There's a crematorium in the cellar, and they are burnt there. That's what will happen to all of you.'

One of the few 'rights' enjoyed by prisoners was that of out-door exercise once a day, although the privilege might be with-drawn for a long time from those in solitary confinement, as happened to myself more than once. In the Lubyanka, which is in the centre of Moscow, everyone had to be in bed and quiet at eleven p.m., but the night was the time for exercise as well as for interrogation. Unlike many others, I used the privilege, as I knew how important it was to health. We were taken by a lift up to the roof, which was fenced with barbed wire lest anyone should be tempted to put an end to his tragic existence by jump-ing off. The prisoners were formed into a ring, and we walked round and round for twenty minutes under the gloomy sky. A tall iron chimney rose up in the middle of the roof, emitting continuously a thin smoke and covering the ground under our feet with fine dust. I well knew what the smoke was, but I tried not to think of it and to convince myself that it was not my fate to be burnt to ashes there. But many women wept during the exercise period, and one of my cell-mates always refused to take part in it. I kept telling her how important it was to our health, even though it was unpleasant to be woken up when we had just gone to sleep; but nothing I could say would make her go up on to the roof. Finally she asked me if I knew what the chimney was. 'That smoke is from the crematorium in the cellar, where they burn people after shooting them. My husband was an officer and disappeared in this prison, and that is why I won't go up there and trample on his ashes.' I was deeply moved, and ceased trying to make her change her mind.

In Lefortovo the prisoners exercised in a courtyard, and my zeal for fresh air once almost cost me my life. My cell-mate, a pleasant and cultivated woman, used always to come with me; on the evening in question the yard was covered in snow, and as usual we walked some distance apart, with a warder ensuring that we did not talk to each other. Suddenly I felt a heavy blow on the head and lost consciousness. When I awoke, I was in bed in my cell and a doctor was holding an ice-pack to my head; when he saw me come to, he left the cell without a word.

'What happened?' I asked my cell-mate.

'I don't know. You fainted, and the warders brought you in.'

I could not understand why I had a large bump on my head

and a violent headache. The doctor came back several times during the next few days, to ask how I felt and apply a new ice-pack.

About a week later the situation took an almost comic turn. The door opened and a stout colonel walked in, flanked by two officers: it was the commandant of Lefortovo in person. My companion looked on in terror as he addressed me in a friendly tone, saying I need not get up. The conversation went as follows:

'What happened to you in the exercise yard?'

'I don't know.'

'Have you any idea what it might have been?'

'None at all. I only know that I woke up here with a bad headache, and the doctor came.'

'What did he say?'

'Nothing. He put ice-packs on my head; I have a big bump, and it hurts badly.'

'Did anyone hit you?'

'I don't know. I felt a blow on my head, and fainted at once.'

'Who was with you?'

'My neighbour here was behind me, and the warder was somewhere near.'

'Do you think your neighbour hit you?'

'Certainly not—we are friends.'

'What about the warder?'

'I don't think so. He wasn't especially close.'

'Then what do you think?'

'I really have no idea.'

Thereupon the colonel showed me two pieces of brick that he had been holding behind his back, and said: 'The matter has been thoroughly investigated, and we think this is what happened. The pigeons that nest under the roof of this old building have pecked away the mortar between the bricks over the eaves; the bricks have got loose, and this one fell and hit you so hard that it broke in two. Do you agree with this explanation?'

I replied: 'I suppose I must,' and at his request I signed a report in which my accident was blamed on the pigeons.

I have related this trivial occurrence in some detail because of the ironical light it throws on the system. Night after night in that building innocent people were being tortured and murdered, but the mishap caused by the pigeons and the bricks was investigated with the utmost care so that no one could be accused of doing me an unauthorized injury.

Here is another instance of tragicomedy connected with the arrests. When I was in the Lubyanka in 1938 a young woman was brought to my cell whom I will call Olga Petrovna. As with all newcomers, we were eager to hear her story. She had been employed in Stalin's household; it was apparently his habit to drink tea all day long, and her sole duty had been to prepare and serve it. She had been chosen for the task as a Party member in whom full reliance could be placed. The process was governed by the strictest rules: the sealed packets of tea were locked up in a special cupboard to which Olga held the key. She had to open it in the presence of a supervisor, whose duty was to scrutinize the packet and make sure that the stamp and seal were intact. The packet was then opened and the right quantity of tea taken out. The rest was thrown away by the supervisor—on no account was tea to be taken twice from the same packet.

One day Olga opened the cupboard under supervision as usual, and saw with horror that the seal of a packet had been broken. There was a fearful to-do: the packet was at once examined for poison in the Kremlin laboratory, and although no poison was found, Olga was packed off to the Lubyanka. She told us likewise of an electrician who had been responsible for the wiring of Stalin's apartment and had been arrested because of a short-circuit. In this case too Olga's vigilance had prevented any further harm, but she did not escape being arrested and charged with attempted poisoning and arson. I don't know what happened to her, but I do know that while in prison she never ceased to sing Stalin's praises!

Perhaps this is the right point at which to say something about Kuusinen's alleged espionage. I often wondered what the basis for the charge might be, and came to the conclusion that it lay in his friendship with Hella Wuolijoki, who came to Moscow on business from time to time and used always to look him up. She was a good linguist and gave parties in Helsinki in the twenties which were attended by many foreigners, including diplomats. Her salon did not have an especially good reputation, in fact it was nicknamed the 'spy centre', no doubt largely because of the Soviet diplomats who frequented it.

I had heard in Helsinki that Hella was connected with the British secret service, and I remembered her saying in Moscow that she saw a lot of Trilisser,[31] the head of Soviet espionage in Scandinavia, and that they had once met by appointment in Berlin. I also remembered that she had called on Otto and myself in the company of a British officer who spoke Russian and had rung up Trilisser from our flat to arrange a meeting. So I now began to conjecture that the charge against Otto was due to his friendship with Hella and Trilisser, that his enemies had got to know of their contacts and that I was now paying the penalty. However, at every interrogation I suppressed this thought in order to let no word of it escape. Nor did I mention Otto's friendship with Hella's sister, Salme Pekkala. As I related in a previous chapter, I made the acquaintance of both sisters in Helsinki in 1920, and Salme was sent at that time on a secret errand to London. Three years later, Otto told me that Salme had paid him a brief visit and had made important contacts in England: he said she was doing a good job. She afterwards divorced Pekkala and married the British Communist R. Palme Dutt, whom I met when working for the Comintern.

Some time in the late twenties I returned from work to find Otto in his study with a lady who spoke English; Allan Wallenius, the Comintern librarian, was acting as interpreter. After she had gone, Otto told me it was Mary Peters, a friend of Salme's; the latter was trying to arrange for her to marry Eino Pekkala, which she afterwards did. Otto evaded my questions about her and I do not know why she came to visit him.

The overheated imagination of the NKVD had apparently blown up these meetings with Hella, Salme and Mary Peters into a tale of espionage for Britain, which of course was nonsense: I have not the slightest doubt that everything Otto did was intended to serve the interests of the Comintern and the Soviet government.

In 1950, when I was under interrogation at the Lubyanka for the second time, I was confronted with an unknown general who said with a baleful look: 'You managed to save your husband in 1938, but no one can help him now: we know for certain that he is a British spy, and we know who recruited him—Sophia Stern.

Do you know her?' I replied that I had never heard of her, but gradually the name came back to me. One day in 1920 I was strolling along one of the main streets of Helsinki and met Hella Wuolijoki with an attractive brunette, evidently a foreigner. Later on in Moscow I mentioned the encounter to Otto, who said he had met the lady in Hella's home, where he had been in hiding for some days: her name was Sophia Stern, and she was a secret agent whom Denikin had sent to Helsinki. I have not the faintest idea how the GPU got to know that he had met her, but it is extraordinary that this trifling circumstance could be dug out of the archives in 1950, thirty years later.

It was only rarely and by accident that prisoners were able to hear any news of one another. In 1938 there were two Americans in Lefortovo, Joe and Stepan (the latter perhaps of Ukranian origin), who managed, every morning, to whisper information to me through a small opening near the ceiling of my cell. I never saw these two young men, but I thought of them as friends, and when they ceased coming I very much missed the scraps of news they were able to give me.

Conditions in Lefortovo were bad enough in any case, but the worst thing was to be kept in a tiny cell in solitary confinement. Through the opening in the ceiling one could occasionally hear a normal human voice, but for the most part only the screams of people being tortured to death. Many of those in solitary tried to commit suicide, but this was not so easy, as the walls were perfectly smooth and the prisoners were watched day and night through a spyhole in the door. Many went mad, and an interrogator once said to me: 'It's a wonder you haven't gone off your head like so many others.' But I summoned up all my strength to prevent myself dying or going mad. I wanted to live, and was sustained by hope that the day would come when I could leave the Soviet Union and describe all the oppression and persecution practised by the society which was building the 'Communist paradise'. In order to do so, I must at all costs preserve my physical and mental health. I knew from my medical studies what a shattering effect long isolation can have on the nervous system. According to one story I had read, a man was marooned by a jealous rival on a South Sea island, where he lived for years in complete solitude, and when he returned to human society he had lost the power of speech. I was determined to avoid such a fate, and I worked out a programme to help preserve my nervous energy and keep myself in 'conversational' practice. I contrived to keep account of dates and times of day, and I divided each day into periods during which I concentrated on specific themes. I would mentally review films I had seen and novels or descriptions of travels that I had read, and would recite the contents of these to myself in a low voice. I held imaginary talks with friends and repeated passages of verse—often the Finnish classics I had learnt at school, such as the Finnish epic *Kalevala* or *Tales of Ensign Stål* by Runeberg, a collection of poems describing the courage of the little Finnish army which fought the Russians in 1808-9. At other times I would sing songs, and on particular days I would talk to myself in one or another foreign language—but all this had to be done cautiously, so that the warders in the corridor could not hear me.

Another exercise I performed was to strengthen my memory by recalling events that had happened to people I knew. Even today, after all these years, I feel that names and dates have been fixed indelibly in a certain corner of my brain. A psychologist whom I met in later years expressed the opinion that it was these mental gymnastics that had saved me from madness.

The interrogations went on interminably; the main theme was still Kuusinen's alleged espionage, but my questioners also began to ask about my Finnish friends in the USSR, who they said were all in prison. Mauno Heimo, I was told triumphantly, was a spy in the French service (I knew he had been in Paris, where he had been skilful in sorting out difficulties for the Comintern), while Niilo Virtanen was in the pay of Germany and Norway as well as Finland. They once tried to persuade me that Virtanen had signed a document accusing me of being a foreign spy; I answered that this was a lie, since I knew Niilo to be too honest a man to say such a thing even under torture, and I added that he was a true Communist in the idealistic sense. This made the official furious and he shouted: 'You spies are all alike, each one covering up for the other!' He added that what I had said would not help Virtanen, as he had been shot the night before. I replied: 'Then you have certainly shot one good Communist.' Niilo had indeed been right in 1935 when he warned me not to stay in the USSR, and spoke of the coming danger and his hope of escaping it by getting to China.

I was of course grilled on the subject of my trips to America and Japan. I told the interrogators that the Comintern had sent me to the States to look into the conflicts between local organizations; in Japan I had obeyed the instructions I was given on departure and confined myself to studying Japanese and observing conditions in general. Questioned about Berzin and Uritsky, I said truthfully that I had met them only twice and could say nothing about their activities.

I was interrogated about Sorge, and told that 'high quarters' were disappointed in him: his reports were unsatisfactory and he spent too much. The authorities wanted me to write asking him to return to the USSR. I thought this very odd, and asked why it should be me. The officer replied that Sorge had been ordered back several times and that Stalin himself had told him to come. There was not much to laugh at at these sessions, but I could not help showing amusement as I replied: 'You surely don't think Sorge will listen to me when he has disobeyed Stalin's personal order.' The officer countered this by saying that Sorge was sure to do what I said as we were 'such close friends'. I retorted that this was pure invention: I certainly knew Sorge, but we were not on intimate terms.

I must have been regarded as a first-class 'enemy of the people', for in the fifteen months of my first imprisonment I was questioned by no fewer than twenty-four different officers. Zaitsev once asked me if I knew why the interrogators, one after another, asked to be taken off my case and given an 'easier prisoner' to deal with. He answered his own question by saying plaintively: 'We assign your case to the toughest and most experienced men, but it's too much for them: your answers are so wily that they don't know what to say or do next.'

Surprisingly, I was never actually beaten, but besides attempting to break down my resistance in the ways I have already described, my tormentors resorted to another which was especially dangerous and malicious: I was made to sit, lightly clad, at interrogations in an icy room while the official opposite me wore a fur coat. It required cast-iron strength to endure this hardship without collapsing. My blood-pressure rose seriously at times, and at Lefortovo I was once taken to the clinic to be treated with leeches, after which I was transferred to Butyrka for a while.

VI

My Eight Years of Forced Labour at Vorkuta

In April 1939, fifteen months after my arrest, I was taken one evening from my cell in the Lubyanka to a tiny room in which about ten women were standing huddled together like sheep and clasping one another. An official behind a small desk, pencil in hand, called our names one by one and ordered: 'Sign here.' When it came to my turn he held out a piece of paper no bigger than my hand: it appeared to be blank, but on turning it over I saw the words scribbled in pencil: 'I have been notified that I am being sent to a distant penal camp for eight years.' Underneath were the letters KRD, which, as I afterwards learnt, stood for 'counter-revolutionary activity'. Some women had on their slips of paper KRTD, the T standing for 'Trotskyist'. I told the NKVD man angrily that I could not sign, but he replied: 'It makes no difference, you'll be sent anyway.'

Thus I had been sentenced without a trial or judicial proceeding of any sort, and in the years that followed I was at no time brought to trial, nor did I see a lawyer. There was nothing exceptional in this: apart from the show trials of well-known figures like Zinoviev or Bukharin, political prisoners were executed or sent to labour camps without any process of law. It is true that press reports and decrees of the Soviet government always mention the Ministry of Justice, and indeed there is such a ministry and it has a large staff, but very few of its members ever come into contact with a political prisoner. Shortly before the 'legal' ceremony referred to above, I had addressed a petition to Andrey Vyshinsky, the chief Public Prosecutor of the Soviet Union, asking for a short interview. I received no answer, and when I asked the interrogation officer why this was, he shrugged his shoulders and said Vyshinsky would not have received my letter.

Many people in the camps wrote letters to the Department of Justice, protesting their innocence or begging for release; usually they got no reply, or if they did it was often to increase their sentence, perhaps from ten to twenty-five years. Habitual complainers were apt to disappear, and it was an open secret that they were executed. On the other hand, there were some who appealed in this way and were in fact released.

On 11 April I was locked into a Black Maria with many other prisoners and driven through Moscow in a direction I could not identify. When the vehicle stopped and the doors were opened, we were somewhere outside the city near a railway line. The warders shut us into a cold, draughty, roofless shed, and it began to rain in torrents. A score of juvenile criminals were already in the shed when we arrived. At dawn we were transferred to a 'Stolypin' carriage—a stout affair, built some thirty years earlier under the Tsarist Prime Minister of that name, but unlit and without windows. The carriage was hitched to a train, and in pitch darkness we set out for an unknown destination. The worst feature of the journey was the juveniles, who were given the upper berths and perpetrated all kinds of indecencies—spitting, uttering obscene abuse and even urinating on the adult prisoners.

We travelled all that night and the following day; next evening our carriage was uncoupled from the train, and the guards told us we were at Kotlas. I did not know where this was, but later I saw on a map that it lies on the Northern Dvina, about three hundred miles from the river's mouth at Archangel on the White Sea.

All I saw in Kotlas were the vast fenced-in areas in which parties of prisoners awaited onward transport to camps within the Arctic Circle. These areas, known as 'zones', were the temporary abode of thousands of prisoners, mostly men; there were, however, some women's zones, and I met the wives of several high officials, who were usually charged with failing to report their husbands' anti-Soviet misdeeds. I also met some other interesting personalities, including a male and a female doctor. The latter was Elisabeth von Fait, a Russian of Cossack descent but an Austrian national: she had studied medicine at Vienna in the twenties and married an Austrian doctor, by whom she had two sons. She had brought the boys to Russia to see her mother, and had been arrested on the ground of espionage. The other alleged spy was Dr Erich Sternberg, a German neurologist and mental specialist, who had accepted an invitation to Moscow University as an exchange professor, but had been arrested before he could give his first lecture.

I was surprised to meet some Finnish women who had been taken from Petrozavodsk to Kotlas, including Hilja Huttunen, Ida Kukkonen, Alfa Pekkala, Saimi Heikkinen, Elvi Koskinen, Ester Nikkari, Maire Salonen, Meeri Vellamo-Salonen, Ester Pihlajamäki, Maria Viitala and Lyyli Äikäs. Most of these had left Finland with their husbands, enticed by propaganda about high wages in the Soviet Union; as soon as the men got to Russia the authorities had decided that they were not workers but spies, and accordingly they had been shot. I saw a good deal of the wives in subsequent years, but I doubt if many of them are still alive. There were several in our group of whom I would like to say more, particularly Anni Kukkonen, or 'Aunt Annie' as we called her. She was a woman of some age who had come from Finland to Russia years before. When Gylling founded the Karelian Republic she was made Vice-Minister for Education, but afterwards she was arrested and imprisoned at Petrozavodsk with many other Finns of both sexes. She was a lively person and described conditions there with humour and sarcasm. The prison was an old wooden building, and the walls were so thin that prisoners could hold conversations, exchange news and even discuss plans to circumvent the authorities. They soon found out that they were all accused of spying and could expect a ten years' sentence, and the news also got about that a prisoner who refused to sign a confession had been beaten and then mauled by bloodhounds. Aunt Annie had been shown the place where the dogs were kept, and her interrogator told her that she too would be thrown to them and mangled if she did not confess. The prisoners were full of alarm at this threat, and agreed that even ten years of forced labour would be better than being thrown to the dogs, so each one invented a fictitious confession before he or she was questioned. In the case of one young man the interrogation went as follows:

'Do you admit that the Finnish secret service sent you here as a spy?'

'Yes, I do.'

'I'm glad to hear you say that. You're a smart lad. If you tell me everything, you'll be let off more lightly. Who recruited you as a spy?'

'Runeberg.'

'First name and father's name?'

'Johan Ludvig.'

'Where did you meet him?'

'In Helsinki.'

'But you weren't living there. Did you go there specially to meet him?'

'Yes, I did.'

'Did you go to his house?'

'No.'

'Where did you meet him, then?'

'On the Esplanade.'

'How was the meeting arranged? A lot of people walk up and down the Esplanade.'

'He stood waiting for me near the place where the band plays on summer evenings.'

'Who told you he would be waiting there?'

'My teacher at school, Hr Leppanen, told me I would see him in front of the rotunda, the first day I got to Helsinki.'

'How did you recognize him?'

'Hr Leppanen said he would be holding a book in his hand.'

'And that was how you met him?'

'Yes.'

Naturally the youth got a ten years' sentence without further ado. I need not tell Scandinavian readers who Johan Ludvig Runeberg was, but to anyone who does not know his name or his monument in Helsinki, I would explain that he is Finland's national poet, who wrote in Swedish in the last century: schoolchildren learn his poems by heart, and his songs of the war of

1808-9 against Russia have inspired generations of Finnish patriots. There is a bronze statue of him on the Esplanade in the middle of Helsinki. Leppanen was in fact the primary school teacher from whom the young man had first learnt Runeberg's poems.

Another interesting prisoner at Kotlas was Ida Sjöberg, a middle-aged woman of good education who had come to Karelia with her husband and brother to 'build socialism'. Her husband, a skilled worker, had been employed all his life in a factory at Kymi. He was quite comfortably off and had built himself a neat little cottage with a pretty garden, of which Ida once showed me a photograph. Shortly before he was due to retire and spend the rest of his days in peace and quiet, the 'Karelian fever' broke out in Finland. As Ida told me: 'Late one evening there was a broadcast from the Soviet Union, and my husband sat in front of the set and listened till midnight. He couldn't understand a word, as it was in Russian, but he wouldn't come to bed till it was over, just because it was a Soviet broadcast.'

The only cure for Karelian fever was to go to Karelia, which this couple did. Together with Ida's brother they crossed the frontier and settled in a Karelian village. The men's place of work was so far off that they could only come home on Saturdays, when Ida had the sauna ready for them. Life would not have been so bad if they had not been half-starved: food could not be bought anywhere, and when the men came home with healthy appetites at the end of the week, Ida had nothing to offer them. Finnish labourers are used to a good square meal, but at work they were given only sour cabbage-soup without bread. Ida was in despair till one day she wondered if a meal might not be made out of the large fat rats, with healthy-looking skins, which were constantly running about the place where they lived. So she set traps and caught a few. 'I cleaned them like rabbits,' she told me, 'and the meat was nice and white: it smelt rather like chicken. I gave my good black dress to a Karelian woman in exchange for some potatoes and onions and a bit of pork. On Saturday morning I heated the cooker, cut the rats into small pieces and put them into the pot with the potatoes. I buried the head and feet and all the other remnants. In the evening the men came home, and as soon as my brother got to the doorway he called out: "It smells like a Sunday joint!"' The men went off to the sauna, while Ida laid the table. When they asked where the meat had come from, she replied: 'Never mind, it's there, that's all. Men don't have to know all their wives' secrets.' So for once the men had a proper dinner and were highly delighted.

I asked Ida if she had eaten the rats' meat herself, and she replied: 'Not at first, but I tried it later, and it was so good that I always ate it after that.' She also said: 'There was a great deal of starvation in Karelia, and many died of malnutrition. I am sure that I saved my husband's and brother's lives by catching and cooking those rats.' I was quite convinced that what Ida said was true.

The month of May came; the sun shone, and Kotlas grew a bit warmer. The women from Moscow were housed in what had been a large cowshed: the floor had been washed down and covered with a thick layer of hay. I must admit that we did not find this too unpleasant, especially as we were allowed to leave the doors and windows open day and night. My neighbour was a Serbian, Nadja Kuberić, whose husband had represented the Yugoslav Party in the Comintern, while she worked as a translator from Russian into Serbian. He had been arrested and she did not know if he were alive or dead; she herself had been imprisoned some time later as a spy. She was a quiet, intelligent woman and we became good friends.

There was fresh air and sunshine, and we could see through the window everything that went on outside. We were free to move about within the zone, while warders with dogs patrolled outside the fence. One day the soldiers started building beneath our window, and after a few days we saw that the new structure was a kind of small tower. They used excellent wood, so that it had a solid and durable look, with a massive door and no windows. At the very top, near the roof, was a six-inch opening protected by a strong iron grating. Every day we looked out with curiosity to see what the tower was for.

When it was finished, the warders appeared with a group of young men, aged twenty or less and dressed only in torn undergarments; they were pushed into the tower and the door locked. We realized now that it was a place of punishment, without light or air, and that the young men would be lucky if they came out alive. We heard them screaming and beating on the door, begging to be let out. They were kept there for days, with only a few scraps of bread tossed through the grating from time to time. When the door was at last opened a few survivors staggered out; the rest had starved or been stifled to death.

A few days later I had a surprise encounter. Although prisoners were not made to work till they reached their final destination, some of the women had volunteered. They had been peeling potatoes outside the enclosure, and as they were returning a man in a neighbouring zone called through a gap in the fence and asked for news of me. The women said I was in the camp, and he asked if they could arrange for him to talk to me. Back in our enclosure, they formed themselves into a pyramid so that I could stand on their shoulders, and I asked in a loud voice who it was that wanted to see me. To my astonishment it was Danko Sapunov, with whom I had spent New Year's Eve sixteen months before. He told me to cheer up and not worry too much: he thought things could not go on as they were for long, and we would all soon be home.

From my place of vantage I could see two other people I knew. One was Dr Dushman, an army medical officer, whom I met again later: he had been sentenced to twenty-five years for the murder of Maxim Gorki (whom I doubt if he had ever seen in his life). The other was Muchulan, a Latvian and a high official of the NKVD; I had first met him through his wife, also a Latvian, who was secretary of the International Relations Section of the Comintern. When I returned to Moscow eight years later I heard that Muchulan had been shot at Kotlas and his wife executed in Moscow.

Towards the middle of May we resumed our journey, travelling northwards on the Dvina in an ancient paddle-steamer, a kind of vessel that none of us had ever seen before. We were not told our destination, but I gathered from a warder that it was Vorkuta, a name which meant nothing to me at the time.

Elisabeth von Fait, whom I talked to a good deal at Kotlas, had been told that she would be in charge of medical arrangements for the prisoners during the rest of the journey. When she heard I was a trained nurse she asked me if I would be her assistant. I hesitated but finally agreed, as I had kept up an interest in medical matters over the years. I am convinced that her offer saved my life during the following eight years of purgatory, as looking after the sick brought with it some material alleviations as well as spiritual ones. I shall always remember Dr von Fait with the deepest gratitude. We worked together in the far north until the German-Soviet war broke out in 1941; then, to my heartfelt regret, that devoted and courageous woman was sent to another camp and disappeared for ever.

But to return to the river journey. We glided slowly downstream in fine, sunny weather; the nights were luminous and warm. I was not without friends, as Sapunov travelled with our group of women. I learnt that he too had been in the Lubyanka for fifteen months on a charge of collaborating with spies from the Balkan countries; he had been condemned to death, but the sentence was commuted to twenty-five years.

We reached Archangel on a beautiful summer night, and, while the population lay peacefully in their beds, we were taken across the city on foot to the other harbour, where a large ship awaited us. All that I remember of the march is that I was wearing birch-bark shoes that I had acquired at Kotlas, as the 'zone' was not suited to high-heeled ones.

We stood on the wharf waiting for orders to embark. The wait was a long one as we thirty-nine women were at the end of a long queue, behind hundreds of male prisoners. Suddenly one of the men called my name, and I was startled to recognize an old friend of Comintern days, the German Hugo Eberlein. He came towards me: he was clearly very ill, and had difficulty in walking. I asked if he had come from Berlin and he replied: 'No, from Paris.' The Central Committee of the German Communist Party had been transferred to Paris on the Comintern's orders in 1934. Eberlein had received a telegram summoning him to Moscow, and had been arrested as he got off the train. He had just time to tell me: 'Don't worry too much, and above all never let yourself cry. When we get out of here, we'll show them what's what.' At that moment a warder grabbed him and pulled him off to a nearby building. He waved to me from the door, and so I was the last of his friends to see him: prisoners who were too ill to travel were taken behind the building and shot. When we got on board I asked the man in charge of the convoy what had happened to Eberlein, and he replied pompously: 'I could not take the responsibility of transporting such a sick man. He was so weak that he would certainly have died en route. He's better off being spared the hardships of the journey.'

Eberlein had been the German Party representative in the earliest days of the Comintern. He was a friend and confidant of Lenin's and married the latter's foster-daughter, Inessa Armand's sister; what became of her, I cannot say. Eberlein was an honest and outspoken man and a great idealist.

Our ship sailed out of the White Sea in the direction of the Arctic Ocean. The Kola Peninsula could be dimly seen on the port side. We were still not told our destination, though we heard more and more frequently of a place called Vorkuta, where there were apparently many coal mines.

I met two Finns on board, Hjalmar Wickström and Vilho Harju. Wickström had made friends with a Russian in Moscow, who taught him the language. In summer 1937 this man asked him to dinner at the Prague Restaurant and accompanied him back to his house, where Hjalmar was bundled into a waiting NKVD car. His 'friend' was an NKVD agent, and the next thing he knew, he was in the Lubyanka on a charge of spying.

Vilho Harju was a tall, fair, handsome man; I never saw him after we reached Vorkuta, but I heard indirectly that he had been killed in a mining accident. I cannot remember how or why he had come to the Soviet Union or what he was charged with.

After tossing about in heavy seas for a week, the ship turned southward into the Pechora delta and put in at the town of Naryan-Mar. Here some of the male prisoners were taken ashore; the rest of us were transferred to a large lighter, where we found other prisoners confined in the hold. We women were left on deck in the fresh air, and managed to make ourselves fairly comfortable. We made a kind of shelter with the help of blankets, used bundles of clothes for bedding and set up the medicine chests we had been given at Archangel; food was available from the galley. Before long our new vessel began to move upstream, towed by a paddle-steamer.

We were not too badly off on deck, but what of those below? After we had been under way for a time the non-commissioned officer in charge visited our shelter and told us there were nineteen hundred men in the hold, of whom only one was a political prisoner: the others were all common-law criminals, thieves, murderers and so on. They were forbidden to come up on deck during the voyage, and we were not allowed to go below—not even Dr von Fait, to look after the sick. 'If you do, the men down there will kill you.' Elisabeth von Fait asked him if we could see the political prisoner, so as to have an idea what was going on, and the man came climbing up shortly afterwards: he was an ordinary Russian workman. He said there were four tiers of bunks in the hold, which was pitch-dark; they were crowded with men, many of whom were sick and needed medical care. After much pleading, Dr Fait and I were allowed to go below, accompanied by several warders. The workman went ahead with a torch and we did our best to find the patients, but could not do much for them as it was so dark. It seemed hopeless, the stench was frightful, and we were glad to get back alive into the fresh air. In the following days and weeks the situation improved to some extent, as some prisoners were landed at camps along the river, but at the end of the voyage many corpses were dragged out of the hold.

One day a young Russian woman asked me if I was really Finnish, and when I said yes, she went on: 'I have only known one Finnish woman before: she was a bit cracked, and a terrible liar. Her name was Malm, and I met her in the prison camp at the Solovetsky monastery. She didn't speak Russian well, but we could tell she was talking nonsense. She said she was a member of the Finnish Politburo, her husband was a university student and was on the Executive Committee of the Comintern, and all sorts of lies like that.'

I replied: 'She wasn't lying, she was telling you the absolute truth—I used to know her well. But what became of her?'

'She drowned herself in the stream that flows through the monastery grounds. They only found her body three days later —it had sunk into the muddy bottom of the stream. Until then they thought she had run away, and the rest of us were punished, as they made us responsible for one another.'

So that was what had happened to Kullervo Manner's wife, the famous, not to say notorious, Hanna Malm. She had once told me her story: she was an illegitimate child and never had any proper family life or schooling. Her mother made a sort of living as a washerwoman, but Hanna had to fend for herself when she was quite small. She worked at a bookbinder's, where her task was to clean the shop and buy drinks for the men, and for some years she sold newspapers on the streets of Helsinki. Her sense of class-consciousness was awakened one day when she was sent to a factory shop full of workers, and from then on she was a devotee of the class struggle. During the Finnish civil war in 1918 she was indefatigable in urging young men to go to the front, and in the summer of 1921 she became responsible for underground Communist activity. How and when Kullervo Manner, a Member of Parliament and an educated man, became interested in her, I do not know; the marriage between him and an untaught girl of lowly origin was unusual and rather puzzling. Hanna was obstinate, self-centred and prone to quarrel over trifles, but the manner of her end bore witness to strength of character.

As regards Manner's own fate, I heard about it at Vorkuta from another Finn, a former member of the anti-Communist *Schutzkorps*, who if I remember rightly had been arrested by the Russians while fishing on the shores of the Karelian Isthmus. He told me that he and Manner had both been in a camp at Chibyu (now Ukhta) on the Pechora, where it was Manner's duty to keep the barber's shop clean and supplied with water. They were sitting together one day by a stove, frying black bread in oil, and Manner's companion said to him: 'Well, here we are—you a Communist Party leader and me a *Schutzkorps* man!'—to which Manner had replied: 'Never mind, friend, we'll meet again one day in Finland and swop stories there.' But it was an idle hope, as Manner had been shot soon afterwards.

Our voyage was a slow one, as the current was strong and we put in at several camps. At one of them the commandant tried to persuade us women to stay, and assured us that he could fix it. 'You'd be far better off here than at Vorkuta,' he said, 'where there isn't so much as a tree.' So we knew at last that Vorkuta was our destination; but we did not dare accept his offer, fearing that it would get us into worse trouble.

It was already August when we turned north-east out of the Pechora into a tributary called, we were told, the Usa. It was getting colder, and the officer in charge said we were getting near the Arctic Circle and would soon be landing. A week after that, we arrived at Kochmes. We were told that the male prisoners would be continuing up the Usa to Vorkuta Vom, whence they would be marched to Vorkuta. I did not find out the location of these places until much later: Vorkuta Vom (the Komi name of Ust-Vorkuta) is the last landing-place on the Usa and is forty miles from Vorkuta, where one of the biggest prison camps in the Soviet Union was then in a state of construction. Huge deposits of valuable coal had been discovered in this far northern area, and many thousands of prisoners were settled there in inhuman conditions to mine and transport it.

In the middle of August 1939 we reached Kochmes, having travelled for four months in all; the railway from Kotlas to Vorkuta was not finished until the end of 1941, and meanwhile all traffic came by river and sea as we had done.

A few of the women, including Dr Fait, were sent on from Kochmes by boat; the rest of us went ashore there, but she and I were to meet once again. Kochmes was a transfer centre for camps in the neighbourhood, two of which, I recall, were at Abez and Inta. There were two barracks for the male prisoners employed in loading and unloading, but as these were full we were housed in a large cellar, formerly a vegetable store, with two tiers of bunks round the walls. The scenery consisted of a vast marshy expanse, with the low range of the Urals dimly visible to the east.

I saw Danko Sapunov at Kochmes for the last time. He came over on some errand from a nearby camp and said he was being released soon and was to wait at Abez meanwhile. I wished him luck, but secretly I feared that I would not see him again, and my fears were justified. After my own release in December 1946 I went to the Sapunovs' in Moscow, where Alexander showed me a telegram that Danko had sent from Abez in December 1941, saying he was on the way home. She had heard nothing since, despite many enquiries of the NKVD, until in 1946 she was officially told that he had died at Saratov and that subsequently 'his honour had been vindicated'. My own suspicion is that Danko never went to Saratov, but was liquidated in December 1941 in the following circumstances. There was a serious railway breakdown at that time at Kozhva near Pechora, on the new line from Kotlas to Vorkuta, and an epidemic of dysentery broke out among the passengers. These included prisoners of military age from various camps, among them 'Trotskyists' who had served their sentences and were returning to freedom. The disease spread to Kozhva itself, and no one was allowed to travel further south. The small town had not enough food or hospitals, and so on Moscow's orders the epidemic was checked by the drastic method of shooting those who had fallen ill. It is my belief that Sapunov was one of the victims.

I spent the winter months of 1939-40 in Kochmes, where my tasks included whitewashing a small new building, picking a special sort of raspberries that grow in those latitudes, and supervising the food supply. Cut off from the outside world, we heard only that a general war had broken out in the west and that Finland had attacked the Soviet Union. So Stalin had begun to put into effect the plan that Otto had discussed with me back in 1935.

In the second half of March several women, including myself, were called up for a medical examination. The doctor gave me greetings from Elisabeth von Fait and a message that she needed my help at Vorkuta Vom, to which some women were being transferred from Kochmes. 'Why not?' I thought. 'Since she asks me to go, it can't be worse than here, and I would sooner look after sick people than food stores.' About thirty women were passed by the examination, and we soon found out the reason for it: we were about to start a hundred-mile march on the ice-covered surface of the Usa river! This involved nearly all the Finnish women who had been my companions on the journey from Kotlas. As we were political prisoners and not ordinary criminals, our morale was good, and even the armed warder, who followed in a sledge with our few goods and chattels, seemed well-disposed. An emergency medicine-chest was put in my keeping.

In the first week of April we set out northwards in a long

single file. Day after day we marched, with no sound but the monotonous tramp of our feet on the melting snow. We spent the nights in wooden barracks used in winter by the transport workers, all convicts, who were employed to collect goods on horseback and bring them to the Vorkuta camp area for shipment in summer to Kochmes. We encountered some of these teams on their way south to pick up further consignments. The yard outside the barracks would be crowded with horses and their loads, while the bunks within were full of resting labourers. Our 'guardian angel' made them make room for us, and so we shared these elegant quarters with criminals for the night. Early in the morning they would move on, and so did we after a scanty breakfast.

The march went on for three weeks, but miraculously only one of us fell seriously ill, a girl from Käkisalmi named Meeri Vellamo-Salonen. She had a temperature before we left Kochmes, and we urged her to stay there, but with Finnish obstinacy she insisted on coming; she knew no Russian and did not want to be separated from the rest of us. She stuck it out for a week, but collapsed in the snow one evening and could not get up. I saw she had a high fever, and stayed with her while the rest of the group, including the soldier-warder, pushed on in order to reach the next barracks before nightfall.

I improvised a bed for Meeri with my coat. Soon it was dark, and we were absolutely alone. I thought with horror of the tales of famished packs of wolves, but I did my best to keep calm and comfort the unfortunate girl. Suddenly I saw a sleigh approaching from the north. It was a Samoyed, with a team of five dogs; he stopped, and I begged him to turn round and ask our warder to send help, but he would not do so, or perhaps he did not understand Russian. He started up his team again, and I was alone once more with the sick girl and my terror of wolves. Then I saw a dark shape coming in our direction, and recognized our own wretched horse and sledge, driven, to my unutterable joy, by our friend Hilja—the wife of an electrician, and another of those who had been lured to the USSR by false promises. We lifted the poor girl on to the sledge and got her to the barracks; at dawn, when we started out again, the warder made room on the sledge for her.

I forget how many weary days had passed when we came to a spot where our way seemed to be completely cut off. It was just beyond Abez, where a narrow but swift mountain stream, evidently from the Urals, came flooding over the ice that covered the Usa. The warder tried to find a crossing-place, but in the end there was nothing for it but to wade through the torrent. Wearing our coats and felt boots, we stepped over slippery ground through the breast-high waters. On the other side we took off our boots to empty them, all except those who had been clever enough to take them off and hold them out of the icy water, wading across barefoot. Only the sick girl remained dry, as she lay on top of the sledge-load while the horse trotted across with water up to its chest. After that we had another three miles to go before reaching our quarters for the night.

We toiled for many more days along the frozen bank of the Usa, till at last, on the first of May, we reached Vorkuta Vom. All of us were utterly exhausted and in a state of near-collapse. We were given a sauna bath and assigned to quarters consisting of sailcloth tents, where we rested for a few days. To my joy I was able to see Elisabeth von Fait, who was working in the local clinic. Poor Meeri was taken to hospital at Vorkuta Vom, where she died soon afterwards of pneumonia. It was not a proper hospital but rather a collection of tents, with medical practitioners of doubtful quality. There was a woman surgeon there, but she was unable to save the life of Maire Salonen, who contracted appendicitis soon after we got there. She and her husband had come from Rovaniemi to 'build socialism'; he had been executed some time before.

Vorkuta Vom is at the spot where the Vorkuta river flows into the Usa. In 1940 the camp there was very small. During the short summer, food and other stores for the camps in the whole area were brought here by cargo boat, and in winter these goods were distributed on horseback. Vorkuta Vom consisted of three groups of tents and three wooden huts which served respectively as the commandant's office, a sauna and a clinic. Later the camp was enlarged and comprised a medical quarter (*sangorodok*) consisting of eight huts, including a larger psychiatric section for men and a smaller one for women.

We heard little news of the free world apart from Soviet propaganda, but occasionally some information filtered through. In summer 1940 I met a young Lithuanian who had been in his own country not long before and told me heart-rending stories of Finland's 'winter war'. Sad as it was, the news filled me with pride and thankfulness. Finnish courage and patriotism were being praised in all countries and all languages, and my country had become famous among people who till then had scarcely heard of it.

That summer a new commandant was appointed to Vorkuta Vom, and one day, to my surprise, I was called to see him. He was a tall man, with no badges of rank on his uniform. He received me in a friendly way, asked if I was well and what I was charged with, and then what I thought of the Soviet-Finnish war. I said I knew from the radio that it had broken out, but that was all. Was the war over? 'Yes, it is,' he replied, 'and what a way for it to end! We simply couldn't make any headway against the Finns. I know what it was like: I was commanding a sector of the front, and I got the blame for the disaster.' He had evidently been a senior officer, and he spoke frankly of his experience and answered my many questions.

'We were submerged in snow on my sector. The Finns are born skiers, and they would pop up for a moment or two and vanish like ghosts. Our soldiers simply crawled about in their heavy coats and stiff felt boots—the boots filled with snow, then it melted and their feet froze. Whole train-loads of wounded and men with frozen limbs were sent back to Leningrad; the hospitals there were full to bursting, and lots of men had to be billeted on private families, who had little enough food as it was. Nearly all my men had frozen feet and were badly frost-bitten. There was nothing I could have done to prevent it, but I got the blame and now here I am in Vorkuta.'

Later, another senior Soviet officer told me his opinion of the Finnish soldiers compared to the Russian. 'Our fellows obeyed orders and went to war, but they showed no enthusiasm and no spirit of self-sacrifice.' I asked him about the Soviet press reports that Finland had begun the war. 'Rubbish! The simplest soldier knew quite well that our government began it because they wanted to turn Finland into a Soviet State. But

I'd sooner shoot myself than fight another war like that again!'

In the late autumn of 1940 we heard a broadcast by Kuusinen, transmitted on all Soviet stations, in which he congratulated the Estonian people on their 'wise decision to seek incorporation into the Soviet Union'. I was standing in front of my hut, knee-deep in snow, and as these words came over the loudspeaker I tried to imagine the feelings of my Estonian fellow-sufferers in Soviet captivity.

I had plenty to do at the clinic, until an event took place which caused me to be given four months' sick-leave. At the end of March 1941 I was told that General Tarkhanov, who was in charge of the whole Vorkuta camp area, had given orders that I was to go to Vorkuta as his 'personal nurse'. I could not refuse, of course, though I felt much apprehension, and so I set out in a horse-drawn sleigh for the north, a journey of some forty miles—it was bitterly cold, but better than trudging for weeks along the frozen Usa. My driver was doing a stretch for murder and robbery, and his colourful tales of the underworld gave me a new insight into criminal psychology.

When I got to Vorkuta I reported to the medical officer in charge and we set out for General Tarkhanov's office, but on the way I slipped on the ice and broke my right wrist. When the general heard this he had me admitted to the hospital for 'free employees', where a double fracture was diagnosed and I was made to wear a splint for four months. The result was that I went back to Vorkuta Vom at the end of July without having set eyes on General Tarkhanov. I travelled by the aircraft that was used only for mail as a rule, and was glad to be back among my fellow-prisoners.

I should explain that the term 'free employees' was used for the administrative staff at Vorkuta, civilians and army officers and convicts who had served their sentences but remained voluntarily to perform certain jobs, attracted by the fact that wages were three times higher than in the south. A good many others, again, were prevented by the authorities from leaving even after they had served their time.

It was in Vorkuta hospital on 22 June that I heard the radio announcement of Hitler's attack on the Soviet Union. The bulletins did their best to conceal that the Red Army was in full retreat, but it was clear things were going badly, and most people attributed this to low morale: the soldiers simply did not want to fight for Stalin and his tyrannous regime. We prisoners instinctively avoided talking about the war, which we hoped would bring us freedom whichever side won it. But it had a dire effect for the Germans and many Finns, who were transferred to the special camp at Inta, and Dr von Fait disappeared along with these.

Apart from my stay at Vorkuta in 1941, I was at Vorkuta Vom without interruption from May 1940 to the beginning of April 1943, and during that time I had some interesting encounters with Finnish prisoners.

In September 1940 some convicts were ordered to make a narrow fenced path in our zone, leading from the main gate to a new group of tents. We could not think what this was for, and the men said jokingly: 'Perhaps it's for some sheep they've arrested.' But it turned out that the new quarters were for Finnish prisoners of war, about a hundred in number. I was told to find out if any of them were ill, but the warder did not let me talk long enough to them, and all I could do was to hand out a few headache pills. Next day these Finns were sent out into the wastes of the tundra, and none of them was ever seen again.

In summer I worked in a small clinic for riverside workers, and one day a foreman, who was also a convict, brought a man to me for examination, saying: 'Is he ill? He's a good worker, but he doesn't understand Russian and he's been sitting on the river-bank for three days saying nothing to anyone.' The man turned out to have a high fever, and I started to make out an order for his admission to hospital, but he made no reply when I asked for his personal details. I tried Russian, German and Swedish, but he simply looked at me with wide eyes and said nothing. I began to look at his clothing and, realizing suddenly that the shabby grey uniform looked familiar, asked him his name in Finnish. He replied joyfully 'Louko,' and added: 'You speak Finnish, do you?' The mystery was solved—he was a Finnish lieutenant. I had not much chance to talk to him, but if I remember rightly he was a frontier-guard. He was found in hospital to be suffering from pneumonia, but soon recovered.

I saw him again briefly, but I do not know what his ultimate fate was.

The mortality among convicts working in the mines increased steadily, and in autumn 1941 an order came from Moscow to build eight hospital wards at Vorkuta Vom with eighty beds each. I was made matron of one of the wards and was assisted by two Finnish youths, Vilho Röpelinen and Reino—I forget his other name. Vilho was a country boy with red cheeks and blue eyes, while Reino was town-bred and was less sturdy. They had both been frontier guards, and were captured by the Russians in a surprise attack. I don't know what became of Vilho, but Reino died of tuberculosis. I did all I could to save his life, and I shall always remember the grateful look in his eyes.

Once an officer called me to the river-side where two prisoners were unloading a barge. 'Perhaps you can solve the mystery,' he said: 'they are both Finns, but they can't understand each other.' One of them proved to be a man I knew, named Keltakallio; the other was a stranger, and when I asked him his name in Finnish he said in Swedish that he did not understand. It turned out that his name was Lindström and that he was a fisherman from the neighbourhood of Hangö. In the summer of 1940 he and his brother had gone out to sea to lay their nets; they were arrested by the crew of a large Soviet motor-boat and taken with their own boat and tackle to Leningrad, where they were thrown into the Kresty prison. His brother had been sent to a camp elsewhere, and he himself to Vorkuta. Both Lindström and Keltakallio disappeared without trace soon after I met them.

In June 1941 a party of female prisoners arrived by river-boat, including an American-born girl named Senta Rogers, the daughter of Latvian parents who had emigrated and done well in the States. We soon became good friends and she told me her story. Her father's original name was Rudzutak; his brother Jan, a friend of Lenin's, was People's Commissar for heavy industry and perished as a 'counter-revolutionary' in 1938. While still in power he invited his brother to come to the USSR as a technical expert and bring his family; both Senta's parents were liquidated shortly afterwards. Senta was thirteen when they came to Moscow; at the age of nineteen she was arrested, accused of spying for the United States and condemned to death. She was already in the death-cell at the Lubyanka when President Kalinin, to whom she had appealed for mercy, commuted her sentence to ten years' hard labour. She was sent from Vorkuta Vom to the camp for dangerous offenders at Vorkuta itself, from which few came out alive.

A different type of 'enemy of the people', whom I got to know much later at Vorkuta, was Madame Ott, formerly in the service of the French Embassy in Moscow and responsible for looking after the Catholic church there. She had been arrested and imprisoned for a 'crime' committed in the latter capacity. When General de Gaulle visited Moscow in 1944 he expressed the wish to attend divine service; this threw the Kremlin into some perplexity, as the Catholic church had been closed for years, but they set about finding a priest and bringing the church into some sort of order. It was here that Madame Ott made her mistake, as besides providing flowers and candles she procured a large armchair from the embassy and set it, together with a valuable rug, in the sanctuary for the General's benefit. For this excess of zeal she and her daughter, aged nineteen, were both arrested. She showed me a picture of this charming girl, who went mad in the Lubyanka and was put into a lunatic asylum.

Madame Ott's best friend was a *grande dame* from St Petersburg, Baroness Clodt; they often played chess together. The old Baroness was a true aristocrat, friendly and obliging to everyone and never uttering a word of complaint. She had been arrested in Berlin in 1945, her only crime being that she had fled to escape the Revolution in 1917. Her father, Baron Clodt, was a well-known sculptor in St Petersburg, his favourite subject being horses. Soon after I met the Baroness she was released from captivity by a fatal heart attack.

One afternoon in the autumn of 1942 I was doing my round of the barracks with a medical orderly when a group of prisoners came in: they had been working all day in pouring rain and were soaked to the skin. They threw their padded jackets on to the floor of the drying-room, and many also left their wet boots there. I opened the door and was met by a revolting smell from the damp, sweaty garments. Then I saw something move under the heap, and the orderly pulled out a man, evidently a Japanese, still wearing his sodden jacket. He tried to stand up, but failed and was obviously very ill. We took him to the clinic *en route* for the hospital. He answered my questions in a faint voice, smiling in the Japanese manner. He told me his name and said he had been the chief delegate of the Japanese Communist Party to Moscow and a member of the Executive Committee of the Comintern. Next day I heard that he had died in hospital. So, although he had not been shot like so many Comintern officials, he had met his end no less surely through years of hardship in prison and labour camps.

In April 1943 I was transferred by rail from Vorkuta Vom to Vorkuta. The line from Kozhva to Vorkuta had been in use since the end of 1941, though work on the track went on for years longer. I was assigned to the position of matron in the camp hospital, where prisoners suffering from undernourishment and vitamin deficiency were treated, not from humanitarian motives but to get them working again as soon as possible: it was not so much a hospital as a kind of 'convalescent home'. The commonest complaint was pellagra, a deficiency disease marked by severe disorders of the gastric and nervous systems. The daily food ration was quite inadequate for heavy work in the mines: the prisoners were given gruel for breakfast and a thin soup in the evening, plus eight hundred grammes of black bread, but no potatoes or vegetables. In later years a pound of sugar per month was added, but only for prisoners who fulfilled their work norm. Those who were not healthy enough to do so received the 'penalty ration' (*shtrafnoy kotyol*) of two hundred grammes of bread. Nobody could live for long on these rations while performing the strenuous labour that was required of them.

The prisoners were generally awoken at five and marched to the mines a mile and a half away; the working day was from eight a.m. to eight p.m., and it was not surprising that nearly all of them suffered severely in health. I must in all fairness record that Dr Semashko of the Ministry of Health did his best to alleviate their lot by procuring necessary medicines and, more important still, fresh blood supplies, milk and raw meat for those suffering from pellagra. Many of my patients recovered after four to eight weeks, but there was still a high mortality among the miners, as we had not enough room for all those who needed treatment. This did not worry the NKVD officials: human life was valued at a low rate, although the regulations ironically provided that a report had to be sent in quintuplicate to the Ministery of Health, indicating the disease and precise cause of death in each case. Most of the deaths were in fact from starvation, but this was not mentioned in the reports.

Every morning the naked, emaciated corpses were stacked in a little room and, when they had frozen stiff, piled on to a sledge and taken away. I once asked a driver where they were buried, and he replied: 'They throw them out in the tundra.' The disposal of the bodies was as simple as that, and benefited the wolves if no one else. It is true that in those latitudes the earth is frozen hard even in summer, and it would be hard work to dig a grave as much as a yard deep. When the snow melted, the reindeer used to feed on the bodies decomposing in the sun and became diseased. These herds belonged to the Komis, the local nomads in whose 'autonomous republic' Vorkuta lies; the republican government appealed to Moscow, but no action was taken.

By the time I was moved to Vorkuta it had become a much larger camp owing to the railway line: materials had been brought by train and the prisoners had built administrative offices, power stations, houses, huts, schools and even a theatre. A surgical hospital was opened, almost entirely for victims of mining accidents, and I spent over three years as matron there. Security regulations in the mines were quite inadequate, and as each new mine was opened the accident rate increased. In 1946 a new first-aid clinic was set up near the mining area, and I was appointed matron of this also.

Thousands of prisoners lost their lives in the course of constructing the railway from Kozhva to Vorkuta. This was an NKVD enterprise, the engineer in charge being a certain Frenkel, who had been one of those implicated in the 'Shakhty case' of 1928. In that year the OGPU claimed to have discovered an 'illegal counter-revolutionary organization for subversion and espionage', in which Soviet engineers and experts were involved with counter-revolutionaries abroad. The organization was known as the 'Industrial Party' (*prompartiya*), its headquarters were said to be in Paris and its purpose was to overthrow the

Soviet regime and restore capitalism in Russia. Its alleged members included an engineer named Ramzin and several other distinguished engineers. Naturally the whole story was a fabrication, designed to provide scapegoats for difficulties encountered in the first five-year plan. A show trial took place from 18 May to 5 July 1928: it was known as the 'Shakhty case' because the alleged wreckers belonged to the coal and electricity centre at Shakhty in the Donets Basin. Eleven of the accused were condemned to death, and over thirty received long prison sentences. Frenkel was one of the latter, but before long he was released in order to supervise the construction of a canal from Lake Onega to the White Sea: this was to provide a waterway from the Gulf of Finland to the White Sea by way of the Neva, Lake Ladoga and the river Svir. Frenkel promised to build the canal in record time if he were given enough labour, and the OGPU met all his demands. Tens of thousands of convicts, chiefly political offenders, were sent to the Karelian wastes and forced to work strenuously in inhuman conditions. Food and health services were inadequate, and the workers died like flies of disease and starvation. The exact number will never be known, but it certainly runs into many thousands. The canal, known at that time as the Stalin Canal, was completed in 1933, and Frenkel's sentence was terminated as a reward.

The next task he was given was the extension of the Kotlas-Kozhva railway line to Vorkuta. The vast quantities of coal from the Vorkuta mines were no use if they could only be transported by water during the short summer months, and so began the work of building a line, 250 miles in length, across uninhabited bogs and marshes. Again Frenkel was promised all the labour he needed, and again the victims died in thousands. Conditions on the Vorkuta line were still more primitive than in Karelia, and the Arctic climate was more severe; but there were unlimited reserves of humanity in the camp, and they were not spared. For years the prisoners attended evening roll-call in deadly fear as the team-leaders appeared with lists and read out the names of those to be sent next day to work on the railway. The selected men were locked up for the night, though there was no possibility of running away. Only a small minority came back, with fearful stories of the fate of those who had to spend weeks at the job. Food was scanty and there was no medical attention; if a man collapsed and was too weak to get up again, he was shot without ceremony.

In summer it was too muddy for the line to operate, but when the ground froze in autumn the supply of Vorkuta coal to cities and factories resumed. How little its users, in their warm, lighted rooms, knew of the inhuman suffering that had been its price, and the emaciated, worn-out bodies of tens of thousands of forced labourers! As for Frenkel, he was more honoured than ever and was promoted by Stalin to the rank of lieutenant-general; but to the prisoners at Vorkuta he was the most loathsome and contemptible of all their tormentors.

Vorkuta developed gradually into a town, from which the 'zones' of the convict settlement were cut off by barbed wire. Each zone comprised fifteen or twenty canvas barracks, with a hundred to two hundred prisoners in each. The zones covered a huge area, and their total population ran into many thousands. Men and women occupied the same zones, and 'politicals' were mixed up with common-law criminals—murderers, thieves and bandits—the slang name for whom was *urka*. These for the most part acted as team-leaders or 'brigadiers', and if one of them refused to work himself there was not much the camp officials could do about it. The major criminals, known as the 'big *urka*', tyrannized over the 'little *urka*', and would thrash or even kill them if they were disobedient. But, strange to say, the 'big *urka*' treated the politicals with respect and did not harm them, nor did they molest the women.

Most of the political prisoners at Vorkuta belonged to the educated classes, and those who were Russian by nationality were often Party members and officials, doctors, professors or army officers. Many had been taken prisoner by the Germans and, instead of committing suicide as POWs were supposed to do, had escaped from captivity and rejoined the Soviet ranks.

The charge against most of the women was that they belonged to 'counter-revolutionary families', i.e. their husbands or fathers were alleged to have committed crimes, but they were not told what these were. They usually knew nothing of politics, let alone counter-revolution, and were referred to in the camp as *zhony*, meaning simply 'wives'. They worked in the zone kitchens, bakeries, laundries and hospital wards and as cleaners generally, and also as domestic servants for NKVD officials outside the zones. Their work was far lighter than in the mines, and their mortality therefore much less than the men's; it may also be true that women in general are better than men at standing up to tough conditions.

A number of prisoners were released in consequence of the war, since the longer it went on, the more acute became the need for officers; many of these were serving long sentences at Vorkuta, and were now recalled to the army. One of them was General, afterwards Marshal, Konstantin Rokosovsky, who had been arrested in the 1937 purge of 'unreliable elements'. When I first knew him in Vorkuta he was batman to a loutish warder named Buchko, his duties consisting of fetching the man's meals, tidying and heating his cottage and so forth. After his release we heard of his brilliant career, and a rumour reached us that he had an important command on the German front; for once rumour was trustworthy. We also heard that he had written a letter to Buchko, his former master, and this I saw with my own eyes: it was shown to me by the commandant's wife, who was taking it to Buchko and who worked in the camp as a dentist. It was short and to the point, and read: 'Comrade senior officer! I have been made a general. The bread ration is satisfactory. Your ex-batman, Rokosovsky.'

All sorts of Soviet nationalities were represented at Vorkuta, including many Ukrainians accused of 'bourgeois nationalism'. They formed a close community with a strong moral sense. As time went on I increasingly admired their spiritual strength and hostility towards the persecuting regime, and their unalterable love for their enslaved country, its language and culture.

There were also many foreigners belonging to almost every nation in Europe and several in Asia. The Estonians, Latvians and Lithuanians were especially numerous, from men of education to simple peasant folk. Towards the end of the war German and Hungarian POWs began to appear, but they were housed in compounds further off and I had no chance of getting to know them, except for an SS battalion of Latvians whom I inoculated against dysentery—they, however, soon disappeared and were not heard of again.

The winter at Vorkuta is ten months long, and the uninterrupted darkness made life even gloomier. The prisoners were wretchedly clad, and the icy cold and snowstorms added to their suffering and caused many deaths. The thermometer often fell to sixty degrees below zero Fahrenheit. Even worse than the cold was the *purga*, the raging blizzard which buried the huts in snow so that only the chimneys could be seen. It was impossible to go out in the *purga*, and men detailed to shovel away the snow often lost their way and perished. If it was absolutely necessary to leave one's hut, a tunnel had first to be dug in front of the door. It may be wondered how we could live in the huts in winter, but from this point of view we were well off: coal was plentiful, the stoves were always heated, and I do not remember ever suffering from cold indoors.

A rumour spread one day that an NKVD officer had disappeared. This caused excitement and surprise: nobody could understand how an officer could simply vanish, since he had no call to expose himself to danger like the prisoners who sometimes got lost in the snow. After the storm had raged for two days, however, he turned up safe and sound and we heard his story. He had set out on horseback for the fifth zone, some miles away across the tundra. His horse was up to its belly in snow, and suddenly it halted and refused to go any further. He dismounted, and the horse lay down in the snow. Night was falling, and the officer decided that the only way to escape freezing to death was to lie alongside his horse. In this way man and beast spent the night in a snowdrift, and returned to camp after the storm had abated. When we asked if it had not been terribly cold he replied: 'Not at all, it was warm underneath the snow, but we were both desperately hungry.' Many people whom I revived after they were half-frozen to death assured me that they felt no pain, but rather a kind of blessed peace when the intense cold overcame them.

The strange, livid disc of the sun appeared above the horizon in June after its winter sleep, but in August it vanished again for ten months. During the two months of summer it shone day and night, though without giving much warmth. While summer did last, we were plagued with myriads of mosquitoes. One year it was still snowing on 14 June, and a light frost already set in on 6 August.

Two native races inhabit the area round Vorkuta: the Komi, also called Zyryans, and the Nentsy (formerly Samoyeds; singular Nenets). There is a large Komi 'autonomous republic', and a Nenets 'national district', but this is only a façade, and all the important posts are held by Russians. Both races were nomads, living in yurts, who bred reindeer and fished in the Arctic Ocean. Bread and vegetables were unknown to them. Their food consisted of raw fish and raw reindeer meat, and they drank the reindeer's milk and blood. A more primitive folk could hardly be imagined.

It was in 1943, if I remember rightly, that forty-eight Finnish women were brought into my zone, all of whom had migrated to Karelia about ten years earlier to 'build socialism'. Their story is a cautionary tale to Finns and others against Soviet blandishments. They had come to Russia with their husbands, many crossing to Leningrad in their own motor-boats; soon they were all safely locked up in the Kresty prison, the men separated from their wives and children. The children numbered eighteen, all below school age except for two boys. The prison diet consisted of sour cabbage-soup and coarse bread, and most of the children died of diarrhoea. The women had no news of their husbands until they met them again one day in the prison corridor, reduced to skin and bone. The whole party were then taken to a site near Chelyabinsk in Siberia, where they worked in the forest building barracks and a brick factory. When the work was completed men were taken off and shot; the woman drifted from one prison to another, and had now fetched up at Vorkuta.

When they heard that I spoke Russian they begged me to ask the commandant what the charge against them was. We went to his office, and I translated their enquiry. He took a pile of papers out of a cupboard and replied: 'Tell them they are charged under Article 58(6) of the Criminal Code, and that every one of them has signed a paper admitting the charge.'

It was no use arguing further, and I went back to the women's hut, where they told me that they had indeed signed a paper in Russian, the contents of which they did not know. Some of them had hesitated, but a man who spoke Finnish had told them that it meant they were being reunited with their husbands. So they had all signed, not having an inkling that the paper was a confession that they had been sent to the USSR by the Finnish State police for purposes of espionage. They had in fact no idea what espionage was; when I explained, they burst out laughing in spite of their despair, and one said: 'Do the Russians really imagine we would know how to set about it?' They had never so much as seen Karelia, although they had been ostensibly engaged to work there, and they now had to perform hard labour in the bitter cold of Vorkuta, which few of them left alive. They were all homesick and longed to see the relatives they had left behind in Finland.

Homesickness was a torment to many who shared our miserable life. A particularly touching case was that of a working man named Heikkinen whom I often saw at Vorkuta. When I asked him how he came to be there, he cursed heavily and said: 'I brought it on myself. I heard so much about what fine jobs there were in Karelia, and so many of our people were setting off that I thought to myself, why shouldn't a lonely old bachelor like me go and have a look? I could always come back if I didn't like it ... I didn't go straight across the frontier, I went up to Petsamo and found my way from there with a compass. When I got to the border I stood for a long while under a tall pine-tree and wondered whether to risk it or not. Then I crossed over, and I've regretted it day and night for the last ten years.'

I tried to console him, saying that one never knew and that perhaps one day we'd be let out and could go back to Finland. He thought for a while, and said: 'I've got nobody in Finland now. But I know the first thing I'd do if I got back, I'd go to Petsamo and look around till I found the pine-tree I stood under that day ... I'd throw my arms round it and kiss it, that's what I'd do. There's nothing else in the world that I want to do more than that.'

I shall always remember how Heikkinen's eyes shone as he spoke of his longing to see that tree again. When I told him, however, that it was not so easy to get to Petsamo any more, as it was now part of the USSR, he said with a deep sigh: 'So they've taken away my Finnish pine-tree as well.'

The prisoners at Vorkuta hoped that the end of the war would mean a large-scale amnesty, but they were disappointed. No politicals were set free, though one or two ordinary criminals were. Before long thousands more POWs made their appearance, this time members of General Vlasov's army who had turned traitor and fought on the Nazi side. Many were in chains. These unfortunates were sent to dig coal in distant zones; I chanced to meet one, a colonel, who was seriously ill and was admitted to our hospital. Learning that I was a political prisoner, he said that he expected to be shot before long, but that his hatred for the regime would live on.

Among the foreigners at Vorkuta I remember a Danish doctor, Alexander Thomsen, who turned up in 1945, having been in charge of an ambulance unit of the Scandinavian Red Cross in Berlin when it was captured by the Russians. They had arrested him and his staff and charged him with espionage. He was allowed to practise as a doctor at Vorkuta, but spoke no Russian, so I interpreted for him several times. On one occasion he asked the chief political officer of the camp for permission to write for vitamins and other supplies to his brother, who, if I remember rightly, was an official of the Danish Foreign Ministry. The officer promised to forward Thomsen's letter, but I very much doubt if he kept his word. Shortly before I left the camp in December 1946 I took leave of Dr Thomsen, and he gave me a letter to his brother which I despatched from Moscow. In 1965, after I left the Soviet Union, I heard that he had not been allowed to return to Denmark from Vorkuta until ten years later.

I saw quite a lot of my old acquaintance Major Sirotkin, who had been adjutant to Berzin and Uritsky in the Military Intelligence Department. We did not ask each other any questions, but I had no doubt that he had been arrested as a 'spy for foreign powers', and it seemed a marvel that he had not been executed like his former chiefs. He was a civil engineer by profession, and many houses in Vorkuta were built under his direction. In 1955, after my release from Potma, I heard by chance in Moscow that he was still at Vorkuta but was to be set free before long.

There seems to be a widespread idea in foreign countries that Tsarist justice was no less inhuman than that of Bolshevism, since in both cases there was or is no legal security. I certainly have no cause to defend the Tsarist system, and have always felt most deeply about its oppressive treatment of my fellow-countrymen. But during my long years of study at the 'highest academy of Communism'—the nickname commonly given to the prisons and labour camps—I was led perforce to make comparisons between the two systems, and there is no doubt that the Communist one is the less humane.

It is true that under the Tsars people could be sentenced by 'administrative action', i.e. without trial, to months or years of exile on Russian soil. But the conditions of life were generally not very arduous, and it also happened that political undesirables were merely expelled from Russia. The exiles within the Empire could live in any manner they wished, and the State paid them nine gold roubles a month by way of maintenance, which was quite sufficient in country districts at that time. If they had means of their own they were allowed to spend them, and they were perfectly free to move about in their place of residence; they could invite relatives to visit them or for a permanent stay. They could send letters by post and order books, newspapers and anything else they needed.

A typical case is that of Lenin's exile in 1898-1900, at Shushenskoye near Minusinsk in central Siberia. He invited his fiancée to join him, and they were married there. His comrades frequently visited him for companionship and consultation. He went out shooting game, and could move about the vicinity as he chose. He corresponded with friends abroad, and in this exile wrote his book *The Development of Capitalism in Russia*. When he returned, he was granted a passport for foreign travel.

The chief difference is that under the Tsars people were not condemned without cause: they usually had a public trial and an opportunity to defend themselves. There were no prison camps; death sentences were rare, and when they did occur were discussed by the press and public.

The number of executions under Stalin will never be exactly known, but it certainly runs into hundreds of thousands. Sentence was passed without any form of trial. Not even Communists were spared, including the Central Committee of the Party. Out of 139 members of this body eighty-nine, i.e. seventy per cent, were executed in 1937-8, and out of 1,966 delegates to the eighteenth Party Congress 1,008—i.e. more than half—were shot, as Khrushchev testified in his famous speech to the twentieth Congress.

In the spring of 1938 I met a woman in the Butyrka prison who had been an exile under the Tsarist regime. There were about twenty of us in a large cell, and one day the warder brought in this new prisoner—a good-looking woman with a pleasant smile, whose first action was to count her cell-mates and set out the right number of aluminium soup-plates on a long table. When the soup-dish was brought, she ladled out the ration with a practised hand. 'You seem to be at home here,' said one of the women, and she replied: 'Yes, it's my third stay.' Then she told us her story.

'The first time was when my husband and I were both students. We were sentenced to a year's imprisonment for revolutionary activity. When we got out we went on conspiring and were arrested again and kept here; but the doctors found I was pregnant, and so we were exiled to Karelia instead of being imprisoned again as the prosecutor had asked. We lived on the State maintenance money in a Karelian village. It was bitterly cold and snowed nearly all the time, and I was worried about when I would need help for the baby's birth. My husband had lung trouble; he was not allowed to leave the village, but I was, and he sent me with a peasant to Petrozavodsk to ask the governor to change our place of exile. The governor listened kindly; he had no power himself to grant the request, but he suggested that my husband should repeat it in writing and send a medical certificate. A few days later, an official messenger brought a parcel of food and baby's clothes from the governor's wife; and not long after that, we were given permission to move to the place in central Russia that my husband had asked for.'

Those of us who heard this story were amazed that political prisoners under the Tsarist 'tyranny' were treated like human beings and sentenced according to law after a fair trial. I don't know what became of that woman who was doing her third spell in the Butyrka, but I am quite certain which regime she preferred.

I have read many first-hand accounts by people who suffered

imprisonment or exile in Tsarist times. They naturally resented their treatment, but not one of them suggests that there was no genuine reason for it. On the contrary, they admit that they devoted all their powers to the conspiracy to overthrow Tsarism. Most of the 'Old Bolsheviks' spent a great part of their lives in Tsarist prisons, but they stayed alive until the Soviet regime itself turned against them. Many of those slaughtered have, of course, since been 'rehabilitated' by the belated recognition of their innocence *vis-à-vis* the regime. As someone grimly put it: 'Christians believe in resurrection after death; Communists believe in rehabilitation after death.'

VII

Soviet Freedom

The day of a prisoner's release should be a day of freedom and the joy of homecoming. How far this is from reality in the Soviet Union can hardly be imagined by anyone who has not lived there. In other countries there are generally some welfare arrangements for a man who has served his time, and when he has found a job he can live with friends or relations more or less as he pleases. In the Soviet Union things are quite different: the day of release marks the beginning of a tough, interminable struggle to build up one's life anew.

First of all, one is debarred from residing in a large number of places. The documents issued to me on my release from Vorkuta showed that I was a former convict, and they contained indications in a code known to every police officer, signifying that I was not to live in any of thirty-nine important urban areas, including of course Moscow, Leningrad and Kiev. But apart from this, the saddest thing for a former political prisoner is that many people avoid him or her like the plague for fear of becoming suspect themselves. It often happens that relatives and old friends do not dare give such people a helping hand or even a night's lodging; though there are also those who go out of their way to be kind to them.

If I had gone back to my husband I could have lived under his protection in Moscow, but I felt too deeply injured to do so. I regarded it as a point of honour and a moral necessity to make a new life for myself away from him and without his help. The first thing I needed was a job and a place to live; so I went to Moscow and looked up my old housekeeper, Alexandra Seldyankova, whom I had told of my impending release from Vorkuta. She and her husband had a pleasant little flat; they welcomed me cordially and invited me to stay there for a while. Before going to Japan I had entrusted my clothes and some other things to Alexandra, and she had kept them carefully.

I could only stay in this peaceful haven for a few weeks, however. The police picked me up for not having a residence permit (which everyone living in Moscow has to carry on him at all times); I was only in jail for a night, but was ordered to leave Moscow at once. Where was I to go? Some of my influential friends thought they could get me a Moscow permit, and the faithful Alexandra found a room for me with some friends of hers elsewhere in the city, where I could wait till it came through. But I did not dare remain for long, and moved to the small town of Rostov, a hundred and twenty miles north-east of Moscow (not to be confused with Rostov-on-Don), where another friend of Alexandra's kindly took me in. But here too I needed a residence permit, which, as in all Soviet cities, one could only get by having a job there—and my quest for work was fruitless. I could think of nothing to do but return to Alexandra in Moscow. There I was again arrested, and had to share a cell with a man accused of burglary: he was genuinely sympathetic when I told him my only 'crime' was living in Moscow without a permit.

I remained in the cell with the burglar for some days, and was called up one night for interrogation. The official was a decent-looking man but was completely drunk. I could not understand what he said, and he could not write my answers. He tried to take my finger-prints without success, and then tore up the forms in a fit of rage. So the hours passed: he kept on trying to fill in the forms, and I sat placidly on my chair and counted them. When he got to the hundred and thirty-fifth attempt, two plain-clothes officers came in and, after asking my name, fetched me away, leaving their drunken colleague staring vacantly into space.

This time I was taken to the office of the general commanding the Moscow police. His manner was not unfriendly, and I was emboldened to explain my difficulties. He expressed indignation at the harassment I had been subjected to, and promised to help me obtain a residence permit. He gave me a telephone number to ring in a week's time, led me to the door and told one of his staff to escort me to any address I liked—so, shortly afterwards, I was back with my old housekeeper. It turned out that she and her husband had mentioned my case to some highly-placed former friends of mine; they had contacted the general, which accounted for his forthcoming attitude. All the same, I did not dare stay longer than one night with Alexandra. I took refuge with her relatives again, and, a week later, rang the number the general had given me, but was told I could not speak to him. So even the chief of the Moscow police was afraid to help me.

Not long afterwards a friend of mine who was a high official procured me an interview with the senior police officer of the Soviet Union, in his office on the Lubyanka (Dzerzhinsky) Square. He was very amiable and also undertook to help; he was going on an official trip to Lvov that evening, but gave me his telephone number and told me to ring on a certain day next week. Then, in a less formal tone, he asked if I knew any of the political figures in Soviet Karelia, such as Gylling, Rovio and Matsson. He clearly knew about the situation in Karelia, and I felt certain that he must have been police chief there at some time.

I rang his number on the appointed day, but got no reply. I spoke to his secretary, who was evasive as to his whereabouts and advised me not to make further attempts to contact him ... The mystery was solved later by the friend who had arranged the interview for me. The general had been sent to the Lvov area to suppress an outbreak of violence, but had reported on his return that the forces at his disposal were insufficient and that in his opinion it was not a question of mere banditry but of Ukrainian nationalism. As a reward for this unwelcome report he had been shot.

In April 1947 I went to see my old friend Alexandra Kollontay, hearing that she had been recalled from the embassy in Stockholm. She was living in a modest, old-fashioned apartment, seemed depressed and ailing and could only move about the room in a wheel-chair, but told me she was writing her memoirs with the aid of a secretary. It was the eve of the First of May, and Moscow was in a whirl of preparations for the holiday. Bread was rationed, but vodka was plentiful; there was no soap, but an abundance of scent and cosmetics. Alexandra Mikhail-ovna complained that when she applied to the food rationing authorities for some special allowance for the festive season, she had been given a coupon for four extra pounds of wheat flour—enough, as the secretary said, to welcome the First of May with a big batch of ginger-drops.

A handsomely framed photograph of King Gustaf V of Sweden, with a cordial inscription, occupied the place of honour on Mme Kollontay's desk: she had been diplomatic envoy to Sweden, Norway and Mexico before ending her remarkable career as Ambassador in Stockholm. She was a cultured woman and an idealistic revolutionary who took part in conspiracies against Tsarism from her early youth and was an intimate of the Communist leaders, including Lenin himself. In 1920-1 she was a leader of the movement known as the Workers' Opposition, and when Stalin rose to power she was excluded from any position of importance in home affairs; she became a diplomat after the customary process of 'self-criticism' or recantation. She spoke cordially of Finland and the other Scandinavian countries; her Swedish was good and she had picked up some Finnish in her youth during summer holidays near Vyborg. She was a shrewd observer and a fluent writer, and her memoirs would have been very interesting, but if she finished them before her death in 1952 they were presumably destroyed.

The execution of the senior police chief once more thwarted my hopes of obtaining a residence permit for Moscow. During my nine years as a prisoner I had learnt much about the Soviet system from my own experience and that of others, and had gradually become convinced that if that system were to extend beyond the boundaries of the Soviet Union it would mean unutterable misery for the whole human race. I could see no sign that the leaders of the free world recognized this danger, and I felt that the time had come to use such liberty as I had to fight a personal battle against Stalinism. For this purpose, and perhaps also in the hope of obtaining some support in my own difficulties, I went to the American Embassy in Moscow at the end of April 1947 to give them such information as I could and to ask if they could help me to leave the Soviet Union. I was desperate and foolish enough to think the Americans could help or at least advise me; but, while the officials were polite and friendly in their boyish way, they showed no understanding of my purpose, either out of naïvety or because they did not trust me. The visit was a failure for which I paid dearly, and its only positive result was that they agreed to forward to Denmark the letter which Dr Thomsen at Vorkuta had written to his brother.

My days in Moscow were numbered, and I debated again what to do next. I remembered an Armenian friend at Vorkuta, who had been released before me and invited me to go and stay with her; I now wrote to her, and soon received a reply. I sold a few things to pay my fare to Kirovakan, where my friend gave me a hearty welcome: she had a job teaching languages, and urged me to try and find similar work. But my past as a political offender continued to be a barrier, and I spent months in search of a job that I could live on.

By this time it was 1948. A new wave of arrests broke out, in the Caucasus as elsewhere; former 'politicals' were a prominent target, and I was afraid to harm my friend by remaining longer. She had a relative, however, at Tiflis in Georgia who was prepared to take me in, and I resolved to go there. I spent some weeks of the spring in that charming city, where I had enjoyed a delightful holiday in the twenties; but I could not get permission to stay permanently, the arrests multiplied and the political situation was clearly becoming worse. My only faint hope lay in returning to Moscow and visiting the American Embassy again, where I tried to persuade myself they might give me work.

I called at the embassy and was received by a general in uniform with whom I had a long talk; I saw him on two further occasions, his secretary being present. He was polite and helpful but explained what I ought to have known already, that foreign diplomatic missions in Moscow are only allowed to employ Soviet citizens with the consent of the Ministry of Foreign Affairs.

I was afraid to stay any length of time in Moscow, so I went back to Tiflis and then to Kirovakan, where I spent Christmas with my Armenian friends. I shall never forget the warmth of their hospitality. But for them I would soon have been destitute, though every now and then Alexandra sent me money from the sale of my possessions, which she disposed of one by one.

Armenia is a beautiful country, and its people are honest and industrious. I met Armenians of all classes and admired their steadfast attachment to their country, which has been under foreign rule almost throughout its history. Tsarist Russia and Turkey fought bloody battles on Armenian soil, and after they made peace they vied with each other in exterminating the Armenians. Today the oppression continues, as political functionaries see to it that Armenia obeys the will of Moscow. If its people were given a chance they could certainly improve their economic and cultural standards, as the soil is fertile and rich in minerals and the population much harder-working than the Russians.

The most striking feature to a Scandinavian, used to wooden houses, is the appearance of Armenian dwellings built of grey, black or red stone with a smoothly polished surface. They look as if they were built for eternity, and give an impression of prosperity with their big balconies and orchards. But this is unhappily an illusion, as the whole area with its dates, nuts, grapes and tropical fruit is organized into collective farms. When the heavy rains come in autumn the harvest is spoilt, as the men prefer to work in the cities and factories rather than for the meagre farm wages.

Once, on a visit to an elderly couple, I was pleased and surprised to see the reproduction of a picture that used to hang in patriotic Finnish homes in my youth. It is by the painter Isto and shows Finland as a maiden clasping her country's code of laws to her breast, while an eagle from the east attempts to snatch it away. My host told me he had studied at St Petersburg as a young man, had seen the picture on a trip to Finland and had bought it because 'it means the same to an Armenian as to a Finn'.

I was astonished to find that many Armenians who had lived outside the Soviet Union used to return to their mother country. Most of them had escaped from Soviet Armenia in the past, and many brought their children who had been born abroad. They came from Iran and other parts of the Near and Middle East, but also from Europe and even North America. What on earth could induce them to return to the Soviet Union? The simplest answer, no doubt, is that patriotism and love of one's own language are ineradicable: these emigrants had preserved their religion and love of home and wanted their children to do likewise. Another reason is that the Soviet government exploited the Armenians' homesickness and sent agents all over the world to persuade them to return. This worked with many Russian émigrés before and after the Second World War, and with the Finns who succumbed to 'Karelian fever' in the thirties. As for the deluded Armenians, to my astonishment one of them who had just returned said to me: 'Here in the land of our fathers there is freedom, everyone has a decent home and a good job, and they say the wine flows like water.' Alas, it was not long before they awoke from this dream and found that their beloved country was so impoverished that even long-standing inhabitants were close to starvation.

The returned migrants were distributed all over Soviet Armenia, and I met several in Kirovakan. Not a single one was glad that he had come back, and they would have jumped at the chance of re-emigrating, but it was not so easy to leave the Soviet Union: not only had their passports and foreign identity papers been taken away, but they had been made to change their foreign money into roubles.

A great fuss was made in 1948 over a group of two hundred Armenians who returned from the USA. A friend described to me the welcoming ceremony at Erivan, the capital. A speaker's platform was erected in the main square, and the homecomers, with tears in their eyes and arms upraised to heaven, expressed their emotion and thankfulness at being allowed to return. The most impressive speaker, an elderly doctor, deplored the folly and ingratitude of his son, also a doctor, who had refused to leave America. Many a native Armenian must have thought to himself how much greater was the folly of those who had chosen to live in the Soviet Union.

A tragicomic experience was that of an Armenian who owned a shoe factory in the USA and wished to present it to the mother country. The huge modern installation was shipped to Batum on the Black Sea, where its owner made a speech describing its productive capacity and offering it as a gift to the Armenian State on condition that he was allowed to assemble the equipment and act as manager. The government representatives solemnly accepted the gift, praised the owner for his munificence and promised to respect his wishes. He was then taken off to Erivan for further ceremonies; the equipment remained at Batum for a few days, after which it disappeared without trace. The laughter-loving Armenians were amused at the credulity of their fellow-countryman, whose factory had gone off to be assembled somewhere in central Russia: neither they nor he ever saw it again, for it was not the kind of gift that Moscow parts with easily.

The wave of arrests that had begun in 1947 engulfed the whole country: Stalin was resolved to tighten his hold on all the republics, including Armenia, as opposition to the Soviet regime and Muscovite control was manifestly growing. As in the past, former political prisoners fell under particular suspicion, and many were re-arrested. When a neighbour of mine, just out of prison camp, was seized by the police after spending only one night at home with his family, I realized that the time had come for me to start on my travels once more. My presence was a danger to my friends, as was shown soon after my departure when my Armenian friend was arrested and imprisoned for eight months.

This time I decided to go to Kazakhstan in central Asia, as there was a rumour that several former inmates of Vorkuta who, like me, were unfit for hard labour had settled there. It was equivalent to living in exile, but there seemed to be some chance of finding a suitable job and also less danger of re-arrest. I therefore wrote to a Karelian woman at Demyanovka, a hundred miles north-east of Kustanay: she advised me to come, and at the beginning of March 1949 I set out via Tiflis and Moscow, where I made a short stop. (This was rather as if one were to travel from Rome to Ankara by way of Stockholm, but there was no direct route from Armenia to Kazakhstan.) The journey from Moscow to Kustanay took five days. It was bitterly cold when I arrived, and I was then told that there was no way of getting to Demyanovka, but after two days I received permission to travel by the postal aircraft. I shall not forget that flight in a hurry! Crouching among mailbags in the tiny open plane, I felt as if all the winds of Tibet had conspired to destroy us.

It soon proved that my long journey had been in vain. I did secure a residence permit, but the hopeful rumours of jobs turned out to be illusory as far as 'politicals' were concerned. I was given shelter by three educated Polish women who lived in a wooden hut; it was cold and dirty, and we never had enough to eat. To this day I cannot understand how the people at Demyanovka endured their privations, which were worse than I had seen at Vorkuta or elsewhere. I had no money left, and was convinced that this was the end.

But Soviet ways are unfathomable, and I was saved in an unexpected manner—by being arrested at the end of May after less than three months of 'freedom' at Demyanovka. Two officers, a Colonel Dmitriev and a major, fetched me away in the middle of the night. We drove across the steppe to Kustanay and stopped in front of a dilapidated shack; they pushed me in and slammed the door. A girl with brown hair was sitting at the only window. She asked what I had been arrested for; I replied I had no idea, and she said: 'Then you must be a political.' She volunteered that she was charged with murder, but added: 'Don't worry—I won't hurt you.' I assured her I was not afraid, and as we were both glad to have company we made friends quickly. She was illiterate, and to pass the time I read to her from a sentimental Russian novel.

However, we were together only a few days. Colonel Dmitriev suddenly announced that he had been ordered to send me at once to Moscow, for reasons unknown to him. He asked if I was satisfied with the way I had been treated; I said yes, and we drove to the station in a rickety old car. A young woman in a captain's uniform sat beside me: she was introduced as Galina Petrovna, and I gathered that she was in charge of me. We got into a third-class carriage, which, for a wonder, was perfectly clean. Just before the train left, fifteen officers got in with their luggage; they proved to be pleasant company on the five-day journey. Colonel Dmitriev had given me some black bread, herrings and sugar to take along, but I did not need them, as the officers bought food at every stop and shared it generously with me. They also gave me newspapers and books to read, and one or other of them would talk to me from time to time. Nevertheless the hot, dusty journey was very tiring, and we were all glad to reach Moscow on 3 June.

Arm in arm with Galina Petrovna I walked out of the station behind the officers, one of whom carried my suitcase. A row of vehicles stood waiting, and I was put into one which had a door at the back only. They helped me in, handed me my suitcase and shut me into the pitch darkness—it was a prison van. We sped off rapidly and soon came to our destination—I could not see the building, but felt instinctively that it was the Lubyanka. The next thing I knew, I was sitting in a tiny cell painted light blue. A warder brought me a piece of bread, but when I said I would like a wash he growled: 'No time. You're to be questioned at once, they're waiting.' He took me to an interrogation office on the fifth floor: a colonel was standing there, and when I appeared he exclaimed: 'Well, we've caught a fine fish today!'

'I'm not a fish, I'm a woman, and I would like to know why I have been arrested.'

'How can you ask that? You know as well as I do, and the best thing you can do is to confess on your knees and ask forgiveness.'

'How can I do that when I don't know what I'm charged with?'

By way of reply he shouted and cursed obscenely, but did not answer my question. So ended my first interrogation, and I thought to myself: 'Well, here I am a guest in the Lubyanka again. What's to become of me, I wonder?'

My detention this time, pending sentence, lasted fourteen months, a month less than in 1938-9. I was usually held at Lefortovo by day, and taken at night to the Lubyanka in the small prison van. Scarcely anything had changed in the routine since I was there ten years previously. The method of questioning was the same, and executions took place as before, although less to-do was made about them. The only improvement was that my interrogation was conducted almost throughout by only two officers: these were Colonel Polyansky, a stupid and unpleasant man, and Colonel Nikitin, who had milder manners. The theme was my alleged espionage for the United States. Week after week and month after month they tried to make me confess that I had visited the American Embassy and talked to the military attaché, but I denied persistently that I had been near the embassy. They kept talking of a visit in the middle of May 1947, which made me think they did not know of my two visits before and after that date. They showed me the photograph of a US general, but I denied ever having seen him or the assistant military attaché; to which they replied: 'We have irrefutable proof.'

Finally, towards the end of February 1950, they played their trump card. I was presented to a general who adopted a friendly, disarming manner and urged me to confess, as they had indisputable evidence. He then produced a photocopy of a document in English which he said was a memorandum of my visit. It consisted of two handwritten sheets: the text was incomplete and there was no indication of the author or to whom it was addressed. It began: 'We had an interesting visit today from Mrs Aino Kuusinen, the well known Communist. She is an intelligent woman.... We agreed on a further meeting.' There was no doubt that this document was authentic, and I had to change my tactics. So, as the general pressed me further, I promised to tell the whole truth next day.

By way of reward and encouragement I was given an unusually good supper, which I shared with my cell-mates, and was allowed to go to bed before the statutory hour of eleven. But I spent a sleepless night working out my 'confession', as any false step at that stage might well be my death-warrant. I remembered vividly Otto Kuusinen's parable about grasping the 'right ring', which was published in *Pravda* and which I mentioned in the first chapter of this book. If there had ever been a moment at which this was important, it was now; but how could I tell which was the ring that would save me from the abyss?

Next morning at nine I was taken to Polyansky's office and, after making him promise not to interrupt me, began to tell the story I had worked out overnight. I spoke deliberately but fluently, as though I were reading from a book, and Polyansky listened for nearly two hours without a word. As regards the main point, I admitted that I had spoken to the 'duty officer' at the embassy about the possibility of a job—my description of this man made him sound quite unlike the military attaché. The embassy had been willing to take me on, but when I heard they could only employ Soviet citizens with the consent of the Foreign Ministry I took it for granted that such consent would be refused to me, and so I went back to Transcaucasia.

When I had finished, Polyansky said I had told my story well but it was a very naïve one, especially for an intelligent, much-travelled woman like myself. I nodded stupidly and agreed with him: 'Yes, I was very naïve, but there you are, that's the way it happened.' At this point the general came into the room and asked Polyansky if I had told the truth, to which he replied that he honestly wasn't sure. The general then said to me: 'You really are incredible! For nine months now we've been battling with this case, and you've been too obstinate to tell us anything.' And, to Polyansky, 'What a time we'd have if our own people were as good at keeping their mouths shut!' Polyansky replied: 'Yes, the Russians can't wait to tell us everything. But this is a Finn, and you know how stubborn they are.'

My 'confession', of course, was not what they had been hoping for; but things had gone off all right, and I felt that this time I had got hold of the right ring. None the less I was interrogated for another five months, though less severely, and traps were laid for me now and again. Once the general said, speaking of the photocopy: 'You needn't imagine that we had to copy this here in Moscow; we could just as easily have done it in London, for instance. As you know, mail goes by all sorts of routes, and we have plenty of methods at our disposal.'

I replied: 'Yes, I'm sure you have excellent methods'—which seemed to please him.

The incessant nervous tension and the frequent night sessions gradually undermined my health: my blood pressure got higher and higher, and I finally collapsed. As a rule the prison doctors were supposed to treat patients as harshly as possible, but there were exceptions, and the doctor who treated me was fortunately one of them. One evening, as I lay half-conscious at Lefortovo, I was put on a stretcher and taken to a small barred cell in the Butyrka prison hospital. The woman doctor there was kind and considerate, but she was only allowed to see me in the presence of a warder, and my illness was the only permitted subject of conversation. I had to lie motionless on my back, and was fed with a spoon and given medicine at regular intervals. I felt no pain, and slept better than usual. I was in fact given a kind of sleep therapy, and I found later that I had been peacefully and almost continuously somnolent for about a fortnight. At mealtimes I was vaguely aware that I was in hospital, but the drugs prevented me worrying about this or anything else. I am sure that doctor saved my life, and I shall never cease to be grateful to her. Gradually I recovered, and in due course I returned to Lefortovo and my fellow-prisoners, of whom I will now give some account.

Elizaveta Oranovskaya was the daughter of a Tsarist colonel and a member of the aristocracy. Her father died young, and his widow sold all their possessions and took her five small children to Paris, where they had a good education. When France recognized the USSR, Elizaveta became an interpreter at the Soviet Embassy. After the collapse of France in 1940 the Nazi conquerors obliged the French to expel all members of the embassy staff, and so Elizaveta and her mother returned to Russia via Greece and Turkey. Although she had been promised a job in the Foreign Ministry, she found that like all ex-émigrés who had been long abroad she was forbidden to live in Moscow. The two women were sent to a lonely spot in central Asia where there was nothing but poverty, hunger and bitter cold. They were given a tumbledown cottage to live in; the mother soon fell ill from undernourishment, and her sick-bed consisted of a chest without any sheets or blankets.

Elizaveta found a job teaching French in a school some miles off, to which she had to battle her way through snow and ice. One day she came home to find that her mother had died, and that rats had already eaten her face away so that it was hardly recognizable. The horrified girl could scarcely stand up, but she ran to fetch a neighbour who kept the rats off with a stick until her husband came and they loaded the body on to his sledge. The three of them pushed it through the snow and buried the old woman in a snowdrift. It had really been a mercy for both her and her daughter that she had not died a more lingering death of starvation. Elizaveta now managed somehow to get to Moscow and ask for a job at the Foreign Ministry, the result of which was that she was arrested as a French spy.

Elizaveta was a sensitive, cultivated person who never blamed others and accepted her cruel fate as the work of destiny. Soon after my own illness and recovery she contracted a form of dysentery and died of it although I nursed her with loving care.

The two other women in the cell were both victims of the lying promises with which the Soviet government enticed Russians to return from abroad. One of them, Lidia, was a celebrated singer in Shanghai, where she was making a good career. In China as in other countries, the Soviet authorities published appeals in the newspapers assuring émigrés that all would be forgiven if they came home. Tens of thousands responded, and a special commission in the Soviet Consulate worked day and night to prepare their papers. They were offered free transport by sea to Vladivostok, and were told they could go from there to any destination in the Soviet Union. Many were distrustful at first, and lively arguments were held at meetings in the Russian Theatre in Shanghai. But the nostalgic fever soon became an epidemic, and those who had made up their minds could hardly await the day of departure.

Some, it is true, guessed correctly what was afoot, and one of these actually committed murder. A shipload was about to sail, and an Orthodox priest stood on the quayside with a crucifix, blessing the travellers. Suddenly a Cossack sprang out of the throng and stabbed him, crying: 'You know these poor fools are being sent to their death, and you dare to bless them!' His prophecy was horribly fulfilled: those who were not murdered on their arrival were usually sent straight to prisons and labour camps. I had met some of them at Vorkuta, and was to meet others at Potma. As for poor Lidia, she was tricked twice over. A General Roshchin at the consulate in Shanghai promised to marry her and get her an engagement at the Bolshoy in Moscow. She yielded to his plea, made the long journey across Siberia and had time, before she was arrested as a spy, to find out that he had a wife and children.

The third member of our company was a dentist who had been lured home from Manchuria, buying before her departure a set of first-rate American equipment. She opened a practice in a Soviet provincial town and married, but was soon thrown into jail as an American spy. I doubt if she or Lidia are still alive, but if they are, they have certainly been cured of homesickness for the Soviet Union.

Once, to my surprise, I was taken from Lefortovo to the Lubyanka in daylight—a thing that had never happened before —and up to the fifth floor instead of the second where the cells for female prisoners were. The warder took me through a small door and down a long, narrow, carpeted stairway, at the bottom of which two guards in uniform saluted—almost like an official reception! Then two steps led up to a kind of balcony with numbered doors opening off it. I supposed that I was being moved to another cell, but to my astonishment it proved to be more of a bed-sitting room: there were a proper bed, a table and chairs and an unbarred window looking on to Lubyanka Street. The officer on duty was most polite and provided me with some books I asked for. To my further surprise, I heard a man and a woman talking in the next room, though I could not tell what they were saying or in what language. Could there be married quarters in the Lubyanka? The door of my room did not shut tightly, and I could hear and smell that they were being served an excellent meal, apparently with wine. I myself, however, received only the ordinary prison rations.

At my subsequent interrogation I was told that I had been brought to the 'foreigners' section' so that I could refresh my memory in comfort about my visit to the US Embassy. However, the authorities soon found that this device did not answer, and back I went to the darkness of Lefortovo. I have related the incident chiefly to show that foreigners in Soviet prisons are sometimes much better treated than Soviet citizens.

On the way to one of my innumerable interrogations at Lefortovo I passed a lad in the corridor wearing such long trousers that he could hardly walk. At first I thought he was a dwarf, but then I saw it was a boy of about ten. I expressed my astonishment to Colonel Nikitin, who laughed and said the boy had been caught leaving the American Embassy. When asked what he was doing there and who had recruited him as a spy, he had replied that he only went to find out how he could get to America, where he had heard life was so good for everybody. The embassy secretary had told him to come back when he was grown up and could get a passport. It is almost beyond belief that the authorities could take a 'spy' of this calibre so seriously as to immure him in the dungeons of Lefortovo.

At Butyrka I came across many Soviet women who had worked for foreign embassies and who, needless to say, were all accused of espionage. I remember especially Margarita Shidlovskaya, who had been a secretary at the Swedish Embassy from 1924 to 1949 and was supposed to have been recruited by Sohlman, the ambassador. She showed the utmost fortitude and bravery, and often sang songs to cheer up her companions in misfortune. She was certain she would not come out of jail alive, and I think she was in fact executed. All Soviet citizens who had anything to do with foreign embassies, even as cleaners or sweepers, could reasonably expect the same charge and the same fate. One such was a frail old woman known as 'Aunt Polya', who had been cook to an American diplomat in Moscow. Her sister had come to see her one day with a friend from a collective farm not far off; they had brought some bread from the farm, and the diplomat asked if he might taste it. Shortly afterwards, an American periodical published an article about Russian farm-house bread. This was sufficient to brand Aunt Polya and the other two women as security risks and they were all thrown into prison.

I should make it clear that not all the interrogators were ruthless, hard-bitten types: some were understanding and considerate, like Colonel Nikitin, to whom I could sometimes talk on general subjects. I complained to him once about Polyansky's rudeness, and he suggested that I should ask the head of the department to put him, Nikitin, in sole charge of my case—prisoners were allowed to make requests of this kind. I did so, and the request was granted. My long sessions with Nikitin could indeed have been much worse than they were. We were both, in a sense, acting a part—he as the stern official demanding answers, I as the stubborn, wrongly accused prisoner—but basically we understood each other and got along quite well. I once told him that I thought he was a kind, well-meaning man with an unpleasant job to do, and this remark pleased him. He himself once said that he found our arguments very interesting, and added: 'When you are set free it would be nice if I could come and see you: we should have a lot to talk about.'

I should also record that, long and exhausting as the interrogations were, I myself was never treated with physical cruelty, though I had to listen to plenty of threats and insults during both periods of questioning, month after month. Sometimes I was threatened with execution, then as often as not would follow the jest: 'You aren't worth the fourteen kopecks that a bullet would cost.'

VIII

Five and a Half Years at Potma

About the end of 1950 I was moved into a large cell at Butyrka. My companions were intelligent women of good education who received me kindly. They said that everyone in the cell was awaiting deportation to a labour camp, though they did not know where. One of them, a Finnish girl called Mäntylä, had studied at the Communist University for Western National Minorities and was charged with being a spy; I do not know what became of her. A young Ukrainian doctor, Olga Kochegub, had been sentenced to twenty-five years for nationalism, and she and I were together in camp for nearly six years.

After nearly a week in the cell we were moved to what had once been the prison chapel. We had to sleep on the floor, but we were pleased at the change of abode, as it was a warm summer and we were free to walk about in the surrounding garden. In the middle of August, however, we were taken in a closed lorry across Moscow to a railway station, and there put into a 'Stolypin carriage' which was coupled to a goods train. So we set off again for an unknown destination. Was it to be within the Arctic Circle, where I had already spent eight long years? ... To our relief, the carriage was taken off the train at a small station named Potma, which, as they told us, was 250 miles east of Moscow on the Kuibyshev line. It was a fine summer's day; the station was surrounded by a dense oak forest, and a narrow-gauge line led to the camp area, to which we were taken in the dark, cramped carriage. The locomotive stopped at the gate of the thirteenth zone, and our carriage door was opened by warders with leashed bloodhounds. So here we were in the camp at Potma, where the discipline was said to be exceptionally severe.

We were lodged in a fenced-in barrack and told that we would soon be transferred to other quarters. Our home was empty except for the bunks, which looked relatively new; but we found with horror that the planking of the floor was so covered with fat bugs as to be almost invisible. We begged the commandant to come and have a look. He replied angrily that our predecessors had been an uncultivated lot, always singing and praying, and had not minded the bugs in the least. This seemed strange to us, but we took his word for it. In any case he allowed us to rip out the boards and scour them with boiling water and disinfectant, after which the bugs disappeared.

When I had a chance to look about me in the zone, I was pleased to find that I was in much better company than at Vorkuta, where the sexes were not separated and common-law criminals and politicals were mixed up together. Here all my fellow-inmates were political, most of them being wives of 'enemies of the people' who had failed to denounce their menfolk to the authorities. Their children had been taken away, nobody knew where, and their husbands were in prison or had already been shot. Many of the women were young Ukrainians. also Lithuanians, Latvians, Estonians and natives of many other European countries.

After my arrival in Potma I was informed that I had been sentenced to fifteen years' hard labour for counter-revolutionary activity. Thus for the second time I had been condemned without trial and without even being told in writing what I was charged with. Like most of my companions I also did not know what court, or *troika* as the special 'boards' were popularly called, had sentenced me for my alleged offence.

Compared with Vorkuta, I am bound to say that Potma was a lesser evil. The climate was much milder and the living quarters and food were better; the discipline, on the other hand, was much more strict. Every prisoner had to sign a statement on arrival acknowledging that he or she might be executed for the slightest infringement of the rules; this was put into practice, and the executions were announced over the camp radio.

Thanks to special instructions from Moscow, I was not made to do forced labour. This was a great alleviation, as female prisoners generally worked in the fields until they collapsed.

The camp extended over a large area and comprised thirty-six zones. It is hard to say how many prisoners there were, but certainly many thousands. I lived in three different zones during my time there, and thus got a general idea of the layout. The camp probably dates back to the Russo-Japanese war of 1904-5; it was enlarged and used for POWs in the First World War.

A curious incident happened soon after my arrival, when a female prisoner came and said that someone outside the enclosure wanted to speak to me. I was surprised that anyone knew I was there, and it was strictly forbidden to talk through the gap in the fence. However, I went to it and heard someone whisper: 'Are you Kuusinen?' When I said yes, the voice went on: 'Are you Hertta Kuusinen?'

'No, I am Aino Kuusinen.'

'Is Hertta in the camp too?'

'No, I believe she's in Finland.'

'When I heard there was a woman named Kuusinen in the last lot of prisoners, I came here to kill her.'

I laughed and replied: 'Please don't kill me, I've done nothing wrong.'

'No, I won't kill you, but I'll kill Hertta Kuusinen when I get out of here. I'll find her and kill her, because it was she who got me sent here.'

Later, when our group was assigned to new quarters, I met the woman who had spoken to me and she told me her story. Her name was Katya: she was a charming girl from Leningrad who spoke Finnish well, though with an accent. She had been captured by Finnish troops on Soviet soil during the Russo-Finnish war and was interned for a time, but was soon released and allowed to seek work in Finland. She became a waitress in an officers' club in a small town on the Gulf of Bothnia; there she found 'a man for a husband', as she put it, and when he left the service they settled on the family farm, where his mother welcomed them both. The couple had a son, and the little family were very happy together. But when the Russo-Finnish armistice was signed, the Soviet government demanded that all Soviet citizens should be sent back to Russia, and Katya soon found herself in the Katajanokka prison at Helsinki, awaiting homeward transport.

One Sunday morning the group of Soviet citizens were told that Hertta Kuusinen wanted to give a coffee-party for them. They were taken to a large hall, and over the coffee and cakes Hertta made a speech about the loving care of the Soviet government and the good life that awaited them. When someone called out that this was untrue and that they would all be put in prison, Hertta replied indignantly that such ideas were bourgeois propaganda. But they proved to be no more than the truth: as soon as the train was over the frontier, the home-comers were told that the first thing in store for them was five years' hard labour. Katya blamed Hertta personally for her misfortune; I argued that Hertta probably had nothing to do with the decision, but Katya said she knew better and would have her revenge one day.

Since our first encounter with the zone commandant I had realized that religious believers were the butt of special persecution. As I got to know the camp, I discovered the exact value of the freedom of religion that the Soviet constitution guarantees to every citizen.

While I was in the fourteenth zone a new hut was built of stout logs, with narrow grated crevices under the eaves in lieu of windows. This was to house a group of deeply religious Russian women who refused to work in the fields and spent their time praying aloud and singing hymns. These 'nuns', as they were sarcastically called, were not fed with the rest of us but were given bread and soup in their own hut; an armed soldier escorted them to the latrine twice a day. From time to time the commandant would visit their quarters with a whip, and the hut resounded with shrieks of pain: the women were usually stripped before being beaten, but no cruelty could dissuade them from their habits of praying and fasting. Besides refusing to perform manual labour they also objected to prison clothes because of the numbers on the back; as they were not allowed to wear anything of their own, the numbers were stamped on their bare flesh instead. Those in the 'religious huts' also refused to attend morning and evening roll-call. Some 'nuns' who lived in our hut were made to attend these parades stark naked in all weathers, and it was heartbreaking to see their emaciated forms.

One day the commandant ordered me to go with him to the nuns' barrack, taking a clinical thermometer. Standing in the doorway he shouted: 'Any sick?' The prisoners pointed to a woman who had a high fever and seemed on the point of death, and she was taken to the camp hospital. While I was attending to her the warder noticed that the women were one short, and the missing one was found under a bed. She refused to stand up when ordered; the warder dragged her out roughly, and she lay naked in the middle of the floor. It was a girl of eighteen, who had just left school and, for attending a religious service, had been arrested as an 'enemy of the people'. As she still refused to get up, other warders came to the first one's aid and she was stood on her feet like a statue, to the accompaniment of jeers and mockery. I took her to her bed, put her clothes on and spoke a few words of consolation, whereupon the warder shouted: 'Don't you be so kind to that she-devil!'

During my time in the fourteenth zone the women in the hut sang hymns and prayed without interruption, until one day the noise ceased—they had been taken away, most probably to a martyr's death.

Another unusual character at Potma was an aged, infirm peasant woman known as 'Moya Radost' ('my delight'), because she bestowed this charming endearment on everyone. She was a true old-style Russian peasant, of simple disposition and profoundly religious. She spoke surprisingly good Russian, with a large vocabulary considering she had never been to school. Her life story was a touching one. Her mother, who was desperately poor, had sold her in 1895 or so for two hundred roubles to a much older man, who married her. He turned out to be a sadist, and treated her so badly as to injure her health. She escaped to her mother several times, but the latter only sent her back, and the priest would not help her either. In the end she ran away and asked a convent to admit her as a nun, but they would not because she was married. She then sought refuge on a farm: the farmer's wife gave her a small room next to the kitchen and sent for a doctor, who said she would never be properly well and must not do any heavy work. However, they kept her on as a kitchen-maid, she learnt to read and her health improved slightly. She went to church every Sunday, and the village priest let her look after the candles and consecrated bread.

So the years went on, and Moya Radost was contented and happy. But then came the Revolution: the farm was burnt down, and the owner and his family murdered. The priest was arrested for 'spying', and so was Moya Radost—though, as she said laughingly to me, 'I still don't know what a spy does.' But there was nothing to laugh at at the time, as she was sentenced to prison camp for I forget how many years for endangering state security.

At Potma she and I were both for a time in the thirteenth zone, together with many young women from Estonia, Latvia and Lithuania. Moya Radost was too old and feeble to work, and we all treated her kindly. One Easter day a miracle happened: she was told that a letter and parcel had come for her and that she was to fetch them at the commandant's office. Having nothing else to do at the time, I went with her. The things were from her old parish priest, who had been set free by this time, and the parcel contained food and a hard-boiled goose's egg with an elaborate picture of the Virgin on it. But alas, this was religious propaganda, so the commandant broke the egg to pieces. At my entreaty he let Moya Radost have it in its broken state, and even this filled her with joy because the egg had been blessed by her priest. She shared the edible part with her friends and kept the shell as an icon, crossing herself before it from that day onwards, and blissful in her simplicity and humility.

Most of the inmates of the thirteenth zone were sent in the fullness of time to collect pitch in the remotest parts of Siberia, whence they sent letters describing their appalling living conditions. But Moya Radost was set free, together with another woman, and I last saw them both as they set out in the direction of their former homes. I wonder if Moya Radost ever saw her old church again—it was the dearest wish of her heart.

Remarkable as it may sound, there was a four-legged prisoner at Potma—a large, ugly, one-eyed horse, a broken-down veteran that had been captured from the Germans. He was used for hauling water, and reminded me of a celebrated horse in *Seven Brothers* by the Finnish writer Aleksis Kivi. The peculiarity of the one at Potma was that it would neigh joyfully if it heard so much as a word in German, but reacted to no other language. The German women in the camp loved this compatriot of theirs, gave him bread out of their meagre rations and told him their sorrows, and doubtless the horse was moved by their attention. One day, however, it met with a sad accident. It was standing in front of the cookhouse after taking a cartload of food to some women working in the fields, when suddenly the empty mess-cans fell off the cart with a clatter. The horse shied, and hit its head against the wall so violently that it killed itself. The German prisoners mourned it sincerely, and were hardly consoled by the fact that the poor beast made an excellent soup.

From the fourteenth zone I was moved to the sixteenth, and in mid-February 1952 I was told to expect another transfer. Next morning I was put on to a lorry with my few possessions and we drove off towards the station. I expected a train journey, but instead we stopped at an enclosed area containing three new-looking houses, two storeys high. There was a sentry at the gate, but no guard-dog. I was taken to a clean, comfortable room where I found two women already installed: Saima Ahmala, a Finn from Oulu (Uleåborg), and Vera Leontievna Nekrasova, a professor of biology from Leningrad. Now I really was in good company! My new home, it turned out, was known as the 'rest-house' (*dom invalidov*) and was a place of residence for prisoners who were shortly to be released. Most of them were foreigners, in particular Germans, Ukrainians, Estonians and Latvians. There was another Finn besides Saima and myself, namely Olga Hietala from Helsinki. The inmates were of all ages, some ill and some not, and the purpose of keeping them here was apparently to soften the memory of their appalling treatment in prison before they were set free. It was a much more comfortable place than the camp barracks; the food was better, and was served by neatly dressed Mordvin girls—the Mordvins, a Finno-Ugrian tribe, are the chief indigenous race in that part of the Soviet Union. We even had a library at our disposal, and could walk freely in the oak woods and enjoy the sight of the flowers and bushes in summer.

Several of my friends were released in the ensuing months, but for some time I heard nothing. Then an event took place which almost dashed my hopes of liberation once and for all. At the beginning of March 1953 I was told to report to the chief political officer of the camp: this was always an ominous sign, and I wondered anxiously what it might mean. I was received by an officer whom I had not seen before; he spoke in a friendly way and even asked me to sit down. He drew out a pile of papers from a brief-case on the desk, slapped it with his palm and said: 'These are the records of your interrogation. My chief in Moscow has sent me here to find out how you are. Have you any complaints?' I replied that I had never complained, since I knew it would be no use. He then began to commend my intelligence, which I knew from experience was a bad omen. He said he had read the documents and knew all about me, including the fact that I spoke several languages; then, suddenly: 'Could you write a letter in English?' I said I could, and asked whom it was to go to. 'Never mind that for the moment; write anything you like, but don't say you're in prison. You must say you are writing from Saransk [the capital of the Mordvinian Autonomous Republic]. It doesn't matter about the address, we'll put that on.' Then he added: 'You'll be going back to Moscow soon, and you can live in style, with all the clothes, hats and shoes you want.' He ended the conversation by saying that he had to go and see the commandant and would talk to me again next morning.

I could not sleep a wink that night for worrying about what I should do. If I refused to write the letter I would be signing my own death warrant, and executions in Potma were carried out every day. But if I agreed, it would come to the same thing, since once I had written the letter the NKVD (or MVD as it now was) would not need me any more and my knowledge would be dangerous. However, I was determined on no account to degrade myself by doing anything at the behest of Stalin or Beria.

Next morning an Estonian woman asked me in the washroom if I had heard the wireless bulletin. I replied: 'No, I never bother with the radio—there's nothing on it that concerns us.'

'Doesn't concern us?' she exclaimed. 'Then you don't know that Stalin has died. We're all sure to be set free now.'

What astounding news! We were all filled with indescribable relief, and were convinced that the reign of terror and lawlessness would be ended at a single stroke. This feeling was strengthened by the confusion and disarray which prevailed among the camp officials, who suddenly ceased to take notice of us. Many of them disappeared, including the handsome officer who had tried to persuade me to write the fatal letter. So Stalin's death came in the nick of time as far as I was concerned, though it was another two and a half years before I left Potma.

For four days on end the camp radio broadcast nothing but funeral marches. Overjoyed as the prisoners were at the tyrant's death, they did not dare to show their feelings at first, and many counterfeited deep sorrow, hoping thus to improve their lot. One old Communist woman, a notorious informer, wept bitter tears and said to me: 'How frightful! How terrible! Why aren't you crying?'

'What for?'

'Haven't you heard the news?'

'Yes.'

'And you're not crying?'

'I have no tears left,' I replied, and cut short the conversation. It was as well to be careful: the leaders had changed, but did that mean that the system would?

About four months later Beria was dismissed; this of course delighted the prisoners too, but it did not speed up liberation from the camp, and caused less confusion than Stalin's death. Only a few more officers disappeared; but when the news of Beria's execution was broadcast, a miracle happened—the MVD men actually demeaned themselves so far as to discuss the event with the prisoners. One morning I was called to the office of the ideological instructor—an amiable, rather stupid man—who offered me a chair and said: 'Imagine it, Beria had been a British spy ever since 1919. What do you think of that?'

'Has it been proved?' I asked with feigned surprise.

'Yes, it has, and all our state secrets have been leaked to the British.' And he gave a deep sigh.

It was astonishing to me that such crude lies should be offered to the Soviet public. Beria had committed enough domestic crimes to justify his execution without inventing foreign ones; the question was rather whether he had been tried by any court. When I got to Moscow in October 1955 there were conflicting rumours about this. A high official told me that Beria and his immediate staff had been sentenced by a court, and that his last words before execution and cremation in the Lubyanka had been: 'The charges are all true, but every single thing I did was approved by Stalin.'

I will say a word here about the experiences of my two Finnish companions in the 'rest-house'. Saima Ahmala came to Petrozavodsk at the time of the Karelian fever, in 1932; she married a Finn there and they had a daughter, Tellervo. Some years later the NKVD 'discovered' that her husband was a spy, and he was shot. Saima was allowed to go on working for a short while as a restaurant cashier; then her home was expropriated, though she and the child were allowed at first to go on living in the attic, with no source of warmth except the chimney. A few months later she was arrested for failing to inform the authorities of her husband's 'treason'. She spent years in various prisons and eventually came to Potma, where she fell ill and was moved to the 'rest-house'. She was in a state of nervous collapse, and was desperate at not knowing what had become of Tellervo. All her efforts to trace the child had been in vain. I helped her to address another appeal to Petrozavodsk, and this time she heard that Tellervo was with foster-parents there. Shortly before, Saima herself had asked to be allowed to return to Finland. This request was granted, and she now wrote to the foster-parents begging them to let Tellervo go to Finland with her. She also wrote to her daughter, but Tellervo replied in Russian that she did not understand Finnish or regard Saima as her mother, and that the Soviet Union was her homeland. This letter was of course dictated to the girl, but Saima could not appeal against it and had to go back to Finland alone.

Olga Hietala's story was equally tragic. In 1918, in Petrograd, she had married a Latvian, who was killed in the Kronstadt rising of 1921. Having left Finland illegally she feared to be punished if she returned, and therefore stayed in Petrograd. In 1932 she met a Finnish-American named Leevi Hietala who, as I related in an earlier chapter, was sent with two other printing experts to assemble the press which was shipped to Leningrad for the use of the Finnish-language newspaper *Vapaus*. When the task was completed his two companions went back to America, but Leevi stayed and married Olga. Soon after, they were both arrested as spies; Olga was sent from one Siberian camp to another and finally to Potma, whence she was set free later than I was. Her relatives tried to obtain permission for her to go to Helsinki, but by this time her mental health was in danger. She returned to Leningrad to try and discover where her husband was, and finally learnt from the public prosecutor's office that he had died in the Arctic gold-mining camp of Kolyma, from which few prisoners emerged alive.

On several occasions I helped fellow-prisoners to write applications for their sentences to be reviewed; sometimes these resulted in the sentence being shortened or even cancelled. One day I decided to take my own case in hand. I wrote a letter to the Procurator-General of the USSR, not asking for release but only for a revision of the judgement against me. I pointed out that I had been deprived of liberty for over fifteen years without having ever been put on trial or informed in what way I had broken the laws of the land. If it should be found on investigation that I was guilty in any way, I would submit to any punishment that might be inflicted according to law.

In October 1955 I received the following reply:

Chief Military Section,
Office of the Procurator-General of the USSR
No. 1d-23235-49

41 Kirov Street,
Moscow.
12 October 1955.

To Aino Andreyevna Kuusinen,
   Zubo-Polyansky Rest-House,
   Potma, Mordvinian ASSR.

With reference to your application of 15 July 1955 to the Procurator-General of the USSR, I have to inform you that by a decision of 29 August 1955 on the part of the Procurator-General's Office, the Ministry of Internal Affairs and the State Security Committee of the Council of Ministers of the USSR, the judgements of the Special Board [*soveshchaniye*] against you in 1939 and 1950 are annulled and the proceedings terminated, owing to the absence of a *corpus delicti.*

For the Chief Military Section,
(signed) Major Dashkevich.

In this way I was informed without a vestige of concern or apology that fifteen years of imprisonment with forced labour were due to a mistake.

IX

My Final Release and Departure for Finland

I left Potma on 17 October 1955 and arrived at the Kazan Station in Moscow at 5 a.m. next day. The city was dark and it was raining in torrents. I sat for a while in the station restaurant, wondering what to do and to whom to apply. I had heard that since Stalin's death two and a half years before, Moscow had become so 'democratic' that one could simply go to an office in the Kuznetsky Most and talk to an officer of the secret police. Exhausted as I was, I resolved to do just that.

It was still raining when I left the station, and I plodded through the wet streets till I found the building. I went in and found myself in a corridor; one of the doors bore a brass plate with the letters MVD. This opened into a small waiting-room in which three women were sitting in deep silence; I took my place beside them. Shortly a man in uniform appeared through another door leading to an office, and said 'Next' in a bored voice. One of the women went in. In a few minutes she came out weeping. After the next two were dealt with I entered the small office, where a colonel of stocky build and impenetrable countenance sat behind a large desk. Without offering me a chair, he asked bluntly what I wanted.

I began hesitatingly to tell him that I had just been released from a labour camp and did not know how to start my new life. He questioned me about my past, and I answered truthfully. Then he read my name on the certificate of release and asked if I knew the Kuusinen who was a member of the Presidium of the Supreme Soviet. I said with careful nonchalance that I did.

'Is he any relation of yours?'

'Yes, he's my husband.'

At this the colonel jumped up in consternation and paced about the room, muttering to himself; then he collapsed on to his chair with a groan, saying: 'Now I've started something, and no mistake!' For a while he was too overcome to continue, but at last he collected himself and said: 'I suppose you'll go back to live with your husband now?'

'No, I shan't.'

'Why not? He's sure to be expecting you.'

'It's against my dignity as a woman. I'm independent now, and I mean to make a new life on my own.'

The colonel shook his head. 'If I were you I'd go straight to my husband and say: "Hullo, here I am again."'

I replied: 'Maybe you would, but I'm not going back to him.' This argument went on for some time, in quite a friendly tone, but I saw I was getting nowhere and took my leave; the colonel asked me to let him know what happened.

It was still raining hard, and I still did not know what to do. Once I had known many people in the great city, but most of them had vanished in Stalin's purges and I did not have the courage to look up any of the survivors, knowing that they would be scared out of their wits if somebody visited them straight from prison camp. No, I meant to make a new beginning and not cause unpleasantness to anyone.

Wandering along the streaming pavements, I finally decided to go to the headquarters of the Party Central Committee and simply ask where I should apply for help. I entered the huge building without hindrance; as I remembered, it was full of glass doors bearing the names of different Party high-ups whom one might see if the receptionist permitted it. Several of the names were familiar, and on one of the doors I read 'Otto W. Kuusinen'—and walked past it.

I went to the waiting-room and wrote a note to the chairman of the Party Control Commission, asking for an interview and saying that I would wait on the pavement outside the building for his reply: there was indeed nowhere else I could go. A girl was seated at a desk with a sign on it saying 'Post', but she explained that this was for official letters and not personal ones; however, as she had a pleasant manner I ventured to tell her my name, and she took my note and promised to pass it to the addressee. So here was at least one person not enslaved to heartless bureaucracy. I was pleased that my appeal was on its way, but having no address to give I felt despondent as to the result.

I went out again into the rain and tried to think things over. I was wet through and exhausted, but I had to do something, so I decided with a heavy heart to look up a family with whom I had been friendly in the distant past, and who I thought might take me in until I could make some plans. I was on Nogin Square and it was a long way to Gogol Prospekt where they had lived, but I somehow managed to get there. I hesitated a long while on the doorstep, wondering if they would refuse to receive an ex-convict, but finally I rang the bell and my friend opened the door: he and his wife were both Old Bolsheviks, and he held a high official position. To my delight and relief they received me cordially, took off my wet coat and gave me breakfast. I told them I had returned from camp that very morning, and asked timidly if I might stay the night. They said I could, and that they had known of my arrest. They also told me what had happened to various friends and acquaintances of ours who had fallen victim to Stalin's tyranny and had not survived, as I had, to tell the tale.

Later my friends went off to work, leaving me to rest and sort out my ideas. I could not help thinking of the past, and of the strange tricks life had played since I came to the 'workers' paradise' in 1922, over thirty-three years ago.

Before long my host came back from his office to ask me more questions, and I told him of my visit to Party headquarters and my appeal to the chairman of the Control Commission. He rang up the Commission's office and handed me the receiver; the man who answered told me to ring a certain number at once and ask for Colonel Stroganov. I did so, and the colonel gave me his address and asked me to go and see him, adding that when my note was received a search had been made for me outside the headquarters building.

I felt too weak and confused to go alone, and asked my old friend to accompany me to the colonel's address. It proved to my surprise to be a large military office: I obtained a pass at the entrance, but realized that I was afraid to make my way anywhere alone. For years I had not taken a step except in someone's company. Although I was now free, it would take time to re-learn the ways of freedom. However, with the commandant's help I found Colonel Stroganov, who had been told of my arrival and greeted me pleasantly. He had instructions from the Commission to look after me, and invited me to say frankly what I wanted, as he knew no details. I sighed with relief —at least this handsome colonel was not a jailer—and replied: 'I really don't know where to begin. I have nothing in the world, absolutely nothing—no food, no money and nowhere to live. Some old friends have asked me to stay with them tonight, but in all conscience I can't ask any more of them.'

The colonel at once sent for a cashier and gave me some money, after which he sent me off to an army hotel in the Sokol district, where I was quartered in a room with two officers' wives. I stayed at the hotel nearly three months, seeing Colonel Stroganov every few days and drawing from him enough money for my bed and board. He treated me with the utmost sympathy and consideration, and I shall always remember him gratefully. He also procured the papers I needed in order to apply to the Moscow authorities for a place to live. Unfortunately the housing committee was extremely corrupt and one could get nowhere except by bribing heavily; the colonel was an honest man, and consequently the papers he obtained were of very little use.

In February 1956 I left the hotel at Sokol, which was really for officers and their families in transit, and moved to Kuchino, about twenty minutes from Moscow by rail; the colonel got me a room with a balcony in one of three villas which had housed captive German generals during the war and were now used as quarters for married officers. I enjoyed resting at last in the peaceful atmosphere, and took many walks in the nearby fir-woods. I made friends by degrees with the officers' wives and children, and it seemed as if my life, all at once, had become one of quiet and security. I sometimes went to Moscow and saw old friends; they urged me to get in touch with Otto, and I felt some temptation to do so, but not enough to overcome my wounded pride. Colonel Stroganov continued to supply me with money and to look out for a flat; I tried hard to find one and stood in queues at the City Soviet office, but in vain. Eight months passed in this way, with repeated visits to Stroganov's office and to housing bureaux. In spite of all the documents I had accumulated, the authorities at every level seemed determined to ignore my application, and I had to return to Stroganov time and again and tell him I had failed.

The housing office of the City Soviet was in a basement: a female receptionist of masterful appearance sat at the end of a rectangular hall filled with an endless queue of people. I paid several visits without getting as far as this young lady, whose desk was beside a door leading to the director's office. One day I lost patience, pushed to the head of the queue and asked to see the director, to which she replied haughtily that he could not be disturbed. I went to Stroganov and told him of this, adding that there was no point in my going back again—I should obviously never get a flat in Moscow. I also told him how I had seen a poorly dressed old woman of the working class collapse in a faint at the receptionist's desk when she heard that there were people who had been coming every day for five years to find out how matters stood with their application. However, Stroganov persuaded me to go once more, and I returned to the basement office on the following day. To my surprise the hall was empty, and I wondered if it was some sort of holiday; but I then saw that the director's door was ajar, so I went up slowly to it and knocked. Inside was a woman I had never seen before; I greeted her politely and she told me she was standing in for the director, who was on leave. I said I only wished to know whether my application for a flat had been considered. 'When was it put in? Only two months ago? Then it certainly won't have been dealt with yet,' she replied with a smile. 'We have too much to do.'

'But I have several recommendations and all sorts of official papers.'

'That makes no difference.'

'I hope I shan't have to apply to other quarters. My friends are people of influence, and they've asked more than once for something to be done. As that seems to have no effect, I suppose

I must try other methods.'

'What other methods?'

'Is President Voroshilov one of your superiors?'

'You can apply to anyone you like. It's our business to allot accommodation, and nobody can dictate to us what we do.'

'But isn't the President of the Soviet Union more important than the Moscow Soviet?'

'We act as we see fit. When it's your turn, if you get a flat at all, you'll get it through us.'

This was enough for me, but before leaving I took care to ascertain the woman's name. I was boiling with rage, and as soon as I got back to my room I wrote a long letter to Voroshilov describing in detail the obstruction that I and other applicants for homes encountered from the Moscow Soviet. I said I had written to its chairman, Bobrovnikov, asking for an interview, but he had neither replied to my letter nor given any instructions concerning my application. I also told Voroshilov of the old woman who had fainted, and of the director's deputy who had told me that the President of the Soviet Union had no say in accommodation matters.

Miraculously, this letter produced the desired effect. As I heard later, Voroshilov sent it to Bobrovnikov with a note in his own hand telling him to grant my application at once. A day or two after sending the letter I was invited to the housing office—not in the basement this time—and, without having to wait my turn, was asked politely what kind of flat I wanted and in what part of the city. 'President Voroshilov's instructions are that you are free to choose.'

It was hard enough for me, as a rehabilitated ex-convict, to start a normal life again. For those who were merely released without exoneration for their 'crimes' it was infinitely harder, and often downright impossible.

Many of my old friends had died while I was away, either in the course of nature or as victims of the Stalin terror. To my great joy Elena Stasova, who had lived in the same house as Kuusinen and I many years ago, was still alive. She was over eighty but still mentally alert, though her sight had failed considerably. I stayed with her several weeks at her invitation. She too had been a victim of the terror, but was now rehabilitated:

she received a small pension and spent every morning dictating memoirs to her secretary.

Elena belonged to a well-to-do family of the nobility and was very well educated: as a child she learnt fluent English, French and German. Her father, Dmitri Stasov, was a prominent barrister in Tsarist times and used to defend persons arrested on political charges; it was from him that Elena inherited her democratic ideals, including that of raising the cultural level of the Russian people. After leaving school she became a student teacher, and at that time met the fiery young Vladimir Ulyanov —Lenin himself—so that, not surprisingly, she joined the revolutionary movement. She was a Bolshevik from her early days at the university; Lenin had much to thank her for, and at his instance she was appointed secretary of the Party's Central Committee—a post of high distinction for a woman, which she held from 1917 to 1920. After the foundation of the Comintern she was sent to Europe as a political adviser, working chiefly in Berlin, and was an outstandingly skilful organizer of clandestine activity. After the collapse of the Communist rising in Germany in 1923 she was recalled to Moscow and put in charge of MOPR (International Aid to Revolutionary Fighters, also known as International Red Relief), which afforded help to political prisoners and other revolutionaries in capitalist countries. In 1938 she became editor of the Soviet periodical *International Literature*, which appeared in German, French and English; but after the war Stalin relieved her of this job and she spent eight months in the *Spetskorpus* prison which was generally reserved for the most dangerous political offenders.

Unlike most of the Bolsheviks, Elena Stasova was a true and unshakeable idealist who saw the good in everything and remained optimistic even in the darkest hour, whatever might happen to herself or those about her. Having been Party secretary she perhaps knew the revolutionaries of the old generation better than anyone else did, and was consulted about personalities by government departments, including the Procurator-General's office. She told me one day while I was staying with her that the latter had rung up to ask whether she knew me from the time of the Stalin purges and what she thought of me. The Procurator himself, moreover, wanted me to write a report on improper methods of interrogation and to say if I knew any cases in which prisoners had been treated in a manner contrary to Soviet law, so that the guilty officials might be prosecuted. After thinking this over for a while I told Elena that Colonel Polyansky had certainly treated me very badly but that I did not care whether he was brought to trial or not. 'Please tell the Procurator that I want to forget that part of my life as quickly and completely as possible. I was interrogated by twenty-six men altogether, and it's all the same to me now whether the government wants to shoot them or promote them to be ministers.'

One rainy day in late October I was walking along the Gogol Prospekt when a man coming towards me exclaimed: 'Aino Andreyevna, is it really you?' This was General Berzin's brother, who had still been at Potma when I was released. He was unkempt and looked tired and ill, much worse than when I had last seen him. Like his brother, he was an Old Bolshevik and revolutionary fighter and had held high office, being public prosecutor at one time; he had been arrested under Stalin like so many others, but had contrived to remain alive and had now been rehabilitated. He asked me how I was getting on and whether I had seen Kuusinen. I replied that I had not seen Otto and did not intend to try, but that on the Central Committee's orders an officer had looked after me, given me money and done his best to get me a flat. Berzin looked astonished and said: 'I'm glad you were so lucky. No one has done anything for me.'

'Where do you sleep at night?' I asked.

'In a wooden barrack on the edge of the town; the Central Committee have taken it over and it houses about a hundred ex-prisoners. That's the best I get—an Old Bolshevik and a former public prosecutor as well. When I think of all the years my brother and I served the Party so faithfully ...' We exchanged a few more words, as gloomy as the weather, and parted wishing each other 'the best of luck'; what more was there to say or do? But the meeting showed once again what Colonel Stroganov's help had meant to me.

And now at last I was able to move into my own home—again with the aid of Stroganov, who gave me enough money to equip it and also arranged a monthly allowance. I felt almost well off, and was glad not to have the worries of those who, on paper, were richer than I was. One day I went to see a doctor friend and was surprised to find her in floods of tears; when I asked why, she said that by a decree published in that day's paper the government had cancelled all State loans. These had been extracted from Soviet citizens over the years by compulsory deductions from their wages and salaries, and now that they hoped to reap the benefit in their old age the bonds turned out to be useless paper. My friend told me between her sobs that she and her husband had forty and sixty thousand roubles' worth respectively and had hoped to buy a little villa for when they retired, but this was now an idle dream. This couple was only one of millions who were bilked by their government in this way. It was a blow that could not befall me, as owing to my many years in prison I held no government bonds. No other regime in the civilized world could have perpetrated such a shameful trick; the population, one and all, were embittered, but nobody dared to criticize. Admittedly this financial juggling was a small matter compared with the horrors of Stalin's rule, which had terrorized people so thoroughly that they could hardly believe the dictator was not still there. Scarcely a single family in Moscow was unscathed by the purges, yet even now nobody said a word about them. I did not tell even my closest friends of my prison and camp experiences, and such was the universal grip of fear that they asked no questions.

It must seem extraordinary in Western countries that, all these years after Stalin's death, the Soviet regime still does not venture to denounce or repudiate the dictator's system. It is true that Khrushchev at the twentieth Party Congress in February 1956 made a speech exposing Stalin's misdeeds, but this was in secret session and the speech has not been published in the Soviet Union: official publications after the congress reproduced the criticism of Stalin in a much diluted form, though a shortened version of Krushchev's speech was read out at closed sessions of Party institutions and, in some cases, of the Communist Youth League. Many Soviet citizens continued to maintain silence concerning the reign of terror, while others at last began to discuss it freely and to hope that a period of liberalization was in sight. I myself did not read the speech till years later, in a book that I bought after leaving the USSR.

Now that my own affairs were to some extent in order, I resolved to find out what had become of my brother Väinö. I had had no news of him for more than twenty years, since he was arrested in the Karelian purge in December 1935 and brought to Leningrad. I now wrote to his wife in Petrozavodsk and, getting no answer, went there myself, but could not find her. For three and a half years, from 1956 to 1960, I bombarded the authorities with requests for information. Finally I received a certificate from the military court of the Northern Military District at Petrozavodsk: this was dated 3 May 1960 and stated that the sentence passed on Väinö on 11 November 1937 had been annulled, as he was guilty of no crime, and that he had been posthumously rehabilitated. So he must have had a few days longer to suffer before reaching the end of his journey. His wife had no doubt been executed also, for failing to report his 'espionage' to the authorities.

Soon after moving into my flat I received a surprise summons to the personnel department of the general staff. I turned up punctually and was shown into a large room in which several senior officers were seated at a long table. The chairman, an admiral, made me sit opposite him and delivered a short speech expressing regret for the arbitrary and unjust way in which I had been treated: he hoped that I would 'erase these unpleasant events from my memory'. This, it seems, was the official re-habilitation ceremony. When it was over, one of the generals saw me out and asked me, as I took my leave, to promise to forget all that had happened. I replied that such a promise would be a lie, as I could never forget what I had undergone; to which he answered in a low voice: 'Yes, I quite understand.'

In 1957 I was present at another evening session in the general staff building. A woman appeared at my flat one morning with an invitation from a party committee: she said that the meeting was to be an important one and that a retired colonel who lived in the building would take me to it. I could not imagine why they wanted me there, but as they had gone to the trouble of providing an escort I accepted. When we got to the hall it was full of high-ranking officers. A civilian whom I did not know opened the meeting on behalf of the Central Committee and said there was only one item on the agenda. Then another man

in plain clothes said: 'Marshal Zhukov was summoned yesterday before the Central Committee to render an account of his
intrigues against the Party. The Committee resolved to deprive
him of his office as Minister of Defence.' The chairman asked if
anyone wished to comment, and to my surprise the colonel who
had escorted me stood up. He said he had fought in both world
wars and, as he knew Marshal Zhukov personally, would like to
hear the reason for his dismissal. The chairman replied angrily:
'How can a Communist of such old standing have the audacity
to ask what Zhukov has done, after the Party has investigated
the facts and taken its decision?' Another senior officer then
spoke and expressed satisfaction at the Central Committee's
resolution; a vote was taken approving it unanimously, and the
chairman dismissed the meeting.

On our way home the colonel made no secret of his wrath
at the disgraceful treatment of such a distinguished and admired
officer. The real reason, he was sure, was that Zhukov had
offended the Party by trying to curb its influence in army
circles.

A few days later I learnt the circumstances of Zhukov's dismissal from some old Party members. On his return from an
official visit to Yugoslavia and Albania he was met by Krushchev
at Vnukovo Airport and taken to the latter's office in the Central
Committee building, where a few other leaders were present
including the Committee's secretary, Ekaterina Furtseva.
Zhukov was given a seat opposite Krushchev, who proceeded to
harangue him on his 'hostile attitude towards the Party', after
which the indictment was pronounced by Furtseva. Zhukov, it
was said, had instituted a cult of his own personality and striven
after public glorification. He had commissioned a painting of
himself on a white horse like St George, inscribed 'Georgi
Zhukov, conqueror and liberator of the German people', and
had it hung in the Red Army museum—yet it was the Red
Army itself, and not Zhukov, that had liberated the German
people from Nazism.

'What have you to say in your defence?' Khrushchev had
asked. Zhukov, according to the story, replied calmly that
Nikita Khrushchev did not know the first thing about military
matters; as for Furtseva, he looked at her with silent contempt

Finally Khrushchev gave an order, the door opened and Zhukov was led off under escort, after which he was apparently kept under arrest for a while. Next day *Pravda* published a leading article maintaining that the war had been won by the Party and the Party alone, and that the Soviet people and the Red Army owed their victory to the Central Committee's leadership. Most of the paper's readers at the time had no idea against whom the article was directed.

There were in those days a remarkable number of Chinese in the streets of Moscow. Relations between the USSR and China were already under strain, but, to cover up this fact, Mao Tse-tung's visit in autumn 1957 was celebrated with great pomp. The whole population of Moscow was called out on to the streets to express its jubilation: many thousands paraded on Gorky Street and the Red Square, waving little Chinese flags and shouting 'Long live Mao and China!' Russo-Chinese friendship was the great topic of the day, and many women in Moscow were heard to say that Mao was the best-looking man they had ever seen. During those stirring days I went to see a doctor friend and found her gazing spellbound at a Chinese newspaper. When I asked laughingly if she could read Chinese she replied: 'No, but don't you see? ... it's printed in *China*!'

Many of course foresaw the Moscow-Peking conflict, but there were plenty of simple Soviet citizens at that time who still believed in friendship between the two powers. One Muscovite said to me: 'We don't need to be afraid of America any more. The Chinese army and our friendship with China have altered the whole world situation, and America can't do a thing about it.'

Pro-Chinese propaganda was incessant and skilful, and everything Chinese was belauded on every hand, but the friendship had its disadvantages for some sections of the community, such as university students. Hundreds of Chinese flocked to Moscow, filling hostels and lecture-halls and making it harder for Russians to pursue their studies. Both Chinese and Africans were highly unpopular for this reason. Many Russian engineers and academic specialists were sent to China to aid in the country's progress, but the Chinese delegations and tourists were so numerous that I think they outweighed the Russian visitors to China.

Then, one day in 1959, the dream came to an end: the friendship suddenly cooled, and the only hope was that this state of affairs would not be permanent. 'The Chinese can't get on without us'; in other words, the withdrawal of Soviet loans and technical aid would mean the end of China's industrial development.

While these political changes were going on, I was much concerned with myself and the fulfilment of my own hopes. I would have liked a job, but was not offered any that I was competent to do. The labour market was in an uncertain state: ordinary people were either frightened of being sacked or waiting for some congenial employment to be offered them on a plate, though they had little real idea of what they wanted. A workman once said to me: 'I'm just going to wait and see.' When I asked what he was waiting for, he replied: 'The same as everyone else.'

What I was waiting for was to know when I could leave the Soviet Union and go back to Finland. For the time being there was only one answer to this: as long as my husband was alive and occupying a high position, then, even though we were living apart, I had not the slightest hope of being given a passport to travel anywhere abroad, least of all Finland. This was shown clearly enough in 1958, when the Finnish government headed by Fagerholm, with Virolainen as Foreign Minister, refused to let Kuusinen into the country when the Finnish Communist Party invited him to speak at the fortieth anniversary of its foundation. Kuusinen having been refused a visa, it would be an affront to his honour and that of the Soviet Union if one were granted to me. I felt certain that the Finns would have nothing against me personally, as I had never done anything to harm my native land, but I was equally certain that I would never be admitted into Finland while Kuusinen was alive.

Altogether it was nine long years, from 1955 to 1964, before I could at last see my country again. During that time I never once met Kuusinen, though he rang up once or twice to offer help or ask me to go back to him. My answer to both suggestions was a resolute 'No'. I did not need his help, and even if I had done I should have been too proud to accept it: the bitter memory that he had not stirred a finger to save me from prison and forced labour was an ineffaceable barrier between us.

I was an independent woman now, and intended to remain so. In May 1964 I heard that Otto was a patient in the Kremlin hospital, and on the 13th I wrote a letter telling him for the first time how I had stood up for him when I was pressed to testify that he had been a spy in British pay. I also reproached him for doing nothing to save our Finnish friends and comrades from liquidation, especially Gylling, Heimo and Manner. Four days later, on 17 May, Otto Wille Kuusinen died at the age of eighty-three. On the 18th, all the Moscow papers appeared with black borders and published obituary articles extolling Kuusinen's friendship with Lenin and his importance as a Party theoretician. The city went officially into mourning and large, crape-bedecked photographs of Otto were displayed in shops and in the windows of government buildings.[32]

Next morning I dressed with unusual care and sat by the window of my flat. I felt sure that something of significance would happen: I was still Otto's legal wife, and it seemed inconceivable that I would not be paid some special attention and invited to take part in the funeral ceremony. Sure enough, at exactly eleven o'clock a large black Cadillac stopped outside my house on Smolensk Boulevard and two men got out, one of whom I recognized as Alexander Shelepin, Deputy Premier of the Soviet Union, his uniform covered with badges and medals. They rang at the door of my flat, and I opened it to them. Shelepin bowed with stiff formality and pressed my hand; the general also bowed. Then Shelepin said: 'Mrs Kuusinen, we have come to escort you to the lying in state, which of course you know about.' Before I could say anything, he made a gesture and went on: 'We know you lived apart from your husband but you realize that appearances must be preserved.' The ceremony begins in an hour's time. May I ask you to put on mourning clothes?' He did not know, of course, that I had a black dress ready, being as well acquainted as most people with the art of 'preserving appearances'. I changed quickly and, wearing a solemn expression, went down to the car with Shelepin and his companion. We drove rapidly through the streets of Moscow, none of us saying a word, and were soon at the Trade Union building (*Dom Soyuzov*), where Lenin once lay in state.

Kuusinen's body lay on a catafalque, in a coffin adorned with flowers and wreaths. A guard of honour was formed by government and Party members who relieved one another from time to time. An endless throng of Muscovites filed past the bier, paying their last respects to the dead. I sat for a few minutes beside the catafalque and was then taken into a side room to receive condolences, which I accepted with some confusion. One after another the mourners pressed up to me with words of sympathy, saying in hushed voices how they felt for me over the death of my husband and what a loss he was to the country. Some time later we returned to the hall and were treated to a speech praising Kuusinen's great deeds and services to the USSR. When this was over I felt that my attendance had served its purpose and that it was time to go. I moved towards the exit; Shelepin remained where he was, and only the general came out with me. He too had played his part, and made no secret of the fact that he was in a hurry. I drove home unaccompanied: even the chauffeur seemed anxious to be rid of me as quickly as possible, and when we arrived he let me open the car door for myself. I got out, feeling truly alone, and went up to my room.

Sitting there, I felt for the first time a ray of hope. Now that Kuusinen was dead, did it really mean that I was free at last? Free of terror and anxiety, free of this hateful city and the country that had trampled on my rights as a human being? Now that nothing was left of Kuusinen but his name, would I not at last be allowed to leave?

My thoughts ranged over the past, present and future, my own fortunes and those of my fellow-creatures. I had no feeling whatever as far as Otto was concerned, except a vague sense of triumph that I was still alive: time and my aversion for him had wiped out everything else. I had survived Vorkuta—what more could I be expected to feel? Only one thing was clear to me: *I* was alive and Otto was no longer there.

I sat for hours trying to sum up my impressions of Otto. I felt sure that if the Kremlin archives were ever investigated it would be possible to form an accurate picture of his character and personality, but, as things were, his memory would always remain a puzzle to future generations, as it was to me. He was a foreigner, born outside truly Russian soil. He spoke Swedish and German and could read a political report in French, but he never learnt to speak Russian with elegance or to rid himself of the accent that betrayed him at every word. And yet, was not this a pointer to his greatest achievement? For nearly fifty years he had been at the centre of both the Soviet government and the Russian Communist Party. This was remarkable enough for a foreigner, but it was downright astonishing that, despite all the vicissitudes of Soviet politics, he had remained at the top to the very end of his life.

Kuusinen outlived both Lenin and Stalin: he was a close collaborator of both, but to Stalin he was something more. Stalin knew little of foreign affairs, diplomacy and the capitalist world, while Kuusinen was an adroit and talented diplomat with a good knowledge of other countries. Like some ever-present Byzantine official, he was able to prompt his master and whisper advice into his ear, the more effectively as he had no desire to parade his knowledge and achievements in public. This was not due to modesty—far from it: he was devoured with the ambition to see his opinions, wishes and plans put into practice, and they nearly always were. But, provided he got his own way, he did not in the least mind if others carried out his ideas and enjoyed the credit for them. He was at bottom a man of immense, rather cynical self-confidence and would never have bowed the knee to anyone. He never for a moment thought anybody his intellectual superior, least of all Stalin; but he was so skilful in making his ideas palatable that Stalin imagined them to be his own.

Otto's success, I thought to myself, might well have been due to the fact that, as a foreigner, he was able simply to disinterest himself from many important questions. For example, he took no interest in the building of Communism in Bolshevik Russia, or in its internal political and economic problems. The tragedy of rural collectivization, the reign of terror and the arrests of innocent Soviet citizens did not worry him in the least. He grew anxious when the purge started to affect the Comintern, but everything else, he used to say, was no business of his or mine.

If he was concentrating on some particular matter, he would withdraw into his own world and pay no attention to what was going on around him. I remember especially an incident in, I think, 1925 when the waters of the Neva rose so high that the whole of Leningrad was threatened with flooding. Thousands of people fled from their houses, and many lost their lives: it was the biggest recorded disaster of its kind, and pictures of devastation appeared every day in the papers. Otto neither looked at them nor read the reports, as he was absorbed in some Comintern problem. Zinoviev, who was then Party secretary for Leningrad, telephoned one day from the Caucasus to say he was interrupting his leave because of the catastrophe. Otto replied: 'Yes, isn't it frightful?' After replacing the receiver, he said to me: 'What on earth has happened in Leningrad, anyway?'

I answered, somewhat shocked: 'Look, every schoolchild in Moscow knows there's been a flood in Leningrad, yet Otto Kuusinen is the one person who knows nothing about it. You might at least look at the front page of today's and yesterday's newspapers. What's the good of my putting the papers on your breakfast table if you don't read them?'

He replied calmly: 'Don't tell anyone that I didn't know about the flood.' I was then convinced that he did not care two straws about it.

His single-mindedness began to be disturbed in the thirties, when the terror spread to members of the Comintern and to his own relatives. When even Stalin's closest collaborators were being arrested and executed, he began to pay serious attention. Until then he had persuaded himself that these were internal affairs of the Russian leadership and did not affect him: he was at pains to be considered a foreigner who had no concern with conflicts inside the Kremlin and no ambition to supplant anyone. He avoided official receptions and ceremonies whenever he could, and the only time he wore his Soviet medals was on the day of his lying in state. Speech-making and popularity-hunting were not for him. All the same, this detachment and playing up his rôle as a foreigner would not in themselves have sufficed to keep him at the top for so long. His strongest qualities were perhaps prudence, caution and a lively instinct for self-preservation. He served the rulers of the day without forgetting his own interest, and always knew exactly when to switch to a new master. This was how he managed to survive the paroxysm of the terror, when heads were rolling on every side.

His relationship with Trotsky affords an example. Originally he was a great admirer of Trotsky's, especially for his gifts of organization and leadership of the Red Army. But Trotsky was one of the few who once dared to attack Otto publicly, stating in a newspaper article that he was not a true Communist, and Otto neither forgot nor forgave this. When Trotsky's theory of 'permanent revolution' fell into disfavour and he himself was ousted by Stalin, Otto became one of his fiercest opponents, though he was careful to wait until there was no doubt about Trotsky's downfall.

Kuusinen once boasted to me in all sincerity that he had 'cast his skin seven times in his life, like a snake'. Seven changes of loyalty, seven transformations of his philosophy and views. As a schoolboy he was deeply religious, assiduous at prayer and churchgoing. At the university in Helsinki he cast his 'religious' skin and became a fanatical patriot and nationalist, but gave up this line during a period when he took to drink. He then became deeply interested in the working class, went into active politics and joined the Social Democratic Party, which he represented in parliament. At the time of the Finnish Communist uprising in 1918 he was a left-wing Marxist and a champion of world revolution. In the thirties, after I left him, he sloughed off this attitude too, having come to believe that it was wrong and anachronistic to expect to achieve world revolution by political means. In his last phase he persuaded himself and Stalin that the only way to achieve it was by military power.

In this way he turned his coat several times, displaying a cold faithlessness towards one comrade after another. I cannot remember any occasion on which he stood by anyone in trouble, with the solitary exception of the Austrian Stange, whose case I described earlier. He did not lift a finger when his own son was arrested in Karelia and sent to Siberia, where he contracted tuberculosis. When Beria discovered who it was he had the boy released, but it was too late, as he soon died of the disease. Similarly Kuusinen did nothing to save his principal Comintern assistants, Mauno Heimo and Niilo Virtanen, or his first wife's brother, Einari Laaksovirta. In a previous chapter I mentioned Einari's fruitless money-changing expedition to Germany; on his return he was appointed at Kuusinen's instance to a post in Karelia, but for some reason was then expelled from the Party, a decision which had to be approved by the Control Commission. As Laaksovirta had mentioned that he was Kuusinen's brother-in-law, Yaroslavsky, the chairman of the Commission, asked Otto's opinion. I have read his answer: 'Laaksovirta has never been a Communist and never will be one. Do as you think fit.' So Laaksovirta was shot as a 'Finnish spy'.

In the same way Kuusinen did nothing to help his Finnish comrades Gylling and Manner, and was partly responsible for their liquidation. Nor did he do anything for me, his lawful wife, even after I stood up for him in prison and refused to admit that he was a 'British spy', despite the fact that we were separated and despite the fearful pressure that was used to make me denounce him.

Even in trifling matters he would refuse to help. For instance, after Manner was arrested he got a friend to ask Otto to send him some long woollen underpants from his flat, as the prison damp and cold were bad for his rheumatism; he also asked for soap. Otto gave instructions that these requests were to be refused.

Kuusinen was very thin-skinned and never forgot an insult, even one inflicted in jest. One evening a Finnish-born officer of the GPU telephoned from Leningrad to inform us of the death of Kuusinen's old comrade Evä, a former Social Democratic Member of Parliament who, after the Red uprising in Finland escaped to Leningrad and became a leader of the Finnish Communist Party in exile. Otto's reaction to the news of his death was to say: 'Good, it's the only useful thing he could have done for the world revolution.' We spoke no more about it, but could not understand Otto's spiteful attitude until I heard that Evä had once opposed a suggestion of his at a meeting in Leningrad, and Otto had never forgiven him.[33]

Otto never had any really close friends except for Nikolai Bukharin, whom he knew well in Moscow in the twenties. Bukharin was editor of *Pravda* for several years; he was a fascinating personality, humorous and lively, and at that time very popular. He was greatly admired by the young Moscow intellectuals, and his lectures at the Red Professors' Institute were always crowded out. Bukharin and Kuusinen differed considerably in their views but shared a taste for political and ideological argument. Bukharin in those days was the only person who was ever allowed to drop in on us unannounced: he lived in the same house and would pay us a visit at night after next day's *Pravda* had gone to press. He and Otto would sit till the small hours discussing Comintern affairs or problems of Marxism and socialism, and fetching snacks from the larder from time to time. Once Bukharin slept on the sofa in Otto's study and went straight from there to his office next morning.

After politics, Bukharin's greatest passion was for shooting game, and whenever he came back from the Caucasus he would bring us pheasants or something of the kind. He once also brought me a monkey from the zoo at Sukhumi, which he handed over with a little speech. This animal learnt in course of time to switch the electric light on and off and to perform other tricks. These began to be a nuisance, and my patience snapped one day when I came home and found him in front of the mirror with one of my hats in his paws: this sealed his fate, and we gave him to the Moscow zoo.

The close friendship between Otto and Bukharin lasted until 1929, when the latter was dismissed from the Comintern and the editorship of *Pravda*: on this occasion Otto himself made a virulent speech against Bukharin in the Central Committee. In the same way, he was always ready to give an extra kick to his Finnish comrades when they were on the way down. In short, he never let feelings stand in his way when his own safety or career seemed to be in any way threatened.

I was in the Comintern building on the day after Bukharin's dismissal and met on the stairs Lominadze, a Georgian who was chairman of the International Communist Youth Organization; his office was on the top floor. Like everyone else he knew of the close links between Bukharin and Kuusinen, and he asked me: 'What does Kuusinen think of things now?'

'How do you mean?'

'Well, it looks to us in the Youth Organization as though he'll be for it next. What do you think?'

'I'd rather not say, but I know nothing will happen to Kuusinen.'

'How can you be sure?'

'It's quite simple—Otto knows how to keep out of trouble.'

Ironically, it was Lominadze, a Georgian and Stalin's friend, who was liquidated some years later, and not Kuusinen.

What did Otto really want from life? Yrjö Sirola, who knew him well in their young days, once told me that he had been a romantic, poetic sort of youth, interested in art and the humanities. He was respected by his friends, but they always found him mysterious, as I was to do later; this sphinx-like quality increased with age, and whatever the company he tended to seem an outsider. He could be shy and unsociable, and his immediate staff often found him frightening. He had no practical knowledge and could never get on terms with ordinary Finnish workers and their families: machines, industry and technology were a closed book to him and one he had no desire to read. He never visited a Finnish or Soviet factory to see what was produced there or what sort of life the workers had: he was, in fact, a theorist in politics and a man who liked to work behind the scenes.

He was not devoid of leisure interests and liked music and the theatre—especially the Meyerhold in Moscow, whose talented director enjoyed Otto's friendship until he too was purged. He was fond of rambling about museums and galleries, and when he spoke to me of the history of art and of the lives of painters he was like a different man, revealing an unknown side of his nature. But he had no taste for modern art, especially when it dealt with political themes, as was so often the case in the Soviet Union.

But all this does not really explain his unapproachability or his ultimate aim in life. After much thought, it seems to me that the true key to his personality was hatred.

Above all, his attitude to Finland was one of intense bitterness. Throughout his life, the failure of the Communist rising in 1918 rankled like an open wound. He seldom spoke about it but he once tried to analyse the reasons for the fiasco in a pamphlet entitled *The Finnish Revolution: a Self-Criticism* which contained the poetic words: 'Amongst us, too, the genius of revolt passed over the country. We did not mount upon its wings, but bowed our heads and let it fly far above us.' He also once said to me: 'Our great mistake was that we did not do away with Svinhufvud's cabinet at once. We should have captured and executed the lot, but we let them slip through our fingers. We shan't make that mistake next time!'

In the short-lived revolutionary government of 1918 Kuusinen played a responsible rôle as Minister of Education. When it collapsed, the leaders fled to Russia and their misguided followers, left behind in Finland, paid with their lives. From then Kuusinen was an implacable enemy of his native country and even of its language. Gylling, with Lenin's approval, had made Finnish the national language of Soviet Karelia, but Kuusinen objected to its being used as a medium of instruction in schools. After Lenin's death and the dismissal of Gylling and his friends, Kuusinen's views were put into effect and Russian took the place of Finnish as the official language.

Otto's hatred of Finland was also shown in a preface he wrote for a commemorative edition of the Finnish national epic, the *Kalevala*,[34] which appeared at Petrozavodsk in 1935, a century after the work was first printed. In the preface he declared that the bourgeois scholars who had investigated the origins of the *Kalevala* had got it all wrong: the poem was a purely Karelian one, which had developed over the centuries without any contribution from the Finnish people, and incidentally it showed no trace of any belief in a Supreme Being—in which he was grossly mistaken.

Everything in fact indicates that the great aim of Otto's life was the subjection of Finland, and that Lenin was right when he nicknamed him the 'Finland-swallower'. This sobriquet, of which Otto was very proud, owed its origin to an article in which he described Finland as a speck of dust that ought to be swept off the map—which Lenin disapproved of as an exaggeration. Kuusinen once told me himself that he dreamed of controlling Finland and, eventually, being 'proconsul' for the whole of Scandinavia; then, after the rest of Europe had surrendered to Communism, he would return to Moscow and be the *éminence grise* of the Soviet empire. These aims, of course, were to be attained by force of arms: as I have already explained, he came to the conclusion in the middle thirties that Communism would triumph by military and not political means. On 30 November 1939 the Red Army attacked Finland, and in all probability Kuusinen's influence played a large part in this. He wanted to return home under the banners of the Red Army, and thus wreak revenge on the country which had rejected him. He bears a heavy responsibility for the losses and sufferings that were visited on the Finnish people, and no man born on Finnish soil can ever have laid a more grievous burden on his conscience.

I retraced in my mind once again the stages of Kuusinen's career. Step by step, he had risen to the top despite all the accidents of politics. A faithful disciple of Stalin, he served the latter's successors no less faithfully. Appointed to the Central Committee of the Soviet Communist Party in 1941, he reached his zenith as a member of the Politburo in 1957. From 1940 to 1958 he was deputy chairman of the Supreme Soviet and, as such, Deputy President of the Soviet Union. From 1940 to 1956 he was President of the so-called Karelian Republic, although he took scarcely any part in running its affairs.

His greatest services to the Soviet Union were no doubt rendered in the field of foreign policy, as Comintern leader for eighteen years and chairman of the Foreign Affairs Committee of the Supreme Soviet. His last assignment was, I have heard, a secret meeting with Mao Tse-tung in 1962 or 1963 for the purpose of regulating some points of contention between the USSR and China.

It seems extraordinary that this man who so profoundly influenced the policy of a great nation was not a Russian by birth but an outsider, who at heart cared nothing for Soviet interests. The purpose behind all his schemes and intrigues, all his devotion to Trotsky, Lenin, Stalin, Khrushchev and Brezhnev, the good deeds and more often bad ones that he aided and abetted was not to help Russia nor even to promote the success of Communism—the one objective, in his own eyes, of all his prestige and power was to march one day into Finland under the banners of the Red Army and show his country who was master in the end.

It took some months for me to obtain a passport and other necessary papers, including a certificate that I was born in Finland: Hertta Kuusinen provided this at my request, on the letterhead of the Finnish Communist Party. In the late autumn of 1964 I submitted my application for a passport. The authorities were helpful; after three months I received a document valid for a year, and the Finnish Embassy issued a visa for a three months' stay. On the evening of the day on which I received my passport I boarded the train for Leningrad, and on 8 February 1965 I crossed the frontier into Finland.

Biographical Notes

BERZIN, General Jan Karlovich (1890-1937)

Party member from 1905. March-May 1919, deputy people commissar for internal affairs; 1924-35, head of defence depa ment of the Red Army; released from this post in 1935 at own wish; deputy commander of the Red Banner special arm in the Far East; senior Soviet military adviser in Spain; recall from Spain 1937; head of counter-espionage of the Red Arm arrested and executed at the end of 1937.

BLUCHER (BLYUKHER), Marshal of the Soviet Union Vasili K stantinovich (1889-1938)

Party member from 1916. Hero of the Civil War; adviser Sun Yat-sen government in China; executed without trial Stalin's orders, 9 November 1938.

BUKHARIN, Nikolay Ivanovich (1888-1938)

Party member from 1906, Marxist theoretician. During t Brest Litovsk negotiations he led the 'Left Communist' oppo tion to Lenin. 1917-36, member of the Central Committee; 19 1924 candidate member, and 1924-9 full member, of the Po buro of the CC; for several years editor of *Pravda* and mem of Executive Committee of the Comintern; executed in 1938 belonging to 'anti-Soviet bloc of rightists and Trotskyists'.

CHICHERIN, Georgi Vasilyevich (1872-1936)

Statesman and diplomat; Party member from 1905. 1918 deputy people's commissar and then people's commissar foreign affairs of the RSFSR (later USSR); signed peace treaty

Brest Litovsk (1918) and treaty of Rapallo with Germany (1922). 1925-30, member of CC of the CPSU.

DENIKIN, Lieutenant-General Anton Ivanovich (1872-1947)

Tsarist officer. After the October revolution he founded a volunteer army with Generals Kornilov and Alexeyev, and became commander of the White forces in southern Russia. Defeated in the Civil War, he fled abroad in April 1920.

DIMITROV, Georgi (1882-1949)

Bulgarian Communist; from 1921 member of Executive Committee of the Comintern and Central Council of the Profintern. Acquitted in the Reichstag fire trial, 1933, and returned to Soviet Union, February 1934. Organized resistance in Bulgaria during the Second World War. 1946-9, chairman of Bulgarian council of ministers; 1948, secretary-general of CC of the Bulgarian CP.

FURTSEVA, Ekaterina Alexeyevna (b. 1910)

Party member from 1930; graduate of Lomonosov Institute for chemical precision technology, Moscow. 1934-6, first Party secretary for the city of Moscow; member of CC from 1956; 1956-1957 candidate member, and 1957-61 full member, of presidium of the CC of the CPSU; 1956-60, secretary of the CC; from May 1960, Minister of Culture of the USSR.

HEIMO, Mauno

Son of a Helsinki lawyer; member of Finnish revolutionary government (1918), and took refuge in Soviet Russia after the Finnish Civil War (1920). Served in the Commissariat for Foreign Affairs and worked among Finnish Communists in Sweden. In the early twenties he became a functionary of the Comintern in Moscow. Appears to have been in France in 1934-1935, and was arrested by the NKVD two years after his return to Moscow.

KIROV (KOSTRIKOV), Sergey Mironovich (1889-1934)

Party member from 1904. 1921-5, secretary of CC of the CP of Azerbaijan; 1923-4, member of CC, 1926-30 candidate member, and 1930-4 full member, of Politburo of the CC of the Russian (later Soviet) CP; 1926-34, first secretary of provincial committee and north-western bureau of the CC of the CPSU in

Leningrad; 1934, secretary and member of Organization Bureau of the CC of the CPSU. Murdered on Stalin's orders; the crime was officially ascribed to an alleged Trotskyist conspiracy and furnished the pretext for the notorious Moscow trials and the wholesale extermination of eminent Party and state leaders.

KOLLONTAY, Alexandra Mikhailovna (1872-1952)
Party member from 1915, diplomat and officer of the international women's movement. 1917-18, people's commissar for supply; 1920, head of women's section of the CC of the Russian CP; 1920-2, leading member of 'Workers' Opposition'; 1923-6, Minister to Norway, 1926-7 Mexico, 1927-30 again Norway; 1930-43, Minister and then Ambassador to Sweden; adviser in Foreign Ministry from 1945.

KUIBYSHEV, Nikolay Vladimirovich (1893-1938)
Brother of the Bolshevik leader Valerian Kuibyshev, after whom the town of Samara was renamed. Occupied various army posts; 1937, commander of military district of Transcaucasia; deputy to Supreme Soviet of the USSR; Order of the Red Banner three times; executed 1938.

KUUSINEN, Hertta (1904-1974)
Daughter of Otto Kuusinen. Member of CC of Finnish CP from 1944, and of its Politburo from 1944 to 1970; 1945-66, chairman of parliamentary group of Finnish People's Democratic League (SKDL).

KUUSINEN, Otto Wille (1881-1964)
Party member from 1905. Studied at Helsinki University; 1906-16, edited *Socialist Journal* (in Finnish) and *Työmies* (Worker), organ of the Finnish Social Democratic Party; 1921-1939, secretary of Executive Committee of the Comintern; 1940-1964, member of Supreme Soviet of the USSR; 1940-57, chairman of presidium of the Supreme Soviet of the Karelo-Finnish SSR, deputy chairman of presidium of the Supreme Soviet of the USSR; 1941-64 member of the CC, 1957-64 member of presidium and secretary of the CC of the CPSU.

MANNER, Kullervo (1880-1935)
Journalist and Social Democratic leader; member of Finnish

parliament, and its Speaker in 1917; head of workers' revolutionary government, 1918. Escaped to Russia after civil war and became chairman of the Finnish CP and member of Executive Committee of the Comintern. 1935, arrested and liquidated in Chibyu (Ukhta) labour camp on the Pechora river, Komi ASSR.

MANUILSKY, Dmitri Zakharovich (1883-1959)
Party member from 1903. Law graduate of the Sorbonne, 1911. 1918, member of All-Ukrainian revolutionary committee, people's commissar for agriculture of the Ukrainian SSR; 1920-3 and 1949-52, member of Politburo of CC of the Ukrainian CP, and its first secretary in 1921-2; 1922, transferred to Comintern; 1922-3, candidate member, and 1923-52 full member, of CC of the Russian (later Soviet) CP; 1924-8, member of presidium, and 1928-43, secretary of Executive Committee of the Comintern; 1944-6, people's commissar for foreign affairs of the Ukrainian SSR, and 1944-53, deputy chairman of council of people's commissars. Author of numerous works on strategy and tactics of the international workers' and Communist movement.

MIRBACH, Count Wilhelm (1871-1918)
German diplomat. Ambassador to Soviet Russia after signature of the treaty of Brest Litovsk. Murdered in Moscow during revolt of the Left Social Revolutionaries, who hoped thereby to overthrow the treaty.

ORDZHONIKIDZE, Grigori Konstantinovich (Sergo) (1886-1937)
Party member from 1903. Special commissar for the Ukraine, 1917, organizing food supplies for the RSFSR; commander and political organizer in the Civil War, afterwards active in Transcaucasia; 1921-6, chairman of Caucasian Bureau of CC of the Russian (later Soviet) CP; 1921-37, member of CC; 1926-30, candidate member, and 1930-7, full member, of Politburo of CC of the Russian (later Soviet) CP; 1926-30, chairman of Central Control Commission of the CPSU, also people's commissar for workers' and peasants' inspection and deputy chairman of council of people's commissars of the USSR; 1930-2, chairman of Supreme Economic Council of the USSR; 1932-7, people's commissar for heavy industry of the USSR; committed suicide, 1937

POSTYSHEV, Pavel Petrovich (1887-1940)

Party member from 1903. One of the chief Bolshevik leaders; occupied important posts in the October revolution and Civil War; 1933-7, member of Politburo and secretary of CC of the Ukrainian CP. Though an organizer of forced collectivization and purges in the Ukraine, he came to the conclusion that these had been arbitrary and harmful to the Party. Recalled from the Ukraine on Stalin's orders and appointed regional Party secretary at Kuibyshev; later arrested, and shot in 1940.

PYATNITSKY, Osip Aronovich (1882-1939)

Party member from 1898. 1917-18, chairman of railway workers' union; 1918-22, member of executive committee of Moscow Soviet and of the All-Russian central executive committee; 1920, secretary of Moscow Party committee; 1920-1, candidate member of CC; 1924-7, member of Central Control Commission; 1927-39, member of CC of the CPSU; from 1923, secretary of Executive Committee of the Comintern; shot in 1939.

RADEK, Karl Bernardovich (1885-1939)

Publicist of Polish origin, and comrade of Lenin's; occupied important Comintern posts; condemned to ten years' imprisonment in 1938, and executed in the following year.

ROVIO, Kustaa

Lenin's host in Finland in the summer of 1917, when the Bolshevik leader was in hiding. In the thirties Rovio was Party first secretary in Karelia, but was dismissed in autumn 1935, as was Edvard Gylling, chairman of the council of people's commissars of the Karelian ASSR. Both men were arrested in 1937 and posthumously rehabilitated in 1956, soon after the twentieth Congress of the CPSU.

RUDZUTAK, Jan Ernestovich (1887-1938)

Born in Latvia; Party member from 1905. Active in the October revolution and Civil War. Under Lenin he was a member of the Supreme Economic Council and held important trade union posts; 1923-34 secretary of the CC, 1926-32 member of the Politburo, 1934-7 candidate member of the Politburo; 1924-30 people's commissar for communications (transport); several times member of the presidium of the Central Executive

Committee of the USSR and the RSFSR; arrested and shot in 1938.

RYKOV, Alexey Ivanovich (1881-1938)
Party member from 1899. Chairman of Supreme Economic Council of the RSFSR, 1918, and directed the nationalization of industry; 1921, deputy chairman of council of people's commissars and council for labour and defence of the RSFSR; 1924-30, chairman of council of people's commissars of the USSR, and 1924-9 of the RSFSR; 1930-6 people's commissar of the USSR for posts and telegraphs; arrested in 1937 and shot in March 1938.

SHLYAPNIKOV, Alexandr Gavrilovich (1884-1937)
Party member from 1901. April-October 1917, chairman of metal workers' trade union; after the revolution, people's commissar for labour of the RSFSR; 1918-19 candidate member, and 1921-2 full member, of CC of the Russian CP; 1919-22, chairman of metal workers' union; 1920-2, organizer and leader of the Workers' Opposition, which he also represented in 1923, 1926 and 1927; 1924-5, counsellor at the Soviet Embassy in Paris; expelled from the Party in 1933 and executed in 1937.

SIROLA, Yrjö (1876-1936)
Originally a member of the bourgeois group of 'Young Finns', but in 1903 joined the Social Democratic Party and became its secretary two years later. Was in charge of foreign affairs in the revolutionary government of 1918; after its defeat, like many of his colleagues, he emigrated to Soviet Russia. Was first chairman of the Finnish Communist Party, founded in Moscow in 1918; member of Executive Committee of the Comintern (twice) and of its International Control Commission. Worked as an emissary in Scandinavia, Germany and the US. Died a natural death in Moscow.

SORGE, Richard (1895-1944)
Great-nephew (and claimed to be grandson) of Friedrich Albert Sorge, an associate of Karl Marx. Member of the German Communist Party from 1919 and of the CPSU from 1925. Soviet agent in Japan from 1933, using the cover of a correspondent for the *Frankfurter Zeitung* (to which he contributed from

1936). Stalin disbelieved his report of an imminent German attack on the USSR; he was arrested by the Japanese police in 1941 and executed after trial in 1944. In 1964 the Soviet authorities for the first time celebrated Sorge publicly as a 'master spy', conferring on him the posthumous decoration of Hero of the Soviet Union.

STASOVA, Elena Dmitrievna (1873-1966)
Party member from 1898. 1912-18, candidate member, and 1918-20, full member of CC of the RSDWP, later Russian CP; 1917-20, secretary of CC of the RSDWP; 1921-6 on staff of the Comintern, and 1926-7 in information bureau of the CC of the CPSU; 1927-38, chairman of CC of International Red Relief and deputy chairman of its executive committee; 1930-4, member of Central Control Commission of the CPSU; 1935-43, member of International Control Commission; 1938-46, editor of *Internatsionalnaya literatura* (in French and English).

TANNER, Väinö (1881-1966)
Finnish Social Democratic leader for nearly three decades; was Foreign Minister during the Winter War of 1939-40 and Minister of Finance during the Finnish-Soviet 'continuation war', 1941-4. Sentenced as a 'war responsible' in 1946, he was paroled in 1948 and remained the chief figure in the Social Democratic party until his death.

TOVSTUKHA, Ivan Pavlovich (1889-1935)
Party member from 1913. 1918-21, secretary and member of the collegium of the people's commissariat for the affairs of national minorities; 1921-4, on the staff of the CC of the Russian CP; 1930-5, deputy director of the Marx-Engels-Lenin Institute and member of editorial board of *Proletarskaya revolyutsia*; 1934-5, candidate member of CC of CPSU.

TRILISSER, Meer (Michael) Abramovich (1883-1938)
Party member from 1901. After the February revolution of 1917 he was secretary of the Irkutsk Soviet; 1920-1, chairman of regional revolutionary committee at Blagoveshchensk; 1921, chief of foreign department of the OGPU; 1926-30, deputy head of the OGPU; from 1930, deputy people's commissar for workers' and peasants' inspection of the RSFSR. His code name in the

Comintern was Moskvin. Executed as a spy in the Yezhov purge.

TROTSKY (Bronstein), Lev (Leo) Davidovich (1879-1940)
Party member from 1917, and chief organizer of the Red Army. He was a Menshevik from 1903, and in 1902-5 worked in London for the periodical *Iskra*. In 1905-8 he edited *Rabo-chaya gazeta*; in 1908 he was arrested and exiled to Siberia, whence he escaped abroad. Edited *Pravda* with A. A. Joffe (Ioffe) in Vienna; in 1914 founded the Petersburg paper *Borba*, which closed in the same year. After the February revolution he returned to Russia, and was a member and then chairman of the Petrograd Soviet. 1918-27, member of the CC, and 1917-26, member of the Politburo of the CC, of the Russian (Soviet) CP; 1917-18, people's commissar for foreign affairs, and 1918-20 for military affairs, of the RSFSR; 1920-1, chairman of the revolu-tionary military council and people's commissar for transport of the USSR. Opposed Lenin over the Brest peace negotiations. Ousted from the leadership by Stalin, he was expelled from the party in 1927 and was exiled first to Alma-Ata and then to Turkey (1929); in 1932 he was deprived of Soviet citizenship. While in exile he founded the Fourth International of world-wide Trotskyist groups. Killed with an axe by a Soviet secret agent in Mexico.

TUPOLEV, Andrey Nikolayevich (b. 1888)
World-famous aircraft designer, member of Academy of Sciences of the USSR since 1953; Lenin prizewinner.

TURTIAINEN, Väinö
Brother of Aino Kuusinen; lived as an émigré in Soviet Karelia, where he became director of an Agricultural Institute in 1932. Married to Hanna Kangasniemi; was known in Com-munist circles as Väinö Kangas. Received an eight-year sentence during the great purge; rehabilitated posthumously after Stalin's death.

URITSKY, S. P. (1895-1937)
Prominent revolutionary, organizer of the Red Army and a front-line commander in the Civil War. 1935, head of counter-espionage department of the Red Army; took part in Spanish

Civil War, 1937; arrested on 1 November on Stalin's orders, and executed shortly after.

VARGA, Evgeni Samoilovich (1879-1964)
Marxist economist of Hungarian birth; lived in the USSR from 1920; adviser to the Comintern and Soviet government on international economic questions.

VIRTANEN, Niilo (1892-??)
Studied at Helsinki University; took part in the workers' uprising of 1918, escaped to the Soviet Union and edited the Finnish-language newspaper *Red Karelia* at Petrozavodsk. Was private secretary to Kuusinen for Comintern affairs. Perished in the 1938 purge.

VOROSHILOV, Marshal of the Soviet Union, Kliment Efremovich (1881-1969)
Party member from 1903. Was a metal worker from 1896 to 1899. 1918, people's commissar for internal affairs of the Ukrainian SSR; 1921-4, commander of the North Caucasian military district; 1921-61 and 1966-9 member of the CC, and 1926-60 member of the Politburo of the CC, of the Russian (Soviet) CP; 1924-5, commander of Moscow military district; 1925-34, people's commissar for the army and navy and chairman of the revolutionary military council of the USSR; 1934-1940, people's commissar for defence of the USSR; held high military command during the Second World War; 1946-53, deputy chairman of Council of Ministers of the USSR; 1953-60, chairman of the presidium of the Supreme Soviet of the USSR.

YENUKIDZE, Avel Safronovich (1877-1937)
Party member from 1898. 1923-37, member of the presidium and secretary of the Central Executive Committee of the USSR; executed in 1937.

ZETKIN, Clara (1857-1933)
Member of the German Social Democratic Party from 1881, and a close associate of Lenin's; occupied important posts in the Comintern. From 1919, member of the CC of the German Communist Party; 1920-33, member of the Reichstag; from

1921, member of the Executive Committee and presidium of the Comintern.

ZHUKOV, Marshal of the Soviet Union, Georgi Konstantinovich (born 1896)

Party member from 1919, Hero of the Soviet Union (three times). 1953-7, member of CC of the CPSU; 1955-7, Minister of Defence of the USSR; 1956-7, candidate member, and June-October 1957 full member, of presidium of the CC of the CPSU. Deprived of all his Party and military functions at Khrushchev's instance, on the ground of seeking to withdraw the army from Party control. Published his memoirs in 1969.

ZINOVIEV (Radomyslsky), Grigori Yevseyevich (1883-1936)

Party member from 1901, and founder member of the Comintern. After the October revolution he was chairman of the Petrograd Soviet; 1919-26, chairman of the Executive Committee of the Comintern; 1923-6, member of the Politburo of the CC of the CPSU; joined Trotsky in 1926, was expelled from the Party in 1927, confessed his 'errors' and was readmitted in 1928; 1928-35, member of the presidium of the central association of consumers' co-operatives of the USSR; arrested in 1935 and shot in 1936.

ZORIN, Valerian Alexandrovich (b. 1902)

Diplomat. Ambassador to Czechoslovakia from 1945 to 1948, in which year he aided the Communists to seize power. Ambassador to the Federal Republic of Germany, 1955-6, and to France, 1965-71.

Notes on the Text

1. O. W. Kuusinen, *'Vernoye zveno'*, in *Pravda*, 3 December 1922, p. 2.

2. Aino Kuusinen's Soviet papers give her date of birth as 5 March 1893, but some Finnish documents, as Professor John H. Hodgson has pointed out, give it as 5 March 1886. This date seems to be the correct one, as it tallies with the details of her early life in Chapter I and the date of her marriage to Sarola. Probably the Soviet authorities took the decision to represent her as seven years younger during the time when she was working for the Comintern: this was quite a usual practice for reasons of camouflage.

3. Aino Kuusinen's maiden name was Turtiainen; she married Leo Sarola on 9 July 1909.

4. Otto Kuusinen was no longer a member of the Finnish parliament at this time: his years of membership were 1908-10, 1911-13 and 1916-18.

5. Kuusinen arrived in Finland in May 1919 under the assumed name of Otto Willebrand.

6. The letter was concerned with the peace negotiations between Finland and Soviet Russia. In a postscript Kuusinen added: 'I hope the innocent bearer of this letter will not be condemned to death.'

7. Yrjö Sirola was in Germany in January 1922 and again in 1923-4.

8. A session of the Central Committee of the Finnish CP was in fact taking pace at this time, but agreement between the

Kuusinen-Sirola and Evä-Rahja-Manner groups had already been achieved at the Party Congress in 1921.

9. After the abolition of 'War Communism' in 1921, the market economy and private property were to a certain extent restored; compulsory deliveries were suspended, and private initiative soon brought about recovery from the effects of the Civil War. This phase of Communist rule was brought to an end soon after Lenin's death in 1924.

10. Sirola was the first director of the Leningrad branch of the 'Communist University for the National Minorities of the West'.

11. J. G. Blumkin, a Left Social Revolutionary, committed the murder of Count Mirbach, but the official version of his fate differs from Aino Kuusinen's. He was released from prison and worked for the security service, but was afterwards arrested and liquidated for maintaining contact with Trotsky.

12. As Professor Hodgson has shown, Kuusinen travelled from Stockholm to Moscow in February-March 1921 via northern Norway, Murmansk, Petrozavodsk and Petrograd.

13. The Inner Commission (*Uzkaya Komissia*) was known in French and German as *'la petite commission'*, *'die kleine Kommission'*.

14. The successive designations of the Soviet secret police are: 1917-22, Cheka or Vecheka; 1922-34, GPU or OGPU; 1933-41 NKVD (People's Commissariat of Internal Affairs); February-July 1941, NKVD and NKGB (People's Commissariat of State Security); July 1941-3, NKVD. In April 1943 the NKVD was divided into NKVD, NKGB and SMERSH ('death to spies'); in January 1946 the NKVD was renamed MVD (Ministry of Internal Affairs), and in October of that year NKGB and SMERSH were combined as MGB. In 1954 the MGB's functions were redistributed between the MVD and the newly-formed KGB, i.e. State Security Committee of the Council of Ministers. Between 1966 and 1968 the MVD was known as the Ministry for the Defence of Public Order.

15. Jacob (Yakov) Mirov-Abramov did not become head of the OMS till the early thirties; in 1921-30 he was in Berlin and was under Pyatnitsky's orders.

16. The Communist Youth International (KIM) was founded

on Lenin's initiative and functioned from 1919 to 1943 as a section of the Comintern. All its chief leaders, such as A. V. Kosarev, V. T. Chemodanov, E. V. Krasnov and R. M. Khitarev, were liquidated in 1937-9.

17. The Krestintern existed from 1923 to 1933. It was founded at a conference of various peasant organizations, and after a series of misadventures was separated from the Comintern.

18. The Profintern, an organization of pro-Communist trade unions, existed from 1921 to 1937.

19. M. Heimo and A. Tivel, *10 let Kominterna v resheniyakh i tsifrakh* (Ten years of the Comintern: decisions and figures), published by Gosizdat, Moscow and Leningrad, 1929.

20. Hertta Kuusinen was sent to Finland in the early summer of 1934 and arrested on 14 June 1934. When Otto Kuusinen heard the news he wrote to her: 'You are closer and more dear to me in prison than ever before.'

21. *Kulak* ('fist'), the term used opprobriously in Communist parlance for peasants with large or medium holdings, whose resistance to collectivization was broken by slaughter, deportation etc.

22. A. Scheinmann (Sheinman) was elected chief of the Helsinki Party Committee in the spring of 1917, and in 1918 was chairman of the Helsinki Soviet of workers, soldiers and sailors.

23. Aino Kuusinen's rather disparaging account of Dimitrov does not agree with that of some Yugoslav and neutral sources: e.g., Vladimir Dedijer, *The Battle Stalin Lost: Memoirs of Yugoslavia*, 1948-1953, New York, 1971.

24. Dimitrov was diabetic, and his health worsened from year to year. He died a natural death in 1949 and received a magnificent State funeral; his embalmed body is preserved at Sofia.

25. The ECCI resolution of 15 May 1943 dissolving the Comintern stated in part: 'The whole development of events in the last quarter of a century, and the experience accumulated by the Communist International, convincingly showed that the organizational form of uniting the workers chosen by the first Congress of the Communist International answered the conditions of the first stages of the working-class movement but has been outgrown by the growth of this movement and by the

complications of its problems in separate countries, and has even become a drag on the further strengthening of the national working-class parties.' (*World News and Views*, 29 May 1943, quoted in Jane Degras (ed.), *The Communist International, 1919-1943, Documents*, London, 1965.

26. Aino Kuusinen states that after her release from Potma in 1955 she was told by friends in Moscow that Tenhunen was arrested in the Soviet Union in 1938 and given a ten years' sentence for espionage. He is believed to have died in 1939.

27. Aino Kuusinen and Kullervo Manner in fact reached Canada in 1930, almost a year after the sixth Congress of the Canadian CP. Aino Kuusinen's daughter, Aila Sarola, died in Massachusetts on 17 October 1930.

28. Nadezhda Alliluyeva (1901-32) was Stalin's second wife. The version of her death given here is one that circulated in Moscow, but differs from the account in Svetlana Alliluyeva's memoirs. Many of the dead woman's friends, especially Molotov's wife Polina Zhemchuzhina, were severely punished by Stalin for spreading the story in question.

29. Virtanen was arrested on 20 December 1933 and, after a spell in a German prison, was expelled to Finland. The Finnish police arrested him on 24 December 1934 and handed him over to the Russians on 22 January 1935.

30. In Professor Hodgson's opinion the friendship between Otto Kuusinen and Hella Wuolijoki went further than is here suggested. After Kuusinen moved to the Soviet Union she looked after his family and provided his daughter Hertta with a home for several months. During the twenties she corresponded secretly for years with Kuusinen, whom she described as a 'beacon' (*valonheittäjä*).

31. Hella Wuolijoki's friendship with Trilisser began in 1906 when the latter was chief of the Bolshevik military organization in Helsinki. He later became a high official of the Soviet security service.

32. The official report of Kuusinen's funeral made no mention of his wife. Accounts of him in *Pravda* and elsewhere ignored his collaboration with Stalin and merely stated that he 'long worked hand in hand with the great Leninist N. S. Khrushchev and other leaders of the CPSU and the Soviet State.'

33. According to Professor Hodgson, Kuusinen's hostility to K. M. Evä dated back to 1920-21 and in particular to a stormy congress of the Finnish CP in 1921, when Evä, supported by a majority of the CC, attacked Kuusinen in violently critical terms: the latter had to defend himself in a long speech.

34. Aino Kuusinen is mistaken here: it was not her husband but Yrjö Sirola who wrote the preface in question. Otto Kuusinen published an extensive commentary on the Finnish national epic in 1949, the centenary of the second edition or *New Kalevala*.

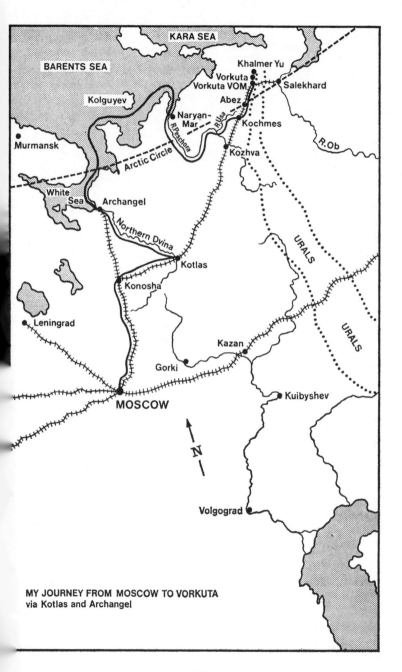

MY JOURNEY FROM MOSCOW TO VORKUTA
via Kotlas and Archangel

249

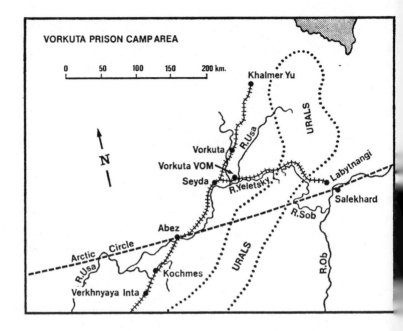

VORKUTA PRISON CAMP AREA

0   50   100   150   200 km.

N

Khalmer Yu

R.Usa

URALS

Vorkuta

Vorkuta VOM

Seyda

R.Yeletsky

Labytnangi

Salekhard

R.Sob

R.Ob

Abez

Arctic Circle

R.Usa

Kochmes

URALS

Verkhnyaya Inta

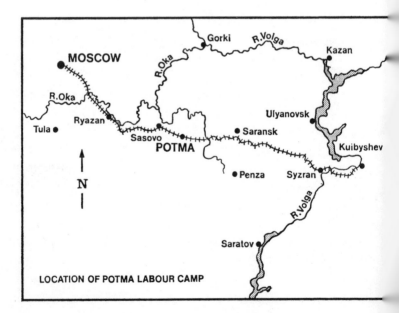

Gorki

R.Volga

Kazan

MOSCOW

R.Oka

R.Oka

Ulyanovsk

Tula

Ryazan

Sasovo

POTMA

Saransk

Kuibyshev

N

Penza

Syzran

R.Volga

Saratov

LOCATION OF POTMA LABOUR CAMP

Index

251

Comintern—*cont.*
  Press Dept, 41, 48, 58
  Profintern (International Trade Union Federation), 44, 59, 71
Communism in Finland, 13
Communist International, 53, 57, 138, 247
Communist Youth League (Komsomol), 139
Conte Verde, S. S., 107, 108, 109, 120, 121
Control Commission of Soviet Communist Party, 47, 211, 212, 213

Daily Worker, 84, 88, 100, 101
Danish Communist Party, 59
Dashkevich, Major, 209
Das Kapital, 32
Dedijer, Vladimir, 246
Degras, Jane, 246
De Gaulle, General, 168
Denikin, Lieut-General Anton Ivanovich, 235
Det Leende Nippon (Smiling Japan), 121, 122
Development of Capitalism in Russia, 178
Dimitrov, Georgi, 67, 77, 79-80, 235, 246
Dmitriev, Colonel, 189
Dutt, R. Palme, 144
Dushman, Dr, 155

Eberlein, Hugo, 35, 156-7
Erich, Rafael, 20
Estonian Communists, 66
Eteenpäin (Forward), 87, 88
L'Europeo, 8
Evä, K. M., 228, 245, 248
Ewert, Arthur, 59, 82
Expressen, 8

Fagerholm, Karl-August, 222
Fait, Dr Elizabeth von, 151, 155-6, 158, 160, 161, 163, 166
Falk (Norwegian lawyer), 106
Far Eastern Study Group, 67
Feinberg, 59, 67
Finnish American workers, 82-102
Finnish Communist Party, 35, 72, 228, 232
The Finnish Revolution: A Self-Criticism, 230
Ford, Jim, 90
Foster, William Z., 82, 83, 89-90
Founding Congress of the Communist International, 36
Fourth Bureau of the Red Army, 51, 100, 103, 105, 107, 114, 119, 123, 124, 126

Frankfurter Zeitung, 239
Frenkel, 170, 171, 172
Frumkina, Dr Maria Yakovleva, 53, 137-8
Frumkina, Rosa, 138
Frumkina, Tamara, 139
Furtseva, Ekaterina, 220, 235

General Strike, 1926 (British), 71
German Communists, 21, 27, 60, 61, 62-6, 79, 80, 82, 156
German Revolution, 61-6, 79
Ginzburg, Evgenia, 11
Glaubauf brothers, 59
Gorin, 94, 95
Gorki, Maxim, 155
GPU, 40, 43, 45, 53, 70, 75, 89, 145, 228, 246
Grollman, 59, 69
Gross, Babette, 13
Guralsky, 62
Gusev, 43
Gylling, Edvard, 95, 96, 117, 120, 183, 223, 228, 230, 238

Hall, Otto, 74-5
Hansson, Mrs Elisabeth (name assumed by Aino Kuusinen), 106, 107, 113, 121, 122, 125, 126
Harju, Vilho, 157
Heikkinen, Saimi, 151
Heimo Mauno, 38, 44-5, 46, 47, 48, 51, 59, 66, 74, 77, 78, 82, 146, 223, 227, 235, 246
Hietala, Leevi, 89
Heitala, Olga, 204, 207, 208
Henrickson, Martin, 96, 97
Hindenburg, Marshal von, 23
Hirohito, Emperor, 122
Hitler, Adolf, 80, 100, 165
Hodgson, Professor John H., 12, 244, 245, 247, 248
Hoxha, Enver, 53
Humbert-Droz, Jules, 59
Hungarian Communists, 75
Huttunen, Hilja, 151

Idelson, 59, 69
Ilf (Soviet humourist), 98
Ilyin, 108
'Industrial Party', 170-1
Inprecorr, 53, 54
International Literature, 216, 240
Inukai, Prime Minister, 107-8
Iskra, 241
Izvestia, 48, 79

Japanese Communist Party, 74, 169
Japanese/Soviet relations, 104-126
Japan Times, 111, 113, 122

254